# The Masterless

# The Master

Self & Society in Modern America

# less

Wilfred M. McClay

The University of North Carolina Press   *Chapel Hill & London*

*Publication of this book was assisted by a grant from the Earhart Foundation.*

© 1994 The University
of North Carolina Press
All rights reserved
Manufactured in the United States
of America

Portions of this work appeared earlier
in somewhat different form in
"Introduction" to the Transaction edition
of Walter Lippmann, *The Phantom Public*
(New Brunswick, N.J., 1993); "The
Strange Career of *The Lonely Crowd*: Or,
the Antinomies of Autonomy," in *The
Culture of the Market: Historical Essays*, ed.
Thomas L. Haskell and Richard F.
Teichgraber (New York, 1993); "A Tent
on the Porch," *American Heritage*
(July/August 1993); and "Weimar in
America," *American Scholar* (Winter
1985–86) and are reproduced here by
permission.

Wilfred M. McClay is associate professor
of history at Tulane University.

Library of Congress
Cataloging-in-Publication Data
McClay, Wilfred M.
The masterless: self and society in modern
America / Wilfred M. McClay.
    p. cm.
Includes bibliographical references and index.
ISBN 0-8078-2117-9 (alk. paper).
— ISBN 0-8078-4419-5 (pbk. : alk. paper)
1. Individualism—United States. 2. Social
integration—United States. 3. United States—
Social conditions. I. Title.
HM136.M3814 1993
302.5'4—dc20    93-9673
                        CIP

98  97  96  95  94    5  4  3  2  1

FOR MAC AND MARY,

*more than conquerors*

# Contents

# Acknowledgments

Before I wrote a book, I used to think the lengthy acknowledgments at the beginning of books were pretentious and superfluous. Now that I have written one, I marvel that authors' acknowledgments are not longer, and more florid and impassioned. I will try my best to abide here by a standard of sober brevity, though I am intensely aware of my intellectual creditors, to whom I have run up many more debts, large and small, than I can adequately acknowledge here, let alone ever discharge. Yet it is an extraordinary pleasure to express my gratitude to them, however inadequately. Each has contributed something important to this book.

First, I should acknowledge the help I received from the staffs of the various libraries and depositories that aided me in my work. I am particularly grateful to the Library of Congress, especially the Manuscript Division; the Harvard University Archives and Houghton Library; the Enoch Pratt Free Library in Baltimore (a wonderful institution now badly in need of financial support); and the libraries of Tulane University, Louisiana State University, Columbia University, the United States Naval Academy, Southern Methodist University, the University of Dallas, and Johns Hopkins University. I am also indebted to a number of persons and institutions for financial support that made the research and writing possible. I would never have made it through graduate school without the financial and moral support of a Danforth Fellowship and a Richard M. Weaver Fellowship, for which I thank, respectively, the Danforth Foundation and the Intercollegiate Studies Institute. More recent sources of financial support have included a junior sabbatical provided by Tulane; research grants from the Smith Richardson Foundation, the Marguerite Eyer Wilbur Foundation, and the Earhart Foundation (the last of which was especially crucial); and constant help, provided in forms large and small, from the Murphy Institute of Political Economy at Tulane and its director, Rick Teichgraeber.

As for my formal education, I still proudly bear many of the marks of my undergraduate training at St. John's College (Annapolis) and will always count myself fortunate for having wandered into that singular place at an impressionable age. As a historian, I have learned to operate upon rather different premises than those undergirding the St. John's program; yet its legacy still lives in me, like an insistent Socratic voice that constantly calls my operating premises into question and insists upon a constant reconsideration of the broadest philosophical questions.

Although I encountered a very different environment in graduate school at Johns Hopkins, I was equally fortunate in the people I came to know there. Hopkins is often regarded as a thoroughbred research institution, at which teaching is but an afterthought; but I was blessed with sterling teachers there. Although I benefited from many members of the faculty, my principal debts are owed to William W. Freehling, Jack P. Greene, Vernon Lidtke, and Kenneth S. Lynn. I draw constantly on what I learned from all four, but the last two deserve special mention. Vernon Lidtke stimulated my interest in the intellectual history of modern Central Europe, and his influence is clearly visible in this book. Kenneth Lynn's influence has been even greater, for he showed me how one can write about ideas as reflections and formulations of the inner lives of those who create them—as ways they, and we, grapple with the mystery, wonder, and terror of things. I am immensely grateful to him for sharing his intellectual intensity, which has constantly spurred me on by holding my work up to the highest imaginable standard and insisting on nothing less. I should also mention with gratitude the sustenance and stimulation I derived from my fellow Hopkins graduate students of that time, including Chris Gray, Sally Griffith, Peter Kafer, Bill Klein, Ken Lipartito, Stu McConnell, Alice O'Connor, and Michael Wolfe.

Several people read all or part of the book and made valuable suggestions and criticisms for which I am grateful. I want to pay particular tribute to Thomas Haskell, whom I first encountered in a memorable Murphy Institute faculty seminar he directed at Tulane for a semester in the spring of 1990, and who has since come to be an exemplary source of intellectual and professional inspiration for me. John Lukacs, who has been a good friend and reliably independent-minded reader for nearly a decade, also gave the manuscript the benefit of his close and critical examination. Others who read the entire manuscript were Casey Blake, Chris Gray, Kenneth Lynn, Tom Pauly, David Shi, Rick Teichgraeber, and Robert Wuthnow; all were very helpful. But at the risk of seeming to slight others' contributions, I want to mention my great indebtedness to Casey Blake, whose wonderfully intelligent, informed, detailed, demanding, challenging, but also fundamentally generous reading of my manuscript was everything an author could possibly want. He has made this book infinitely better than it would have been otherwise, and I cannot thank him enough. In addition, my editor at Chapel Hill, Lewis Bateman, who is in a class by himself, offered numerous good suggestions and shrewd observations about the book even as he was expertly steering it into print; my thanks to him and to Fred Siegel for bringing us together.

Thanks are also due to those who read parts of the manuscript, or read it in earlier drafts, and made valuable suggestions; these include Patrick Allitt, Joyce Appleby, Bob Asahina, Thomas Bender, Lee Congdon, Joseph Epstein, Eric Gorham, Paul Gottfried, Irving Louis Horowitz, Gary Huxford, Mike Lowenthal, Matt Mancini, John Shelton Reed, David Riesman, Douglas Rose, Peter Schwartz, Edward Shils, Richard Snow, David Steiner, Louise Stevenson, Henry Tom, and Gregory Wolfe. I am especially grateful to Thomas Bender for his fruitful suggestion that I take a look at the life and work of John W. Burgess, and to David Riesman for his generous remarks on my treatment of his life and work in chapter 7. Many of the ideas herein have been tested in conversations with Ian Dowbiggin, who was my colleague in Dallas for a year and who has been a valued and trusted friend thereafter. I am grateful to numerous Tulane colleagues, especially George Bernstein, Charles Davis, Ken Harl, Dick Latner, Paul Lewis, Colin MacLachlan, Linda Pollock, Sam Ramer, Rick Teichgraeber, Terry Toulouse, and Lee Woodward, who have been sources of strong support. Ruth Carter of the Murphy Institute was of incalculable help in the process of bringing the manuscript to completion; she deserves an award for patience as well as one for efficiency. I have also been fortunate enough to have many gifted and stimulating students at Tulane who have constantly challenged and clarified my thinking; I am especially grateful to Danton Kostandarithes and Blake Pattridge for their helpful readings of this book in manuscript.

I cannot close without mentioning others outside the scholarly orbit whose inestimable help deserves acknowledgment. Jim Woods helped me in ways I could never explain but will never forget. My brothers and sisters at St. Philip's Episcopal Church, and others scattered throughout the diocese of Louisiana, and elsewhere, especially Chris Colby and Ian Montgomery, support me in ways that also pass understanding and give shape and substance to my own evolving understanding of the beloved community. (My special thanks to Mary, Sue, Fran, and Joyce.) My mother, Mary Bear McClay, and my sister Susan M. Foote and her husband, George, have been wonderfully supportive;

so too has the vast army of my Oklahoma-based in-laws, particularly my mother-in-law, Barbara Holt. My children, Mark and Barbara, surely must have contributed something important—perhaps a sense of urgency?—warranting acknowledgment; in any event, I won't leave them out. As for my wife, Julie Holt McClay, sometimes it is best to resist saying what resists being expressed in words. She knows anyway.

# The Masterless

*Liberty is all very well, but men cannot live without masters. There is always a master. And men live in glad obedience to the master they believe in, or they live in a frictional opposition to the master they wish to undermine. In America this frictional opposition has been the vital factor. . . . [America is] a vast republic of escaped slaves[,] . . . [of] the masterless. . . . But men are free when they are in a living homeland, not when they are straying and breaking away. Men are free when they are obeying some deep, inward voice of religious belief. Obeying from within. Men are free when they belong to a living, organic,* believing *community, active in fulfilling some unfulfilled, perhaps unrealized purpose. Not when they are escaping to some wild west. The most unfree souls go west, and shout of freedom. . . . The shout is a rattling of chains. . . . Liberty in America has meant so far the breaking away from all dominion. The true liberty will only begin when Americans discover . . . the deepest* whole *self of man.*
    —D. H. Lawrence

*The most profound theme that can occupy the mind of man . . . What is the fusing explanation and tie—what the relation between the (radical, democratic) Me, the human identity of understanding, emotions, spirit, &c., on the one side, of and with the (conservative) Not Me, the whole of the material objective universe and laws, with what is behind them in time and space, on the other side?*
    —Walt Whitman

*Lead me to the rock that is higher than I.*
    —Psalms 61:2

# Introduction

In my beginning is my end, wrote T. S. Eliot, and the book before you exemplifies this double-edged truth. Like many books, it began less with an idea than with a question—or rather, a problem. I was perplexed to find that, in the extensive literature on American "national character," from Tocqueville on, Americans seemed to be consistently charged with two faults: first, that they are too prone to individualism, and second, that they are too prone to conformism. To make matters worse, I found myself willing to assent readily to both charges—not, to be sure, simultaneously, but in sufficiently rapid succession as to make me question my own consistency. How could both such contradictory assessments be valid? Or, I wondered, might there be some other, better frame of reference, by whose standard these seeming opposites might be understood as complementary?

Such questions eventually led me to the present study, which is a general consideration of the tension between individualism and social cohesion, and between centrifugal and centripetal impulses, in modern American social thought. Such an inquiry must, of course, be conducted on more than one level at once. I have offered an interpretation of the shifting ways American thinkers have formulated conceptions of their society in the years since the Civil War; at the same time, I have explored the changing profile of the individual person as conceived by and within that changing order. Such a linkage of individual and polity, self and society, has long been a mainstay of Western social and political thought. Indeed, from Plato's *Republic* onward, conceptions of the social order and conceptions of the self often appear in tandem, one serving as mirror to the other. Such linkage came naturally

3

enough to ancient political thought, which was grounded in the Aristotelian understanding of man as *zōon politikon*, a being whose very nature was fulfilled socially, unlike the proverbial beast or god who could dwell outside the *polis*. In the modern United States, however, precisely because of our "modernness" as a people, we have found it especially difficult to conceive a stable, reliable, and necessary relationship between the two. Perhaps nowhere else in history have "self" and "society" been more likely to be conceived in diametrical opposition to one another, as a virtual Kierkegaardian either/or. Like the proverbial deep-sea fish that never knows itself as an underwater creature, our experience of our individuality is often remarkably oblivious to the structures that enable and shape it.

To be sure, this condition is by no means uniquely American. It is a singular feature of what is imprecisely called Western civilization, whose spiritual trajectory has been marked, particularly since the Renaissance, by an intense concern with the immense worth of the individual human personality in all its heroic splendor and all its Faustian waste and wreckage. Yet that concern has perhaps found its most undiluted expression in the American setting, precisely because of the weakness there of all traditional forms of authority. Hence the intrinsic interest and significance in observing the problem's twists and turns through the past century and a half of American social thought. Hence, too, my appropriation of D. H. Lawrence's term *the masterless* as a title that seems to me expressive of both the promise and the peril of that condition.

In a sense, the book's central concerns are encapsulated in the three epigraphs. Lawrence, writing in the great tradition of European observers (and perhaps from a particularly British perspective), saw the great problem of American life as the riddle of authority: the difficulty of finding a way, within a liberal and individualistic social order, of living in harmonious and consecrated submission to something larger than oneself. Whitman's poignantly convoluted words speak to the dualism of my subtitle, for they ask how the bracing (and sometimes terrifying) experience of radical, unconditioned selfhood can be brought into enduring and nourishing relationship with the larger whole to which it belongs. The psalmist's plea reminds us that a yearning for self-transcendence and submission to authority, a cardinal feature of the Christian intellectual tradition and a recurrent theme in the pages that follow, is just as deeply rooted as the lure of individual liberation. The problems wrestled with herein, then, though in one sense intensely historical and particular, also reflect the enduring task of political and social philosophy: the reconciliation of the one and the many.

In this volume I explore the psychological ramifications of such questions as they have flowed from changing models of social and political life, and conversely, I investigate the way that a certain kind of "self" calls for, and reinforces, a certain kind of society and polity. I am especially interested in assessing the effects, in both the realm of ideas and of social and political institutions, of the general movement I call "consolidation": an umbrella term describing the process of national economic, political, social, and cultural integration and centralization that has been such a prominent feature of post–Civil War America.

By dubbing this phenomenon consolidation, I have deliberately appropriated a word that was instantly (and negatively) suggestive to many Americans of the pre–Civil War years, precisely in order to illustrate how dramatic a reversal the Civil War wrought in projective social ideals. I also mean to suggest by its use that the growing power of the nation-state, and the waning political authority of states and localities (and therefore of the federal idea itself), have had a profound effect upon ways of understanding the self, both in its proper relationship to the social and political order and in its most intimate experience of itself. An examination of the conflict between federalism and centralism in American governance, always a rich and resonant subject, can be made to yield even more abundant fruit when that conflict is also understood analogically, as an expression of a more pervasive struggle between visions of dispersion and coalescence, or diversity and unity, in social organization. A similar opposition has played itself out not only in politics but in society, economy, and psyche—in microcosm as well as macrocosm.

In order to give flesh-and-blood concreteness to this extended meaning of consolidation, I begin the story with an account of one of the most fertile symbolic expressions of the great national coalescence wrought by the Civil War: the Grand Review of the victorious Union armies in May 1865. Then, after exploring the review's antebellum antecedents and probing for fissures beneath the surface of antebellum individualism, I examine what seems to me the most striking and indicative expression of the social philosophy embodied in the Grand Review: the work of Edward Bellamy, particularly his influential utopian novel *Looking Backward* (1888), a veritable ode to the virtues of national consolidation, social solidarity, and self-sacrificial transcendence.

Using Bellamy's vision as a touchstone, I continue my account by tracing successive efforts to work out the details of that vision, and a correspondingly social understanding of the self, which would transcend the harmful pathologies of individualism by offering in their stead a transpersonal, public ideal of disinterestedness. In so doing, however, one also soon encounters the complications and intellectual struggles that those efforts stirred up—sometimes in the form of striking ambivalences and contradictions within a single thinker, such as Frederick Jackson Turner or Lester Frank Ward, or, by the 1920s and

1930s, in the more concentrated resistance of Walter Lippmann, who doubted the very existence of a genuine public, or Reinhold Niebuhr, who doubted whether social groups were even capable of disinterested behavior.

Eventually the idea (and reality) of totalitarian *Gleichschaltung* would transform Bellamy's rosy vision into a grim nightmare, leaving the attractiveness of the consolidationist vision and the social self badly undermined. As the powerful intellectual influence of refugees from Hitler, such as Hannah Arendt and Erich Fromm, filtered into post–World War II American social thought, it gave persuasive shape to a mounting fear of devouring social totalism, a distrust of "the people" and a corresponding veneration of individual autonomy, expressed notably in such a quintessential postwar work as David Riesman's *The Lonely Crowd*. Yet, as I suggest in chapter 8, this neoindividualist preoccupation with autonomy, far from representing a counter to the effects of consolidation, may have proved a mere adaptation or accommodation to it. The pathology of the unencumbered self, as Michael Sandel has observed, does not occur in a social vacuum; it is, in fact, the logical correlative of a bureaucratic, impersonal, centrally directed "procedural" republic. The two, in short, seem to go together—a partnership made possible, in turn, by an odd bureaucratization of the soul into social and authentic selves.

Today, much as in Edward Bellamy's time, American social thought has once again begun to focus upon our society's tendency toward individualism, identifying it increasingly as one of our most urgent problems. If this book has any contribution to make to that discussion, it would be to propose that individualism cannot be profitably addressed in isolation. We must also address the need for social and political forms capable of embodying the characteristics of moral community—and those characteristics include genuine sources of moral authority and moral obligation. Once the question of the proper size and shape of those forms is raised, then so will questions about consolidation itself, and the forms of pluralism it is able to accept. Does the fading primacy of national identity in our time, and its increasing replacement by more narrow and particularist forms of identification—such as race, gender, ethnicity, class, age, occupation, sexual preference, lifestyle, and so forth—represent an understandable reaction against the inadequacies of consolidation, and a movement in the direction of more tangible and intimate forms of social connectedness, forms more congruent with the moral needs of the individual? Or does it represent the conquest of the social and political world by the egoistic voice of the emotivist self, amplified into the contemporary din of clashing special-interest groups? Does the latter prospect represent a divergence from consolidation, or a consequence of it? The answers we find to these questions will have much to say about the pattern our efforts at fostering national community and social cohesion will follow in the next century.

This, then, is a history of evolving ideas—ideas about the proper constitution of the social or political order, ideas about the self, and ideas about the relationship between the two. Let me emphasize at the outset that I have by no means pretended, or intended, to trace the development of American society, economy, politics, or culture in the past 150 years. Whatever other follies may have informed the composition of this book, that was not one of them. Yet in the end it is neither possible nor desirable to segregate the study of ideas from those other subjects entirely. The history of ideas sometimes is treated as an indoor spectator sport, as if we were merely watching a chess tournament between mentally overdeveloped oddities, cloistered in soundproof rooms. Nothing could be further from the truth. It is, or should be, a record of individual thinkers' full-blooded, creative struggles with the most urgent conditions of their (and our) existence.

Such records must concern themselves with a wide variety of conditions. It is impossible, for example, to ignore the effects of wars in shaping the history of ideas—particularly since war has been the preeminent builder of modern nations—and I have therefore devoted a good deal of attention to the broad cultural aftereffects of the Civil War and the two world wars. It is equally impossible to ignore the degree to which, for nearly all the thinkers examined herein, the issues at stake seemed to be woven into the texture of their personal lives. Many of them were caught up in contradictory desires to feel both autonomous and connected and were involved in a search for a principle of self-sacrifice or self-transcendence—"the rock that is higher than I"—sufficiently powerful and authoritative to serve as a source of social order. Such issues may be posed in abstract language, but that should not conceal how ineluctably concrete and compellingly personal they really are, for all of us.

Partly as a consequence of this contextual and biographical approach to ideas, I have sought to concentrate, for the most part, upon thinkers who combined intellectual power and insight with a degree of popular reach and accessibility—the sort of thinkers that have of late come to be called public intellectuals. This rough criterion of combined depth and breadth will serve to define two sorts of history I have not attempted herein, except episodically. First, this book is not a history of sociology, psychology, or the social sciences, particularly as considered in their most sophisticated professional or institutional academic aspects. I have been highly selective, allowing the intellectual problem itself, rather than the agenda of the specialized professional disciplines, to dictate my choice of subjects—which is why I have felt free to include poets, novelists, and political scientists. (As George Santayana once observed, the visions of philosophers may deserve more attention than their arguments.) Second, to move to the opposite end of the spectrum, it is not a history of broadly popular attitudes, the sort of ideologies, mentalities, persuasions, climates of opinion, and so forth that would more properly be the province of a social or cultural historian. My approach presumes the existence of a middle ground between these two paths and attempts to situate itself there as much as possible. It is most certainly a book about intellectuals, but about intellectuals whose works combined intrinsic importance with broad cultural significance.

I would like to think that the decision to focus upon such an admittedly elusive *via media* has a compelling intellectual rationale. There certainly are sufficient drawbacks to the alternatives. The work of professionalized specialists is too often in thrall to an esoteric language, an internal logic, and an institutionalized system of rewards that have little meaning or resonance in the larger society—indeed, may seem bizarre and willfully unintelligible from that perspective. The echoes of popular sentiment are not automatically a better guide to historical significance, however; they are too often turbulent, raw, confused, and derivative, lacking the clarity, the independence, the composure, and the diagnostic and prescriptive power of the disciplined intellect.

Perhaps, to borrow the parlance of economics, the law of diminishing returns and Gresham's law present the two most threatening pitfalls of contemporary intellectual life: the division between professional culture and popular culture, our era's version of Van Wyck Brooks's familiar antagonism of highbrows and lowbrows. But that dichotomy is hardly one to rest in. The middle ground, far from being the ground of compromise or sellout, may be the most intellectually fertile, partly because it must take seriously the genuinely *public* obligations of the disciplined intellect. Indeed, if mind is to have a place of authority in the unfolding drama of our lives and our institutions, it must speak in a resoundingly public voice. In the process, it will not only have a salutary effect on the public to which it speaks. It will also discover that addressing the public is itself a salutary form of intellectual discipline.

# I

## Grand Review

*One rapid but fairly sure guide to the social atmosphere of a country is the parade-step of its army. A military parade is really a kind of ritual dance, something like a ballet, expressing a certain philosophy of life.*
—*George Orwell*

On May 18, 1865, thirty-nine days after General Robert E. Lee surrendered his Army of Northern Virginia at Appomattox Court House, the U.S. War Department ordered a final review of the large Federal armies still in the Washington area. The principal elements in this celebratory procession, to be held in the nation's capital for the benefit of President Johnson and his Cabinet, would be General George Meade's Army of the Potomac and the rather roughneck combined western armies that had slashed through Georgia and the Carolinas under the command of General William Tecumseh Sherman. All together, the parade would include some 200,000 of the Union army's most skilled and battle-hardened fighting men. More than any event in the confused and conflict-ridden months after the war's conclusion, this large military parade was designed as a terminal punctuation mark, a decisive and memorable public recognition of unity and national triumph. Yet few anticipated just how impressive this Grand Review would be. Reporting from

Washington on the eve of the review, the *New York Times*'s correspondent saw little to get excited about. Although he did notice a "great rush of visitors" coming into town "to see the boys in blue," he was confident that "those who see the show to-morrow will be indifferent about seeing it the next day. Few people will have the patience to gaze for seven or eight hours in the hot sun at the never-ending stream of troops that will pour through the city to-morrow."[1] He did not think the Grand Review would make grand theater.

He was wrong. In fact, the parade attracted throngs of "deeply interested spectators," as the *New York Tribune*'s correspondent described them, men and women of every station and race who stayed and stayed and, in many cases, came back for more the next day. It soon became clear, when the huge national forces had assembled and begun to move through Washington, that their presence did more than commemorate a great victory with a great spectacle. The parade also tellingly dramatized some of the specific meanings of that victory. A massive, highly disciplined national army, locking into its "cadence-step" in the shadow of the Capitol dome and moving in an inexorable, continuous flow along the mile and a half up Pennsylvania Avenue to the White House, then filing in perfect order past the admiring eyes of their commander in chief and his Cabinet: such imagery suggests how dramatically the country seemed to be leaving behind the dreams of a decentralized agrarian republic that had animated so many of its founders, and was embracing a dramatically new image of itself. Through its waging as well as its results, the war had thrust the United States into the ranks of the consolidated modern nation-states, with the increasingly powerful and centrally directed national institutions that such a transformation implies.

Indeed, the immense Grand Review that ensued on May 23 and 24 became a remarkable pageant of fully achieved nationality whose sheer scope eclipsed any comparable event in previous American history. Attending journalists agreed that it was "the greatest military pageant ever witnessed on this American continent."[2] "Washington," said the now-enthusiastic *Times*, "was filled as it never was filled before," even for Lincoln's funeral—so filled, in fact, that the out-of-town visitors pouring in by road and rail could not find overnight accommodations. Their reaction seemed to be anything but impatient or indifferent: "With many it is the greatest epoch of their lives; with the soldiers it is the last act in the drama; with the nation it is the triumphant exhibition of the resources and valor which have saved it from disruption and placed it first upon earth."[3] On the northern side of the Capitol building, at the spot where the parade was to begin, a banner was unfurled with the following words:

"The only national debt we can never pay is the debt we owe to the victorious Union soldiers."[4]

Early each morning the seemingly interminable lines of men, stretching backward as far as twenty-five miles, began to move; all day long a steady stream of marching blue wound its way through the heart of the Federal city "like a tremendous python."[5] It was as if all the accumulated power that had won the war were being gathered, concentrated, and placed on display for the edification of the citizenry: an object lesson in the new civics of nationalism. Few who witnessed the sight—the many thousands of martial participants, the countless fascinated civilian onlookers, the politicians and generals observing from the reviewing stand, their incessant feuds and intrigues momentarily submerged—were likely to forget it. Walt Whitman, for whom the war had been a great salvific struggle engaging his deepest personal passions, made it a point to be present. His observations, too, evoked the immense sprawl, in both space and time, of the review's panorama: "For two days now the broad space of Pennsylvania avenue along to Treasury hill, and so up to Georgetown, and across the aqueduct bridge, have been alive with a magnificent sight, the returning armies." Although Whitman had over the course of the war seen countless regiments parading through the streets of Washington, he was so drawn to the sight of the armies' "wide ranks stretching clear across the Avenue" that he watched their passing in review through both days.[6]

Many other outpourings of celebration occurred across the northern states in the wake of Appomattox, and like all such public festivities, they offer clues to the historical and social meanings imputed to the events they venerate.[7] Occasionally those observances betrayed an edge of conquering and gloating animus on the northern side, of just the sort Lincoln had so greatly feared and to which the shock and fury unleashed by his assassination by a southern zealot would contribute so greatly. Some of that sentiment inevitably surfaced in the War Department's ceremony at Fort Sumter, the Lexington and Concord of secession, on April 14, 1865, four years to the day after the Confederate takeover (and the very same day, it would also turn out, of Lincoln's assassination at Ford's Theater). Following Secretary of War Edwin Stanton's specific directive, the ceremony climaxed with Brevet Major General Robert Anderson's defiant rehoisting of the identical flag "which had floated over the battlements of that Fort during the rebel assault" four years before and which Anderson had at that time been forced to strike. With the Stars and Stripes flying again above Charleston harbor, the heartland of rebellion, the Reverend Henry Ward Beecher treated the crowd to a fiery oration directed against the "traitorous" rebels.[8]

Such sentiments were the exception rather than the rule, however. Any desire to rub the South's nose in defeat or to avenge Lincoln's death was generally overshadowed for the moment by emotions of intense relief and exhilaration. Cities, towns, and villages scattered across the face of the republic organized their own celebrations—often indistinguishable in character from the usual Fourth of July revelry—when their own local regiments at last came marching, or drifting, home from war. Although such celebrations gave evidence of American nationalist sentiment, they were more patriotic than nationalistic in flavor, more closely identified with the *patria*, with attachment to locality, to one's immediate home turf.[9]

The Grand Review, though, was not merely a bigger version of the customary American Fourth of July parade. It was a genuinely emblematic event, one that, as the contemporary journalists remarked again and again, was without any real precedent in American history. There had been no such Grand Review at the conclusion of the revolutionary war, or the War of 1812, or the Mexican War.[10] To be sure, patriotic and nationalistic sentiments were very much quickened by those earlier conflicts, but afterward, Americans quickly reverted to their long-standing republican distrust of standing armies, military professionalism, and excessively powerful central authority. Large armies were, for the most part, quickly dispersed or dissolved back into their state-based constituent militias as soon as the immediate military need had passed. The decision to hold a Grand Review showed how much a burgeoning nationalism had displaced the local and regional loyalty that had still prevailed in the early republic. As a majestic national pageant, the Grand Review affirmed the primacy in American life of national power, national governance, and national consciousness. If the flag-raising at Charleston gestured toward the antebellum status quo, even to the orchestrated return of Fort Sumter's erstwhile Federal commander, the setting and scope of the Grand Review conveyed a rather different message: the dramatic and perhaps irrevocable changes the war had wrought upon America.

Whitman surely committed a revealing slip of the pen when he called the participating troops "returning armies." They were, of course, nothing of the sort; most of the soldiers and units striding and riding down Pennsylvania Avenue those two days hailed from places like Ohio, New York, Illinois, or Massachusetts, and many were seeing Washington for the first time.[11] By all accounts, they had been very reluctant even to participate in this march, for they were anxious to return—not to Washington, but to their real homes—and to say good riddance to army life.[12] Yet there was figurative truth in Whitman's literal error. In the first place, they *were* returning from enemy territory. Notwithstanding Lincoln's sincerely conciliatory professions and intentions, the war for the Union quickly became a war of unification, that is to say, an exceptionally bitter war of conquest and occupation, fought with great tenacity and ruthlessness against an equally tenacious and ruthless regime whose hostility was fueled by powerful and contrary interests. A great public display like the Grand Review, meant to serve as a grand celebration of national unity, also served to define the nature of that unity—inevitably, from the vantage point of the winners. One ought not forget the wound over which the balm is spread, however. *Unity* and *Union* tend to be talismanic words in nations, institutions, committees, families, and other forms of social organization; yet their use often serves to deflect the impertinent question of *whose* unity and blurs the distinction between agreement and acquiescence, consensus and hegemony, reconciliation and domination. The Grand Review was conducted in an atmosphere of national assurance, not sectional vindictiveness. But it could never, for example, have included Confederate participants; the nation the victors celebrated did not yet contemplate that degree of reconciliation.

There was another, even more significant, sense in which the armies were returning: the orderly blue rows of men marching to Washington were also flowing back, as if pulled by diastolic force, to their ultimate political source. The small-town Yankees, the midwestern farm boys, and the Irish city-dwellers, volunteers and conscripts alike, that made up the Union army had, in a sense, been transformed by their experiences; they had become "national" men, initiated into a new kind of collective identity by their collective rites of passage—not only through the severe rites of modern war itself but also through their assimilation into the apparatus of a modern, thoroughly nationalized military organization. There was no more palpable sign of the new national dispensation than that long river of blue uniforms. It stood in striking contrast to the motley garb of the first northern regiments arriving in Washington in response to Lincoln's early recruitment calls, regiments whose irregular outfits reflected the natural diversity and diffused authority of a more loosely organized federal republic. Some states had dressed their fighting men in blue; others were in various combinations of grey, emerald, black, or red, while the New Yorkers sported baggy red breeches, purple Oriental blouses, and red fezzes in sartorial tribute to the French Zouaves. Given such a crazy quilt of martial apparel, the first Union forces assembled in Washington looked less like a serious army than "like a circus on parade."[13] Not so the Grand Review, four years later. Its steady flow of blue uniformity, interrupted only here and there by a sprinkling of variations, stilled the laughter and replaced it with awe.[14] That river of blue was visual confirmation of a sea change, the emblem of a powerful new political order whose authority would emanate increasingly from Washington.

---

Whitman was not the only one to find himself transfixed by the unfolding spectacle. The streets, sidewalks, doorsteps, windows, and balconies were crammed to overflowing with equally enthralled spectators, some of whom had journeyed hundreds of miles on jam-packed railroad cars, hoping to witness the great assembled armies in their moment of glory. Ladies and gentlemen came, stylishly turned out in their most resplendent holiday attire, carrying lovely bouquets of flowers or handkerchiefs to be bestowed upon passing heroes or favorite regiments; many of the well-off or well-connected watched the review from the elevation and relative privacy of an upper-story window or balcony. Others unable to secure one of the more favorable spots stood on curbs, climbed onto lampposts, milled about on sidewalks, and loitered on doorsteps, craning their necks to catch glimpses of the rolling show. The parade's cynosure was the spot near the White House where two large reviewing stands had been erected for VIPs: one, on the southern side of the avenue, for the president, his Cabinet members, and honored military guests, and the other directly across the street, for members of Congress, governors, and judges. Everywhere the eye turned, it encountered flags—state flags, division flags, brigade flags, and regimental flags—often tattered and soiled from battles and exposure to the elements on long marches, and flying from staffs decorated with flowers. But, fittingly, it was the national flag that seemed to dominate the field of vision up and down the parade route, decorating nearly every home and shop, dangling out of windows and fluttering from flagpoles.

The main attraction, however, was not the colorful and jubilant mise en scène but the armies themselves, for they seemed to embody in their forceful discipline and relentless momentum the awesome strengths and untried potentials of the newly reforged national unity. On the twenty-third, the Army of the Potomac, commanded by General Meade, passed in review; the following day, General Sherman led his western armies in like manner, filing down Pennsylvania Avenue, threading through the dense crowds, and taking the flowers, handkerchiefs, adoration, and accolades offered them by the cheering multitudes. When Sherman reached the Treasury building, he wheeled his horse around and paused to take in the full measure of the moment—the gigantic spectacle of his own troops stretching back toward the Capitol, proceeding smartly toward him in their final moments as a great army. Even the most unsentimental of men would have to be stirred, as Sherman was. The moment allowed him to savor a full measure of personal vindication.

Sherman was a complex man who, like his general in chief, Ulysses S. Grant, had overcome a dark past of personal failure and psychological turmoil to achieve the glory of this moment and become transformed into a byword of military history. That past, which included a nervous breakdown about which his detractors whispered, had left him prickly and perpetually insecure.[15] Even as the Grand Review was proceeding, he was fuming and brooding over embarrassments he had recently suffered at the hands of his political enemies, especially Secretary Stanton.[16] The sight now spread before him, however, lifted his spirits incalculably, and the reflections he later recorded in his memoirs not only bespoke his understandable pride in his own generalship but also resonated with an awareness of the review's deeper symbolic implications. His army was no longer merely an organized aggregation of individuals comprising units drawn from all over the northern states; instead, it had metamorphosed into a single, well-oiled marching mechanism of fearsome power and efficiency: "The sight was simply magnificent. The column was compact, and the glittering muskets looked like a solid mass of steel, moving with the regularity of a pendulum. . . . It was, in my judgment, the most magnificent army in existence—sixty-five thousand men, in splendid *physique*, who had just completed a march of nearly two thousand miles in a hostile country, in good drill, and who realized that they were being closely scrutinized by thousands of their fellow-countrymen and by foreigners."[17]

It was not often that Sherman and the journalists saw eye to eye, but on this occasion they did.[18] The *Times*'s reporter, his earlier skepticism now thoroughly banished, enthused that Sherman's men appeared to be "the most superb material ever molded into soldiers."[19] Although all the leaders and their troops were greeted by spirited cheering over those two days, Sherman was clearly the man of the hour and attracted the most rapturous reception. When he reached Lafayette Square, his attention was drawn to the figure of William Henry Seward, who, still weakened from the stab wounds inflicted by one of John Wilkes Booth's coconspirators, was viewing the parade from an upper-story window. The general doffed his hat in heartfelt tribute to the great Republican patriarch and diplomat, who had caused a firestorm seven years before when he predicted that the sections were heading toward "irrepressible conflict" arising from their "antagonistic systems" that could no longer coexist within the boundaries of a rapidly coalescing American nation-state.[20] The Grand Review marked the fulfillment of Seward's prediction: both the end of that conflict and the coalescence of that nation-state. Seward returned the greeting, and Sherman proceeded toward the White House. As he and his retinue approached the presidential stand, they saluted by drawing their swords, which flashed and gleamed in the spring sunlight. All on the stand rose to their feet in response. Then the general dismounted and took his place on the reviewing stand as the band offered a rousing rendition of "Marching through Georgia."[21] The two days of Grand Review had reached their climax.

---

"Marching through Georgia," written by Henry C. Work to memorialize the already fabled March to the Sea, was fated to become (to Sherman's intense annoyance) the general's lifelong tribute, struck up invariably in his honor whenever he made public appearances.[22] Sherman had every reason to dislike the song, for its bouncy, upbeat lyrics immortalized an incredibly sanitized version of the Georgia campaign. The architect of total war knew only too well that in deliberately cutting a path of destruction and terror from Atlanta to Savannah to Columbia, he had done something more complex than making "a thoroughfare for Freedom and her train," in whose path throngs of grateful, Union-loving Georgians had "wept with joyful tears, / When they saw the honor'd flag they had not seen for years," even as the Georgians' "sweet potatoes even started from the ground" and into the hungry bellies of his foraging army.[23] He had not earned the epithet Attila of the West and provoked enduring southern enmity as a reward for his liberatory benevolence. It had been his deliberate (and defensible) strategy to do whatever could be done to obliterate the southern will to resist by convincing southern civilians that their army and government could no longer even minimally protect them.[24]

But no matter: "Marching through Georgia" was a perfect song for this climactic moment of the Grand Review, partly because it so effectively highlighted Sherman and his army and partly because it so neatly edited the plight of the vanquished, but mainly because of its splendid evocation, both in its words and in its infectious rhythm, of the enterprise of marching. Indeed, the war songs of the Civil War were especially rich in marching imagery, which dominates many of the best-known refrains: "Tramp, tramp, tramp, the boys are marching," "When Johnny comes marching home," "When Sherman marched down to the sea," "March on, March on," "On, on, on the boys came marching," "We are marching to the field, boys, we're going to the fight, / Shouting the battle-cry of Freedom." Perhaps the most famous is the ringing assertion, declaimed with hammerlike insistence at the end of every verse and every chorus of "The Battle Hymn of the Republic," that the will of God himself "is marching on" in and through the Federal army's exertions. The emphasis upon marching in these songs, to be sure, partly reflects the wearisome activity they were designed to accompany and enliven; war songs are the soldier's work songs, and Civil War armies did more than their share of monotonous trudging. But the activity of marching itself also has a mystique, and it seemed especially to work its wonders on the enthralled crowds lining Pennsylvania Avenue during those two days in May 1865. In a very real sense, the Grand Review was consecrated to the act of marching itself, for marching made a rich symbol of a new American dispensation: of national power, discipline, and resolution.

Sherman's description of the review suggests how easy it was for the marching Union army to symbolize the unfolding political character of a newly energized national government:

> The steadiness and firmness of the tread, the careful dress on all the guides, the uniform intervals between the companies, all eyes directly to the front, and the tattered and bullet-riven flags, festooned with flowers, all attracted universal notice. Many good people, up to that time, had looked upon our Western army as a sort of mob; but the world then saw, and recognized the fact, that it was an army in the proper sense, well organized, well commanded and disciplined; and there was no wonder that it had swept through the South like a tornado. For six hours and a half that strong tread of the Army of the West resounded along Pennsylvania Avenue; not a soul of that vast crowd of spectators left his place; and, when the rear of the column had passed by, thousands of the spectators still lingered to express their sense of confidence in the strength of a Government which could claim such an army.[25]

Not only did the review make an impressive spectacle, but its success seemed to prefigure forms of organization that might lie in the nation's future. In that sense, the review was also preview.

---

To begin thinking about what those prefigured forms might be, one can reflect on the phenomenology of marching itself. At its most glorious, marching was a visible sign of complete social solidarity, the welding of a mob of isolated, unruly, puny, petty, flawed, self-interested, and inconsequential individuals into a massive, disciplined, dedicated, formidably powerful unit that could move with force and decisiveness, summoning full coordination of men and resources, in the pursuit of lofty, transpersonal ideals and grand objectives. Marching was thus an incomparable metaphor for the benefits to be derived from a thoroughgoing coalescing, reconceiving, and redirecting of the structure of modern industrial society. In addition to its structural and social dimensions, marching also had psychological and personal implications. The discipline of marching required suppressing and renouncing the impulse to initiate one's own movements; it meant finding freedom instead in submission to a clear, sure, decisive, repetitive order of prescribed movements and pre-ordained directions, of rhythmically stepping feet and precisely swinging arms, moving in tandem with many thousands of others, propelled by the crisp and insistent rhythms of pounding drums and blaring brass.[26]

For those who enter fully into its spirit, the experience can be intensely exhilarating, intoxicating, energizing, and liberating. Even those from a highly provincial background were likely to be overcome by a sudden, surging sense of connection to the nation. A Wisconsin private wrote thus of the Grand Review to his parents: "That day we all fell in, and it seemed the minute the order was given, our boys took on an apperance [sic] of glory and holiness, and they *marched*, *oh* how they marched, never before did they stride like that. Just imagine the scene, Mother and Father, if you can! . . . How proud we were. . . . President Johnson with his Government Officials, some Foreign Officers and General Grant stood up and cheered as we passed. I thought we would all lose some more buttons for our chests swelled up and our hearts throbbed."[27]

Notice the easy association of marching with glory and holiness. The lure of marching has an ecstatic, even spiritual, side to it, just as a prompting toward military vocation may have much in common with the call of spiritual vocation. Both the iron cross and the Calvary cross offered the vision of a consecrated life of discipline and sacrifice devoted to the overcoming of self through commitment to a greater, transpersonal power whose authority took precedence over one's own chaotic and unruly will. That parallel has been particularly salient in the Christian intellectual tradition, under whose unquestioned cultural auspices the Grand Review marchers dwelled and whose imperatives therefore largely defined what "holiness" might mean. The central figure in that tradition had taught that "he that loseth his life for my sake shall find it"; that he had come "not to send peace, but a sword"; that he had come even "to set a man at variance against his father," daughter against mother, household (and nation) against itself; and that those who would gather under his banner had to be willing to lay aside all other loyalties, even the most primal and venerable, in favor of the cross, because the man "that loveth father or mother more than me is not worthy of me."[28] St. Paul further elaborated this teaching, pronouncing himself "dead to the law" and sin, so that he "might live unto God"—"crucified with Christ" so that, though "I now live in the flesh," it is not "I" that lives, "but Christ [that] liveth in me."[29]

Who would save his life must lose it. That knotty paradox is, in its truest acceptation, the most fundamental imperative of Christian life: for one saves it *only* by losing it for the sake of Christ, losing self in order to become a part of

his body. There are no substitutes; he who "finds" his life in some oth[er]
worships a false god and shall thereby lose it without possibility of rest[ored].
Yet it is an inevitable feature of Christianity's cultural impress that su[ch]
sacrificing imperative would often spill over into other areas of life. [Such]
imperatives may produce or reinforce a characteristic way of thinking that can
easily be projected or insinuated, consciously or unconsciously, by analogy or
transference, into quite different situations and concerns. Indeed, as students
of American religion have repeatedly pointed out, this kind of displacement
has long been a persistent feature of American national identity; it was just
such a national characteristic that led G. K. Chesterton to call the United
States "a nation with the soul of a church."[30] America has often linked its
national self-understanding to a national creed that includes a perceived provi-
dential mission of spiritual regeneration, redemption, or millennial destiny—
or, to put it more negatively, it has had a tendency to confuse devotion to the
nation with devotion to God.[31]

In short, the same urges that drew the individual soul toward the self-
transcendence of the Christian faith might also draw it toward the self-
transcendence of military marching, of righteous warfare, of devotion to the
national cause. Sherman recalled how, as his soldiers marched away from a
smoldering Atlanta, they sang a song associating the martyr of radical abolition with God's glory: "before us the Fourteenth Corps, marching steadily and
rapidly, with a cheery look and swinging pace, that made light of the thousand
miles that lay between us and Richmond. Some band, by accident, struck up
the anthem of 'John Brown's soul goes marching on;' the men caught up the
strain, and never before or since have I heard the chorus of 'Glory, glory,
hallelujah!' done with more spirit, or in better harmony of time and place."[32]
Because the temper of American Protestantism encouraged the conjunction of
the sacred and the national, it was not difficult to adapt the tune of "Glory
Hallelujah" (whose original opening words were "Say, Brothers, will you
meet us, on Canaan's happy shore?") for the purposes of war. In the closing
verse of "The Battle Hymn of the Republic," Julia Ward Howe's adaptation of
"Glory Hallelujah," one finds two very similar kinds of self-mortification
effortlessly conjoined, carried along together, as it were, by the rhythm of the
pounding drums: "As [Christ] died to make men holy, let us die to make men
free, / While God is marching on." This amalgamation of holiness and freedom, of the Crucifixion with the Union casualties, of the sacred order and the
secular nation, suggests the distinctive contours of the American (or at any
rate northern) political religion.[33]

In this light, it is not surprising that as the conflict wore on, Lincoln spoke
more and more frequently of "the nation"; and when he did speak of "the

Union," he presented it as an end in itself, one eminently worth sacrificing for, to such an extent that his old friend Alexander Stephens marveled that "the Union with him in sentiment rose to the sublimity of a religious mysticism."[34] In other words, the strictly nationalistic elements in his political thinking increased in power and prominence, and they did so in tandem with his increasingly quasi-religious perception of the meaning of the conflict. That latter perception is well borne out in Lincoln's wartime speechmaking, as his rhetorical appeals on behalf of the Union began to vibrate with more and more explicitly biblical overtones. As John Patrick Diggins has pointed out, Lincoln's most powerful and resonant rhetoric during the war years was not drawn from the reservoir of liberal or republican ideologies; rather, he reached back increasingly into the thought and imagery of the King James Bible.[35] In the second inaugural address, he depicted the war as a necessary atonement, an expiatory sacrifice offered a "true and righteous" God for the nation's ghastly original sin of slavery.[36] This imagery itself was cast, as was so much of the "Battle Hymn," in the mold of the Pentateuch and the Prophets; but an even more impressive feature of the second inaugural, given its wartime circumstances, was its breathtaking New Testament humility: "Let us judge not that we be not judged. The prayers of both [parties to this conflict] could not be answered; that of neither has been answered fully. The Almighty has His own purposes." Such an attempt at self-sacrificial evenhandedness, at conscientiously distinguishing the intentions of men from the intentions of God, in itself marked a great moral advance over the dichromatic self-righteousness of the "Battle Hymn"; but its being delivered by the leader of a belligerent nation during an unexpectedly bloody, passionate, divisive, and exhausting war seems nothing short of astonishing.[37]

The unmistakably Christian overtones of his message were startlingly reinforced by his assassination on Good Friday and by his subsequent transformation into a national martyr. The three-week-long spectacle of Lincoln's seven-car funeral train traversing the northern states, greeted by somber crowds of mourners who were willing to stand in the rain and the darkness just to witness the passing train, was perhaps the Grand Review's only rival as a defining postwar public spectacle.[38] It too reflected upon the meaning of the nation and on the way that, as Lincoln expressed it in his first inaugural address, the "mystic chords of memory" could "swell the chorus of Union."[39] The funeral train was, in fact, a harmonic inversion of the Grand Review, and not only because it represented Washington extending its hand to the country rather than the country coming to Washington. It was an affirmation of Union expressed, not through the power of marching, but through the pain of shared loss—through sacrificial, expiatory, hallowed death of the sort he had commemorated in the Gettysburg Address.[40] In time, Lincoln's dedication to the Union seemed to merge with his increasing conviction that a just God punishes the iniquity of nations and that there was a redemptive purpose for suffering—both his country's and his own. The conciliatory, unvindictive, nonpunitive peace toward which the second inaugural address looked, and for which Lincoln was still planning and yearning, anticipated a change of heart, a true conversion, the replacement of malice by charity, a crucified ego—a willingness to release the desire for vengeance and submit to something larger than oneself, something with its own purposes. Whether Lincoln would have been able to bring the country successfully into such a gentle reunion is imponderable. Having died as the carrier of the national sins, he was reborn into the full flower of national redemptive myth. If victory can unify, so too can affliction.

"With the tolling tolling bells' perpetual clang," wrote Whitman, evoking the memory of Lincoln's funeral train, "Here, coffin that slowly passes, / I give you my sprig of lilac."[41] "When Lilacs Last in the Dooryard Bloom'd" immortalized Whitman's fervent love for, and identification with, the dead president, and the depth with which he mourned his hero's passing. Whitman felt and registered both forms of the impulse toward Union—not only the animating uplift of marching but the crushing weight of suffering, and not only the selflessness of righteous solidarity but the selflessness of agape—and, further, of willing death.[42] That attachment to Lincoln was inseparable from Whitman's own even more mystical commitment to the Union. Lincoln, he believed, had exemplified "a new virtue, unknown to other lands," called "UNIONISM"; and Whitman's description of it subsumed the glory of military self-sacrifice under the mantle of national apotheosis: "He was assassinated—but the Union is not assassinated—*ça ira*! One falls, and another falls. The soldier drops, sinks like a wave—but the ranks of the ocean eternally press on. Death does its work, obliterates a hundred, a thousand—President, general, captain, private—but the Nation is immortal."[43]

Clearly, part of what Whitman meant by unionism was that willingness to subordinate not only one's egoistic desires and personal interests but also one's local identity and particularist loyalties—to be incorporated into those interests, identities, and loyalties that were national in character. For it was the nation that endured, the nation that was worth sacrificing for. "From Paumanok starting I fly like a bird," he wrote, a bird that learns the songs of all the states, but prefers always "to sing first, (to the tap of the war-drum if need be,) / The idea of all."[44] Like the panorama of the Grand Review, in which disparate individuals, regiments, localities, and states were welded into a consolidated whole (moving "to the tap of the war-drum"), Whitman's invocation of "the all" reflects a more general shifting of perspective, both in reality and in imagination, from older ideals of individualism, dispersed authority, federalism, and localism toward a more comprehensively knitted-together ideal: the marching nation. Why an archindividualist like Whitman would be so powerfully drawn to "the idea of all" is an important question, to be taken up shortly. For now, it is enough to point out that the Civil War, for him as well as for other Americans, was the crucial moment in the coming of that national, consolidational ideal in American life, in ways both obvious and subtle, empirical and intangible, macroeconomic and intimate.

---

If we conceive modern American history by mapping it in relief, then there can be little doubt that the Civil War still stands at the symbolic crest of that history's watershed. The long, meandering, often indistinct boundary that defines modern America passes along the grassy rise of Cemetery Ridge; and, as is true of any momentous historical event involving the fates of many individuals and myriad interests, the Civil War will always bear the weight of multiple meanings. The lure of its enigmas will continue to attract scholarly investigation and stir the public imagination. The most powerful symbols hold a wide range of ambivalences and polarities within their ambit, and the Civil War accordingly will always admit of varied, and valid, interpretations: a great crusade of freedom; a democratic or bourgeois revolution; a tragic clash of divergent economies, political ideologies, and cultures; an upheaval of modernization; or perhaps even in some as yet unimagined categories.[45] One of the most fundamental of all the issues addressed by the war, and largely settled by it, however, was the supremacy of national institutions in American life.[46] In that sense, the American Civil War may be regarded as part and parcel of the larger evolution toward national unification and consolidation that runs through the history of the nineteenth century; indeed, it may be usefully compared to the roughly contemporaneous battles for national unification that were then dramatically changing the map, and the political geography, of continental Europe.[47]

Clearly, for Americans that idea takes some getting used to. Lincoln as Cavour, Lincoln as Bismarck: such comparisons may seem jarring, incongruous, even irreverent to Americans, who not only tend to see the war as a great moral struggle but also tend to segregate the issues animating their own nineteenth-century history from that of Europe; and there are ample reasons not to press such comparisons too energetically.[48] They do serve, however, to emphasize certain features of the Civil War that our fascination with its uniqueness, its many layers of intensely human drama, the tantalizing complexity of its origins and results, and the ambiguity of its ultimate meaning may obscure somewhat. So it is useful to recall the obvious: to whatever extent the Civil War served to define the future shape of the American nation, it did so through the proverbial Bismarckian formula of blood and iron, forcing the divergent aspirations of the southern states into the hard mold of a true modern nation-state. Lincoln's unionism was a form of nationalism, and the reunification of his "house divided" occurred at the insistence of northern arms, just as German unification would occur under the coercive hand of Prussia. In each case, the prosecution of war and the progress of national consolidation were indissolubly linked.[49]

National consolidation, then, accomplished initially (though not exclusively) by northern military domination, could well be designated the watchword of the postbellum decades. War is the most powerful of all engines for fostering national self-consciousness, and the most reliable of all centralizing and unifying agents in human affairs. Its inevitable byproducts immeasurably strengthen the hand of national political institutions, as Randolph Bourne's lapidary dictum, "War is the health of the state," has paid bitter tribute.[50] More than the subduing of the rebellious South was at stake; the Civil War, as much from its conduct as from its outcome, boosted the powers of the national government, the scope of the presidency, the size of the executive branch, and the powers of the Congress and the federal courts, and established a national social-welfare agency (the Freedmen's Bureau) and even a national income tax. War's centralizing force was so inescapable that even Confederate president Jefferson Davis was forced to begin constituting the South as a nation-state, collecting his own income tax and dictating to the several states on such sensitive matters as habeas corpus, conscription, and martial law—thereby eliciting the howls and opposition of more devoted states'-rights advocates, including his own vice-president, Alexander H. Stephens.[51]

Perhaps that experience of betrayal, on top of the secession crisis itself, about which he had been highly ambivalent, had made the Georgian Stephens deeply sensitized to these issues; for in his *Constitutional View of the Late War between the States* (1868–70)—as its title would suggest, a thoroughly pro-southern and pro-secession apologia, which has since fallen into obscurity—he nevertheless offered illuminating observations regarding the war's political meaning and effects.[52] The fundamental conflict, in Stephens's view, was not over slavery versus freedom, or northern versus southern economies or cultures, but over "two different and opposing ideas as to the nature of what is known as the General Government," pitting "those who held it to be strictly Federal in its character" against "those who maintained that it was thoroughly National." It was a battle, he contended, "between the principles of Federation, on the one side, and Centralism, or Consolidation, on the other."[53] As a historical explanation of the coming of the Civil War, this downplaying of the slavery question, as well as other social and economic issues, made for an exceptionally narrow and legalistic perspective—one notably at odds, moreover, with Stephens's own earlier insistence in 1861 that slavery was the "cornerstone" of the Confederacy, a cornerstone that "rests upon the great truth, that the negro is not equal to the white man; that slavery . . . is his natural and normal condition."[54] If read in descriptive terms, however, as an account not of the supposed nature of the contest but of its results, Stephens's perspective highlights an indubitable truth about the war. Moreover, it helps us bring into the picture the long background of the formation of Anglo-American political institutions, which had been wrestling with the problematic nature of divided sovereignty since colonial times, and particularly so during the American Revolution—itself an evolving dispute over the proper allocation of political authority within the context of the British Empire. The Federalist-Antifederalist debates, the Hamilton-Jefferson conflicts, and the nullification and interposition controversies all reflected the dialectical interplay of Stephens's two principles. The Civil War itself represented yet another stage in the progress of that lengthy Anglo-American debate, but it was a decisive stage, in which the centripetal strength of national cohesion and coalescence finally gained the upper hand over looser patterns of federal dispersion.

The Civil War was a similarly significant moment in the economic history of the nineteenth century, one in which the forces of northern domination and national consolidation become fused into near-synonymity. It is certainly tempting, in this connection, to recur to the Beardian argument that the war represented a second American Revolution, in which northern commercial and industrial interests achieved clear dominance over southern agrarian interests—thus resolving the conflict that Seward had foreseen by redefining the national economy.[55] One can also point to the substantial economic stimulation produced in the northern states by the war, including sizable increases in coal and iron production, manufactured goods, shipbuilding, and agricultural products; these gains, moreover, were accompanied by catastrophic losses of wealth and productive capacity in the South, producing a massive northward redistribution of national economic resources.[56] Yet as Charles Beard himself noted, "The real revolution—the silent shift of social and material power—had occurred before the southern states declared their independence," and therefore the South would have had to yield, one way or another, gracefully or violently, to the economic regime of industrial capitalism.[57] Moreover, there were steady consolidating forces at work throughout the century, such as the growing nationalization of markets made possible by ongoing revolutions in transportation and increasingly refined techniques of mass production and distribution. The war had no decisive effect upon these long-term changes, except that of accelerating them in some cases or confirming them in others.[58] In some respects, then, the Civil War's economic significance was symbolic as well as direct, a confirming push to developments already well under way.

The growing saliency and predominance of national political and economic integration in the postbellum decades of the nineteenth century had more personal, and even intimate, ramifications. Such developments reflected and furthered a pervasive challenge to the patterns of local political and economic affiliation that had shaped the consciousness and daily life of most Americans in the country's first nine decades—the challenge poeticized in Whitman's image of the flying bird who sings "the all." That change again recalls the central meanings that Stephens had imputed to the war and suggests that the conflict between the federal and the general, far from being confined to the political realm, may also serve as a powerful root metaphor whose meanings may be fruitfully extended into the social, cultural, and economic spheres. One of the most influential renderings of modern American history has envisioned the great underlying story of postbellum America as a gradual movement from a society of "island communities"—more or less insular, homogeneous, and provincial communities whose sense of connection to the nation was highly attenuated, outweighed by the considerable degree of autonomy they enjoyed—to a society in which that sense of autonomy had been penetrated and undermined by the emergent (and frequently profoundly disruptive) forces of political, economic, and cultural nationalization.[59] Economic and political features lay at the base of the transformation; the growth of the railroads had a particularly inescapable impact. Such changes could not help but manifest in what can only be called a growing nationalization of consciousness.

One should be careful about claiming too much too soon for this term. By no means did it imply, then or since, the sudden and complete obliteration of local affinities,[60] nor should it imply that American nationalism suddenly burst upon the scene in 1865 without considerable antecedents.[61] Yet an event like the Grand Review, whose participants were caught up in an almost tangible experience of the nation, did mark the inauguration of something new. This newness was perhaps even more tellingly prefigured in the interstate spectacle of Lincoln's funeral train, an event that would not have been thinkable without the single most nation-integrating technology of the nineteenth century, which made it possible literally to nationalize an event whose impact would formerly have been confined to a single place. Indeed, it is impossible to escape the railroads' structural centrality to virtually all the major social and economic transformations of the postbellum era. In human terms, however, perhaps the most telling examples of growing national influence were the most commonplace, accumulating piecemeal: rural free delivery, parcel post, the railroad depot, the Montgomery Ward and Sears mail-order catalogs, the McCormick salesman, the agricultural jobbers and middlemen, the chain stores (such as Woolworth's or A&P), Swift's meat, Borden's condensed milk, *The Ladies' Home Journal*. The nationalization of experience also meant a certain standardization of experience.[62]

Perhaps no development symbolized this ongoing process, and the way it inexorably touched and transformed individual consciousnesses, more potently than the establishment in 1883 of the standard time zones. The need for them was clear; they arose from the formidable structural requirements entailed in scheduling and operating a sprawling transcontinental railroad system—the quintessential modern business enterprise. One could hardly expect to run a nation-spanning railroad effectively and reliably by continuing to schedule according to local mean time, in which noon simply meant the time at any given place when the sun reached its zenith. But the standardization of time (which was, in effect, imposed by the railroads, not the federal government, on November 18, 1883) was consequential, as momentous in its way as the invention of the mechanical clock. Lives that had formerly been measured by, and entwined with, the rhythms of agricultural life or the promptings of the local church (or factory) bells now found themselves radically delocalized as the measurement of time—the fundamental grid upon which human experience is plotted—was made to conform to a national standard.[63] The standardization of that grid, for better and worse, exemplified the fruits of nationalization and consolidation, the socially unsettling combination of benefit and dependency, of connection and invasion, wrought by the intrusion of the railroad and other modern, vertically integrated, national-scale business enterprises.[64]

---

Perhaps the Civil War, then, can be seen both as a catalyst of certain dramatic changes and as a potent symbol for those longer-term, steadier, more structural developments that transformed nineteenth-century America; both meanings, in any event, seemed to be aimed at the same broadly integrative, nation-building end. The success of the knitting-together process was far from uniform; witness the continuing marginalization of certain groups and regions and, perhaps most notable, the immiseration and economic backwardness of the postbellum South, which did not begin to recede significantly until the Second World War. The general drift, however, toward consolidation and nationalization over the entire course of the nineteenth century, in both social fact and social imagination, in description and prescription, seems clear. Equally clear are the elements of changing consciousness that accompanied that general drift, elements that manifested themselves powerfully in the intellectual history of the period—in dramatically altered understandings both of society and of the individual and in profound alterations in the projective social ideals that flowed from such understandings. *Consolidation* not only describes a changing world but also the changing ways of imagining it, accounting for its pathologies, and prescribing for it.[65]

The word *consolidation* has to be used with numerous disclaimers and caveats. From the privileged vantage point of grand historical panorama, the complex spectacle of a coalescing nineteenth-century America invites a host of images and metaphors but defies adequate containment by any one of them. It was an enormous drawing-together of a continent, the transformation of an archipelago into a single landmass, a great coalescence, a great centripetal contraction, a shrinking of space and time. These words and images are less than completely adequate, yet all suggest a process of unifying, or drawing together, and a consequent or correlative shifting of fundamental assumptions. As Alan Trachtenberg has argued, *incorporation* may be one of the most fruitful terms with which to label the fundamental dynamic of this era, since that word's range of meanings embraces both the fact of national coalescence and the coercive elements in that coalescence, particularly through the rise of the large business corporation. *To incorporate* may mean (1) to merge disparate elements into a unified whole; (2) to absorb something into another, larger entity; and (3) to form a corporation, a legal person or *corpus*, a body with rights, privileges, and liabilities distinct from those of its members. All three meanings are readily applicable to features of the postbellum scene, and they interplay and ramify outward in infinitely suggestive ways. The first definition carries an impartial sense of integration and unionism; the second suggests the integration of regional and sectional diversity into national unity; the third, most importantly to Trachtenberg, points to the increasing concentration of power and authority in America in the hands of a few dominant institutions, especially the heavily capitalized modern industrial corporations.[66]

Although somewhat redolent of the language of corporate mergers or organizational streamlining, the word *consolidation* is a more neutral, less charged term that encompasses a multitude of sins and virtues without prejudicially labeling them as such from the outset. It suggests something closer to an archetypal or paradigmatic pattern of movement and thought, whose characteristic forms may manifest in a variety of discrete ways. The growing perception of the nation as a single unified political and social entity falls under its rubric; so does a recognition and acceptance of the profound interdependence inherent in modern forms of social and economic organization; and so too does the desire to systematize the efficiencies offered by such forms, and to offer systematic redress for the unprecedented social inequalities that such forms seemed to produce and perpetuate. *Consolidation* applied to this era can be merely a descriptive term, denoting an ever more pervasive social reality. In other respects, however, and more importantly for our purposes, it can stand for a tantalizing prescriptive ideal yet to be adequately realized. It was not only tied to changing perceptions of the American nation. In the hands of the most thoughtful writers, it expressed a changing vision of human nature itself and of the appropriate aims of social reform in an increasingly interdependent industrial order.

The usefulness of the term in the present context lies in the way it permits us, from the distance and altitude of the historical reviewing stand, to see how even contemporary antagonists can be understood as different facets of a more encompassing cultural whole—to make, in short, a revealing cultural generalization about characteristic patterns of thinking. The term cuts across some of the usual lines and unites some surprising bedfellows. Contrary to the familiar view of a postbellum America intellectually dominated by credos of rampant individualism and social Darwinism, one is likely to be struck by the degree to which visions of consolidation, in one form or another, were an increasingly commonplace feature of late nineteenth-century intellectual life. Some version of that ideal, rather than a vulgarization of Herbert Spencer, better describes the Weltanschauung of John D. Rockefeller, J. P. Morgan, or others among the pioneering modern corporate leaders.[67] Something like consolidation also informed the vision of influential labor leaders, socialist utopians, middle-class reformers, and conservative nationalists. For all their obvious differences, all were drawn to certain paradigmatic assumptions. They shared a tendency to project imaginatively a centripetal and integrated social ideal. They regarded unfettered individualism with fear or disdain and stressed instead the needs of the group, the fixity and dignity of institutions, the importance of functional differentiation, the satisfactions of social solidarity, the illusory quality of individual autonomy.

The extent to which this shared outlook or agenda represented a dramatic shift of emphasis can best be gauged against the background of what had preceded it. As John Higham has pointed out, the enormous American popularity of Spencer in the mid-nineteenth century derived less from his putative endorsement of buccaneering individualism than from his convincing articulation of a cosmic evolutionary principle of consolidation, in which the universe itself was seen as tending "from a relatively diffused, uniform, indeterminate arrangement, to a relatively concentrated, multiform, and determinate arrangement." The existence of such a universal support made the bewildering changes occurring in postbellum industrial America more intelligible and tolerable; however chaotic things might seem at any given moment, we may feel confident that they are moving in the way of the universe itself. The operational influence of such a principle could account for, among other things, the shifting ideals of American culture in the mid-nineteenth century: from an expansive emphasis upon fluidity, decentralization, localism, individual liberty, "self-culture," diffusion, and growth to a more cautious, self-effacing, and stewardly concern with institution building, integration, nationalization, and social cohesiveness. Higham succinctly expressed the dichotomy as a movement "from boundlessness to consolidation," and although not every important cultural phenomenon of the time fits under that canopy, there are enough to make it a suggestive generalization.[68]

The history of the term *consolidation* itself tells part of the story, and that is another compelling reason for using it. *Consolidation* had long been a controversial term, appearing again and again, generally used in a highly pejorative tone, in the political discourse of pre–Civil War America. In the debates over the adoption of the Constitution, for example, one frequently encounters Antifederalists charging that the proposed document was designed to bring about the tyranny of a consolidated government (and proponents of the Constitution responding by strenuously denying the charge).[69] Perhaps most famous of these laments were those of Patrick Henry, who railed against the Constitution at the Virginia State Ratifying Convention: "The fate of this question and of America may depend on this. Have they said, We the states? Have they made a proposal of a compact between states? If they had, this would be a confederation. It is otherwise most clearly a consolidated government . . . [which is] abhorrent to my mind." Henry's ire reflected the persistent small-scale republicanism underlying much of the argument against national consolidation:

Shall we imitate the example of those nations who have gone from a simple to a splendid government? Are those nations more worthy of our imitation? What can make an adequate satisfaction to them for the loss they have suffered in attaining such a government—for the loss of their liberty? If we admit this consolidated government, it will be because we like a great, splendid one. Some way or other we must be a great and mighty empire; we must have an army, and a navy, and a number of things. When the American spirit was in its youth, the language of America was different: liberty, sir, was then the primary object. . . . We drew the spirit of liberty from our British ancestors: by that spirit we have triumphed over every difficulty. But now, sir, the American spirit, assisted by the ropes and chains of consolidation, is about to convert this country into a powerful and mighty empire. . . . Such a government is incompatible with the genius of republicanism. There will be no checks, no real balances, in this government. What can avail your specious, imaginary balances, your rope-dancing, chain-rattling, ridiculous ideal checks and contrivances?[70]

Patrick Henry's view might be dismissed as sectional and extreme, but the specter of consolidation haunted countless other Antifederalist documents, North and South. According to the dissenting minority of the Pennsylvania convention, "Consolidation pervades the whole constitution. . . . The powers vested by this constitution in Congress, will effect a consolidation of the states under one government, which even the advocates of this constitution admit, could not be done without the sacrifice of all liberty."[71] The Albany Antifederal Committee felt "they have not formed a *federal* but a *consolidated* government, repugnant to the principles of a republican government; not founded on the preservation but the destruction of the state governments."[72] "Agrippa" of Massachusetts wrote, "The direct tendency of the proposed system, is to consolidate the whole empire into one mass, and, like the tyrant's bed, to reduce all to one standard. . . . Large and consolidated empires may indeed dazzle the eyes of a distant spectator with their splendour, but if examined more nearly are always found to be full of misery. The reason is obvious. . . . To promote the happiness of the people it is necessary that there should be local laws; and it is necessary that those laws should be made by the representatives of those who are immediately subject to the want of them."[73]

Equally worthy of note is the fact that supporters of the Constitution were generally at great pains to echo their own horror of consolidation and to offer assurances that they had no such intention in mind and that the document would surely not produce such dire effects. For example, the staunch Federalist Fisher Ames agreed that "too much provision cannot be made against a consolidation. The state governments represent the wishes, and feelings, and local interests of the people. They are the safeguard and ornament of the Constitution; they will protract the period of our liberties; they will afford a shelter against the abuse of power, and will be the natural avengers of our violated rights."[74] James Madison himself, in *Federalist* 39, felt called upon to address the specter of consolidation directly: "'But it was not sufficient,' say the adversaries of the proposed Constitution, 'for the convention to adhere to the republican form. They ought with equal care to have preserved the *federal* form, which regards the Union as a *Confederacy* of sovereign states; instead of which they have framed a *national* government, which regards the Union as a *consolidation* of the States.'" In a long and subtle answer to this objection, Madison concluded that the proposed constitution actually was "neither a national nor a federal Constitution, but a composition of both."[75] Madison claimed that the very thought of the new central government wresting preeminence from the states was wholly illusory and that it was "beyond doubt that the first and most natural attachment of the people will be to the governments of their respective States"—and even were that to change somehow, perhaps as a result of "the people . . . giving their confidence where they may discover it to be most due," still "the State governments could have little to apprehend, because it is only within a certain sphere that the federal power can, in the nature of things, be advantageously administered."[76]

Even after adoption of the Constitution, *consolidation* was still a term to conjure with and quibble over, though eventually a sectional polarization set in. In the Kentucky Resolutions of November 1798, Thomas Jefferson warned that "consolidating" the states "in the hands of the general government" would be "to surrender the form of government we have chosen."[77] The 1828 "South Carolina Exposition and Protest," largely drafted by John C. Calhoun, complained that a federal tariff policy for purposes beyond revenue collection implied an "absolute control over all the interests, resources, and pursuits of a people, and is inconsistent with the idea of any other than a simple, consolidated government."[78] In the great 1830 Senate debates between Robert Y. Hayne and Daniel Webster, Hayne used the issue of the sale of public lands to raise more fundamental questions about the effects such revenues might have upon the power of the central government. Echoing the words and thoughts of his mentor, Calhoun, he opined that such a "consolidation" had been the long-term sinister intention of some of his nationalist-republican colleagues. Webster ridiculed this claim ("Consolidation!—that perpetual cry, both of terror and delusion—consolidation!"), pointing out that the framers of the Constitution themselves had declared an interest in the "consolidation of the Union." Hayne rejoined that consolidation of the Union meant nothing more than was meant by the Preamble's expressed aim "to form a more perfect Union"—but that was very different from consolidation of the government, by which was meant supersession of the states' sovereignty by the central authority. That was the change Hayne opposed so strenuously, and on that point he met with no disagreement from Webster, who was readily willing to aver that he would find "odious" any "consolidation" which might mean "an accumulation in the Federal Government, of the powers properly belonging to the States."[79] But Webster continued to insist that the Union had been created not by a compact of the states but by the people, and that it was therefore not dissoluble or rescindable without recourse to that authority.

To a large extent, as always, one's position in these matters of political theory seemed to turn on the question of whose oxen were being gored. Just as Calhoun's political thought moved from Whiggish nationalism to states'-rights sectionalism, Webster's opinions on issues of national sovereignty had not been notably consistent. Earlier in Webster's career, sectional interests and anti-Jeffersonian convictions had led him to support the doctrine of state interposition against the Embargo Act—and, his disingenuous disclaimers to Hayne notwithstanding, to support the Hartford convention, praising its resolutions as "moderate, temperate, & judicious."[80] Now sectional interests and a growing commitment to nationalism were inclining him the other way. This time, however, that shift had positioned him in coordination with the gathering centralizing tide of American history. Webster's ringing final response to Hayne, which included his famous invocation of "Liberty *and* Union, now and forever, one and inseparable"—a widely reprinted, instant classic of a political sermon that almost certainly shaped Lincoln's own conception of the Union—left little doubt that old republican ideas of confederated government, and of the Constitution as a compact between states, were losing their grip and were destined to become more and more the exclusive property of the South, eventually to be routed from the stage.[81] From Thomas Jefferson to Jefferson Davis, *consolidation* had been a word held in more or less ill repute in American life. After the war, though, only a few eccentric proslavery diehards, like Alexander Stephens, were left to pronounce it with the former measure of poisonous disdain.

---

Even so, one wonders how many onlookers standing in the cheering crowds lining the Washington streets on those two sunny Grand Review days in May might have quietly harbored complex feelings, perhaps admissible only in the privacy of their hearts, about what they were witnessing. Did anyone feel anxiety about the metamorphosis of the old republic into a new nation—the many-faceted transformation symbolized by this passing colossus of marching men? Were there any vestiges of Patrick Henry's fears for the future of liberty in "those nations who have gone from a simple to a splendid government"? Was there any of the premonitory angst expressed by Charles Francis Adams, Jr., about the disruptive effects of the nation-spanning transcontinental railroad: "an enormous, an incalculable force, practically let loose suddenly upon mankind, exercising all sorts of influences, social, moral, and political . . . the most tremendous and far-reaching engine of social change which has ever either blessed or cursed mankind"?[82] Did anyone anticipate Lewis Mumford's even more bitter opinion that "the war was a struggle between two forms of servitude, the slave and the machine . . . and the human spirit was almost as much paralyzed by the victory as it would have been by the defeat"?[83] Did anyone wonder whether "the idea of the all" that they watched striding so smartly to "the tap of the war-drum" could be elicited and mastered by other rhythms, other promptings, for other ends? Was the ebullient marching spirit of the occasion disturbed or chastened by such vagrant thoughts? Perhaps so, perhaps not. History is filled with moments of inscrutable depth, where what is latent, potential, unconscious, and unspoken can never be reliably known, let alone adequately documented.

In any event, such complexities of sentiment would emerge in due course. Consolidation could claim no great virtue or honor for itself unless it was animated by a sense of higher purpose. (Charles Adams's brother Henry acidly remarked, "The generation between 1865 and 1895 was already mortgaged to the railways, and no one knew it better than the generation itself.")[84] A collective aim or guiding aspiration was wanted, a master goal as socially powerful, comprehensive, and irresistible as that animating the marchers. But *was* there another motivation as powerful? War, as William James mused almost a half-century after the Civil War, was the greatest of all social organizers, "the only force" so far devised "that can discipline a whole community." Although he was a pacifist, James well understood the many facets of war's appeal and admired many of them, particularly war's respect for the "spiritual" values of honor, discipline, service, self-sacrifice, cooperation, self-forgetfulness, disinterestedness, and devotion. He well understood, moreover, how effectively the "chords of memory" might unify us, since our memories of Civil War bloodshed and sacrifice had become, by the early years of the twentieth century, "the most ideal part of what we now own together, a sacred spiritual possession worth more than all the blood poured out." Far from rejecting the organizational structures that modern warfare between nation-states had given rise to, James embraced them: "The conceptions of order and discipline, the tradition of service and devotion . . . which universal military duty is now teaching European nations, will remain a permanent acquisition, when the last ammunition has been used in the fireworks that celebrate the final peace."[85]

Somehow, he felt, it was necessary to find a desirable substitute, a "moral equivalent," for war, which would allow us to preserve the precious martial virtues without the carnage of war. James thought it eminently possible, being "but a question of time, of skillful propagandism, and of opinion-making men seizing historic opportunities." Indeed, he contended, the example of priests and doctors had already showed that there could be room in an unmartial mode of existence for such unselfish and honorable virtues. The key to a more general diffusion of those virtues, apparently, was the cultivation of a sense of service, especially service to the state: "We should all feel some degree of [martial character] imperative if we were conscious of our work as an obligatory service to the state. We should be *owned*, as soldiers are by the army, and our pride would rise accordingly." If the inherent top-down purposefulness characteristic of military organizations could be translated into the more general relationship between national state and national society, it would result in enormous payoffs in terms of material progress alone, James contended. He cited approvingly the words of H. G. Wells: "Beside the feeble and irregular endowment of research by commercialism, its little short-sighted snatches at profit by innovation and scientific economy, see how remarkable is the steady and rapid development of method and appliances in naval and military affairs! Nothing is more striking than to compare the progress of civil conveniences which has been left almost entirely to the trader, to the progress in military apparatus during the last few decades." The only thing needed is "to inflame the civic temper as past history has inflamed the military temper," a process James believed would be far easier for mankind to achieve than the movement from cannibalism to "civilized" warfare.[86]

That James's essay appeared four years before the First World War would suggest that for all its optimism and its enduring subsequent appeal to energetically inclined American presidents, it was anything but prescient. Yet if its prescriptions were not borne out by events, it nevertheless stands as a summarizing testimony to the depth of yearning for unity, purposefulness, and social connectedness, even to the point, in James's words, of being owned, that undergirded so much of the social thought of the post–Civil War decades. That yearning was perhaps even more trenchantly exemplified, both intellectually and personally, in the works of James's contemporary Henry Adams. "For the young men whose lives were cast in the generation between 1867 and 1900," Adams wrote, very much including himself among that number, "Law should be Evolution from lower to higher, aggregation of the atom in the mass, concentration of multiplicity in unity, compulsion of anarchy in order."[87] Adams, too, was caught up in a vision of consolidation. For all his elaborate multiple facades of insouciance and cynicism, he was at bottom desperately concerned to find a way of bringing his meandering, doubt-ridden, fragmentary consciousness into a full accord with that centripetal movement of universal law—of a coalescing universe that might also offer the lonely atomic self a sense of peace and place through aggregation.

That hunger for the centripetal, so fully on display in his magnificent and loving study of a thoroughly consecrated civilization in *Mont St. Michel and*

*Chartres*, was also uncannily figured in the scientistic Adams's mystical fascination with the phenomenon of magnetism. In a peculiar, yet strangely moving, passage of his *Education*, he related a moment of emotional and intellectual anguish when, not knowing "in what new direction to turn," he aimlessly "covered his desk with magnets, and mapped out their lines of force by compass. Then he read all the books he could find, and tried in vain to make his lines of force agree with theirs." Like his more famous encounter with the great forty-foot dynamos at the Paris Exposition of 1900, this experience with the energies of electromagnetism imitated the dynamics of prayer, for it was an effort to bring his unruly, broken individuality into accord with the will of God—of God, that is, in the only form left in which Adams could plausibly conceive him. Adams had contended for years that "the laws that govern animated beings" were the same as "those which rule inanimate nature"; it was a conception that he found he could "receive with pleasure," and one that surfaces again and again in his attempts to elaborate a "scientific" philosophy of history.[88] But now he discovered, to his horror, that the two could not be brought into alignment. How, he wondered, could it be so difficult for him to comprehend, and make fruitful connection with, "a force which must have radiated lines of energy without stop, since time began, if not longer"? Rather than standing reassuringly for unity, for the organization and convergence of multiple lines of force, the magnet "in its new relation" offered him only "evidence of growing complexity, and multiplicity, and even contradiction, in life. He could not escape it; politics or science, the lesson was the same."[89]

The lesson seemed to be that the forces of coalescence were incommensurable with, and therefore unfavorable to, individual consciousness; that the splintering of the world Adams experienced, the radical disjunction of self and society (or self and cosmos) was not likely to be overcome. The yearning for aggregation was not to disappear, but neither was it to be satisfied:

> All one's life, one had struggled for unity, and unity had always won. The National Government and the national unity have overcome every resistance, and the Darwinian evolutionists were triumphant over all the curates; yet the greater the unity and the momentum, the worse became the complexity and the friction. One had in vain bowed one's neck to railways, banks, corporations, trusts, and even to the popular will as far as one could understand it—or even further; the multiplicity of unity had steadily increased, was increasing, and threatened to increase beyond reason.[90]

Adams spent the Civil War years in Europe, serving as an assistant to his diplomat father, and so did not witness the Grand Review. It is not hard to imagine, however, that his reaction to it would have followed a similar pattern of ambivalence. On one hand, the victory itself would have doubtless elicited his joy and praise, and the consolidation of national power that the review represented was, in any event, something he regarded as inevitable—as irrepressible as the pattern of coalescence underlying any number of natural phenomena. The Constitution, he asserted, "had become as antiquated as the Confederation"; the Civil War had "made a new system in fact," and the country now had to "reorganize" itself "in practice and theory."[91] The industrial system, too, had an inexorable deterministic logic: "Once admitted that the machine must be efficient, society might dispute in what social interest it should be run, but in any case it must work concentration."[92]

Hardheaded acceptance of the "concentrated" new order was hardly the whole story with Adams, however, and very likely the review would have impressed upon him the essentials of what became his characteristic lament: that "the whole mechanical consolidation of force" going on in postbellum American life would end up "ruthlessly stamp[ing] out the life of the class into which Adams was born"—even as it "created monopolies capable of controlling the new energies that America adored."[93] In other words, while the scientistic and nationalistic tendencies in Adams's makeup pushed him toward the acceptance of consolidation, his stubbornly Adamsian independence of mind, his moral preference for traditional American republicanism, and his embrace of the family's "inherited quarrel with State Street" simultaneously pushed him the other way.[94] At times Adams even betrayed a strong, if perverse, attachment to the Old South, a warmth perhaps most transparently evident in his novel *Democracy*. The story's heroine is Mrs. Lightfoot Lee, an attractive widow bearing a great southern surname—only change *foot* to *horse* to create the name of the hero of the American Revolution, father of Robert E. Lee—who is searching in the darkness of postwar Washington politics for an "object worth a sacrifice." The novel's most admirable male character is a Virginia-born lawyer and former Confederate officer. Its most thoroughly corrupt (though not wholly contemptible) villain is a prominent Illinois senator known as the Prairie Giant of Peonia. One of the book's pivotal scenes is that of the principals' outing to George Washington's house at Mount Vernon, a journey that stimulates an extended meditation upon the corruption that had befallen the founders' original republican experiment.[95] Perhaps Adams needed a novelistic medium—with, significantly, a feminine alter ego as the story's moral compass—to convey his own inner resistance to the very scientistic, consolidationist triumphalism he had so dogmatically championed. How else to keep the right hand unaware of what the left was doing?

The brilliant Grand Review itself had a shadow side, then. "Had the eye of the spirit been opened" in the exultant observers of the review, mused General Francis A. Walker, they would have beheld something far more somber; they "would have seen by the side of each man who moved firmly and proudly in the victorious column three wounded and crippled men, limping and stumbling in their eager desire to keep up with their more fortunate comrades, while with the four stalked one pale ghost."[96] That ghastly shadow side was even more uncannily evoked in a strange, uncharacteristically searching poem by Bret Harte, "A Second Review of the Grand Army." Harte was a staunch Unionist, known principally for his romantic, local-color tales of the Old West, but with "A Second Review" he broke through his chronic sentimentalism to a more somber and ambiguous reflection upon the human price of national consolidation. In his hands the Grand Review became transformed into an even more potent, because powerfully dark and equivocal, symbolic event.[97]

The poem opens with a fairly typical evocation of the review, full of happy throngs, stirring music, and precision marching, which attests to the powerful effect of the review even upon one who did not witness it firsthand:

> I read last night of the grand review
> In Washington's chiefest avenue,—
> Two hundred thousand men in blue,
>     I think they said was the number,—
> Till I seemed to hear their trampling feet,
> The bugle blast and the drum's quick beat,
> The clatter of hoofs in the stony street,
> The cheers of people who came to greet, . . .

Reflecting upon the scene, the narrator falls into a "reverie, sad and sweet," a reflection upon the war's losses and achievements. But that mild, reflective state soon gives way to "fitful slumber" dominated by an appalling vision of another, very different procession: a spectral march of the anonymous Civil War dead on an utterly deserted Pennsylvania Avenue at midnight, many hours after the cheering crowds had gone home.

First to appear on the scene is a sight filling the poet "with fear and dread": the stern and solitary Reviewer, who rides deliberately up the avenue in advance of the parade, accompanied by a "phantom bugle's warning." The Reviewer is a bronze statue of a well-known American figure who "in State and field had led our patriot sires" (he is not named but very likely is George Washington).[98] The statue has come to life to supervise this spectral review, after sitting motionless all day, observing the passing of the "living column" without once bowing his head. Now, in the dead of night, he silently removes his hat out of respect for the procession to follow, of which he and the poet are the only observers:

> And I saw a phantom army come,
> With never a sound of fife or drum,
> But keeping time to a throbbing hum
> > Of wailing and lamentation:
> The martyred heroes of Malvern Hill,
> Of Gettysburg and Chancellorsville,
> The men whose wasted figures fill
> > The patriot graves of the nation.
>
> And there came the nameless dead,—the men
> Who perished in fever swamp and fen,
> The slowly-starved of the prison pen;
> > And, marching beside the others,
> Came the dusky martyrs of Pillow's fight, . . .
>
> So all night marched the nation's dead,
> With never a banner above them spread,
> Nor a badge, nor a motto brandishèd;
> No mark—save the bare uncovered head
> > Of the silent bronze Reviewer;
> With never an arch save the vaulted sky;
> With never a flower save those that lie
> On the distant graves—for love could buy
> > No gift that was purer or truer.
>
> So all night long swept the strange array,
> So all night long till the morning gray
> I watched for one who had passed away;
> > With a reverent awe and wonder,—
> Till a blue cap waved in the length'ning line,
> And I knew that one who was kin of mine
> Had come; and I spake—and lo! that sign
> > Awakened me from my slumber.[99]

Harte's poem communicated a weird and unsettling combination of reverence and horror through this Black Mass–like inversion of the triumphant Grand Review: instead of sunny day, pitch-black night; instead of the living, the dead; instead of crowds, deserted streets; instead of the unimposing

Johnson presiding, the silent shade of a great southern soldier-statesman, a father of the old republic; instead of the profusion of flags and flowers, not a single banner or other sign of national appreciation or recognition—only the ancient Reviewer's unspoken gesture of transcendent respect and the flowers placed on scattered individual graves across the land, flowers left, bouquet by bouquet, in isolated and private expressions of grief. Surely this suggests an alternate view of the meaning of the war, a view that lends a different tone to Lincoln's famous Gettysburg assertion that it was the fighting men themselves, and not the speeches of national leaders, who consecrated the ground upon which they fell.

In a sense, Harte's poem also points to the need to find war's moral equivalent, but it goes even further. It grants the full measure of honor and veneration to the martial virtues, to the sacrificial valor of the fallen men. But it has nothing to say about the worthiness of the collective cause and the nation for which the men fell. Indeed, it implies that their sacrifice may not have been at all redemptive, for it depicts those men as true unfortunates—"wasted figures" trapped in perpetual limbo, as it were, still crying out in agony over the bitter hideousness of war, and wounded over lack of appreciation from those for whom they sacrificed ("never a banner . . . Nor a badge, nor a motto . . . never an arch . . . never a flower"). The grateful banner that had been unfurled during the day on the northern side of the Capitol—stressing "the debt we owe to the victorious Union soldiers"—was nowhere to be seen. Theirs was not the glorious brotherhood of *les enfants de la patrie* but the brotherhood of blasted hopes and shared suffering: the brotherhood of Hemingway's First World War veterans, who recoiled from the rhetoric of sacrifice and national glory and preferred to hear merely the names of places.[100]

It was also a brotherhood in which all vestiges of individuality are absorbed into a spectral unity, and the consolidation of force that the original Grand Review so impressively celebrated becomes reversed, rendered sinister, life-robbing, and harrowing. It is appropriate, then, that the dream's spell upon the poet breaks at the moment when he recognizes, and is moved to speak to, an individual person, a known man—indeed, a kinsman—for whose countenance he had been scanning the passing sea of anonymous faces. Was this Harte's way of affirming the preciousness of the individual, and the more intimate bonds of kinship and locality, against the sweeping, cosmopolitan claims of the nation? If so, then he was offering an affirmation with a long American pedigree. But it was also a view standing directly athwart some of the most powerful intellectual tendencies of his own age.

# 2

## Paradoxes of Antebellum Individualism

We have speculated that the unnamed Reviewer supervising the ghostly Grand Review in Harte's poem was probably George Washington. The poet might well have had in mind another southerner from the pre–Civil War era, however, another heroic American patriarch who had served the country with great distinction in both war and politics: Andrew Jackson.[1] The substitution of the rough-edged, raw-tempered, self-made, entrepreneurial westerner for the grave, patrician, old-republican tidewater Virginian allows a slightly different perspective on the poem. How indeed, one might ask, would Old Hickory have reacted to the Grand Review itself, had he survived another two decades to witness it? The question is, of course, both anachronistic and impossible to answer with certainty. But it is also especially intriguing to contemplate, since Jackson was one of those rare American individuals of such powerful impress that his very name became the eponym of a historical era, an era stamped by certain distinctive qualities. There is good reason to believe that, despite his deep devotion to the preservation of the Union, Jackson might not have joined wholeheartedly in the lusty cheering along Pennsylvania Avenue.

Consider the gravamen of the warnings permeating the farewell speech he gave on his last day as president, in March 1837. He began by praising the Constitution's preservation of the "liberties of the people" and their "free institutions," which permitted "citizens of every quarter" (particularly the "agricultural, the mechanical and the laboring classes") the wide-open opportunity to succeed in a degree proportionate to "their own industry and economy." Then he sounded an alarm, directed not only at the threat of his bêtes noires, the banking and paper-money interests, but at the specter of consolidation itself. "It is well known," he asserted, that there are "those amongst us who wish to enlarge the powers of the general government" and "overstep the boundaries marked out for it by the Constitution." Americans who value their freedom will firmly oppose "every such attempt," for "if the principle of constructive powers or supposed advantages or temporary circumstances" is used to "justify the assumption of a power not given by the Constitution, the general government will before long absorb all the powers of legislation, and you will have in effect but one consolidated government." Such a development would not only be injurious to our liberties but would be unworkable, for given the size and diversity of the United States, "it is too obvious for argument that a single consolidated government would be inadequate to watch over and protect its interests." Therefore, those who count themselves friends "of our free institutions should be always prepared to maintain unimpaired and in full vigor the rights and sovereignty of the states and to confine the action of the general government strictly to the sphere of its appropriate duties."[2]

Nothing indeed was more remarkable about the Grand Review than its coming so close on the heels of the Jacksonian era, which was known for its bumptious, wide-open, factionalized, nakedly partisan and class-conscious democratic politics and for a general cultural spirit of boundless aspiration, entrepreneurial initiative, and radical individualism. That fact bears further witness, if more were needed, to the change in projective social ideals that had been wrought by the war's end. If the postbellum ideal figured by the Grand Review envisioned society as a vast organism or mechanism within whose embrace individual members realized themselves precisely by shedding their individuality and by finding their energies flowing in coordination with the whole, then the prevailing antebellum ideals could not have been more different. Indeed, at first glance, the two eras seem to be best characterized by virtually inverse terms of description and definition: instead of a prevailing commitment to integration, an embrace of differentiation; instead of consolidation, diversity; instead of control, laissez faire; instead of a broadly social or national principle of organization, an individual or local one; instead of following the lead of established institutions, following the promptings of the boundless self.

Such a striking change in emphasis, if such a characterization is accurate, cries out for explanation. Did the Civil War really effect so profound a change in intellectual topography as to reverse in one stroke the entire flow of American social thought? Or might the apparent changes actually be reflecting, upon closer examination, a plausible bend in the river's course, a developmental logic or evolutionary continuity that envisions individualism and nationalism standing in a complementary, sequential, or even symbiotic relationship rather than as mutually exclusive opposites? To suggest ways of answering these questions, we must again veer back into the antebellum decades and look at the emergence of the notion of what Walt Whitman would call "the simple, separate person"—an atomic and boundless self that would turn out, in the end, to be not very simple at all.

Perhaps the second quarter of the nineteenth century is forever destined to be labeled the Age of Jackson despite the multitudinous reservations and corrections historians have continued to offer to that appellation.[3] But there is little reason to doubt that, despite its diversity and the persistence of important conservative or "republican" currents, the era was marked by the emergence of a restless, individualistic, egalitarian, wide-open, romantic, liberatory, antinomian, and antiauthoritarian spirit. The emergence of this temper can easily be correlated with the democratization of politics and culture generally associated with the rise of Jackson, including the decline of deferential politics and the status of older governing elites, the intensifying disdain for all forms of privilege and ascriptive status, the veneration of "the common man," the general weakness of institutional authority, the seeming fluidity of social boundaries, the sense of immense economic opportunity presented by a vast and unexploited American continent, and the swell of enthusiasm for a plethora of social reforms, each driven by its own impassioned dream of the perfectibility of man. All these elements seem to merge and coalesce into a heroic fantasy of boundless individual potential, a vision of personal infinitude that impatiently brushed aside the severe and impassible limits imposed by custom, by history, by the accidents of birth, or even by the venerable doctrine of original sin. The spread-eagle rhetoric of Manifest Destiny and continental expansion seemed to find its counterpart in a spread-eagle, expansive understanding of the self. The social historian will have difficulty knowing how pervasive such notions might have been, but for the history of ideas, the emergence of such an individualistic vision seems difficult to dispute.

The locus classicus for this understanding of antebellum American culture, and therefore a good place to begin our own investigations, is Alexis de Tocqueville's *Democracy in America*, particularly the analysis of individualism in the second volume.[4] Yet it should be made clear at the outset that Tocqueville's definition of individualism differed in subtle but significant ways from what generally goes by that name—ways that revealed the French aristocrat's reverence for the classical civic-humanist and republican ideal of the duties of active citizenship.[5] Tocqueville's individualism was far closer to what we would today call privatism, the withdrawal of members of the community from active participation in public life, a disposition in which a man "willingly leaves society at large to itself," in favor of more and more exclusive involvement with "a little circle of his own," made up of "family and friends." Tocqueville regarded this dispersing, disaggregating tendency of *individualisme* as an unprecedented, and inherently dangerous, moral and ideological tendency of egalitarian societies. American *individualisme* was not just a prevalent emotion or passion; it was a settled, more or less consciously held and elaborated theme in the moral outlook of Americans. As such, it was quite distinct from the age-old vice of *égoïsme*, or selfishness. Yet in the end, Tocqueville argued, an unchecked excess of individualism could well lead beyond privatism into a state of generalized social atomism, in which only selfishness would be left to serve as a principle of action.

Although Tocqueville did not, as is sometimes insinuated, view America through the gloomy spectacles of a nostalgic Old World legitimism, he saw much that was deplorable and worrisome in the phenomenon of American individualism, and he insisted that these deplorable traits arose from precisely the same features that were most admirable and attractive about the fluid and socially mobile environment of Jacksonian America. In one of the most celebrated and striking passages of the *Democracy*, Tocqueville directs our attention to the shadow side of social mobility, conjuring the specter of an individualism carried to its barren logical conclusion:

> Among democratic nations new families are constantly springing up, others are constantly falling away, and all that remain change their condition; the woof of time is every instant broken and the track of generations effaced. Those who went before are soon forgotten; of those who will come after, no one has any idea: the interest of man is confined to those in close propinquity to himself. . . . As social conditions become more equal, the number of persons increases who . . . owe nothing to any man, [and] expect nothing from any man; they acquire the habit of always considering themselves as standing alone, and they are apt to imagine that their whole destiny is in their own hands.
>
> Thus not only does democracy make every man forget his ancestors, but it hides his descendants and separates his contemporaries from him; it

throws him back forever upon himself alone and threatens in the end to confine him entirely within the solitude of his own heart.[6]

The ultimate result of such a social state, he feared, would not be a Hobbesian war of all against all but, rather, a Leviathanian despotism—for despotism thrives upon the very vices that equality fosters. The separation of men from one another is "the surest guarantee of [despotism's] continuance."[7]

Of course, Tocqueville did not think matters had yet come to so dire a pass in America, chiefly because the Americans had so far found effective ways to counter the pathologies of individualism. He applauded the existence in America of voluntary public associations and of republican political institutions constellated within a federal system of government. The former encouraged the civilizing "reciprocal influence of men upon one another"; the latter, which stood in such stark contrast to the long-standing centralization (and only intermittent republicanism) of French politics, had the salutary effect of forcing men to recognize their interdependence and therefore accustoming them to act together in public ways regarding matters affecting their mutual interests. The framers of the U.S. Constitution, he assumed,

> did not suppose that a general representation of the whole nation would suffice to ward off a disorder at once so natural to the frame of democratic society and so fatal; they also thought that it would be well to infuse political life into each portion of the territory in order to multiply to an infinite extent opportunities of acting in concert for all the members of the community and to make them constantly feel their mutual dependence. The plan was a wise one. . . . Far more may be done by entrusting to the citizens the administration of minor affairs than by surrendering to them in the control of important ones, towards interesting them in the public welfare and convincing them that they constantly stand in need of one another in order to provide for it. . . . Local freedom . . . perpetually brings men together and forces them to help one another in spite of the propensities that sever them.[8]

As this description implies, such a scheme did not depend upon the virtuousness of Americans; indeed, the axiomatic assumption that made effective political and social association in America possible, he believed, was the principle of self-interest rightly understood (*l'interêt bien entendu*). To ask an American to do virtuous things for virtue's sake was quite possibly to waste one's breath, but the same request would readily be granted if the prospect of some personal benefit could be shown to flow from it. The challenge of moral philosophy in such an environment, then, was to demonstrate repeatedly the ways in which "private interest and public interest meet and amalgamate" and how one's devotion to the general good would therefore also promote his personal advantage. Belief in that conjunction—belief that one would do well by doing good—was what was meant by the "right understanding" of self-interest, and the prevalence of that belief could be gauged by the characteristic forms of moral discourse Tocqueville observed in Jacksonian America. In the United States, he asserted, "hardly anybody talks of the beauty of virtue, but they maintain that virtue is useful and prove it every day." American moralists, in short, did not attempt to deter men from following their self-interest. Instead, they fully accepted the primacy in human life of each person's self-propulsive engine, the fundamental premise of individualism. Since such self-seeking was an "irresistible force" in the democratic age, the only alternative was to acknowledge it and to direct and channel the force it generated by educating the public to believe "that it is the interest of every man to be virtuous."[9]

Such was Tocqueville's attempt to rescue what he could of the classical notions of moral obligation through a kind of halfway covenant, one that conceded the primacy of unregenerate individualistic vice, being satisfied, to paraphrase Oscar Wilde's witticism, to coax that vice into paying willing tribute to virtue. Such a strategy would be fully consonant with the overall objective of the *Democracy* to provide guidelines whereby the transition into a new democratic order could be effected with the least possible loss of what was precious and estimable in the old ways.[10] That view was, in any event, Tocqueville's sine qua non for all future moral calculations and education: "I am not afraid to say that the principle of self-interest rightly understood appears to me the best suited of all philosophical theories to the wants of the men of our time, and that I regard it as their chief remaining security against themselves. Towards it, therefore, the minds of the moralists of our age should turn."[11] And the educators as well, for since the increasingly explicit pursuit of self-interest was destined to "become more than ever the principal if not the sole spring of men's actions," it became all the more critical to promulgate the "right understanding" of that pursuit, if political liberty and social cohesion were to be preserved. Fortunately, he believed, this was a realizable goal: "The system of self-interest . . . contains a great number of truths so evident that men, if they are only educated, cannot fail to see them. Educate, then, at any rate, for the age of implicit self-sacrifice and instinctive virtues is already flitting far away from us, and the time is fast approaching when freedom, public peace, and social order itself will not be able to exist without education."[12] Although Tocqueville admired the ideals of disinterestedness and duty-bound citizenship, he could no longer regard them as feasible means of governing the thoughts and appetites of an egalitarian society.

---

For all his eminence, Tocqueville is not an uncontroversial source to turn to for strictly historical information about Jacksonian America. Whether he provided a meticulously accurate description of the social contours of Jacksonian America, whether he was correct in the degree of social equality and cultural uniformity he attributed to the country, whether his ex-Federalist American friends exerted undue influence upon his viewpoint, whether he had an adequate feeling for the revivalistic character of evangelistic Protestantism, whether he had even had Europe primarily in mind when writing the abstract and brooding essays of the second volume, years after his American visit: all these matters are, and will remain, contested issues among historians of the United States.[13] Our present interest in Tocqueville is much narrower and less controversial. It revolves around the degree to which the tendencies he so memorably depicted, founded upon an egalitarian belief in the separate self as the ultimate ground of moral judgment and the ultimate mainspring for all purposeful action, can provide a useful organizing principle for an examination of antebellum American political ideology and speculative social thought. For what was most striking about Tocqueville's analysis was not the degree to which it deplored atomistic, self-interested behavior and judgment, but the degree to which it accepted them, insisting upon the futility of challenging the individualistic principle frontally, seeking rather to contain and refine its effects. If even the simulacrum of virtue were to be retained, Tocqueville argued, it would have to be retained on terms satisfactory to individualism. This suggests that belief in the separate self formed a point on which there was broad consensus, a salient unifying tendency underlying the competing intellectual perspectives of the period, a backdrop against which the novelty of postbellum developments may be rendered more distinct.

Certainly the same pattern emerges in the general outlook and characteristic concerns of the era's most important political players. The Jacksonian Democrats are especially easy to associate with it, for they evinced a fierce devotion to the principles of individual liberty and equality of opportunity, including laissez-faire entrepreneurial capitalism, free trade, and imprescriptible natural rights (for white men). They generally accepted a high degree of moral and intellectual laissez-faire as well, showing a strong aversion to such Whiggish moral-purity crusades as temperance or antislavery, preferring instead to adopt a warmer, more inclusive tolerance for politically useful marginal groups such as freethinkers, Catholics, and immigrants. Perhaps their most distinctive characteristic was a profound hostility to alliances of government with business (such as protective tariffs), monopolies, particularist interests, hierarchies, special privileges for any person or group, paper money, experts, entrenched civil servants, and any other would-be aristocrats who might lord it over the common man. "Governments," declared William Leggett, in a characteristically libertarian Jacksonian flourish, "have no right to interfere with the pursuits of individuals . . . [or] to tamper with individual industry a single hair's breadth beyond what is essential to protect the right of person and property. . . . The sole reliance of the labouring classes . . . is the great principle of Equal Rights . . . [and] a system of legislation which leaves all to the free exercise of their talents and industry."[14] It is worth noting that, notwithstanding Jackson's enlargement of the presidential office, the practical effect of much Jacksonian policy, most notably the dismantling of the Bank of the United States, was to support local elites over national ones and therefore to favor the principle of federal dispersion over the principle of national consolidation.[15]

Given the dramatically contrasting perspectives offered by Whigs on so many issues of the day—on questions of social organization, class relations, agencies of moral authority, social reform, Protestant evangelism, education, economics, and the scope of the national government—it would seem surprising that similarly individualistic premises undergirded even such seemingly opposite positions. The analytical separateness of the individual, however, was a generally accepted point of reference, a point of consensus even for those arguing from a more corporatist or consolidationist perspective, as the Whigs so frequently did.[16] This is not to say that the Whigs' reliance upon these premises was immediately apparent. On the contrary, the Whigs were economic and political nationalists, proponents of system and planning, largely without the laissez-faire propensities—economically, morally, intellectually, or culturally—of their Democratic opponents. They tended to express a distaste for, or even horror of, unregulated individualism, preferring to promote the rational and comprehensive reorganization of American society through the creation of institutions with directive, ordering, and prescriptive powers. Their emphasis upon the moral and religious element in such reform derived its force from the power of a culturally insurgent evangelical Protestantism. There are even compelling reasons to identify them, and the strain of evangelical piety from which so many of them took their bearings, as instruments in the service, wittingly or not, of national, collective, or corporate interests—forces molding hearts and minds into compliance with the imperatives of economy and society.[17]

As Daniel Walker Howe has persuasively argued, however, the evangelical impulse toward moral reform that was such a pervasive feature of the Jacksonian era and that rested at the heart of Whig ideology (particularly in the northern states) cannot be adequately described by the term *social control*. Instead, evangelically driven antebellum moral reform was directed toward the achievement of *self* control, an objective that, whatever its social effects, also confirmed that the individual was regarded as the mainspring of social action, and it made clear the close links between the "liberatory" features of eighteenth-century evangelicalism and the "controlling" concerns of the nineteenth century.[18] Authoritative and disciplining social institutions were designed less for the achievement of social control than to create a society in which all individuals had the opportunity to function as free (that is, rational, self-directed, responsible, and self-disciplined) moral agents. Such an emphasis upon inner discipline was, moreover, in keeping with the evangelical insistence upon a distinct, personal, saving experience of Christian conversion. "The goal of the reformers," Howe asserted, "was to substitute for external constraint the inner discipline of responsible morality."

In short, the evangelical sensibility was able, with surprising ease, to fuse the requirement of a complete individual submission to the lordship of Christ with a profoundly modern understanding of the self as a rational and autonomous agent. Control and liberation were two facets of the same coin: "two sides," in Howe's words, "of the same redemptive process."[19] Such an objective was by no means restricted to those of evangelical hue; it had been equally characteristic of the Unitarian William Ellery Channing, whose thoroughly Arminian conception of "self-culture" emphasized "[our] power . . . of acting on, determining, and forming ourselves," a power "not only of tracing our powers, but of guiding and impelling them; not only of watching our passions, but of controlling them; not only of seeing our faculties grow, but of applying to them means and influences to aid their growth," a growth "to which no bounds can be set."[20] As Thomas Haskell has pointed out, the same emphasis was reinforced by the characteristic thought processes fostered by market capitalism.[21]

Perhaps the ideological difference between Jacksonian Democrats and Whigs may be usefully sharpened by reference to Isaiah Berlin's distinction between negative and positive liberty.[22] The Democrats, with an outlook rooted in feisty antiauthoritarian American traditions and Enlightenment notions of equality and natural rights, tended to see liberty in wholly negative (and largely secular) terms—as a freedom of the individual to pursue happiness to the full extent of his wants and abilities, without the unwanted interference of governments, churches, and other busybodies. Whigs, however, in keeping with the Reformed view of human nature, would be more likely to define true liberty in Christian terms, as morally enabling and inherently teleological. Positive liberty was something enabled, then achieved, not something given: it was self-realization through moral and rational self-control. Such freedom would not simply occur by allowing things to take their natural course, especially considering the inherent inadequacies of human nature; it would require careful formation and education designed to check, redeem, and perfect the perverse tendencies of our fallen natures, and thereby enable us to govern ourselves properly. The voluntaristic premises of such moral perfectionism, however, with their stress upon the efficacy of the individual will and of well-organized human agencies of reform (such as the studied techniques of the revivalist preacher or the social reformer) represented a clear departure from the tenets of orthodox Calvinism in the direction of Arminianism and beyond. The moralistic Whigs no less than the libertarian Democrats granted pride of place to the freedom and autonomy of the individual, although they defined it in distinctive ways.

In practice, moreover, the two kinds of liberty intermingled to the point where they were often difficult to distinguish. Take the case of Abraham Lincoln, for example. Lincoln's devotion to the principle of natural rights was evidenced in his consistent and reverent invocation of the principles of the Declaration of Independence, especially as a moral support for his opposition to slavery. Lincoln endorsed the vision of an equal-opportunity producer society that granted every man, no matter how humble his birth and station, a chance to succeed or fail entirely on his own efforts. His own life seemed to exemplify these negative-liberty virtues, and he thought it the glory of American society to allow "the humblest man an equal chance to get rich with anybody else."[23] In the ideal free-labor system, the wage earner always had the opportunity of moving up in the world through his efforts; any immobility he encountered was "not the fault of the system" but of either his "dependent nature" or his "improvidence, folly, or singular misfortune."[24]

Who would save his life, then, must work for it, and who did so controlled his own destiny. Lincoln also felt the moral-perfectionist currents of his times, however, and he realized that those afflicted with flaws of character such as dependence, improvidence, drunkenness, and folly would not stand a chance in life's race; hence their infirmities had to be remedied. It was with this end in mind that the young Lincoln had so enthusiastically embraced what he called the "temperance revolution," which he compared favorably even to the "political revolution of '76": "In [the temperance movement] we shall find a stronger bondage broken, a viler slavery manumitted, a greater tyrant deposed. . . . Happy day when—all appetites controlled, all poisons subdued, all matter subjected—mind, all conquering mind, shall live and move, the monarch of the world. Glorious consummation! Hail, fall of fury! Reign of reason, all hail!"[25] The coexistence of such different conceptions of liberty, in short, was a problem in theory but not in practice, for belief in the unlimited potential of the individual person as *fons et origo* was something both held in common.

---

It would, of course, be wrong to assert that such individualistic perspectives dominated the antebellum years in a monolithic and exclusive way, to the extent of driving out all alternatives. Such complete ideological unanimity seldom occurs and never persists, particularly in the arena of practical political and social discourse, where the press of competing material interests ensures that issues rarely stay settled for good. Older or alternative political languages do not necessarily die out; they often can find rhetorical niches in which to survive, sometimes to be later resurrected or adopted in unanticipated ways.[26] Sometimes those uses include the granting of moral legitimacy, for even the Tocquevillean regime of "self-interest rightly understood" ultimately paid tribute to republican virtue, however indirectly and instrumentally. As Marx ruefully observed, even revolutionaries feel irresistibly compelled to translate the new into an older language, clothing their pioneering deeds in the language of restoration, of *revolvere*, rolling back.[27] The Jacksonians themselves, even as they extolled the benefits of freewheeling individualistic economic competition, spoke of their task as one of recovery, of restoration of the eroding and endangered moral qualities of the virtuous Old Republic, and warned that liberty could not be sustained without the cultivation of a virtuous citizenry.[28]

One should also not overlook the presence of frankly corporatist perspectives in antebellum social thought—although, in their distinctively nineteenth-century, post-Calvinist manifestations, they tended to be aflush with the glowing hopes of empowered will. Utopian Robert Owen cursed the "individual system" as the chief obstacle to "peace on earth and good will to man" and advocated its replacement by a "social system."[29] Fascinating communitarian experiments running the gamut from Brook Farm to the Shakers to the Oneida community were scattered across the antebellum American landscape; their existence perhaps attests to a search for social connectedness amid the growing fragmentation and centrifugal tendencies of American life.[30] Certainly the heightened sense of personal agency characteristic of Whig and evangelical reformers went hand in hand with a strong conviction of the organic and historical (as opposed to abstract and contractual) character of society, with an expanded awareness of one's social obligations, and with a growing concern about the social consequences of one's actions—and, as importantly, one's inactions.[31]

Then, too, as Tocqueville was only too aware, the self-interested individualistic ethos of the antebellum years was almost exclusively the property, and burden, of white males. African slaves and Indians, by social definition, had no part to play in public life; they did not breathe the rarefied air of boundless possibility. Though it is more difficult to generalize about women as a group, it is safe to say that what actual power they possessed was generally confined to the private domestic sphere, where they were asked to serve, in the classic Victorian pattern, as custodians of moral virtue, source points of feeling and sentiment thought to radiate life-giving warmth within the precious sanctuary of family and home. Their considerable authority within that arena should not be minimized; nor, by the same token, should we overlook the dramatically different valuations of personal autonomy implied by the prevailing notion that both men and women had their appropriate but separate spheres of responsibility.[32] Both facts would contribute to the frequency with which idealized feminine personae would appear as instruments and radiant sources of social and personal salvation and reintegration in the writings of nineteenth-century male authors, from Whitman to Bellamy to Henry Adams.

Some qualifications are in order, however, since such sentiments never represented an ironclad consensus. Adherence to the ideal of classical-liberal autonomy was implicit in both the style and the content of the parody of the Declaration of Independence adopted as a Declaration of Sentiments by the convention of pioneering American feminists meeting at Seneca Falls in 1848.[33] The contemporaneous writings of the freewheeling Margaret Fuller ring with similar exhortations to intellectual independence.[34] But such expressions were the exceptions to the rule.[35] Autonomy did not figure in the worldview or admonitions of an important, and far more influential, writer like Catharine Beecher. Her *Treatise on Domestic Economy* (1841), which was deeply influenced by a reading of Tocqueville, insisted that strict separation of spheres by gender fulfilled the principle of division of labor and would create the proper conditions for the ongoing ennobling of civilization.[36] Even Margaret Fuller, though a critic of separate spheres and an advocate of self-reliance, envisioned distinct male and female principles at work in the world and saw the latter principle ("Femality") as an "electrical" force that, rather like a cosmic Victorian matriarch, "flushes, in blossom, the face of the earth . . . daily renewing and purifying its life."[37]

To find the individualistic credo crystallized in its purest and most consistent form, then, one must look at the untrammeled visions of the era's possibility offered by the era's most influential philosophical and literary male

writers [...] undiluted expression of radical individualism
is nearl[y] [...] alized distaste for the disfiguring constraints
of socie[ty] [...] w expressed more memorably, and influen-
tially, th[...] Waldo Emerson, the supervisory spirit of
Americ[a] [...] and a half decades, from the opening salvos
of his fir[st] [...] the mellower *Society and Solitude* (1870) of
his old [...] laced his writings with invocations of the
limitless [...] d, specifically, the American's) capabilities.
He frequently yoked such invocations to expressions of raw disdain for the
bogus constraints imposed by custom, history, tradition, institutions, and
ultimately, by society itself. He began his literary career challenging the timid,
retrospective, and derivative character of his era, demanding "an original
relationship to the universe" with its "own works and laws and worship." His
faith in the infinite capacity of the individual consciousness ruled out the
mystery and alienation of a Calvinist *deus absconditus* in favor of an Enlightenment transparency tinged roseate with romantic correspondence: "Whatever
curiosity the order of things has awakened in our minds, the order of things
can satisfy. Every man's condition is a solution in hieroglyphic to those
inquiries he would put."[38] The very notion of boundaries to be set upon to the
human prospect was wholly repugnant: "The only sin is limitation."[39] "Before
the immense possibilities of man," he asserted, "all mere experience, all past
biography, however spotless and sainted, shrinks away." "Who," he cried, "can
set limits to the remedial force of spirit?"[40]

As for society, to Emerson it represented little more to him than governance
by the herd, fatal to the kind of self-generative agency he conceived to be the
central fact of man's highest functioning. One can find this sentiment throughout his work, but its most forceful expression occurred in the essay "Self-
Reliance":

> The voices which we hear in solitude . . . grow faint and inaudible as we
> enter into the world. Society everywhere is in conspiracy against the
> manhood of every one of its members. Society is a joint-stock company,
> in which the members agree, for the better securing of his bread to each
> shareholder, to surrender the liberty and culture of the eater. The virtue in
> most request is conformity. Self-reliance is its aversion. It loves not
> realities and creators, but names and customs. . . . Nothing is at last sacred
> but the integrity of your own mind. . . . No law can be sacred to me but
> that of my nature. Good and bad are but names very readily transferable
> to that or this. . . . A man is to carry himself in the presence of all
> opposition as if every thing were titular and ephemeral but he. I am

ashamed to think how easily we capitulate to badges and societies and dead institutions.[41]

Small wonder that Emerson's admiring readers would i͟ Friedrich Nietzsche.[42] Tradition and custom were no ma͟ supreme "confidence in the unsearched might of man," fo͟ tance given to the single person," the task of embodying wh͟ all motives, by all prophecy, by all preparation, to the Ame͟

Clearly the deforming power of society itself was the mortal enemy of such confidence: in such a state "the members have suffered amputation from the trunk, and strut about so many walking monsters—a good finger, a neck, a stomach, an elbow, but never a man."[44] If solitude was "proud," then "so is society vulgar." Society brought out the worst in people, eroding their independence of mind, making them dependent and envious of all distinction. Therefore "the people are to be taken in small doses":

> In society, high advantages are set down to the individual as disqualifications. We sink as easily as we rise, through sympathy. So many men whom I know are degraded by their sympathies; their native aims being high enough, but their relation all too tender to the gross people around them. Men cannot afford to live together on their merits, and they adjust themselves by their demerits—by their love of gossip, or by sheer tolerance and animal good nature. They untune and dissipate the brave aspirant.[45]

Only a rare heroic figure would have the stamina to forsake "the ease and pleasure of treading the old road, accepting the fashions, the education, the religion of society," and instead taking up "the cross of making his own" way, thereby confirming "the state of virtual hostility in which he seems to stand to society." Such a liberatory figure would be so socially disengaged as to hold even his own kin of small account: "I shun father and mother and wife and brother when my genius calls me."[46] But he would in the end enjoy the fullest reward for his aloofness, since he would be "exercising the highest functions of human nature. . . . He is the world's eye. He is the world's heart."[47]

Strange, that it was precisely by shunning the various coils and snares of "society" that the American Scholar could best serve it, that by standing scrupulously aloof from his brethren he actually stood closest to them. This seeming paradox could only be explained through the mystical correspondences inherent in a capacious transcendentalist understanding of Nature. By pouring his energies outward into an apprehension of the meanings of the natural world, the Emersonian individual simultaneously came to understand and heed the promptings of his own inward nature, for the two were mysti-

Cf. w/ Lett

[ead by following "following"

stand aloof in order to get closer

cally connected and coextensive; that inmost self was perpetually figured and precisely embodied in the rich emblematic field of Nature—and vice-versa. ("Every natural fact," Emerson asserted, "is a symbol of some spiritual fact," and "the whole of nature is a metaphor of the human mind.")[48] By apprehending the ultimate unity of Nature and Soul, one gained access to the universal ground he shared with all persons, and that was the only authentic ground for community. It was as if the truest link between individuals was not to be obtained either directly or laterally—not face to face, as it were—but instead had to be arrived at indirectly, mediated by the solitary heroic journey into Nature and Oversoul; as if the ideal Emersonian society could be imagined as a rimless wheel, whose spokes were united only through their shared connection to the numinous hub. This logic was made visible in Asher Brown Durand's famous 1849 painting, *Kindred Spirits*, which portrays Thomas Cole and William Cullen Bryant "communing" with nature, a picture in which it is clear that the "kindred spirits" include Nature itself and, indeed, that Nature is the necessary ground of the men's rich communion.[49]

So a thoroughgoing individualism was the main prerequisite for a superior collective life, and a specifically *social* thought, if that term designates the logic of social aggregates—the logic, so to speak, of the wheel rim—seemed at best a distraction and at worst a fatal enclosure, antithetical to the real sources of creative achievement. According to Emerson, in the hortatory final words of his "American Scholar":

> Is it not the chief disgrace in the world, not to be an unit—not to be reckoned one character—not to yield that peculiar fruit which each man was created to bear, but to be reckoned in the gross, in the hundred, or the thousand, of the party, the section, to which we belong. . . . Not so, brothers and friends—please God, ours shall not be so. We will walk on our own feet; we will work with our own hands; we will speak our own minds. . . . A nation of men will for the first time exist, because each believes himself inspired by the Divine Soul which also inspires all men.[50]

If we will just watch the individual pennies, Emerson seemed to say, then the societal pounds will take care of themselves.

In 1880, when Emerson reflected with some degree of historical detachment upon the years of antebellum intellectual ferment through which he had lived, he still characterized that time in broad strokes of dispersion and individualism, in which social association was merely a means to an end, that end being "the enlargement and independency of the individual." In place of "the social existence which all shared," he recalled, there "was now separation.

Every one for himself; driven to find all his resources, hopes, rewards, society, and deity within himself." Former generations had "sacrificed . . . the citizen to the State" for the sake of "a shining social prosperity," but "the modern mind" asserted that "the nation existed for the individual"—nay, that "the individual is the world."

> This perception is a sword such as was never drawn before. It divides and detaches bone and marrow, soul and body, yea, almost the man from himself. It is the age of severance, of dissociation, of freedom, of analysis, of detachment. Every man for himself. . . . The social sentiments are weak. . . . There is an universal resistance to ties and ligaments once supposed essential to civil society. The new race is stiff, heady and rebellious; they are fanatics in freedom; they hate tolls, taxes, turnpikes, banks, hierarchies, governors, yea, almost laws.[51]

If Emerson was the philosopher of that zealous, stubborn American individualism, then Walt Whitman was its poet. No writer then or since has celebrated the boundless capacity of the individual more exuberantly: "Never was the representative man more energetic, more like a god, than today. He urges on the myriads before him, he crowds them aside, his daring step approaches the arctic and antarctic poles. . . . He unearths Assyria and Egypt, he re-states history, he enlarges morality, he speculates anew upon the soul, upon original premises; nothing is left quiet, nothing but he will settle by demonstrations for himself."[52] Nor did any writer assign himself a more momentous role in proclaiming the new individualist dispensation: "For the great Idea, the idea of perfect and free individuals," he chanted, "the bard walks in advance, leader of leaders. . . . The great Idea, / That, O my brethren, that is the mission of poets."[53] The true heroic individual "walks at his ease through and out of that custom or precedent or authority that suits him not."[54] The literary persona Whitman created for himself purported to model that individual. He was a Broadway swaggerer who did not blush to "celebrate myself, and sing myself," and declare that "nothing, not God, is greater to one than one's-self is." He urged his countrymen to "unscrew the locks from the doors! Unscrew the doors themselves from their jambs!," hold all "creeds and schools in abeyance," and value their own "head more than churches, bibles, and all the creeds."[55] The free soul takes to the open air of Nature and to the open road of a free life, unconstrained by mores and conventions: "All religion, all solid things, arts, governments—all that was or is apparent upon this globe or any globe, falls into niches and corners before the procession of souls along the grand roads of the universe."[56]

Like Emerson, then, Whitman celebrated the glory of a boundless self, but unlike the ethereal ex-minister, the ex-journalist Whitman took a city-boy's passionate interest in the specific and varied textures of the human condition and was possessed of genuinely expansive, inclusive, democratic tastes.[57] He was enduringly fascinated by the spectacle of what he liked to call the *en-masse*; he loved to catalog, at Homeric length, the myriad sights and sounds of his beloved city streets (or as in his "Salut au Monde!" the cultural and geographical panorama of the entire world). The breadth of his vision, however, was always subordinated to the lifework of self-creation and self-elaboration that he had so breathtakingly undertaken with the 1855 edition of *Leaves of Grass*.[58] Whitman's work enacts its drama within the theater of an infinitely extensible, all-registering, all-enveloping consciousness—the consciousness of "Walt Whitman, a kosmos," who asserts, "I am large, I contain multitudes. . . . I hear all sounds running together, combined, fused or following, / Sounds of the city and sounds out of the city, sounds of the day and night . . . it is a grand opera, / Ah this indeed is music—this suits me."[59] The disparate phenomena of the world become recast as art in the mind of this singular audience. But he is an audience, not a participant. That is why his long descriptive catalogues of the infinite variations he encounters among his fellow men and women so often have a strangely anonymous and abstract feeling to them, as if they were the registrations of a highly sympathetic alien—"Crowds of men and women attired in the usual costumes," he mused in "Crossing Brooklyn Ferry," "how curious you are to me!"—a remark far more suggestive of detachment than engagement.[60]

So his expansive vision was ultimately founded upon the postulate of his own boundless and all-embracing consciousness, and his passionate embrace of the natural and human worlds was predicated upon his limitless capacity for identification.[61] Whitman himself was that child he described in the *Leaves* who

> went forth every day,
> And the first object he looked upon and received with wonder or pity
>    or love or dread, that object he became,
> And that object became part of him for the day or a certain part of the
>    day . . . or for many years or stretching cycles of years.[62]

Like that child, Whitman could discover elements of his own image reflected back to him from almost any place in the folds and lineaments of the natural and human world. "I find I incorporate gneiss and coal and long-threaded moss and fruits and grains and esculent roots," he chanted, "And am stucco'd with quadrupeds and birds all over."[63]

I am of old and young, of the foolish as much as the wise,
Regardless of others, ever regardful of others,
Maternal as well as paternal, a child as well as a man . . .
Of every hue and trade and rank, of every caste and religion . . .
A farmer, mechanic, or artist . . . a gentleman, sailor, lover or quaker,
A prisoner, fancy-man, rowdy, lawyer, physician or priest.
I resist anything better than my own diversity. . . .[64]

Such catholicity of consciousness made Whitman assume an evenhanded view of the debate between positive and negative liberty, though his sympathies clearly lay with the latter:

What blurt is it about virtue and about vice?
Evil propels me, and reform of evil propels me. . . . I stand indifferent,
My gait is no faultfinder's or rejecter's gait,
I moisten the roots of all that has grown.[65]

And that catholicity made him claim for himself the role of cosmic mouthpiece and prophetic spokesman: "Through me the afflatus surging and surging . . . through me the current and index."[66]

---

Whitman and Emerson exemplified an Age of Boundlessness's paradigm of heroic assertion. Yet one need not probe too far beneath the luminous surfaces to discover a shadow cast by the solidity of that assertiveness, a hint of individualism's opposite number—a countercurrent of acquiescent yielding, or compensatory passivity, carried even to the point of regressiveness, eddying back across the assertive surface. The contrary motion may be detected in the most celebrated lines from Emerson's *Nature*, such as the familiar passage where he described the "wild delight" that runs through man in the presence of Nature, "a perfect exhilaration" making him "glad to the point of fear": "Standing on the bare ground,—my head bathed by the blithe air and uplifted into infinite space,—all mean egotism vanishes. I become a transparent eye-ball; I am nothing; I see all; the currents of the Universal Being circulate through me; I am part or parcel of God."

With these words, Emerson recounted an experience of ecstatic self-transcendence, of the self becoming at once everything and nothing, releasing the definition of its contours into the infinitude of cosmic God-space. As Emerson's next words indicated (if there could be any doubt), this ego-whelming rapture did not open a passage toward greater human connected-ness, toward a recognition of the social dimension of human existence, but closed it off with finality, declaring the near-solipsistic plenitude of the romantic self: "The name of the nearest friend sounds then foreign and accidental; to be brothers, to be acquaintances, master or servant, is then a trifle and a disturbance. I am a lover of uncontained and immortal beauty."[67] Such an uplifting transport of mystic delight has, then, its disquieting, even chilling, aspects; it recalls Tocqueville's somber warning that individualism's liberatory blade would prove double-edged and might well lead a man to feel radically cut off from his ancestors, his descendants, and his contemporaries, isolated within the solitude of his own heart. But the example from *Nature* goes further than the mere limning of an atomized social state. It suggests the possibility that, in the very flood tide of its fullest realization, the logic of individualism might turn and be unexpectedly transformed through ironic reversal into its opposite—into a profound yearning for self-negation, for absorption into something incomparably greater than oneself.

A similarly incongruous melding of assertion and passivity was noted by Tocqueville (and years later by James Bryce) as a baffling coexistence of individualism and fatalism in the American psyche.[68] The empowerment of all individuals in a democratic society, Tocqueville observed, had the paradoxical effect of making those individuals feel painfully isolated and relatively weak, incapable of overcoming their rivalrousness to experience genuine community or effect any meaningful political or social change. Hence their growing tendency to believe that the state of their society had not been shaped, and therefore could not be altered, by the conscious and efficacious wills of men and women, but instead was determined by general laws over which no one had any control.[69] Hence, too, their odd sense of priorities, an eagerness to guard their liberties ferociously against other individuals' incursions, yet a curious willingness to yield them readily, even happily, to a growing concentration of power in the hands of the impersonal central state:

> As in periods of equality no man is compelled to lend his assistance to his fellow men, and none has any right to expect much support from them, everyone is at once independent and powerless. These two conditions, which must never be either separately considered or confounded together, inspire the citizen of a democratic country with very contrary propensities. His independence fills him with self-reliance and pride among his equals; his debility makes him feel from time to time the want of some outward assistance, which he cannot expect from any of them, because they are all impotent and unsympathizing. In this predicament he naturally turns his eyes to that imposing power which alone rises above the level of universal depression. Of that power his wants and especially

his desires continually remind him, until he ultimately views it as the sole and necessary support of his own weakness.[70]

Although Tocqueville had in mind here a specific pathology—the social-psychological features of democracies that predisposed them to embrace increasingly centralized and consolidated political institutions—his observations are highly suggestive in a number of other applications. The conjunction of independence and powerlessness he identified has many more general resonances. Indeed, it begins to provide an account of how and why an ethos of individual empowerment and assertion seemed to prepare the ground of its own reversal and would revolt against itself in the fullness of time.

The rise of the humanitarian sensibility animating the reform movements of the nineteenth century points to a similar paradox, particularly if, as Haskell argues, it commenced as a byproduct of the mental practices required of those participating in a modern market-capitalist economy. These practices included a reliance upon the making of covenants or promises, and an ability to make reliable calculations of chains of causal attribution stretching far into the future—a "recipe knowledge" of the way certain causes would produce certain desired effects. Such habits of mind, and such assurance about the attribution of causes for given effects, surely reflected a more confident, general, and greatly expanded sense of the potency, efficacy, and responsibility of one's rational will—and therefore of one's personal responsibility as a potential agent of change, capable of influencing even the most remote effects, including the degradation and suffering of others in faraway places.[71] As Haskell has pointed out in a recent study of John Stuart Mill, however, this empowering position itself was actually on rather slippery ground. Mill well understood, not least because of his own unusually controlled personal formation at the hands of his father, that all present conditions could be understood as effects resulting from a chain of anterior causes and that with the proper interventions, those anterior causes could be changed and sources of human suffering could be relieved. But the very same logic could, and did, sometimes lead Mill into a slough of despondency and depression as he faced the unhappy (but logically inevitable) conclusion that his own seemingly "autonomous" will itself was nothing more than an effect, a product of anterior causes.[72]

Such an inherently conflicted outlook on the self, engendered by its heroic efforts to grasp firmly the levers of causal power, also turns up in the intense theological and soteriological debates that bedeviled American Protestantism during the antebellum years. The efficacy of free will and the necessity of divine grace for salvation, the principal issues that had ignited both the Arminian and the Pelagian heresies, were forced into active reconsideration by the era's immensely popular and influential revivalistic ministries, such as that of Charles Grandison Finney, their most forthright advocate and apologist. Far from believing that revivals of religion were the work of an inscrutable grace whose miraculous effects must simply be awaited, Finney saw the revival as a phenomenon falling within "the ordinary powers of nature" and, therefore, one that could be "worked up" by a skilled minister through the use of "philosophical" techniques of psychological steering and orchestration. In short, Finney seemed to be claiming for himself and his revivalistic process an efficacy that had formerly been reserved for the power of the Holy Spirit. Although Finney was careful not to make any such claim directly, he nevertheless scorned the doctrine that "religion has something peculiar in it, not to be judged of by the ordinary rules of cause and effect," a belief "that there is no connection of the means with the result, and no tendency in the means to produce the effect." No doctrine, he believed, was more "dangerous" and "absurd."[73]

So Finney's approach to evangelism, too, was bound up in the same expansion of the horizons of causal attribution. The connection is hardly surprising, since his later career as a spokesman for abolitionism and perfectionism also make him an excellent example of the humanitarian sensibility. Inevitably, too, his own evangelism also fell into similar dilemmas. His so-called New Measures, which included protracted nightly meetings, dramatic use of the "anxious bench" for earnest seekers, praying for people by name, encouraging public prayers by women, and immediate admission of converts to the church—all promoted by extensive publicity—were founded upon a confidence that the proper techniques, properly administered by the right person under the right circumstances, would reliably produce the experience of conversion in all but the most "sluggish" men. Aside from the Pelagian implications of such practices, the institution of such New Measures threatened to debase the very religious experience they sought to bring under the well-meaning evangelist's causal control. The greater the claims made for such New Measures, the more the process of conversion could appear to be induced by a humanly manipulated "excitement," and the more the souls of the converted themselves might be regarded as mere putty, mere effects to be passively worked by the hands of powerful and histrionic human persuaders. So far as affirming and empowering the individual will was concerned, the New Measures seemed to withdraw with a second hand what they had proffered with the first.[74]

The problematic status of the separate self was especially acute for the secular intellectual, an emerging social type for which both Emerson and Whitman served as pioneering embodiments in the antebellum decades. Both

Whitman and Emerson believed fervently in the boundless possibilities of democracy. They sang and expatiated upon its virtues. They luxuriated wholeheartedly in their age's rejection of privilege, expertise, distinctions of rank, claims of authority, and encrustations of *nomos*; both were among the most articulate exponents of the fertility of that era's centrifugal liberatory whirl. They declared themselves willing to accept the rigors of heroic isolation, but their beliefs were frequently tempered by their profound impatience with the constraints placed upon would-be intrepid individuals by the tyranny of the majority. An uneasy pairing of democratic expansiveness and aristocratic disdain defined the creative tensions as well as the difficulties (and frequent disappointments) that would be the lot of intellectuals in a democratizing and commercial society.[75]

Nowhere are Tocqueville's observations regarding the conjunction of independence and powerlessness, self-reliance and debility, more apropos than in their application to the antebellum American intellectual. For intellectuals, the democratic faith proved far easier to enunciate boldly than to follow consistently; for what might it mean to be a high priest of intellect in a fluid, fiercely egalitarian society? It was exhilarating to throw off the intellectual confinements of all ecclesiastical priesthoods, as Emerson had shed even the loosefitting robes of his own Unitarianism, and to walk on one's own feet on the bare ground. But there was also a great risk involved in thus casting off institutional supports and protections. There was no guarantee that by going one's own way, one would not find oneself terribly alone and vulnerable in the end, a prophet unarmed, unheeded, and perhaps even outcast. For why should anyone in a democratic social order pay special attention to an intellectual? "You shall no longer take things at second or third hand," proclaimed Whitman near the beginning of the 1855 *Leaves*, "nor look through the eyes of the dead . . . nor feed on the spectres in books, / You shall not look through my eyes either, nor take things from me. . . ."[76] Why should the would-be reader not take him at his word? A more ancient kind of priesthood had surely presented many obstacles to the thinker, but the promise of a relatively secure and well-defined social identity was not one of them.[77] For intellectuals, boundlessness entailed glories and perils all its own.

The tension had antecedents at least as far back in American history as the great ecclesiastical ruptures of the Great Awakening, and was indeed implicit in the country's Protestant, antiauthoritarian origins. If the religious pluralism of early America granted something like consumer sovereignty to churchgoers, it did so at the distinct expense of clerical authority. The problem was only exacerbated when some ministers became secular intellectuals in the democratic, fluid, individualistic, and evangelical age of Emerson and Whitman. How to exalt the peculiar worth of intellectuals and their sometimes esoteric and challenging productions, when all men equally were bathed in the light of that same Divine Soul? Were not the men in whom that Divine Soul dwelled precisely the same dreary, petty knaves who, said Emerson, incessantly counted "high advantages" as "disqualifications"? How to defend *any* arrogation of intellect in an age in full revolt against all such priesthoods and arrogations, an age that extolled "the infinitude of the private mind," which would readily assent that "every atom belonging to me as good belongs to you"?[78]

It was a state of affairs tailor-made for lingering ambivalences and disappointments. From the beginning, Emerson and Whitman had passionately asserted both the Promethean heroism and the redemptive social significance of the intellectual's mission. Emerson's "Man Thinking" held the responsibility of embodying "delegated intellect," thereby serving as a kind of grand expression of the *volonté générale*, articulating and fortifying the masses' mute and stumbling wishes; "the poets," he proclaimed, "are thus liberating gods."[79] Whitman, drawing inspiration from Emerson's essay "The Poet," understood his function in much the same lofty terms, although, as ever, showing a more thoroughgoing democracy of attention: "I make appointments with all, / I will not have a single person slighted or left away."[80] The preface to the 1855 *Leaves* soars with Shelleyesque grandeur at the prospect of the poet's glorious function: "The American poets are to enclose old and new for America is the race of races. Of them a bard is to be commensurate with a people. . . . His spirit responds to his country's spirit . . . [and] he incarnates its geography and natural life and rivers and lakes. . . . Of all nations the United States with veins full of poetic stuff most need poets and will doubtless have the greatest and use them the greatest. . . . The proof of a poet is that his country absorbs him as affectionately as he has absorbed it."[81] Or so Whitman hoped.

What a slide those hopes would later experience, however, from the breezy confidence of that last assertion to the dyspeptic postbellum second thoughts that would appear in his 1871 *Democratic Vistas*:

> I say we had best look our times and lands searchingly in the face, like a physician diagnosing some deep disease. . . . America needs, and the world needs, a class of bards. . . . It is useless to deny it: Democracy grows rankly up the thickest, noxious, deadliest plants and fruits of all—brings worse and worse invaders—needs newer, larger, stronger, keener compensations and compellers. . . . Amid these whirls, incredible flippancy, and blind fury of parties, infidelity, entire lack of first-class captains and

leaders, added to the plentiful meanness and vulgarity of the ostensible masses. . . . What prospect have we?[82]

In some respects, his plea was transparently personal, the intense querulousness of a vain and talented man who believed his prophetic voice deserved better than it was getting in Gilded Age America. Whitman, far more than Emerson, lived a life caught in the democratic pincers Tocqueville had described, finding himself both boldly independent and pathetically unappreciated, a voice unheard and unechoed, surrounded at the end of his life not by an adoring working-class public of which he wrote so adoringly but by a tiny coterie of true-believing intellectual friends.[83]

The plaint also had a more general resonance, for it went to the heart of any such intellectual's status in a democratic social order, echoing dilemmas as ancient and familiar as Plato's, experienced with similar alienation and anguish by leading intellectuals of the Old South.[84] In the end, *Democratic Vistas* pleaded for the creation of a "new and greater literatus order," a unifying task Whitman compared, in an extended metaphor, to that of the medieval faithful, who "so long, so well, in armor or in cowl, upheld and made illustrious, that far-back feudal, priestly world." To offset the loss of those "vanish'd countless knights, old altars, abbeys, priests, ages and strings of ages," America required its own "knightlier and more sacred cause."[85] Whitman's highly uncharacteristic adoption of medievalist figures of speech in this context, particularly surprising given his livid and lifelong contempt for priests, is highly significant. The poet unlaureate of boundlessness was pushed to argue for an intellectual priesthood, having discovered to his dismay that a vulgar democracy may fail to reward, or even take notice of, its most ardent exponents.

---

The metaphors of knighthood and priesthood did more than give shape to Whitman's understandable desire for a secure social standing in an increasingly fluid and unreflective world. They also suggest a compensatory yearning to submit to discipline, to find a place of service, and to discover an identifiable collective good, a "more sacred cause" worthy of one's self-sacrifice. It is precisely this seemingly contradictory element in Whitman's makeup that makes his work so eloquent a testimony to the psychological and social complications of radical individualism and, therefore, worthy of our close examination. Emerson had asserted that "nothing is sacred" but the integrity of one's own mind, the law of one's own nature. Whitman's frankness and boldness of self-expression had followed this lead very far, farther than almost

anyone of his time, down the path of consecrating separateness and individuation. Perhaps that was precisely why the countercurrent of yielding and
yearning to connect, when it came upon him, did so with such overwhelming
force. Because Whitman had the courage of his convictions—or, perhaps
equally, the inability to resist his pathologies—he experienced the terrors of
heroic isolation far beyond anything the comfortable Emerson would ever
know. Indeed, Whitman's poetry, which had from the start been notorious for
its grand and arrogant gestures of heroic self-assertion, had also contained
eddying elements within its multitudes, manifested most starkly in his enormous, recurrent, desperate, and seemingly unfulfillable need to connect with
others. It was Whitman's authorial pose to pretend that his work was artless
art, a mere effortless extrusion from the life he lived. But Yeats's hard adage,
that one must choose between the perfection of the life or the perfection of the
art, clearly applied to Whitman's incessantly troubled career. It was not from
his bold and extravagant expressions of polymorphous ambisexuality but from
their thwarting, from his confrontation with the searing pain of solitude and
perpetual unrequited passion, that his greatest poems crystallized.

That ceaseless lust for connection manifested itself early, in the 1855 *Leaves*,
when Whitman beckons the reader directly, rudely:

> Come closer to me,
> > Push closer my lovers and take the best I possess,
> Yield closer and closer and give me the best you possess.
> This is unfinished business with me. . . . How is it with you?
> I was chilled with the cold types and cylinder and wet paper between
> > us.
> I pass so poorly with paper and types. . . . I must pass with the contact
> > of bodies and souls.[86]

In the 1860 edition, he has become even more outrageous, even more disdainful of the conventional author-reader relationship:

> Camerado, this is no book,
> Who touch this touches a man,
> (Is it night? are we here together alone?)
> It is I you hold and who holds you,
> I spring from the pages into your arms.[87]

Such passages reflect the odd combination of brazen assertiveness and pathetic
vulnerability, of strutting self-confidence and bottomless emotional hunger,
that permeated Whitman's work from the start. They also suggest the extent to
which Whitman understood the making of human connection as a strictly

individual, atomic process. Like Emerson, Whitman had little use for social bonds as conventionally understood.[88] "What indeed have I in common with [institutions]?" he scoffed, prophesying instead the establishment "without edifices or rules or trustees or any argument / [of] the institution of the dear love of comrades."[89]

This statement might lead one to think its author had derived much fulfillment and contentment during his life in "the dear love of comrades," but such, of course, could hardly have been further from the truth. Whitman's poetry is saturated with the frustration of one whose desires never approach satisfaction and whose feelings of apartness and overheated longing cause him to conjure half-mad fantasies of intense intimacies, enjoyed with countless persons of indistinct identity or sex:

> From pent-up aching rivers, . . .
> Singing the muscular urge and the blending,
> Singing the bedfellow's song, (O resistless yearning!
> O for any and each the body correlative attracting!
> O for you whoever you are your correlative body . . .)
> From the hungry gnaw that eats me night and day. . . .[90]

> I am he that aches with amorous love;
> Does the earth gravitate? does not all matter, aching, attract all matter?
> So the body of me to all I meet or know.[91]

> Passing stranger! you do not know how longingly I look upon you,
> You must be he I was seeking, or she I was seeking, (it comes to me as
> of a dream,)
> I have somewhere surely lived a life of joy with you. . . .[92]

Sometimes the blurry identity of his erotic *objet du jour* seems to dissolve entirely, leaving in its wake an objectless pansexuality that is virtually indistinguishable from autoeroticism. In fact, despite Whitman's famed homoerotic explicitness, bordering on the pornographic in the "Calamus" poems of 1860; despite his implicit boasts and bravado; and despite the long lists of young men's names he compulsively compiled, the possibility clearly exists—though it is impossible to know for sure—that the bulk of his sexual escapades were more fantastic than actual, installments in his project of poetic self-creation. It is also possible that such affairs, when they actually occurred, turned out to be sordid, horrendously conflicted, and guilt-producing nightmares for him. We do know with certainty of Whitman's crazed fixation upon Washington streetcar conductor Peter Doyle in the late 1860s, and we can clearly see the paroxysms of self-loathing and loss of self-control this obsession induced in him. The evidence comes from his own manuscript notebook entries, in which he excoriates himself for such

> childish abandonment of myself, fancying what does not really exist in another, but is all the time in myself alone. . . . *It is* IMPERATIVE, that I obviate & remove myself (& my orbit) *at all hazards* from this *incessant enormous* . . . PERTURBATION . . . GIVE UP ABSOLUTELY & *for good, from this present hour,* [all] this FEVERISH, FLUCTUATING, *useless undignified pursuit of* 164*—too long, (much too long)* persevered in,—so humiliating . . . LET THERE FROM THIS HOUR BE NO FALTERING, [or] ANY MEETING WHATEVER, FROM THIS HOUR FORTH, FOR LIFE.

"Depress the adhesive nature," he commanded himself, sounding surprisingly mechanical and more like a sermonizing Victorian preaching will power and self-control than a prophet of free and undraped sensuality; "It is in excess, making life a torment . . . All this diseased, feverish disproportionate *adhesiveness*."[93]

The poignancy of these self-recriminations is only heightened when they are read alongside some of Whitman's loveliest poems, which speak with both feeling and exquisite poetic control of his profound need to be connected to others. See, for example, "I Saw in Louisiana a Live-Oak Growing":

> All alone stood it and the moss hung down from the branches,
> Without any companion it grew there uttering joyous leaves of dark green,
> And its look, rude, unbending, lusty, made me think of myself,
> But I wonder'd how it could utter joyous leaves standing alone there without its friend near, for I knew I could not. . . .[94]

Also consider his reflections in "A Noiseless Patient Spider," where he compares the steady launching forth of filament to his own efforts:

> And you O my soul where you stand,
> Surrounded, detached, in measureless oceans of space,
> Ceaselessly musing, venturing, throwing, seeking the spheres to connect them,
> Till the bridge you will need be form'd, till the ductile anchor hold,
> Till the gossamer thread you fling catch somewhere, O my soul.[95]

"O my soul": that stock phrase, which Whitman used more and more often as he grew older, represented more than a verbal sigh or a genteel euphemism. It was addressed to something real, something he experienced as distinct and autonomous within himself. He frequently portrayed himself as having a dual nature and regarded his soul as something distinct from his ego-self (in rather the same way that Jung later wrote of the semiautonomous anima), with needs that must be respected: "I believe in you my soul," he declared in the 1855 *Leaves*; "the other I am must not abase itself to you, / And you must not be abased to the other."[96] Given the tensions within which Whitman lived, however, that was easier said than done. During the years between the first publication of the *Leaves* and the beginning of the Civil War, Whitman struggled increasingly with these conflicting natures, with his competing needs to control and to connect, and with his increasingly undeniable homo-eroticism. He often found himself subject to crippling fits of gloom and melancholy. "Was it I who walked the earth disclaiming all except what I had in myself?" he taunted himself; "Was it I boasting how complete I was in myself?"[97] In "As I Ebb'd with the Ocean of Life" he laments:

O baffled, balk'd, bent to the very earth,
Oppress'd with myself that I have dared to open my mouth,
Aware now that amid all that blab whose echoes recoil upon me I have
    not once had the least idea who or what I am,
But that before all my arrogant poems the real Me stands yet
    untouch'd, untold, altogether unreach'd,
Withdrawn far, mocking me . . .
Pointing in silence to these songs, and then to the sand beneath.[98]

The ebullient Whitman had suddenly become consumed by self-doubt. Some of the reasons may easily be guessed. The *Leaves* had not been the popular and financial success he had hoped for, and he was forced to revert to newspaper work (and was then fired from his job at the Brooklyn *Daily Times* in June 1859). Perhaps, too, Whitman may have had an earlier Doyle-like affair during those years, which could have helped cast him into a "slough" of despondency.[99] Whatever the causes, by 1859 Whitman felt his self and soul locked in extreme conflict and felt himself increasingly helpless before the latter's undertow, the ebbing countercurrent. He brilliantly captured the essential nature of that conflict, that sense of being pulled two different ways on a verge or boundary, by using the imagery of pounding surf in a magnificent series of shore poems:

As I ebb'd with the ocean of life,
As I wended the shores I know . . .
I musing late in the autumn day, gazing off southward,
Held by this electric self out of the pride of which I utter poems,
Was seiz'd by the spirit that trails in the lines underfoot,

The rim, the sediment that stands for all the water and all the land of
   the globe. . . .
Fascinated, my eyes reverting from the south, dropt, to follow those
   slender windrows,
Chaff, straw, splinters of wood, weeds, and the sea-gluten,
Scum, scales from shining rocks, leaves of salt-lettuce, left by the
   tide. . . .
As the ocean so mysterious rolls toward me closer and closer,
I too but signify at the utmost a little wash'd-up drift,
A few sands and dead leaves to gather,
Gather, and merge myself as part of the sands and drift.[100]

The alternative to an assertion of the proud electric self was a yielding to the
elements and to the spirit that "trails in the lines underfoot"—the act of
ultimate adhesiveness, so to speak, of dissolution into the universe itself. The
lure of death, the confessed desire for oblivion, or surcease from the perpetual
tortures of an overheated, lovelorn, insatiable yearning to connect had become
a sustained presence in Whitman's work by 1859, a mere four years after the
cockiness of the 1855 *Leaves*. In "Out of the Cradle Endlessly Rocking," first
published that Christmas as "A Child's Reminiscence" in the *Saturday Press*,
Whitman searched his memory (perhaps anxiously) for the sources of his
creative powers, envisioning himself as a young boy wandering alone on the
beaches of Long Island. The boy has for many days observed two migrant
birds who have made a nest together near the ocean; suddenly one day, one
bird mysteriously disappears. The remaining bird sings a devoted, imploring,
plaintive song for its absent mate, in the course of which it comes to realize its
beloved is now gone forever. The bereaved bird becomes an unrequited lover,
a "singer solitary," the boy realizes, "singing by yourself, projecting me"; from
that moment, the perpetuation of that bird's sorrowful song, and of "a thousand songs, clearer, louder, and more sorrowful," would be the boy's life
task—"what I am for." But the wandering boy pleads for a better understanding of his destiny, a question to which the sea (described in unmistakably
feminine terms) "lisp'd" to him in response,

   the low and delicious word death,
   And again death, death, death, death,
   Hissing melodious, . . .
   . . . edging near as privately for me rustling at my feet . . .
   . . . laving me softly all over,
   Death, death, death, death, death. . . .

> The word of the sweetest song and all songs, . . .
> The sea whisper'd me.[101]

With the daring repetition of "death"—which, when read aloud with conviction, becomes like an aural laving, powerfully reinforcing the meaning of the text—Whitman also paid homage to the final force of reintegration, which he inevitably described as a woman: a "crone rocking the cradle, swathed in sweet garments." Drenched in oceanic eroticism, this *Liebestod* of unrequital— "Never more," the boy-poet vowed, shall "the cries of unsatisfied love be absent from me"—traced the evolution of heroic egoism into heroic negation, into passive absorption and affectlessness. It sang not of triumphant self but of the obliteration of self-consciousness, the release into nirvana, the return to the watery womb. Extremity of romantic ego had prepared the ground of its own extreme reversal.

---

The Civil War, source of so many monumental changes, also deeply affected Whitman. Most of all, it gave him some relief from his despondency, although it did not do so immediately. Not until he learned in December 1862 that his brother George had been wounded at Fredericksburg was he moved to connect with the war effort, leaving New York that very day to search for his sibling.[102] The wound turned out to be quite minor, but Whitman was transfixed by what he had seen at the front and was irresistibly drawn to remain in Washington, as close to the war as possible. The battlefield drama had lifted him out of his personal agonies by linking them to the agonies of the countless wounded young soldiers as well as the agony of national disunion. The Civil War came as a miraculous balm, healing his sense of isolation, restoring a sense of social worth and connectedness, and banishing for a time the dividedness of heart he had felt overwhelming him. Throwing himself with wholehearted enthusiasm into his self-assigned duties as nurse and wounddresser, he was able to win a release from the anxieties bedeviling his "simple separate person" by relinquishing them to the relentless momentum of the war effort. His remarkable ability to project himself into the sufferings of others made him exceptionally well equipped for his self-appointed task as comforter to the young soldiers. The panorama of war and its suffering brought literary benefits as well. It provided Whitman with a wealth of new literary material and the beginnings of a new poetic voice that was less intrusive and self-referential and more purely descriptive, transparent, and understated. From the start, Whitman recognized that there were the makings of at least one book in these experiences, and he was careful to take copious notes on all he saw.

But no mere recourse to Whitman's calculated literary ambitions can begin to account for the extraordinary zeal with which he plunged into the experience of the hospitals—the experience, be it remembered, of voluntarily surrounding himself, day after day, with suffering, mutilated, dying young men. The only plausible explanations are psychological or spiritual. It seems that he had discovered in this self-appointed ministry a temporary knighthood and priesthood—a sacred cause, that is, to which his personal passion could be yoked.[103] Why else would he have chosen to remain in Washington during the war years, living monastically in a tiny, austere room on L Street, subsisting on a bare pittance acquired through occasional hack freelancing, just so that he would be able to go into the hospitals daily and attend to the wounded, bearing them small gifts and the tonic of his healthy and cheerful presence? The horrors he witnessed there and on the battlefield seemed only to augment his strength and resolution, for these visits to the convalescent and dying became a daily communion, satisfying at last his profound need to feel his passion requited. "I never before had my feelings so thoroughly and (so far) permanently absorbed to the very roots," he effused to a friend, "as by these huge swarms of dear, wounded, sick, dying boys."[104] "O what a sweet unwonted love (those good American boys, of good stock, decent, clean, well raised boys, so near to me)—what an attachment grows up between us, started from hospital cots, where pale young faces lie & wounded or sick bodies."[105] His craving for connection had finally found a suitable object and a properly sublimated channel within which it could express itself freely. His intimacy with the wounded sometimes included caresses and long kisses, but more importantly, it was tailor-made for his emotional ideal, being both intensely, intimately individual and broadly national in its resonances. It was a fraternity of shared suffering, made possible under the righteous aegis of the Union.

Such personal satisfactions, as well as the entire range of experiences that the war had entailed, reinforced a captivating vision of the mystical meaning of the national Union that had steadily taken hold in his mind over the past two decades, in periods of despondency and elation alike. Whitman was wont to pronounce his faith in the Union in the same breath that he would praise the perfection of the independent self, and thereby to boldly conflate the whole range of his ideals from the most intimate to the most public. See, for example, the following passage from the 1860 *Leaves*:

I announce uncompromising liberty and equality,
I announce the justification of candor and the justification of pride.

I announce that the identity of these States is a single identity only,
I announce the Union more and more compact, indissoluble,
I announce splendors and majesties to make all the previous politics of
    the earth insignificant.
I announce adhesiveness, I say it shall be limitless, unloosen'd,
I say you will yet find the friend you were looking for.
I announce a man or woman coming, perhaps you are the one, (*So
long!*)
I announce the great individual, fluid as Nature, chaste, affectionate,
    compassionate, fully arm'd.[106]

Whatever may be left unclear or puzzling in this remarkable list, one point should be unmistakable: Whitman saw the emergence of the sovereign individual, his own personal project of self-making, the satisfaction of his erotic yearnings, and the coalescence of American nationhood as different facets of the same process. That was why Whitman was able to begin the 1867 edition of the *Leaves* with the famous words "One's-self I sing, a simple separate person, / Yet utter the word Democratic, the word En-Masse."[107] Similarly, his invocation of "adhesiveness," the very erotic gravitational force he would feverishly seek to "depress" during the Peter Doyle crisis, shows the natural link he felt between the starkly personal and the broadly political. The Union not only served as a model for the integration of sovereign individuals into a comprehensive whole; it had become for him a spiritual entity, even a kind of godhead:

And here and hence O Union, all the work and workmen thine!
None separate from thee—henceforth One only, we and thou, . . .
Think not our chant, our show, merely for products gross or lucre—it
    is for thee, the soul in thee, electric, spiritual!
Our farms, inventions, crops, we own in thee! cities and States in thee!
Our freedom all in thee! our very lives in thee![108]

Needless to say, Whitman's deification of the Union left little room for the compact theory of the Constitution, which stressed the complexity of the Union's antecedents and asserted the sovereignty and historical priority of the individual states. Indeed, in "By Blue Ontario's Shore" Whitman addressed himself to the point directly, taking Lincoln and Daniel Webster one or two steps better:

Underneath all, individuals,
I swear nothing is good to me now that ignores individuals,
The American compact is altogether with individuals,

The only government is that which makes minute of individuals,
The whole theory of the universe is directed unerringly to one single
    individual—namely to You.[109]

When Whitman attempted his own explanation for what he called the war of attempted secession, he again seems to conflate the sacred cause with his own struggle to sustain the integrity of his own personality; for in his view the war was "not a struggle of two distinct and separate peoples, but a conflict (often happening, and very fierce) between the passions and paradoxes of one and the same identity—perhaps the only terms on which that identity could really become fused, homogeneous, and lasting."[110]

Whitman's formulation also recalls and confirms the correlation Tocqueville saw between egalitarian individualism and political centralization and, more particularly, the tendency of the isolated and socially deracinated individual to look toward an "imposing power" rising "above the level of universal depression" to serve as "the sole and necessary support of his own weakness." Indeed, there was a quintessentially Tocquevillean polarization inherent in Whitman's social philosophy, for it seemed to posit an immense social gulf between the only two things that were certain: the sprawling abstraction of the En-Masse and the simple separate person in whom the theory of the universe supposedly converged. Where, one might well ask, were the other quotidian and mediating forms of relatedness that might, like Burke's "little platoons," bridge the giant chasm yawning between the individual and the mass? Was the very structure of social matter to be broken down into the two categories, atoms and visible objects, without the laborious and complex mediation of other levels of physical and chemical organization, such as molecules and compounds? Was it true that, as Tocqueville speculated, the growth of the central state would accelerate, and be accelerated by, the growth of individualism and be accompanied by a proportionate decline in all more localized, less comprehensive forms of public association? Would it be true, in turn, that "the more [the state] stands in the place of associations, the more will individuals, losing the notion of combining together, require its assistance," thereby leading to a cycle of "causes and effects that unceasingly create each other"?[111]

Perhaps it is unfair to thrust such rude questions in the face of Whitman, who certainly never posed as an advanced and rigorous theorist of the national state and, moreover, always spoke with the poet's (or journalist's) license, never much fearing self-contradiction, inconsistency, lacunae, or imbalance in his utterances. Yet his life and his vision provide us with powerful insights into his times, for two reasons. First, their internal tensions were so beautifully articulated and sharply etched, thanks to his artistry and candor. Second, they arose from a particular coloration of his life and psyche that was highly specific to, and indicative of, the imperatives of his own time. As Whitman himself observed, "I know very well that my 'Leaves' could not possibly have emerged or been fashion'd or completed, from any other era than the latter half of the Nineteenth Century, nor any other land than democratic America, and from the absolute triumph of the National Union army."[112] Whitman was hardly typical of his time, but that does not mean he was not profoundly representative of it.

Whitman's powerful, pious reverence for the Union served to underscore the strong affinity that individualism and nationalism had for each other in nineteenth-century America—indeed, the extent to which the latter could grow logically from the former. Viewed in that light, the consolidated modern nation-state was likely to become the preferred medium of connection for a world of separate, radically empowered individuals operating in a modern, competitive, egalitarian social order, free of any traditional, ascriptive, or aristocratic ties. As Tocqueville asserted and Whitman demonstrated, democratic men who would not so much as remove their hat for their neighbor would find themselves ineluctably drawn, even with great eagerness and sense of relief, toward absorption into the nation—into, that is, a paradoxical self-negation or self-transcendence, a sacred cause.

In a word, then, the relationship between individualism and nationalism revealed in Whitman was intense, but complex. His effort to hold the two together demonstrated their inevitable affinity, but his agony in so doing demonstrated their inevitable tension. The characteristics of a radically independent selfhood could not preclude the old imperative of self-sacrifice; indeed, in Whitman's case, they seemed paradoxically to give impetus to it. But for the centripetal energies of nationalism to reign supreme, as they had done so tangibly in those two magnificent days of marching in May 1865, the problematic nature of individualism would have to be addressed more decisively than could be done by a poet who stubbornly insisted upon singing *both* the simple separate person and the En-Masse. That would have to be accomplished by a different kind of poet and a different kind of poetry.

# 3

## The Prisonhouse of Self

Like it or not, the Grand Review seemed to put forward war itself as a principle of social organization, bringing direction and order to a confused milieu of simple, separate selves, forging and reinforcing the powerful and reassuring bonds of nationhood. Perhaps most impressively, war symbolized the disciplined and orderly collective effort needed to overcome huge obstacles and achieve great public ends. This symbolism took on added significance in the great postwar scramble for wealth and advancement (or, what is more important in the end, the general perception of such a postwar scramble). In Gilded Age America, the selfless resolve that was thought to have animated the war effort now seemed nowhere to be found. As that happened, the war's iconic status as a moment of transcendent unity and selflessness in American life, of self-overcoming dedication to a cause larger than oneself, inevitably grew. Some of this growth was liberally fertilized by the intense efforts of organizations like the Grand Army of the Republic, which never tired of reminding the nation of their members' immense sacrifices (even as they lobbied for increased veterans' benefits).[1] But the spirit and the organizational structures of modern war also suggested in some minds the contours of a new *social* vision, of the awesome possibilities opened by the intelligent orchestration of human effort in large-scale combination.

Not the least of the authors for whom this was true was Edward Bellamy, whose utopian novel *Looking Backward* (1888) became a publishing sensation, one of the most widely read books of the nineteenth century, surpassed in sales at century's end only by *Uncle Tom's Cabin* and *Ben-Hur*. Indeed, *Looking Backward* was a book of phenomenal influence, "the most famous, popular, and successful utopian novel ever written," and it left an enduring mark upon the rising generation of American intellectuals and writers, including such notables as John Dewey, Thorstein Veblen, Norman Thomas, Eugene Debs, and William Allen White. In fact, Dewey and Charles Beard both placed *Looking Backward* second only to Marx's *Capital* in their lists of the most influential books published since 1885.[2] Such fabulous success led to a spate of literary imitators; between the publication of Bellamy's novel and the end of the century, some forty-six other utopian novels appeared in the United States.[3] Not only did *Looking Backward* sell like hotcakes to the general public and attract the intense interest of serious thinkers; it gave rise, virtually overnight, to a significant mass social-reform movement, some 165 Bellamy clubs throughout the nation that were dedicated to the implementation of the social vision and reform agenda that the novel propounded.[4] Few books in modern American history can make so strong and uncontroversial a claim as *Looking Backward* to have expressed a powerful and widespread disposition of its time and place.

*Looking Backward* was perhaps not an exceptionally profound or pathbreaking work of social thought; one would want to look elsewhere for more rigorously elaborated versions of a non-Marxian socialism. But such was not what Bellamy had in mind anyway. It was a compelling and inspiring work of the social imagination, not a meticulous work of social philosophy, that *Looking Backward* offered to millions of readers. As a highly popular and accessible piece of utopian literature, it registered the thoughts and yearnings of its audience in two different directions. A utopia is not only an imaginative projection of a radiant social ideal; it is also a way that, indirectly, a society confesses how and why it is unhappy with itself. *Looking Backward* accomplished both tasks, offering a compelling image of a new paradigm of social organization, coupled with a searing critique of the dissociated, inhuman conditions of postbellum nineteenth-century industrial America. For Bellamy, just as for Whitman, that social vision crystallized from his own internal struggle against dissociation and toward social connection, a struggle both highly personal and culturally resonant.

---

In 1890, two years after Ticknor and Company had released the first edition of *Looking Backward*, the once-obscure author, who found himself thrust to the head of a great movement for social reform, indulged for a moment in personal reflections on the aims that had led him to write the book. These reflections, appearing in the pages of *The Nationalist*, a journal founded to propagate the social vision that *Looking Backward* articulated, reveal that Bellamy had started with a quite different book in mind, one more closely resembling the fabulistic novels and strange, dreamy short stories he had been writing over the previous fifteen years. Such an intention would have been consistent with what we know of Bellamy's beliefs. Before publishing the book, he confessed, he had never had "any affiliations with any class or sect of industrial or social reformers nor . . . any particular sympathy with undertakings of the sort." *Looking Backward* was not envisioned at the outset as a "serious contribution to the movement of social reform" but, rather, "a mere literary fantasy, a fairy tale of social felicity . . . a cloud-palace for an ideal humanity." In its first draft, the tale was set in Asheville, North Carolina, in the year 3000, rather than the Boston of the year 2000, for Bellamy wanted to situate his tale in a place and time sufficiently remote from the grimy and oppressive conditions of his own nineteenth-century industrial Massachusetts in order to offer no direct or pointed commentary upon the present. He would soften the impact of a prospective new social order by the ample cushion of eleven centuries of evolutionary change.[5]

In that eventually discarded first draft, the book's opening scene presented the reader with a Grand Review of sorts: "a grand parade of a departmental division of the industrial army" for the occasion of the annual "muster day," when men were to be mustered in or out of "the national service." Although in the end he reluctantly deleted this event from the book, since it did not fit the narrative line he eventually settled upon, his reading and rereading of this scene always gave Bellamy immense pleasure, as he later related:

> The solemn pageantry of the great festival of the year, the impressive ceremonial of the oath of duty taken by the new recruits in presence of the world-standard, the formal return of the thanks of humanity to the veterans who received their honorable dismissal from service, the review and march past of the entire body of the local industrial forces, each battalion with its appropriate insignia, the triumphal arches, the garlanded streets, the banquets, the music, the open theatres and pleasure gardens, with all the features of a gala day sacred to the civic virtues and the enthusiasm of humanity, furnished materials for a picture exhilarating at least to the painter.[6]

The scene was constellated around a metaphor central to Bellamy's rethinking of social organization under modern industrial circumstances. His notion of "committing the duty of maintaining the community to an industrial army" analogous to the defensive role of a military army occurred to Bellamy through the "grand object lesson of the organization of an entire people for national purposes presented by the military system of universal service." The possible uses of this idea had been "vaguely floating" in his mind for one or two years. Only when he began to write *Looking Backward*, however, and attempted to flesh out the particulars of the way that a utopian industrial social order might actually function did he perceive the full possibilities of the military model. By the time he started writing the book, though, he had "recognized in the modern military system not merely a rhetorical analogy for a national industrial service, but its prototype, furnishing at once a complete working model for its organization, an arsenal of patriotic and national motives and arguments for its animation, and the unanswerable demonstration of its feasibility drawn from the actual experience of whole nations organized and manoeuvred [*sic*] as armies." So it was that Bellamy, by his own account, "stumbled over the destined corner-stone of the new social order," and a world of fantasy became recast as "the vehicle of a definite scheme of industrial reorganization." The book's setting was moved closer, to the year 2000, since the increasingly excited Bellamy felt certain that the barriers to his ideas would easily fall away, and surely by the end of the twentieth century "the order of things which we look forward to will already have become an exceedingly old story."[7]

Thus did Edward Bellamy take his place in a long line of prophets of the New Jerusalem on the American strand. He seemed an unlikely candidate for that role, however, and even more unlikely to have seized upon military models for his vision. Born at mid-century in the industrializing Connecticut Valley town of Chicopee Falls, Massachusetts (near Springfield), he was by all accounts a dreamy, reserved, reclusive man, full of generous sentiments but plagued by chronic physical frailty and by recurrent storms of inner turbulence. In the photographs of Bellamy that have come down to us, some hint of this distress seems to be detectable, swimming in the depths of his faintly troubled eyes. Some of that strain arose from Bellamy's profoundly religious sensibilities, a disposition only partly attributable to the long line of New England clergymen from which he was descended—a line stretching from his father, Rufus, a Baptist minister, back to Edward's distinguished great-great grandfather Dr. Joseph Bellamy, a disciple and associate of Jonathan Edwards. But Rufus, in fact, was not a man in the Edwardsian mold, for he was better known for easygoing geniality than for theological asperity. It was not Edward Bellamy's father but, rather, his austere and zealous mother, Maria, who supervised his religious formation with a firm hand and unbending discipline that would surely have met the strictest standards of her husband's distant forebears. Edward grew up imbued with characteristic Calvinist ideas and sentiments about the depravity and fallenness of man, and these notions he quite naturally translated into an especially powerful conviction of his personal unworthiness—a self-imposed agony to be overcome only, Maria stressed to him repeatedly, by observing the inexorable duty to escape the prison of one's self in service to others.

If Jonathan Edwards's legacy made for the relentless goad to self-examination inherent in the Calvinist's agonized conscience, it also promised the ecstatic, ineffable rapture brought by yielding to the grace of God's presence. As a youth, the painfully shy and introspective Edward would rush home from school each day, his heart filled with an ardent desire "to be with God." He found his deepest and most sustaining happiness in those moments of prayer, when he could disengage himself from the sin-tainted fruitlessness of the interpersonal world and feel the hated burden of his stained selfhood lift miraculously from his shoulders as his soul "fused and melted in perfect union with the divine."[8] This pattern of his quest for felicity as a deliverance from the storms of his intensely personal angst into the calm of a higher transpersonal reality, with the concomitant obliteration of memory, would become a template for much of Bellamy's subsequent adult thought. It was not an entirely improbable combination for someone of his Calvinist background, but it did make a curious starting place for a man who would eventually become a prophet of transfigured social organization.

Just how distinctly etched that early pattern was would become clear in his 1873 exploration "The Religion of Solidarity," an essay that, despite the fact that he chose not to publish it in his lifetime, Bellamy later asserted to be "the germ of what has been ever since my philosophy," his "ripe judgment of life," the document that he said he wanted to "be read to me when I am about to die."[9] The essay began to develop Bellamy's youthful yearnings for transcendent release in terms that were at once richer and more generic, less exclusively Christian. When we contemplate a beautiful landscape, Bellamy began, we find ourselves not only thrilled but filled with sadness and "wistful yearning," for we wish to "be a part of the beauty," to enjoy a "perfect communion" with it. The potency of this impulse in our souls demonstrates how deeply our inward being corresponds with that of "external nature," and therefore how confining a prison is created in us by our "narrow, isolated, and incommodious individuality." The personal life is but "a bubble on a foam-flecked ocean," and its significance is "so infinitesimal as to defy the imagination." But there is also within us "a spark of the universal life," a "second soul, an inner serene and passionless ego" that "regards the experiences of the individual with a superior curiosity" and reminds us of our "solidarity with all things and all existence." Human nature and destiny are defined by this duality of our consciousness, both "personal and impersonal, as an individual and a universal." The state of "personality" is characterized by "pettiness," but to the impersonal is attributed "the noblest, broadest, and most inspired, the most intense and satisfying of our psychical felicities." We need not be condemned to pass our days in "the narrow grotto of the individual life," he believed, "counting as strange, angelic visitants the sunbeams that struggle thither, not being able to believe that the upper universe is our world to live in, the grotto of the personality a mere workshop." Our souls are not "islands in the void" but, rather, "peninsulas forming one continent of life within the universe."[10]

Much of our misery in this world, Bellamy thought, was caused by our misplaced emphasis upon selfhood, "this vicious habit of regarding the personality as an ultimate fact instead of an mere temporary affection of the universal." When such an individualist illusion overtakes the mind, we inevitably find ourselves overcome by "a sense of utter and unnecessary isolation, of inexpressible loneliness, of a great gulf fixed between the successive personalities of a single individuality and all others." A man compounds his unhappiness when he tries to "crowd his universal life into his personal experience" and thus to "make too much of the joys and sorrows and circumstances of the person." This common human error explains why "human joy has such an undertone of sadness," why the desires of love are "mocked" by its reality; for whoever seeks "complete significance" in "the joys and sorrows of the individual" is sure to meet with "disappointment." Instead, the passion in us "for losing ourselves in others or for absorbing them into ourselves, which rebels against individuality as an impediment," should be regarded as "the expression of the greatest law of solidarity," the noblest impulsion of our natures. Hence that man who "has but glimmering visions of the universal stands on a plane infinitely above" the Napoleons and Caesars of the world, mere "men of affairs" whose greatness is only "a sort of pygmy greatness not to be desired."[11]

Clearly the contours of Bellamy's religion of solidarity drew upon the residuum left by his mother's tireless efforts. But it just as clearly owed much to the thoughts and sentiments of the New England transcendentalists, even to its unmistakable attempt to mimic the vatic style of Emerson's flowing and epigrammatic prose. The pervasiveness of Oversoul, the profound and emblematic qualities of Nature, the mystic correspondence between the two, the possibility of rapturous union with Universal Being, the absence of any specifically social vision of solidarity: all were abundantly present in Bellamy's early account. Even more strikingly evident, however, is that ground of reversal to which Whitman would be driven, racked by the loneliness and unsatisfied yearnings that seemed to lurk in the shadow of individuation's radical freedom. Indeed, Bellamy's repeated avowals of the soul's need to cast off the burdens of particularity by forgetting itself and merging with the vastness of the elements recall the similar currents of absorption and negation that eddied, with growing force and frequency, through the poetry of Whitman. Such a similarity begins to hint at a shared intellectual motif, a psychological counterpart to the fantasy of consolidation limned in Bellamy's metaphor of "peninsulas forming one continent of life." It also also bespeaks, with a transparent clarity, the powerful and conflicting emotional needs running through so many of the writings of this reclusive, lonely, abstracted author.

Those needs were conflicting because the attractions of mystical union and unworldly piety should not conceal the fact that Bellamy was also an ambitious man. Here too, despite the example of his widely admired father, the likely source of this drive was his strong-willed mother, who demanded that her children—particularly Edward, her favorite—set themselves lofty goals in life. From the time Edward could read, his mother insisted that he devote his spare moments to the study of self-improving works, and so Edward's favorite reading fare became the biographical accounts of great men and noble deeds. So absorbed in this reading did the young Bellamy become that he began to identify with these great men and smugly began to feel himself superior to the "common people" in the world about him—"as utterly out of joint with the world," he later ruefully admitted, "as Don Quixote in his library." As he fantasized prodigious achievements for himself, though, he still felt the tug of a nagging worry: perhaps these "lofty aspirations might spring from a selfish love of fame," a tawdry individualistic motive that his stern conscience, and his mother, would find unacceptable.[12] He was torn between the lures and terrors of prospective autonomy.

The only solution to this conundrum, as ever, was to find a way of discharging his ambitions in self-sacrificing service to others, and so the serious young Bellamy's thoughts turned to the profession of arms. When Bellamy was ten, as he watched his country plunge into the anguish of disunion, he recorded in his journal a list of the soldierly traits that he would need for the military career upon which he had now set his heart. The coming of the Civil War moved him to rage at the rebellious South's treachery and to swell with pride in the righteousness of the Union's cause. A growing interest in military themes is evident in his school essays on such subjects as military tactics, treason, ensigns, and great military heroes such as Philip, Alexander, and Napoleon.[13] All signs pointed in the direction of a career of military service. When Edward attempted, at the age of seventeen, to enroll at West Point, however, he was flatly turned down because of his recurring poor health. It was a bitter blow to his most cherished plans and saddled him with a long and difficult search for a comparably aimed vocation.

Still, his fascination with things military did not disappear, for it contained some of the same appeal that had drawn the young Bellamy into ecstatic prayer. "The Religion of Solidarity," although it appeared to reclassify his old childhood heroes Napoleon and Alexander as pygmies, in virtually the same breath paid tribute to "the soldierly forms of solidarity," in which the "heart melts in a happy rapture" that makes the soldier "impatient to throw his life away . . . as a sacrifice which he can make for his country, even as the priest rejoices in a victim for the altar of his god."[14] Bellamy's son, Paul, also vividly recalled his father's childlike delight in playing soldiers with him, occasions in which some of the old passions would reappear: "We used to clear off the dining table, set up the little images and shoot at them in turn with a spring toy gun which discharged a small wooden projectile. The troops were maneuvered in all sorts of interesting ways, amid a running commentary about Napoleon, whom [Father] considered by all odds the greatest military genius." The normally taciturn and restrained Bellamy became so animated when narrating these war games that he swept his auditors up in his enthusiasm: "He could construct so vivid a picture of the battle of Waterloo," recalled Paul, "that the blood of his young son coursed through his veins as though he were verily a cuirassier falling into the sunken road." Although this "military bent" in Bellamy always captivated his son, at the same time it "greatly puzzled" him, for it seemed to run so counter to the spirit of his father's "socialistic philosophy."[15]

If part of the lure of war resided in its promise of a place of high honor for the noblest, most self-sacrificing, least pecuniary motives animating human beings, and its ability to dissolve the illusion of the separate self into the overriding reality of the militant whole, then the puzzle is not so difficult to resolve. For Bellamy, there was a continuity and consistency linking his religion of solidarity with his understanding of war—an understanding, let it be noted, completely uncontaminated by any direct experience of war. The two elements merged easily, for example, in his short story "An Echo of Antietam," which tells the simple tale of a small-town soldier who must leave his sweetheart to go off to fight in the Union army. The young man, significantly named Philip King, assures his beloved Grace that no harm will befall him and that he will return in a year to marry her. Yet Grace remains inconsolable in her grief, except during her final glimpse of him, as the whole town gathers to see the regiment off. The scene is one of those military reviews that appear repeatedly in Bellamy's work, an unmistakable sign of their special significance to him:

Presently there is a burst of martial music, and the regiment comes wheeling round the corner into view and fills the wide street from curb to curb with its broad front. As the blue river sweeps along, the rows of polished bayonets, rising and falling with the swinging tread of the men, are like interminable ranks of foam-crested waves rolling in upon the shore. The imposing mass, with its rhythmic movement, give the impression of a single organism. One forgets to look for the individuals in it, forgets that there are individuals. Even those who have brothers, sons, lovers there, for a moment almost forget them in the impression of a mighty whole. The mind is slow to realize that this great dragon, so terrible in its beauty, emitting light as it moves from a thousand burnished scales, with flaming crest proudly waving in the van, is but an aggregation of men singly so feeble.[16]

When we next encounter Philip, it is twilight some weeks later, and he is strolling on a knoll outside his regimental camp near Antietam, meditating upon the great battle that was to ensue the following morning and upon the possibility of his demise. Yet Philip felt no fear of death. "The heroic instinct of mankind," proclaims the admiring narrator, "with its high contempt of death is wiser and truer . . . than superstitious terrors or philosophic doubts," for it "testifies that man is greater than his seeming self" and that his mortal life is "but an accident of his real existence, the fashion of a day, to be lightly worn and gaily doffed at duty's call." What a shame, he concludes, that "the tonic air of battlefields . . . cannot be gathered up and preserved as a precious elixir to reinvigorate the atmosphere in times of peace, when men grow faint of heart and cowardly, and quake at thought of death."[17] The prospect of death in combat gives rise to exhilaration, since it lifts him from the closed prisonhouse of self and carries him into the heroic solidarity of cosmic God-space.

Philip is, of course, killed in glorious battle, and his body is brought home to be buried. Not until the funeral eulogy does the sorrowing Grace, who has wondered why she ever let her dear Philip go to war, grasp and accept the meaning of her suffering. The bereaved, too, make their own sacrifice; they too have their own "high calling of martyrdom," which should be understood as precisely the same spirit in which Philip unhesitatingly offered his own life. Although those who remain behind "must needs weep," they should not weep "with hearts bowed down" but instead with "uplifted faces, adopting and ratifying . . . this exchange they had made of earthly happiness for the life of their native land." As Grace listens to the minister's words, she disengages from her sufferings and feels her soul moving into "some place overarching life and death" where it is "made partaker of an exultation" that no religion or philosophy could match.[18] The appeal to this impersonal place, the second soul's exultation in its complete identification with the nation, distanced Bellamy's story from the more hortatory and tragic overtones of Lincoln's Gettysburg Address and marked the tale instead as a parable of solidarity.

Perhaps a more direct encounter with the horrors of modern war might have challenged the dreamy and tenderhearted Bellamy to reconsider this picture, which has about it more than a hint of parlor sentimentality tinged with a child's bookish quixotism—light-years removed from the cool, tough-minded war existentialism of Oliver Wendell Holmes, Jr., for whom patriotic gore was more than a song lyric. Perhaps it was because he never encountered war firsthand that Bellamy continued to see it as a matter of grand reviews, of swelling hearts and stirring parades. The passionate identification of true human happiness with the experience of solidarity did not depend exclusively upon the reality of war, however, valuable as war might be as a root metaphor and organizing principle. Still, if he was not to be a soldier, what could he be? How might he solve the problem of channeling his considerable personal ambition into a lofty and selfless cause? Apparently the most obvious choice, the possibility of following in his father's footsteps, was never a serious option for Edward, a fact perhaps partly attributable to his firsthand awareness of the ministry's sharply declining status in postbellum America. Indeed, Bellamy's vocational problem was mirrored in the searches preoccupying many other similarly inclined American intellectuals who came of age in the years between the Civil War and the First World War—energetic and intelligent men (and women) who might have been drawn into a more traditional ecclesiastical affiliation in a previous era but who had not yet found a comfortable niche in the emerging new one. If not the ministry, then what vocation might offer them similarly lofty and influential scope? Bellamy spent the next seventeen years struggling to answer that question, enduring what he would later call a "ministry of disappointment" before finding a niche for himself as a writer.[19]

After his disappointment at West Point, Bellamy followed his brother Frederick to Union College in Schenectady, where he undertook a program of independent reading that probably included his first exposure to the giants of socialist thought.[20] That discovery would be crucially reinforced by a subsequent visit to Germany with his cousin William Packer in 1868–69. During that time Bellamy not only had an opportunity to take in the writings of German socialists at first hand but to observe extreme disparities of wealth and poverty; in Europe, he later claimed, his "eyes were first fully opened to the extent and consequences of man's inhumanity to man."[21] It is hard to gainsay the effects of that eye-opening experience. Exposure to Comte and other explicitly post-Christian thinkers surely began to move Bellamy away from the old verities his mother had taught and toward the questionings that led in the direction of a religion of solidarity. His experiences appeared to have little immediate effect, however, as he returned to Massachusetts, undertook the study of the law, and passed his bar examination with distinction. But in 1871, with a promising legal career palpably in his sights, he abruptly (and mysteriously) decided to abandon it, after handling but a single case.[22] His vocational crisis was unresolved.

Now twenty-one, Bellamy decided to plunge into journalistic work, leaving Chicopee Falls and the influence of his mother to make his way as a freelance writer in the great metropolis of New York. This foray into autonomy failed; he lasted less than a year there. Retreating in 1872 to the safety of his family, in whose home he would continue to live for most his remaining life, Bellamy took an editorial position with the nearby Springfield *Union*, in his spare time writing short fiction and delivering lyceum speeches. Both activities helped him explore the thoughts that had crystallized into his 1873 religion of solidarity. His facility as a writer grew rapidly, and by 1878 he had published a first novel, *Six to One*, followed in short order by two others. Two years later, he and his brother Charles decided to start a newspaper in Springfield, and both poured nearly all their energies into building the *Penny News* (later renamed the *Daily News*) into a Democratic competitor to the town's two Republican papers. Although the paper eventually experienced considerable success, by 1884 Edward had yet another change of heart about his vocation and decided to withdraw from journalism and devote himself exclusively to his own writing, leaving the struggling paper in Charles's hands.[23]

Despite the detours and discontinuities this zigzagging outward life might suggest, the intellectual and emotional themes appearing in Bellamy's writings during these years of literary incubation were building in a remarkably steady way. Over the years of vocational peregrination, his fiction had evolved into a vehicle of exploratory fantasy, a series of thought experiments or experience simulations in which he probed the possibility of a life lived according to his cherished principle of solidarity—and the perils of a life lived otherwise. Quite possibly, too, such fictions offered him compensatory relief from, and insight into, the tensions of his own life, including his prolonged indecision about the course of his career, an issue upon which all the most onerous burdens of selfhood came most intensely to bear.

One sees this personal subtext emerge with especial clarity in his repeated unpublished and fragmentary (and literarily clumsy) attempts to create a fictional character named Eliot Carson, who would serve as a fully realized model for the new, postsolidaritist man. "I find," said Eliot, "a sense of lofty calm in imagining my future life as being so far impersonal and even unconscious as may be implied in an entire lack of individualities. I love to dream of my spirit as something interfused in the light of setting suns, broad oceans, and the winds. If you say that such impersonality means a merely unconscious existence, I will not quarrel with you. I am quite content that it should be so."[24] Though not always as plangently reminiscent of Whitman's dark yearning to be rocked by the sea crone and hear her "low and delicious word death," a similar personal subtext appears, in one way or another, in nearly all the published fiction Bellamy produced before *Looking Backward*; more often than not, a salvific woman character figured prominently in the male characters' quest for solidarity and restoration. His vision was both empowered and constricted by the very wounds that engendered his need to write—above all, by the pain generated by the powerful grip of individual consciousness and of memory. Each in his series of Hawthorne-like romances, their plots replete with cases of mistaken or blurred identity, tortures of lingering guilt, dreams that became real, and realities that became dreams, was also a reconnaissance of occupied territory, an imaginative foray meant ultimately to weaken the occupier's grip. Each, moreover, contains important elements that would eventually find their way into *Looking Backward*.

For example, in *Six to One*, Bellamy explores the serenity of the "second soul" by embodying it in the figure of a woman. That first novel seems transparently autobiographical, relating the tale of a high-strung New York journalist who comes to Nantucket to recover from a nervous breakdown. He is brought to a state of spiritual peace through the beneficent influence of an enlightened island woman who heals him by bringing him into solidarity with the elements, the "impersonal" mysteries of the sea.[25] In the story "A Summer Evening's Dream" (1877), Bellamy explores the psychological possibilities of blurred identity. A young couple muses about the long Platonic romance of neighbors Miss Rood and Lawyer Morgan, an aging woman and man who had silently and chastely loved each other for forty years but had mysteriously allowed the consummation of marriage to pass them by. On an August evening walk, though, when Lawyer Morgan expresses to Miss Rood the wish that they might once again see one another as they were when young, the young couple magically appears in the shadows, looking uncannily like the fulfillment of that wish. The young girl not only indulges Morgan's wish by walking with him and pretending to be the young Miss Rood, but she pushes him past the barrier that had always held him back from marriage. When he returns to the "real" Miss Rood, he embraces her passionately, in a way he has never done before. At the story's end, the two have at last married.[26]

The story "Two Day's Solitary Imprisonment" (1878) explores the grip of individual consciousness, and particularly the grip of memory, in a different way by depicting the agonies afflicting a guilt-prone, imaginative man whose world disintegrates when he becomes convinced that he was responsible for a murder that, in fact, he did not commit.[27] This theme is presented even more dramatically in *Dr. Heidenhoff's Process* (1880), in which a woman is so racked by remorse over a past sexual indiscretion that she cannot allow herself to respond to the ardent and totally accepting love of her noble and patient suitor, for fear of polluting his life with her sin. The suitor's frustration seems to be answered by his discovery of Dr. Heidenhoff, who has invented a cure for painful memories: "the Extirpation of Thought Process," achieved through "galvano-therapeutics," a medical breakthrough that will make it possible for humankind to live, at last, wholly in the present, unburdened by memory. Our belief in the continuity, persistence, and integrity of the individual person, explains the doctor, is an illusion created by "the obnoxious train of recollections," to which problem his process offers a definitive solution—or would have offered one, had it not turned out that the doctor, and his process, are nothing more than the suitor's wistful dream. There is no quick fix for the problem of remembrance.[28]

The most indicative of Bellamy's early writings was the science fiction tale "The Blindman's World" (1886), which not only immediately preceded *Looking Backward* but directly prefigured it. Indeed, it is significant that "A Blindman's World" itself contained, in embryonic form, so many of the literary devices Bellamy would employ in *Looking Backward*, including the central device of a bemused visitor from the "backwardness" of nineteenth-century America who stumbles into a Martian utopia and has that brave new world's virtues (as well as the pathologies of his own world) patiently explained to him by a bright and articulate spokesman for the perfected order. Of course, too, the characteristics of the perfected order clearly reflect Bellamy's other concerns. The story admiringly describes the superior character of Martians, who possess foreknowledge of their personal future and, being wise enough to "despise the past, and never dwell upon it," are freed by their prevision from "the disease of memory," that "morbid and monstrous growth" that so afflicts inhabitants of the earth. Indeed, the Blindman's World is the Martians' epithet for the earth, whose denizens, alone among the universe's intelligent beings, are "doomed to walk backward, beholding only what has gone by, assured only of what is past and dead." Perhaps, concludes the narrator, the Martians "represent the ideal and normal type of our race, as perhaps it once was, as perhaps it may yet be again."[29]

It is tempting to wonder why Bellamy saw memory as such a serious obstacle to spiritual growth and was therefore so obsessed with its extirpation. Why was he so convinced that memory was merely a snare and not a potential source of life-giving nourishment? Was it out of a reformer's future-oriented zeal? Or was there something in his own past that he could not bear to contemplate? Was his childhood too blighted to bear examination? Did he, as was said of Hawthorne, harbor some inadmissible and unforgivable sin? Or was his loathing for memory merely a logical outgrowth of the *puer aeternus*'s denial of the imperatives of individuation and particularity: that is, denial of the crushing realization that one is no longer a manchild with multivalent possibilities but is merely, for better or worse, one particular person among millions, the sum product of all the things one has been along the way?[30]

It is impossible to know for sure. It is clear from Bellamy's early fictions, however, that the psychological themes that appear in "The Religion of Solidarity" had early permeated his mental life: the burdensomeness of individual awareness, the intolerable weight of the past, the tortures of a too-active memory, and the relief to be found in casting aside the dubious wisdom to be derived from such guideposts and, instead, turning one's attention toward the future, yielding one's perpetually inadequate, insecure self to the all-absorbing embrace of the collective. Although these early tales are often clumsily didactic and sometimes seriously deficient in their plotting and character development, they laid important intellectual groundwork for *Looking Backward*, which Bellamy began to draft in 1886, the same year he completed "A Blindman's World."

If there were such apparent continuities in Bellamy's work, one cannot deny that *Looking Backward*, at least in its ultimate form, represented a substantial shift of emphasis from the dreamy introversion and subjectivism of the earlier fiction toward a more active, vigorous, extroverted, and far-reaching commitment to the transformation of industrial society through specific reform measures. The extent of this shift should not be exaggerated, however, to the degree that *Looking Backward* is made to seem a wholly revolutionary departure for Bellamy, or the result of a profound conversion experience, rather than the result of incremental and logical changes of perspective and emphasis. The fact is, nothing of importance presented in *Looking Backward* lacked clear antecedents in his earlier work. Bellamy had not suddenly discovered "the social problem." From early in his life, he felt a deep concern over the degradation and wrenching dislocation wrought by the industrial system, whose effects he could observe in his own rapidly changing town. He had attached himself firmly to the basic ideals of utopian socialism as early as his late teens and had long been pondering possible solutions to the industrial age's social problems, as is evident from the content of his lyceum talks and many of his journalistic writings.

Moreover, although his fictional writings rarely addressed questions of social inequities in America, there was a notable exception to that rule: his 1879 historical novel *The Duke of Stockbridge: A Romance of Shays's Rebellion*. Written and published in serial form for the *Berkshire Courier*, a small paper published out of Great Barrington, Massachusetts, *The Duke of Stockbridge* put forward a sympathetic portrayal of Shays's Rebellion as a justifiable popular uprising by poor, debt-ridden, and sorely oppressed western Massachusetts farmers. In Bellamy's telling, many such men had returned home after fighting for liberty in the revolutionary war, only to find that a corrupt and undemocratic wealthy elite had in the meantime taken control of their lives and were only too willing to throw the returning patriots into debtors' prison. The tyranny of the British king, it seemed, had merely been replaced by a tyranny of the American moneyed class, and under such circumstances a rebellion was understandable, even fitting, given Americans' sacred revolutionary heritage. With this carefully researched novel, Bellamy broke new intellectual ground, for his interpretation of the rebellion flew directly in the face of nearly a century's conventional wisdom and anticipated the more jaundiced view of the new federal order that soon began to emerge in the scholarship of Charles Beard, as well as the more favorable view of the rebellion that largely holds sway today.[31] More importantly, the story served Bellamy as a revealing allegory of the plight of industrial America. Although this drama was played out on an eighteenth-century stage, it pointed to the same dilemmas of structural inequality and the same betrayal of the great American republican and revolutionary ideals that Bellamy so greatly feared in his own time.

Bellamy had not, then, recently "discovered" the inequities of the social world, but neither had he found a way to conjoin his social concerns with the force of his more personal yearnings. Some inner imperative had kept his introspective side, which informed most of his fiction, separate from the social-reform side, which informed much of his journalism. With *Looking Backward*, however, he appeared to find a means of incorporating both aspects in a single text, a social-political tract resonating in the form of a novel, and that development begs to be interpreted. Bellamy himself believed the explanation was to be found in the growing importance to him of his own domestic life, and there is considerable plausibility to the claim. Despite the warmth of his emotional nature and his readiness to fall in love, for years Bellamy had strenuously resisted marriage, which he feared would reduce him to a mere breadwinner and give "god, nature, and the books the go-by." Such resistance may have reflected a well-founded concern that, to paraphrase Oscar Wilde, capitalism might take up too many evenings (and days), but it was even more obviously the sign of a man stuck in the psychological station of the *puer aeternus*, fearful of the descent into connectedness and dependency, the imperfection and mutability of the flesh, the forging of a relationship with a real, not ideal, woman. Bellamy finally succumbed, however, marrying young Emma Sanderson, who had been for many years a ward of the household and hence had become like a sister to him. Even then, he had only been pushed to marriage from a fear that he might lose Emma to another suitor. Their marriage occurred, significantly, on Decoration Day: May 30, 1882. That day had been consecrated by the nation for the purpose of honoring those who had surrendered their individuality for the sake of the Union. Perhaps that choice of wedding day indicated his faith that his marriage to the sisterly Emma was an equally worthy sacrifice, fully assimilable to the religion of solidarity.[32]

Fatherhood, however, presented a greater challenge, and the appearance of son Paul (1884) and daughter Marion (1886) soon gave "the problem of life" a "new and more solemn meaning" for Bellamy. Parenthood constituted the true descent into the flesh for him, one that forced upon him a deeper sense of connection to, and dependency upon, the social order, and at the same time a stubborn unwillingness to accept that his children should have to endure a world made miserable with the suffering and injustice he saw all around him. It gave a new and highly personal urgency to "the social question," paving the way for the reconciliation of opposites inherent in *Looking Backward*. Bellamy wrote from his own experience when he declared that child rearing was "the problem of all problems to which the individualistic method is most inapplicable":

> Your fear for your child is that he may fall into the ditch of poverty or be waylaid by robbers. So you give him a lantern and provide him with arms. That would be all very well if you could not do better, but would it not be an infinitely wiser and more efficient method to join hands with all the other equally anxious parents, and fill up the ditch and exterminate the robbers, so that safety might be a matter of course for all? However high, however wise, however rich you are, the only way you can surely safeguard your child from hunger, cold and wretchedness and all the deprivations, degradations and indignities which poverty implies, is by a plan that will equally safeguard all men's children. This principle once recognized, the solution of the social problem becomes a simple matter. Until it is, no solution is possible.[33]

His "Eliot Carson" sketches of that time mirrored these developments, relating changes of heart in Eliot when he married and began a family, developments that "cured" him of "Hermitism and self-absorption" and caused him to plunge "with enthusiasm [and] tremendous earnestness into the study of social conditions" and the formulation of a philosophy of "nationalism."[34] Bellamy undoubtedly hoped *Looking Backward* would be a commercial success, a motive to which he naturally would have been reluctant to admit, perhaps even to himself, but one to which his growing family obligations— and Bellamy was by all accounts an exceptionally tenderhearted and solicitous father—lent added force and legitimacy.

One cannot neglect the form and pressure of the immediate times in describing the genesis of *Looking Backward*. The nation's growing labor unrest, symbolized by the bloody Haymarket affair in May 1886—that "year of ten thousand strikes"—must have made a powerful impression upon the former journalist as he began to lay out his magnum opus.[35] This is not to say that he was moved to defend the eight anarchists who were accused of the Haymarket bombing and brought to trial in Chicago, as so many others, like his friend William Dean Howells, had been. His ultimate sympathies, as he made clear in those 1890 recollections, did not lie with anarchists, Marxists, or militant radicals of any sort, whom he frequently accused of delaying progress more than they advanced it. Nor did he find much to admire in the narrow interest-group orientation of mainstream trade unionists, whom he predictably derided as petty and selfish, a mirror image of the greedy capitalists and naked individualism that labor purportedly opposed.[36] His soldierly inclinations notwithstanding, Bellamy detested conflict of any sort and found himself most spiritually and intellectually at home with the kind of peaceful, broadly Christian, unclass-conscious, cooperative-commonwealth vision of industrial and social reorganization espoused by such groups as the Knights of Labor. But as Bellamy pushed ahead with the drafting of his book, the acrid smoke of labor strife still lingering in the air and the afterimages of Haymarket's violence lingering in his mind, he could not help but fear that widespread polarizing class conflict might become a permanent fact of American life. For a thinker who had long brooded over the possibility that America's revolutionary legacy had been corrupted and squandered, and who cherished solidarity above all other social values, few prospects could have seemed more ominous.

Still, even allowing the full force of these explanations of the origins of *Looking Backward*, it is remarkable, particularly in light of the book's astonishing public success, how fully it continued to express the same psychological needs that had given rise to Bellamy's earlier, introspective writings. In that sense, the continuities in his work seem far more impressive and interesting than the departures. This observation in turn gives rise to another puzzle, a mystery that rests at the heart of so much influential writing: how could a book so deeply idiosyncratic have struck a chord so publicly resonant? Psychological investigations of ideas and thinkers often run the risk of demonstrating the extent to which the thoughts of an admittedly atypical person are confined to the peculiarities of that person's psyche alone, without any larger purchase upon the world he or she inhabits. This need not be so, however. A proper sense of the psychological rootedness of ideas, or of "their significance as psychic events," as James Hillman puts it, can lead us to understand them not merely as formal and disembodied thought-units or as rationalizations of instinctive drives, but as ways of seeing, or archetypal patterns of envisioning—just as the ophthalmological roots of the word *idea* clearly indicate that we should.[37] In Bellamy's case, a proper appreciation of his work's psychological dimension, of its "way of seeing," actually forges a link between the particularities of the man and the contours of the culture. To an extraordinary degree, Bellamy's inner struggles, idiosyncratic though they may have been, also faithfully registered, and indeed reverberated with, the larger issues of individualism confronting his age. In *Looking Backward* he provided a powerful way of envisioning and answering both the inner and the outer concerns by imagining a healing ideal of consolidation and then looking back upon the turbulence of his own times through that imaginative lens.

It is tempting to read *Looking Backward* as a utopian tract clumsily grafted onto a nineteenth-century sentimental romance, rather like a "serious" television docudrama that throws in a gratuitous romantic subplot to hold the attention of casual viewers. Perhaps the strongest support for that reading comes from Bellamy himself, who asserted that when he decided to transform the book from a "fairy tale" into a "definite scheme of social perfection," he retained the form of a romance only "with some impatience" and, being mindful of the needs of the general reading public, left "barely enough story . . . to decently drape the skeleton of the argument."[38] We need not, however, treat those remarks as the final word on the subject. Authors are not always their own best critics, particularly authors who become eager to be regarded as social critics involved in world-transforming labors. Readers of Bellamy's previous fiction will find *Looking Backward* replete with all the characteristic devices he used to enliven his romances: time travel, blurred or doubled identities, the confusion between dream and reality, the horrible isolating power of individual guilt, and a woman's love as path to a larger sense of social or cosmic belonging. Moreover, these devices are deployed with considerable authorial care and precision, in ways that compliment and amplify the book's long expository passages and consistently echo elements of the religion of solidarity to which he always professed allegiance. Bellamy may not have been an inspired literary craftsman, but that is no reason to regard the fictional framework of *Looking Backward* as somehow less than integral to his achievement, to be taken less seriously than its utopia-envisioning dialogues.

It is no coincidence, then, that Bellamy chose to open the story on Decoration Day, a day saturated with meaning for him. Julian West, the protagonist-narrator (and authorial alter ego) of *Looking Backward*, after dutifully paying his respects at the grave of his fiancée's brother in Mount Auburn Cemetery, returns to Boston to dine that evening with her family, the Bartletts. It is soon evident that Julian and the Bartletts live in a world of privileged wealth and refined leisure, circulating within the upper strata of Bostonian society. But we also soon discover that Julian is a deeply troubled man. Some of his plaints, and those of his circle of acquaintances, stem from external factors: the disordered state of the times, marked as they are by increasing class divisions and accelerating social tensions, labor agitations, and strikes. For his own part, the well-insulated Mr. West feels no sympathy for or appreciation of the insurgent laboring classes; indeed, at the height of his exasperation he wishes (as Caligula wished of the Romans) that "they had but one neck that he might cut it off."[39] He especially resents the fact that strike-related work stoppages have repeatedly delayed completion of his new house and thereby postponed his eagerly awaited marriage to the lovely Miss Edith Bartlett.

The roots of Julian's own trepidation seem to run far deeper than these troublesome external events, however. Julian has been fighting an ongoing battle with chronic insomnia, regularly finding it impossible to sleep for two or more consecutive nights. To combat this problem, he built a secret sleeping chamber beneath his old house, a subterranean refuge into which "no murmur from the upper world ever penetrated," and because of its inaccessibility and secrecy, it is also an ideal place for him to protect his valuables from theft or fire. But even with the help of this bunkerlike enclosure, wherein he finds himself enveloped by "the silence of the tomb," secure in the knowledge that his worldly wealth is safe and close by, he is still unable to sleep reliably, and he frequently has to call in desperation on the services of a mesmerist to lull him into slumber. His unease runs much deeper than a question of worldly worries. Julian's dark, private chamber serves as a startling figuration of the deathly "grotto" of the purely individual life, which stubbornly cuts itself off from contact with the "upper" world in its frantic pursuit of personal peace and ease. Through the image of Julian West's inexpugnable anxiety and discontent, the mysterious and nagging guilt that lies behind his inability to sleep nights, *Looking Backward* seems to suggest that even the most perfectly implemented isolation of the individual self cannot succeed in exorcising the demons that afflict it.

As night falls on this Decoration Day 1887, the agitated Julian finds he must once again employ his mesmerist, Dr. Pillsbury, for relief. But after he finally drifts off to sleep, a fire apparently sweeps through his house and consumes its contents—including, it is believed, Julian himself. In fact, however, Julian survives the holocaust and continues to sleep undisturbed, unbeknownst to all, sealed in his secret chamber, his bodily processes completely suspended, until the year 2000. At that time he is finally discovered and is taken into the house of Dr. Leete, who resuscitates him and then introduces an astonished and disbelieving Julian to the spectacle of a drastically transformed and perfected millennial Boston. Thereafter the book alternates between long, highly didactic discussions between Julian and the Leetes about the contours and operating principles of this radiant new world, and episodes in the subplot of Julian's psychological development, the latter revolving around Julian's anguish over his now riven sense of his personal identity and his growing attraction to Dr. Leete's daughter, a graceful and reassuring young woman who is, like his nineteenth-century fiancée, named Edith.

From the beginning, the descriptions of utopian Boston offered by the Leete family touch upon Bellamy's characteristic themes, never missing an opportunity to contrast the sordid spectacle of nineteenth-century selfishness and wastefulness with the lustrous twentieth-century ideals of solidarity and efficiency. That contrast is prepared by Bellamy's justly celebrated extended comparison of nineteenth-century American society to a "prodigious coach," in which men and women scrambled and clawed at one another for the sake of a few privileged seats on top, where they could be pulled along in airy comfort by the tightly harnessed "masses of humanity," men and women reduced to beasts of burden. Dr. Leete's discourses soon reinforce that theme: the need to overcome competitive individualism by the triumph of a spirit of cooperation and combination. When the disbelieving Julian is allowed to view the new city of Boston from Dr. Leete's rooftop, he is especially astonished by the orderliness and opulence of the city's streets and buildings. Yes, responds Dr. Leete, he had heard of the squalor of nineteenth-century cities, a blightedness so clearly a result of that era's "excessive individualism," which had prevented the sustenance of any meaningful "public spirit."[40]

The utopia of *Looking Backward* does not attempt to overthrow industrialism but to humanize and purify it. Consider, for example, the "labor problem" that so bedevils the world Julian has left behind. Dr. Leete explains how that problem simply "solved itself," in the process giving an account of the new organization of economy and society in his own time, and of how and why it stands in such marked contrast to what preceded it. The great labor disturbances of the nineteenth century, he patiently explains, had merely been inevitable outgrowths of the increasing concentration of capital under a more and more consolidated industrial system. Although that system resulted in enormous social inequities and degradation of labor, it also produced staggering economic efficiencies, which made thinkable, for the first time in human history, the universal dispersion of a high level of material wealth; thus, such a system was not to be lightly abandoned. The key to managing this problem lay in the very process of economic consolidation, which "had been so desperately and vainly resisted" by those who yearned for preindustrial simplicity. Consolidation was not the enemy; it was, in fact, "a process which only needed to complete its logical evolution to open a golden future to humanity." In other words, the nineteenth century's enormous pains and dislocations should be attributed not to the forces of consolidation but to an *unfinished* consolidation. By the early twentieth century, however, "the evolution was completed by the final consolidation of the entire capital of the nation," whereby the governance of the nation's industry and commerce was turned over to a single syndicate "representing the people" and therefore devoted to pursuit of "the common interests for the common profit." Indeed, the nation itself had become "the one great business corporation . . . the one capitalist . . . the sole employer . . . the final monopoly." Perhaps most remarkable, this colossal transformation had occurred without pressure of violence or coercion; indeed, it had been proposed by the great corporations themselves and was readily accepted by a people who had gradually become convinced of the virtues of large-scale enterprises. The epoch of industrial consolidation, "the era of trusts," found its consummatory fulfillment in the establishment of "The Great Trust."[41]

In this new order, the diffuse energies of solitary selves had found a home, where they concentrated in and fused with the new social order, precisely as Philip King and his comrades in arms had coalesced from an aggregation of ordinary men "singly so feeble," into a single magnificent organism, a coursing river of blue that had the power to overcome all before it. Bellamy could not adequately describe this new order without returning, again and again, to military root metaphors and analogies. Once the nation had come to assume proprietorship of all industrial enterprises, a citizen's service in what is called "the industrial army" became a universal obligation, precisely analogous to the obligation of universal military service. The industrial army follows a time-honored military organizational chart; it is divided into ten great departments, with the chiefs of these divisions being comparable to "commanders of army corps, or lieutenant generals, each having a dozen to a score of generals of separate guilds reporting to him." Above these ten officers, "who form his council, is the general-in-chief, who is the President of the United States."[42] The administrative oversight of the industrial army and the Great Trust comprises the president's chief duties; his political duties (as well as those of the Congress) have dwindled to few or none.

This military style of administrative bureaucracy had yielded efficiencies unimaginable even under the highly productive regime of nineteenth-century capitalism, and Bellamy did not hesitate to define those benefits in the language and imagery of warfare. "The effectiveness of the working force of a nation, under the myriad-headed leadership of private capital," explains Dr. Leete, "as compared with that which it attains under a single head, may be likened to the military efficiency of a mob, or a horde of barbarians with a thousand petty chiefs, as compared with that of a disciplined army under one general—such a fighting machine, for example, as the German army in the time of Von Moltke."[43] Of course, the mere achievement of such efficiencies, however remarkable, would not alone have sufficed to satisfy Bellamy's deeper moral concerns. But these concerns too were answered by the reconceptualization of the nation as an army, for the martial virtues of unselfish valor could now be incarnated in the ordinary labors of the ordinary civilian. "Now that industry," Doctor Leete tells Julian West, "is no longer self-service, but service of the nation," it follows that "patriotism, passion for humanity, impel the worker as in your day they did the soldier. The army of industry is an army, not alone by virtue of its perfect organization, but by reason also of the ardor of self-devotion which animates its members."[44]

How appropriate, then, that the social-reform ideology and movement to which *Looking Backward* gave rise adopted the name of Nationalism—even if Bellamy's principal reason for using that term was to evade the opprobrium, as well as the unwanted emphasis upon class division and class conflict, attached to the word *socialism*.[45] To be sure, no discerning reader was likely to be fooled; anyone familiar with the already considerable literature of American socialism and labor movements could readily recognize the similarities between Bellamy's projections and those of Owenites, Fourierites, Christian socialists, and the Socialist Labor party as well as innumerable other social visionaries going back to antebellum times.[46] Nationalism was more than just a prudent name, however; it was also an honestly descriptive one. It acknowledged the degree to which the coalescence of the United States under the overwhelming force of the national principle, victorious over all other contenders in the clash of the Civil War, served as an important inspiration and animating principle for Bellamy's social vision. The "national party," explained Dr. Leete,

> could not well have had any other name, for its purpose was to realize the idea of the nation with a grandeur and completeness never before conceived, not as an association of men for certain merely political functions . . . but as a family, a vital union, a common life, a mighty heaven-touching tree whose leaves are its people, fed from its veins, and feeding it in turn. The most patriotic of all possible parties, it sought to justify patriotism and raise it from an instinct to a rational devotion, by making the native land truly a father-land, a father who kept the people alive and was not merely an idol for which they were expected to die.[47]

Despite Bellamy's attempts to render the lineaments of his utopian Boston in crisp and analytical terms, his deeper yearning to find individual redemption through corporate solidarity, so consistent a feature of his earlier writings, was ever ready to burst to the surface.

*Looking Backward*'s narrative component, the unfolding psychological drama of Julian West, carries much of the weight of that yearning. As we gradually learn, through Dr. Leete's rather tedious monologues, more and more about how this utopian Boston actually works—how people choose their occupations, how they are paid, how equality of social condition is reconciled with personal freedom, how goods are distributed, how relations between men and women are understood, how meals are provided, how washing of clothes is done, and so on—we are also periodically reminded that this paradisiacal vision has also had profound effects upon the story's protagonist. When Julian awakens after his first night in the Leete household, he feels a total disorientation that soon turns to despair as he contemplates the immense gulf between the 1887 Boston in which he began his long sleep and the strange new environment in which he now finds himself. He feels the amorphous, shoreless terror of crumbling identity, a "mental torture . . . this helpless, eyeless groping for myself in a boundless void." The light of a brave new world beckons to him, yet the pernicious chains of memory, forged from his diminished former identity, hold him back. As he struggles to grasp some reliable bearings in that whirling vortex of despair, the notion takes hold that perhaps "I was two persons, that my identity was double," an answer that soon "began to fascinate" him as a "simple solution of my experience."[48] Like the tomblike image of Julian's sleeping chamber, this dualism too points back to "The Religion of Solidarity" and in particular to its thesis that two souls contest within us: the individual soul, the soul of personality in all its pathetic weakness and dullness; and a "second soul" that dwells in peaceful, impersonal communion with the "upper universe" and thereby with the universal life of all things.

For Julian West, a "second soul" had been called forth by his experience of this brave, unselfish new world of the future, and this in turn had brought the grotto-self of his native nineteenth century into question. Evident as the derivation from his earlier writings was, it is at the same time worth noting the significant intellectual ground that Bellamy had traversed since the neotranscendentalism of his younger work. "The Religion of Solidarity" had argued that personality itself was largely an illusory entity, and the essay had prayed for the happy obliteration of the grotto-self through the willing absorption of that self (and its meddlesome consciousness) into the lush commodity of Nature. In the earlier work, the understanding of solidarity, in short, was not concerned especially with the social dimension of human existence. In *Looking Backward*, however, the emphases have changed dramatically. Nature has given way to culture, as the impersonal embrace of the cosmos is replaced by the impersonal embrace of a perfected society. In a sense, Bellamy had been moving from the cosmic sensibility of Emerson toward the earthly sentiments of the social gospel, but it was not an unforeseeable or incongruous trip, since both standpoints shared a belief in God's immanence, differing mainly in their projections of where and how he might turn up.

The rapid flowering of Julian's romance with Edith Leete, however, presents special problems, both inside and outside the text. Clearly the challenge presented to his nineteenth-century self by his emerging love for Edith is itself a considerable source of Julian's intensifying anxiety and crisis of identity. Like a latter-day Beatrice, she lures him onward toward a committed embrace of the new order, her unfeigned charm and natural allure drawing him even more powerfully than Dr. Leete's dry expositions. But romantic love seems, in some respects, a curiously flawed symbol for the ultimate ascent to the impersonality of the second soul. Had not "The Religion of Solidarity" itself repeatedly warned against investing too much of one's transcendent desires in the personal world? Didn't romantic love make precisely that error? Had not Bellamy, in his own choice of spouse, opted for the sisterly Emma rather than some Yankee Lorelei?

Bellamy knew an audience-pleasing formula when he saw it, however, and his depiction of Julian's profession of love to Edith, for example, could not have been better suited to the sentimental predilections of his nineteenth-century readership. Moreover, given Bellamy's attraction to the image of woman as force of reintegration, romantic love could have a more than merely individual significance—which perhaps explains why he added his own odd and distinctive twist to the conventional formula by revealing that Edith Leete was actually the great-granddaughter of Edith Bartlett, Julian's nineteenth-century fiancée. Such an identity-switching is reminiscent of that employed in "A Summer Evening's Dream," and such a device serves to depersonalize Julian's romance (and thereby render it more legitimate, by solidaritist standards) by blurring the identity of its object: "When at last, in an ecstasy of gratitude and tenderness, I folded the lovely girl in my arms, the two Ediths were blended in my thought, nor have they ever since been clearly distinguished. . . . On Edith's part there was a corresponding confusion of identities. . . . 'You must not love me too much for myself,' she said. 'I shall be very jealous for her. I shall not let you forget her. . . . You need not trouble to love me at all, if only you are true to her.'"[49]

If this strange consummation seemed also to blur the distinction between centuries, Bellamy solved that problem in the book's fevered, phantasmagorical concluding chapter. As the chapter begins, Julian finds himself suddenly transported back to the nineteenth century. It appears, for the moment, that his entire experience of utopian Boston has been nothing more than a dream, as painfully illusory as the dream of Dr. Heidenhoff's mind cure. Now he finds himself cursed by his glimpse of glory, for he must see the social iniquities and horrors of his native century through eyes informed by a vision of future perfection. Julian's look backward thus becomes a journey through hell, in which the disparities of wealth, the shameless cynicism of advertising, the programmatic wastefulness of a capitalist economy, the disarray of the organization of industry and labor, the "debauching influence" of money and banks, and the "drawn and anxious" faces of the people in the streets combine to overwhelm him with "pity and amazement." The only hint of comfort comes, characteristically, when he happens upon a military parade marching down Tremont Street. He responds to the sight with grateful relief: "Here at last were order and reason, an exhibition of what intelligent cooperation can accomplish" through "perfect concert of action" and "organization under one control."[50] Stumbling upon this small-scale grand review brings him the grace of momentary composure by reminding him of his own glimpse of the New Jerusalem.

Finally, after wandering around his hometown in a daze, Julian turns up in front of his fiancée's house on Commonwealth Avenue and is invited to join the family and its guests for dinner. Like a sonata, Julian's tale has returned to the place where it began, but the recapitulation has shifted into an agitated minor key. After his experience in the street, he finds himself nauseated by the disproportionate splendor and luxury of the Bartletts' table and by the exceedingly jolly spirits of the complacent, self-satisfied diners. Like a biblical prophet who cannot contain his disgust, he explodes into a condemnation of them for their indifference to the suffering all around them: "Do you not know that close to your doors a great multitude of men and women, flesh of your flesh, live lives that are one agony from birth to death?"[51] Yet, he adds, it is not some conspiratorial malice or unredeemable hard-heartedness that underwrites this inequity; it is nothing but human folly and, moreover, folly that can easily be reversed once we open our eyes to it. The stunned company, far from being moved to self-examination by this reproach, grows impatient and then angry with Julian, until finally Mr. Bartlett orders the men to throw him out of the house. At that climactic moment, Julian awakens and discovers he has been saved: to his great joy, he is still in Dr. Leete's house. What had seemed genuine turned out to be false. His harrowing return to the nineteenth century had been the dream; the splendor of the year 2000 was reality. As the book concludes, we see a tearful Julian kneel before his beloved Edith Leete and confess to her his unworthiness "to breathe the air of this golden century," counting himself "fortunate" to have found in her "a judge so merciful."[52]

Certainly the deeply Christian patterning of Bellamy's sensibility is never more evident than in these final pages. The scene at the Bartletts resounds with biblical overtones, not the least among them being the language and symbolism of crucifixion—"I have been in Golgotha," raves the half-mad Julian at his dinner hosts; "I have seen Humanity hanging on a cross!"[53] The crucifixion becomes his own, however, a symbolic death suffered when Mr. Bartlett casts him out of the house; being thus ostracized and forsaken becomes the stern price of his intercession. But Jesus assured his followers that those persecuted for righteousness' sake would be blessed with the kingdom of heaven; and Julian's passion is followed by resurrection, in the form of his awakening to the "real" world of the year 2000.[54] His social death fulfills the Pauline dictum that the "natural man" must die to both world and self before Christ can live in him and he be thereby ushered into new life.[55] The same underlying logic, however, also satisfied the religion of solidarity, which proclaimed that the infinitude of the upper world inhabited by the second soul possessed a far deeper reality than the finite, sublunary realm occupied by the ego-personality. Such, too, following the same kind of logic, was the superordinate reality possessed by Bellamy's cherished vision of the New Jerusalem, a consolidated social order to which the troubled and inadequate ego could turn, as the Christian turned to Christ or as Julian turned to Edith, and yield itself wholly, finding relief and fulfillment there. How, after all, could that superior world be thought somehow less genuine than the squalor and disorder of the present industrial system, the substance of which turned out to be, in Julian's story, as fleeting as a dream?

That last analogizing step, however, from upper world to perfected social world, was a giant one, challenging the essential meaning of the Pauline dictum. It was essentially the same step that would be taken by the proponents of the social gospel, reform-minded liberal Protestant ministers such as Washington Gladden and Walter Rauschenbusch. Believers in the traditional doctrine of original sin envisioned an impassable wall separating the imperfection of this world from the glory of the next, a wall to be breached only through the narrow gate of Christ's atoning sacrifice.[56] But to many this doctrine seemed illusory and imprisoning, and for them the redemptive mission of the Incarnation had now come properly to rest in the social and economic reorganization of this world, the making of a postmillennial earthly paradise.[57]

By embracing this conviction, Bellamy not only showed his affinity with the reform currents of his own time. He also showed that he was carrying on in the optimistic spirit of Emerson and other antebellum reformers who were passionately convinced that human potential was boundless.[58] Far from disclaiming connection to such reformers, Bellamy was eager to depict them as forerunners of his own Nationalist movement.[59] In other words, the shift of perspective from Emerson to Bellamy may have been more complex than can be captured by the opposition of boundlessness and consolidation, since for Bellamy those categories were not precise opposites. *Looking Backward* eschews boundlessness only as an aspiration of atomistic individuals. Indeed, the more perfectly consolidated the society is, the more boundless its corporate aspirations and, therefore, those of its members could rightfully be.[60]

In *Looking Backward*, the nature and extent of these aspirations find their most comprehensive expression in the long and eloquent sermon of Mr. Barton, to which Julian and the Leetes listen, over the "telephone," in the Leetes' music room. Delivered in recognition of Julian's "visit," the sermon soon turns into a lengthy philosophical and moral summation of, and apologia for, the civilization of the year 2000, set against the somber background of Julian's own nineteenth-century way of life. The prospect of human boundlessness is invoked repeatedly:

From the moment men allowed themselves to believe that humanity after all had not been meant for a dwarf, that its squat stature was not the measure of its possible growth, but that it stood upon the verge of an avatar of limitless development, the reaction must needs have been overwhelming. . . . Nothing was able to stand against the enthusiasm which the new faith inspired.[61]

In place of the dreary hopelessness of the nineteenth century, its profound pessimism as to the future of humanity, the animating idea of the present age is an enthusiastic conception of the opportunities of our earthly existence, and the unbounded possibilities of human nature. The betterment of mankind from generation to generation, physically, mentally, morally, is recognized as the one great object supremely worthy of effort and of sacrifice. We believe the race for the first time to have entered on the realization of God's ideal of it, and each generation must now be a step upward. . . . The long and weary winter of the race is ended. Its summer has begun. Humanity has burst the chrysalis. The heavens are before it.[62]

As for original sin, this unlovely notion had merely served to reify the unattractive results of faulty social organization, leaving the false impression that such results were caused by a fixed human nature. Now that social conditions no longer serve "to develop the brutal qualities of human nature," Barton asserts, "it was for the first time possible to see what unperverted human nature really was like" and to realize that "human nature in its essential qualities is good."[63]

Mr. Barton's understanding of the sources of human nature, in short, is radically environmental: "It is not necessary to suppose a moral new birth of humanity," or the extermination of the wicked, to explain the new order's coming, for it "finds its simple and obvious explanation in the reaction of a changed environment upon human nature."[64] When the ministers of religion in the nineteenth century looked on "the bitter spectacle of society, these worthy men bitterly bemoaned the depravity of human nature; as if angelic nature would not have been debauched in such a devil's school!"[65] Barton makes this view vivid through the parable of the sickly rosebush, whose development symbolizes that of humanity. So long as the rosebush was planted in an unhealthy, miasmatic swamp, it was afflicted with numerous diseases and was never able to blossom. Philosophers and expert gardeners had studied the problems and attributed them to the inadequacies of the plant, offering a host of elaborate, learned, and ingenious rationalizations for maintaining and managing the status quo, all the time ignoring the handful of daydreamers who suggested the bush might do far better if moved to a more favorable setting. But when, in a time of desperation, the experimental suggestion of transplanting was revived and found favor, and the bush was moved into better soil, it immediately flourished and soon was "covered with the most beautiful red roses, whose fragrance filled the world."[66] So, too, did humanity flourish when placed in the proper societal soil.

In some respects, such a perspective was not new to American history; it was the physiocratic Crèvecoeur who had remarked, a century before, that "men are like plants; the goodness and flavour of the fruit proceeds from the peculiar soil and exposition in which they grow."[67] Bellamy was showing how fully he had absorbed the broader intellectual currents of his time, however, which were not only increasingly propounding a gospel of human interdependency but were challenging the very conception of the autonomous individual, rendering individuals more and more deeply embedded in their formative circumstances.[68] This growing awareness of the character-shaping power of external forces would prove an ambivalent weapon, however, with both liberating and imprisoning consequences. It was liberating, as was the case for Bellamy, in that it seemed to vanquish the limitations of the inadequate self and thereby grant unlimited range to the project of reform, since no existing evil could any longer be regarded as immovable or inalterable. But it was also imprisoning, as when the experience of freedom was revealed to be, at bottom, so radically conditioned. Mr. Barton's environmentalism would have paradoxical effects, for under its regime the consequentiality of the human will was at once vastly expanded and profoundly undermined. If the eclipse of self represented, for Bellamy, a consummation devoutly to be wished, it would be a source of terror or melancholy for others—as it had been for John Stuart Mill, who had experienced a paralyzing fear of the "transitivity" of his own will, of being rendered literally inconsequential.

Bellamy not only accepted the prospect of social interdependency and embeddedness; he embraced it and urged others to do so as well. It is safe to say, however, that he did not not grapple with the shadow side of these positions, largely because of the urgency with which his own psychological makeup and the exigencies of his times pressed a rather different set of issues upon him. Nor was he able to focus on the possibility that there might be stubbornly persistent tensions between the needs of self and society even in a consolidated social order and, in fact, that full social empowerment might come at a very heavy price to the individual, as well as to the intermediate institutions that stood between individual and state. Perhaps his confidence was bolstered by his analogical step beyond the religion of solidarity, his assumption that surrender to a perfected social order was tantamount to surrender to Christ or to the infinitude of the cosmic order—a surrender of self, therefore, that actually opened the way to the most meaningful kind of freedom.

To any apprehension that this might not be so, that so monolithically centralized a state might be a formula for tyranny, *Looking Backward* seemed to turn a deaf ear, a fact that may well constitute the book's most striking feature for today's reader. Bellamy's faith in the fairness and efficiency of central administration appears complete. Dr. Leete assures Julian that all occupational choices in his society are strictly voluntary and that "it is the business of the administration" to assure that "the supply of volunteers is always . . . fully equal to the demand" (though "frequent and merely capricious changes of occupation are not encouraged or even permitted," and the administration is empowered to make use of a "call for special volunteers, or draft"). Julian is told that all state governments had been abolished because they "interfered with the control and discipline of the industrial army"; that money was no longer necessary because "everything was procurable from one source, and nothing could be procured anywhere else"; that conspicuous consumption was no longer possible or necessary because in utopia "everybody's income is known"; and moreover that the credit account of "every person, man, woman, and child . . . is always with the nation directly, and never through any intermediary, except, of course, that parents, to a certain extent, act for children as their guardians. . . . It is by virtue of the relation of individuals to the nation, of their membership in it, that they are entitled to support; and this title is in no way connected with or affected by their relations to other individuals who are fellow members of the nation with them."[69] If a "mass society" is one in which nothing is permitted to stand between the individual and the authority of the state, then the Boston of 2000 seemed well on its way to achieving that end. Certainly it carried the logic of national consolidation to its ultimate conceivable extent.

Bellamy may be thought naive, even foolish, for having failed to ponder how easily such centralization and nationalization could lead to enormous abuses, but it is not our present purpose to make such a judgment. When an image of utopia attains the widespread popularity of *Looking Backward*, it bids fair to be regarded as a kind of collective fantasy, an artifact in which a culture reveals itself by the very process of making a self-diagnosis of its own pathologies and their possible cures. The priorities implicit in *Looking Backward* serve to illuminate the geography of social thought within which it took its place. Social thought, when it is most powerful and incisive, is also inevitably pragmatic, directed toward particular situations and particular problems arising from the immediate and urgent imperatives of social life. An army engaged in the heat of battle against an invader from one direction cannot pause to consider the possibility that someday the potential enemy behind it may prove a far greater foe. The enemy, in the eyes of Bellamy and his readers in 1888, was a chaotic, disorganized society still ruled by the tenets of an unsatisfactory, outmoded, and subjectively intolerable individualism. In such circumstances, the potential dangers of consolidation seemed hard to credit.

In that case, it may be more valuable for us to step back and look at *Looking Backward*, not for the originality of its contributions to American political and social thought, but as an especially vivid rendering of a social archetype whose structure would mold and filter American social thought well into the twentieth century. This exemplary use of *Looking Backward*, moreover, is in no way mitigated by the fact that Bellamy himself was clearly a transitional figure, whose principal influence was more mythopoeic than analytical, inspirational rather than prescriptive. Much that was effective about *Looking Backward*— from the ambiguous nature of its precise genre, in tension between novelistic romance and social-reform blueprint, to its split-minded division between nostalgia for the preindustrial past and worship of the corporatist future, and between idealizations of woman-as-reintegrator and of army-as-consolidator— also reflects this transitional character. Bellamy was not a social thinker whose "serious" ideas were struggling to break out of their romantic-fictionalist cocoon; he was at his most effective when he was combining both approaches, for only in that way could he give proper weight to both his objective diagnosis and his subjective longings. Indeed, when Bellamy attempted in a sequel, *Equality* (1897), to dispense with the romantic subplot of the story, the result was nowhere near as engaging.

Startlingly new though its corporatism seemed, Bellamy's vision grew from venerable New England roots.[70] He was still traveling the road from a severe (though rapidly relaxing) Protestantism into which he was born, through the liberating temper of antebellum transcendentalism to which the religion of solidarity was so deeply indebted, and striding toward the beckoning goal of a comprehensively reordered social universe, whose fundamental structures would be devised by the disciplined power of the organized human intellect. Yet even in that new world, the fundamental imperative was still the great Christian principle: who would save his life must lose it. Whether and how yielding to society (or, for that matter, to Nature) was really comparable to yielding to Christ, however, was a question not easily stilled or answered. As the vision Bellamy limned began to find serious expression, so too would that impertinent, and highly pertinent, question.

# 4

## Ambivalent Consolidators

At the very moment *Looking Backward* was beginning its meteoric ascent to the heights of intellectual and political influence, a more eminent American writer than Bellamy, a westerner well-known for his sharp observations of the postbellum American scene, was finishing an *anti*-utopian novel—but one whose concerns and techniques were strangely symmetrical with Bellamy's. In *A Connecticut Yankee in King Arthur's Court* (1889) Mark Twain also explored the literary uses of time travel by sending the nineteenth-century Yankee mechanic Hank Morgan back to sixth-century Camelot, where Morgan proceeded to attempt to reform cruel feudal institutions according to modern American industrial methods. These efforts to produce an earthly paradise through induced modernization culminated instead in the worst horrors of civil war, pitting the old order against the new, feudalism against industrial capitalism, in a manner Twain meant also to be deeply reminiscent of the American Civil War. Finally the magician Merlin, Hank's archenemy, puts the troublemaker Hank asleep until the nineteenth century—when he could presumably cross paths briefly with the troubled Julian West. Unlike Bellamy, however, Twain did not seem to know which century was to be preferred in the end. Instead, his art was forced to carry the weight of his ambivalences—ambivalences that, in turn, offer a window onto some of the dilemmas generally experienced in his time.

The harsh portrayal of medieval life in *A Connecticut Yankee* merely continued Twain's fierce polemic against Sir Walter Scott, whose false and deceiving images of a romantic premodern past were, in Twain's view, "in great measure responsible" for the South's debacle. For all Twain's disdain for the distant past and his disgust with those who wished to restore it, however, he was hardly more enthusiastic about his own times or the kind of man they seemed to call forth. As Kenneth Lynn has observed, Hank Morgan—though his name may have alluded to archconsolidationist financier J. P. Morgan—was much like the other heroes emerging in Twain's fiction of the 1880s and 1890s: a loner and stranger, free-floating and unencumbered, the *reductio*, in a sense, of the nineteenth-century fantasy of boundless, autonomous man. Hank faithfully mirrored the practical ingenuity and freedom-loving "can-do" optimism of his Yankee milieu. Yet he also, reflecting the growing pessimism of his creator, was a utopian who actually harbored "a relentless and unforgiving contempt for the human race." If Bellamy was compelled to break out of the prisonhouse of self and escape to the relief of a social identity, Twain could not concur and could not follow.[1]

In the haunting unfinished tale *The Mysterious Stranger*, however, Twain seemed to acknowledge the horror of the solitary path he had chosen—a confirmation of the reality of Bellamy's central concerns. The heroic alter-ego figure of that tale not only embodied the detachment and disconnection that Bellamy so greatly feared. The stranger was Satan himself. As the stranger tells the story's narrator, all transcendent or natural points of potential moral connection for the self are illusory; ours is a solipsistic world. "There is no God, no universe, no human race, no earthly life, no heaven, no hell. It is all a dream, a grotesque and foolish dream. Nothing exists but you. And you are but a *thought*—a vagrant thought, a useless thought, a homeless thought, wandering forlorn among the empty eternities."[2] Drinking more deeply of the same undercurrent of despair that had sometimes run through Whitman's work, Twain's stubbornly independent western American soul resisted all consolation, preferring a pose of extravagant nihilism to any form of social submission.

In fact, as his choice of Satan as alter ego would indicate, Twain well understood the same self-sacrificial and corporative Christian imperatives Bellamy embraced. But he had chosen—as D. H. Lawrence thought was the characteristic American pattern—to live "in a frictional opposition to the master" he wished to undermine but whom he had, implicitly, not yet ceased to acknowledge; for Satanism is but Christianity inverted. Twain's roaring defiance led precisely nowhere, however, and no one knew that better than he. Poised between unsatisfactory worlds, he made art from the arguments with himself—one of the deeper meanings in Howells's famous labeling of him as "the Lincoln of our literature," since both men's lives were destined to be consumed in the task of reconciling the irreconcilable. Hence, the well-known difficulty Twain encountered in writing endings for his books (notably *The Adventures of Huckleberry Finn*) may have indicated something deeper than mere personal idiosyncrasy was at work when he found himself unable to come to a satisfying closure. If Twain's turbulent psyche formed a kind of microcosm of the Civil War, he was not the only American carrying on such arguments with himself.[3]

Bellamy's success, then, had showed how effectively the energies and anxieties released by individualism, in tandem with a concrete, insistently social understanding of Christian moral obligation, could be channeled into a powerful centripetal and corporate vision of the nation. Yet Twain's example shows that, notwithstanding the widespread popularity of *Looking Backward*, it can hardly be thought to exhaust the significant intellectual reactions to consolidation, even among its advocates. So enthusiastic and wholehearted an embrace of solidarity was not easily endorsed or emulated, as the discussion that follows will indicate. It examines a range of more ambivalent or nuanced reactions by looking at three roughly contemporary thinkers: the historian Frederick Jackson Turner, the pioneering sociologist Lester Frank Ward, and the Columbia political scientist John W. Burgess. Though a highly disparate group, they exhibit certain features in common. All three well understood, and were deeply affected by, the dynamics of the Civil War and sectional strife. All recognized that the preconditions for antebellum individualism were rapidly fading away. All had been drawn into a profound awareness of the growing importance of consolidation, coalescence, convergence, and unity as alternative American social ideals. And all, to a greater or lesser degree, found themselves struggling with those ideals and with the same vestigial individualism that Bellamy had so summarily banished.

---

It was only five years after the publication of *Looking Backward* that the thirty-two-year old Frederick Jackson Turner, speaking at the World's Columbian Exposition in Chicago, delivered his famous address "The Significance of the Frontier in American History." Over the years, the occasion of this talk has become progressively embellished in historians' imaginations, transformed into a recognizably epochal moment in American intellectual history, a historiographical Rubicon-crossing. Nothing could have been further from the case. In fact, Turner's audience that evening at the 1893 World's Congress of Historians and Historical Students seemed thoroughly indifferent to his paper. This was a distinguished professional audience, one he had not wanted to disappoint. His former teacher Herbert Baxter Adams of Johns Hopkins, the institutional mastermind of the American Historical Association, had wrested control of the congress from the local committee and had managed to persuade a fair number of distinguished eastern historians to venture west to the wilds of Chicago in order to lend legitimacy and prestige to this affair. Adams had also taken great pains to screen the participants carefully, weeding out the "amateur historians and sensational theorists"; in addition he had seen to it that the congress convened not in the exposition's glamorous White City, but in the more sober confines of the Art Institute of Chicago, as far as possible from the madding crowds. This was, in short, to be a gathering of thoroughbred professional historians, the kind of audience that the Hopkins-trained Turner, as an accredited member of that self-designating elite, was especially eager to impress. Even so, Turner waited until virtually the last moment to write his paper and was still flailing away at it furiously in a Chicago dormitory room until the eve of the historical congress.[4] This small detail, as we shall see, spoke volumes about Turner the man.

Only an exceptionally motivated audience would have had the stamina to sit through the entire panel upon which Turner sat. Four long papers preceded his that evening, running the gamut from "English Popular Uprisings in the Middle Ages" to "Early Lead Mining in Illinois and Wisconsin." By the time Turner began, even the most disciplined attention spans had surely been strained, if not exhausted. Moreover, despite his Hopkins credentials, the youthful Turner himself did not command any a priori respect from the assembled eastern eminences, who were likely to regard him as little more than a provincial greenhorn instructor from a western backwater school. Those auditors who stayed awake enough to listen to his talk evidently either felt that his bold challenges to the reigning historiographical orthodoxy of "germ theory" were hardly worth responding to, or they were just in a hurry to get home, for the Turner paper elicited no discussion. We have no record of Turner's reaction to this deafeningly silent reception, but Ray Allen Billington probably understated the matter in guessing that the ambitious Turner walked away feeling "burdened with a heavy sense of failure."[5] Turner had risked more than just his professional reputation by putting forward so strong a brief for the significance of the West, for his thesis was freighted with deeply personal emotions as well.

Yet public recognition would eventually come. Walter Hines Page, editor of the *Atlantic Monthly*, quickly grasped the significance of Turner's essay and urged the young Wisconsan to write an article contrasting western with eastern character traits. The resulting essay, "The Problem of the West," finally appeared just before the 1896 presidential election and produced the kind of public response that put Turner's thesis on the historiographical map for good. Turner's contention that the availability of free land on a western frontier "explained" American development would become, arguably, the single most influential such historical interpretation of American society ever propounded, one that has given rise to several generations of spirited and fruitful debate and reinterpretation.[6] There is some irony in the fact that the professional historians were slow to recognize what Page saw at once. But that fact also reflects the degree to which Turner's thesis was, first and foremost, a reflection of, and comment upon, its own times. It is in that aspect of the Turner essay, its place in the history of ideas rather than its highly questionable adequacy as a historical hypothesis, that our present interest lies. Indeed, few works of the American fin de siècle expressed the growing sense of national closure, the tension between diminishing boundlessness and rising consolidation, more memorably, more hauntingly, and at the same time more diffusely than this ostensibly detached and scholarly interpretation of America's westward expansion. There was no more potent topographical symbol of boundlessness than the frontier, and the process by which frontier-bred individualism yielded, little by little, to the characteristic social formations of European settlement and civilization dramatized the nation's reckoning with organization, coalescence, and consolidation. In its own way, the frontier thesis engaged precisely the same issues as did *Looking Backward*, albeit in more ambivalent, and at times revealingly confused, ways.

Both Bellamy and Turner saw themselves living through a watershed period, and each writer posited a forceful challenge, coming to fruition around the close of the nineteenth century, to the individualistic ethos that had dominated previous American history. It was perhaps no more than a wry coincidence that both works looked backward and featured a protagonist named West. Where Bellamy looked backward in horror and pity, laboring to leave the prisonhouse of the past and eagerly anticipating the world that was to emerge, Turner's essay bore on a different pressure point: a countervailing reluctance to leave the past behind. Turner seemed disinclined to contemplate the lineaments of the new order, whatever it might be. Instead, he chose to remain silent on that point, proclaiming only that, with the closing of the western American frontier, an era of American history had decisively ended, and with it had also disappeared the material factors that had hitherto served to "explain American development." His "The Problem of the West" in the *Atlantic* ventured slightly further, but only to the extent of acknowledging the general need for "original social ideals and social adjustments for the American nation."[7]

The frontier essay's abrupt ending, however, with its bold proclamation that "the first period of American history" had now come to an end, inevitably raised urgent questions about the "second period" that was just getting under way.[8] Would the American individualism nurtured by the frontier also become a thing of the past, once the frontier was gone? Or, to put it in different words, would the disappearance of boundlessness as a persistent feature of American space and perception force a decisive alteration of American expectations, American character, and American institutions? Would the loss of frontier as "a field of opportunity, a gate of escape from the bondage of the past," lead the American character to solidify, then ossify, becoming over time more and more indistinguishable from that of the Europeans? Or would it be possible to retain the precious elements of American national character even without the frontier's magical effects? The reader could only wonder.

Born in the remote central Wisconsin village of Portage, Turner spoke in Chicago, the great metropolis of the West, as a partisan of the West. He even seemed to exemplify representative western virtues, as a handsome, outdoorsy young man of robust simplicity and optimism. Yet he was a complicated man, who sometimes felt acutely the weight of his provincial origins. As is so often the case with such self-perceived provincials, Turner carried a bit of a chip on his shoulder, which informed some of the regional bias and boosterism in the Chicago paper. Turner was intent upon showing that the West, far from being marginal to American history, as easterners and Europeans had always so facilely assumed, was in fact the *most* American of the sections. (Or, as Patricia Limerick wittily summarizes his argument, "The center of American history . . . was to be found at its edges"—meaning only the western ones.)[9] The West was the most powerful agent of national consolidation, the section most responsible for the "vitalizing of the general government," the most progressive and democratic in its political and social life, the cradle of the finest democratic statesmen, the source of America's unique "composite nationality," the section that forced the nation to confront the slavery issue—the only section providing a reliable perspective from which the American national experience could be understood.[10] For "the true point of view in the history of this nation is not the Atlantic coast," he asserted, but rather "the Great West."[11] Above all else, he wished to show that the frontier had given rise to the distinctive traits of "the American intellect," such as its "coarseness and strength combined with acuteness and inquisitiveness," its "practical, inventive turn of mind," its "dominant individualism" with "that buoyancy and exuberance which comes with freedom," its "freshness, and confidence, and scorn of older society, impatience of its restraints and its ideas, and indifference to its lessons."[12]

Turner saw no compelling reason to believe that these traits could not be passed on. "He would be a rash prophet," he prophesied, "who should assert that the expansive character of American life has now entirely ceased."[13] The reasons for this confidence were not entirely clear, however. Early in the speech he argued that "each frontier leaves its traces behind it, and when it becomes a settled area the region still partakes of the frontier characteristics."[14] Indeed, Turner seemed to believe, by analogy with the neo-Lamarckian brand of biological evolutionism that still found favor with some social scientists of his day, that a society or culture too could retain and pass on some of the characteristics it had acquired. The American character formed by the frontier was in some manner fixed and, once fixed, would not be altered by changes in circumstances. Such a prospect was deeply attractive to Americans anxious over the possibility that their country might be entering a period of decline at the turn of the century; they could find in the Turner thesis grounds for hope, grounds for belief that the cherished values of individualism would survive the frontier's disappearance. The West, in Turner's understanding, could even serve to refresh and purify the outlook and morals of the ever-declining East— or so believed the proud and patriotic young westerner, whose education as a professional historian had already taken him east to Baltimore and would eventually lead him back to a position at Harvard. Even though the material development of American society streamed steadily in an east-to-west direction, its moral development, which was linked to the purity of its American-ness, was profoundly affected by a west-to-east eddying, an invigoration from the frontier source.

Turner was also heavily indebted to theories of environmental determinism, which were an indispensable influence upon his frontier thesis.[15] Institutions and forms, according to that view, developed from the "vital forces that call these organs into life and shape them to meet changing conditions." Here was the central thrust in his challenge to the germ theories dominating the heavily Germanic professional historiography of the time, a rigidly deductive and idealist approach that professed to trace the origins of American democracy to the sowing in New World soil of European, and particularly Teutonic, institutional seeds. No, said Turner; it did not happen that way. The environment of the frontier was like a powerful solvent, which broke down and then re-fashioned the habits and thoughts of those Europeans who came to the New World: "The frontier is the line of most rapid and effective Americanization. The wilderness masters the colonist. It finds him a European in dress, industries, tools, modes of travel, and thought. It takes him from the railroad car and puts him in the birch canoe."[16] Needless to say, the same effects might work themselves upon overcivilized Europeans and easterners who went West to seek renewal, as Theodore Roosevelt had done; for the point of maximum Americanness occurred precisely at the frontier—the locus of boundlessness, so to speak—the place where "savagery" confronted "civilization," where "the tendency is anti-social," antipathetic to "any direct control," where "the bonds of custom are broken, and unrestraint is triumphant."[17]

There were two obvious difficulties with this perspective. First, if the environment of America's first period had made such short work of the Europeans' deeply ingrained ancestral ways, which were presumably (in part) a residue of their own earlier frontier experience, and had substituted in their place the fresh and restless characteristics of American individualism and democracy, then what reason was there to believe that the drastically altered environment of the frontierless second period of American history would permit these cherished American traits to stand? Did environmental logic not point inevitably in precisely the opposite direction, toward yet another comprehensive reshuffling or refashioning of national character? Or, if cultural characteristics were heritable, why were they heritable in some instances and not in others? Second, despite Turner's own optimism about the American future, the developmental model to which he was so strongly committed suggested an inexorable logic of national decline. Turner enthusiastically embraced the Italian economist Achille Loria's proposition that "America . . . reveals luminously the course of universal history," adding that the United States "lies like a huge page in the history of society," in which we can read "line by line . . . from west to east . . . the record of social evolution."[18] How flattering to think the country's social history was in effect that of the world, rendered in microcosm; what pride of place that scheme granted to the slighted and ignored American West! If the now-decadent European nations had already followed the same universal process of social evolution, however, vanquishing their own frontiers and driving toward a more organized, more constricted civilization, how could it be plausibly denied that the United States was headed inexorably toward the same eventual fate? How could Turner deny that the closing of the frontier might be the beginning of an American decline?

Turner's essay sent mixed signals on that count, an ambivalence that went to the heart of the questions of national destiny his essay raised without answering. The essay itself seemed to suggest that a moral equivalent of the frontier could and would be found, since, given the fixity of American character, "American energy will continually demand a wider field for its exercise."[19] A good deal of the popularity of the Turner thesis over the years, including the search for new frontiers on land and in space, has derived from the hope implicit in that postulate.[20] Other remarks, however, hint at the coexistence of a more conservative conclusion, which respected the logic of closure and

consolidation rather than that of boundlessness. Such an outlook is particularly evident in his comments on the negative legacy of American frontier
individualism: the social indiscipline, the moral impurity of the spoils system,
the lax and disorganized business, banking, and currency practices—the last of
which, as he sniffed in his aside on the Populists, impeded the recognition that
"a primitive society can hardly be expected to show the intelligent appreciation of the complexity of business interests in a developed society."[21] Turner
found himself, and his time, poised between guiding metaphors of boundlessness and consolidation, and his essay rendered that dilemma like a page in the
history of ideas.

Those conflicting perspectives are also manifested in Turner's surprisingly
unsteady political convictions, which bounced back and forth between political parties, taking him through a somewhat incongruous series of commitments. Turner's admiration for the frontier reflected a liking for an informal,
self-reliant egalitarian ethos, and that sentiment was probably as close to
bedrock as could be found in his repertoire of political beliefs. Yet he supported McKinley in 1896 (and probably also 1900) out of ingrained conservative opposition to the inflationist Bryan. In due course, he came to lionize
Theodore Roosevelt, but he was at the same time distrustful of trust-busting,
following in this respect the consolidationist views of his former Wisconsin
colleague Charles Van Hise, whose *Concentration and Control* (1911) de-
nounced the breakup of trusts and argued instead for their strict regulation.
Such distrust, and a deep personal distaste for the Republican stalwarts,
deriving partly from political troubles at the University of Wisconsin, may
help explain his vote for Bryan in 1908.[22] In 1912, although feeling powerful
reservations about the decentralist thrust of the "New Freedom," he preferred
his old friend and former teacher Woodrow Wilson to Roosevelt. Finally, by
the end of his life, his political hopes settled upon Herbert Hoover, a fellow
midwesterner whose work for Belgian relief after World War I had impressed
Turner, and whose moderately laissez-faire manifesto *American Individualism*
(1922) Turner envisioned as "the platform on which all genuine Americans
can stand, a noble statement of the fruits of our past and the promise of our
future."[23] To be sure, though, Hoover's political philosophy is not easily
pigeonholed; his work both as secretary of commerce and as president showed
him to be as much a prophet of consolidation as an exponent of the "rugged
individualism" so often associated with his name.[24] Such complexities mirrored the ambivalences of Turner himself.

In any event, the existence of such marked ambivalences may explain why
Turner was unable to produce an oeuvre commensurate with his gifts, energies, and knowledge, despite the immense esteem in which he was held by his

fellows. As the account of Turner's sympathetic biographer makes clear, while Turner the teacher and historian was an enormously strong, capable, and attractive figure, Turner the writer was no calm fortress of orderly and scientific thought. On the contrary, his work habits showed all the tempestuousness, volatility, and neurotic compulsiveness of a struggling artist or a man torn by conflicting intellectual and emotional imperatives. He had great difficulty concentrating his formidable energies on any project for long, and in dealing with his manuscripts and his editors he was chronically overambitious, overcommitted, distracted, unreliable, dilatory, blocked, exhausted, physically sick—as tightly and emotionally wound as any romantic novelist, in ways that proved fatal to his literary efficacy. Eight years after the young greenhorn had presented his frontier thesis to an indifferent audience in Chicago, he found himself besieged by enthusiastic book publishers and had appended his name to no less than nine contracts for book projects. In the remaining thirty-one years of his life, he did not finish a single one of them.[25]

No doubt, as has often been observed, he was an extreme perfectionist. It is equally true, however, that despite that trait (or perhaps because of it), he sometimes cast his embryonic thoughts before the public with surprising insouciance, even recklessness—as he did, for example, with his important 1914 paper on the significance of sectionalism in American history—well before he had arrived at clear definitions of terms or sufficient evidence to sustain his positions. He complained of the drain on his research time caused by his teaching and other duties at the University of Wisconsin, but even a move to the more favorable circumstances of Harvard in 1910 made little difference in his output. In 1924 Turner finally decided to retire altogether in order to devote himself completely to finishing "THE BOOK," his long-awaited study of sectionalism in antebellum America. Predictably, the book finished him before he could finish it, and when the incomplete manuscript was posthumously published in 1935, it showed, even after a remarkable editorial cleanup operation by two gifted younger historians, how hopelessly tangled Turner's thoughts had become and how distant he was from ever really completing his magnum opus. His close friend Max Farrand sadly quipped, with mercy tempered by justice, that Turner would never have completed THE BOOK, even if he had lived forever.[26]

Perfectionism, distraction, overcommitment, blockage: the encroaching perils to which Turner fell prey are demons amply familiar to any serious writer. Richard Hofstadter's characterization of Turner as a "constitutional non-writer whose work was wrung out of himself at immense psychic cost" seems psychologically acute and on target, although it is a description that could fit any number of other writers just as well.[27] The particulars of Turner's case, however, suggest more than a man somehow tragically miscast for his role in life. They suggest that he was in thrall to ideas he could neither entirely affirm nor entirely abandon. Because his divisions of heart and mind found their way into the substance of his work—in much the same way that similar divisions had found their way into the work of his fellow westerner Mark Twain—they perforce had broader meaning. The ambiguity of that great American "record of social evolution," running from "west to east," would play itself out in both men's lives.

Such was one reason why Turner's move to Cambridge, which was in most respects an unexceptionable, professionally advantageous change, turned out to be a bittersweet choice, for it wrested this western Antaeus from his life-giving soil and deposited him in the alien heartland of the genteel tradition. It is hard to gainsay the final balance on that decision. Turner always played his professorial role admirably well at Harvard, but his heart was never completely in it; he never felt comfortable there and never developed any abiding affection for, or loyalty to, the institution comparable to what he had felt for the University of Wisconsin. "I am still a Western man in all but my residence," he once confessed, with both defiance and sadness in his voice, to his friend the Chicago medievalist James Westfall Thompson.[28] Again, one is struck by the potential parallels to Twain's move to Hartford, Connecticut, after his marriage to genteel Olivia Langdon—a move that, while not diminishing his productivity, may, as Van Wyck Brooks later argued, have affected the quality of his work.[29]

During those Cambridge years Turner often felt an intense longing for the wilderness and sometimes spent warm nights sleeping in a tent on the back porch of his Brattle Street house. It was an endearing and poignant eccentricity, as if this erstwhile president of the American Historical Association were yet a young boy on his first make-believe camp-out—or a grown man wanting somehow to reach back in time and space, to feel communion with a precious but elusive westering spirit that, however circumscribed its present and future condition, he was not yet willing to relinquish. Small wonder that Turner, who enjoyed poetry, so greatly cherished Tennyson's "Ulysses" as a perfect expression of the restless "Western spirit":

> Come my friends.
> 'Tis not too late to seek a newer world.
> Push off, and sitting well in order smite
> The sounding furrows; for my purpose holds
> To sail beyond the sunset, and the baths
> Of all the western stars, until I die.

Turner so loved "Ulysses" that, though he prided himself upon his scientific approach to history, he could not resist citing these stirring words at the conclusion of his 1914 essay "The West and American Ideals."[30] His use of these lines indicated how powerfully his western affinities shaped his outlook on American history and drew him toward a kind of Emersonian heroism. Just as revealing of Turner and his vision of America, however, were the lines immediately preceding, which Turner curiously—or perhaps not so curiously—elected to omit. The speaker is Ulysses himself:

> you and I are old;
> Old age hath yet his honor and his toil.
> Death closes all; but something ere the end,
> Some work of noble note, may yet be done,
> Not unbecoming men that strove with Gods.
> The lights begin to twinkle from the rocks;
> The long day wanes; the slow moon climbs; the deep
> Moans round with many voices. Come, my friends.

Suddenly the poetry Turner had quoted to buttress an upbeat Emersonian reflection upon the American spirit shows itself to have a richer, more complex meaning—a meaning Turner surely grasped and was moved by, even if his attitude of official optimism refused to allow its recognition and therefore edited it out. One would never suspect from Turner's selective quotations that Tennyson's poem is actually the frustrated lament of an aged and terminally becalmed heroic figure, a disconsolate "idle king" living in "barren crags" with an "aged wife"—so much for his many years of longing to be reunited with the faithful Penelope and restored to the comfort of home and hearth!—who knows that his days of greatness are now behind him, but who cannot bring himself to accept it. His turbulent thoughts "cannot rest from travel," for his action-packed life was spent "always roaming with a hungry heart." He now dreads, above all else, having to sheath himself like an unused sword, "to rust unburnished, not to shine in use!" Better to go out in a blaze of glory than retire at home on a pension.

This Ulysses is, in short, an incurable adventurer and man of action, whose primal masculine disposition echoes the putative physical, mental, and moral qualities of Turner's frontier individualist. Like that man, he is leaving to the next generation, represented by his son Telemachus, the task of civilization— "to make mild / A rugged people, and through soft degrees / Subdue them to the useful and the good." (Though he takes pride in his son, he also makes it clear that such a "labour" would bore him: "He [Telemachus] works his work, I mine." The task of Eriksonian "generativity" does not interest him.) What

Ulysses wishes for is not a death nestled in the warm bosom of family but one last shoot-out, one more heroic foray "not unbecoming men that strove with Gods":

> It may be that the gulfs will wash us down;
> It may be we shall touch the Happy Isles,
> And see the great Achilles, whom we knew.
> Tho' much is taken, much abides; and tho'
> We are not now that strength which in old days
> Moved earth and heaven, that which we are, we are,—
> One equal temper of heroic hearts,
> Made weak by time and fate, but strong in will
> To strive, to seek, to find, and not to yield.[31]

It is revealing that, of the above nine lines, Turner chose to quote *only* the last in "The West and American Ideals." Such truncation completely omits the undercurrent of gloom and even fatalism driving the thoughts of the aging hero, and the romantic disdain for the settled, civilized life implicit in Tennyson's lines. This Ulysses whom Turner so admires is a cowboy who desperately wants to die with his boots on, and we are made to feel that the domesticated life and reign of Telemachus, even if it is prosperous, will be a quotidian, unglorious, feminized letdown by comparison. Tennyson's poem touched directly and revealingly upon the same problem that lurked more covertly at the heart of Turner's frontier essay: the possibility that the coming of settled civilization and the end of the western frontier may signal the beginning of an American decline, a decline that would certainly lead to the eclipse of a certain cherished style of manhood. Small wonder Turner and his readers were so drawn to the subject.

If the westering individualistic impulse was to be preserved in post-frontier America, then perhaps the best hope for it lay in somehow preserving the distinctiveness of the western section as an incubator for adventurous, pioneering values. At any rate, perhaps some such thought may have been behind Turner's obsessive and increasingly quixotic and fruitless crusade to prove the validity of his "sectional" hypothesis, another conceptual form in which he grappled with the tensions arising from national consolidation. Turner desperately held to the idea that sectional distinctiveness could and would be retained and augmented in modern America. He believed he could prove that the United States was too vast and diverse ever to consolidate itself fully; it would perforce always be divided into distinct geographical sections, which would be perpetually in conflict with one another. As he put it in his 1925 essay, "The Significance of the Section in American History,"

The natural advantages of certain regions for farming, or for forestry, or for pasturage will arrest the tendency of the Eastern industrial type of society to flow across the continent and thus to produce a consolidated, homogeneous nation free from sections. At the same time that the nation settles down to the conditions of an occupied land, there will be emphasized the sectional differences arising from unlike geographic regions.[32]

A better way to understand what the United States was becoming, he believed, was to look to Europe as an example. Although Americans were wont to "think of the United States as we might think of some one of the nations of the Old World," Turner believed it was actually more correct to compare the United States to "Europe as a whole," and the sections, therefore, to the European nations. In this understanding, the American sections took on "a new dignity" as "potential nations" with qualities of a European country but "denatured of its toxic qualities."[33] American history, then, had been and henceforth would be characterized chiefly by an ongoing conflict and rivalry between and among various shifting alliances of sections: "a checkerboard of differing environments."[34]

No one today would deny the importance of sectional distinctiveness and antagonism in American history, and that fact may be in some measure due to Turner's insistent voice.[35] It took a historian shaped by Turner's particular experience, however, moving from the provinces to the metropolis, from west to east, to elevate it to such a preeminent position as the master principle in the interpretation of American history. In any event, the sectional hypothesis was to enjoy none of the success of the frontier thesis. There were clear and painfully obvious problems with it from the start. The "section" that seemed so lucid a concept in theory turned out to be too fluid, too imprecise, too productive of blurred, fragmenting, and overlapping examples to be of any general use in empirical investigations. Turner's uses of statistical techniques and maps to demonstrate sectional antagonism were wholly inadequate, as he himself recognized.[36] Perhaps most flagrant was his confident (and wildly inaccurate) prediction in 1925 that "sectional self-consciousness and sensitiveness is likely to be increased as time goes on and crystallized sections feel the full influence of their geographic peculiarities, their special interests, and their developed ideals, in a closed and static nation."[37] Perhaps Turner was engaging in wishful thinking, hoping against hope that invoking the European analogy, sloppy and improbable though it was, would protect America (and that precious westering spirit) from creeping consolidation and homogeneity and ensure that not all America would have to resemble "civilized" Yankeedom— that there would remain some strongholds of other, older ways.

The thought of such clashing sectional ideals recalls again the charming image of Turner, the loyal midwesterner unhappily transplanted and stuck in genteel Cambridge, who comforts himself by sleeping in a tent on his porch. The symbolic qualities of that image not only capture some of the quandary into which Turner's life led him but point to what made Turner's work so culturally significant, so indicative of its historical moment. That tent on the porch was a token not only of the frontier's enduring power, but of its containment, and even its domestication. As such, it encapsulated the problem of perpetuating "the American intellect" in a form that Turner and most Americans could still cherish. If it insisted upon the preservation of the wild, the open, and the raw, it also bespoke their enclosure within the tamed, the delimited, and the cooked. Such was the problem behind the patrician Theodore Roosevelt's westering forays into "the strenuous life," infusions of primal frontier energy to defend against the degenerative disease of overcivilization. It spoke to the heart of William James, another physically vigorous Cantabrigian who favored the same sort of sleeping arrangements and who feared the atrophy of the martial virtues in the advent of a peaceful and corporate world.[38] Such, too, was the background for the rise of a mythic image of the Old West immortalized by Roosevelt's friend Owen Wister, a gloomy, infirm, overcivilized patrician from Philadelphia. Wister's novel *The Virginian*— appearing nine years after Turner's Chicago address and twelve years after the 1890 census had announced the closing of the frontier—fixed what would become an inexhaustible image of perpetual frontier that would be drawn upon again and again in several generations of twentieth-century American novels, radio programs, films, and television series.[39] The Western would become, so to speak, modern America's imaginative tent on the porch.[40]

The popularity of the Western, like the popularity of the frontier thesis, arose from the contradictory impulses it conjoined, the contradictory tendencies it accommodated. Did it bespeak an inextinguishable frontier spirit, the essence of distinctive Americanness? Or that spirit's utter obsolescence, consigned as it was to the realms of safe fantasy? No one would deny the frontier's mythic dimensions, and indeed the thrust of recent scholarship on the American West has been to render the frontier very mythic indeed, and little else besides. The timing of *The Virginian* suggests that myth was at the heart of the matter, right from the start. But the question is, What kind of myth? Was it the kind of vital, life-giving myth that shapes and nourishes the very structure of a distinctive consciousness? Or the sort of myth that is really nothing more than a self-deception, a barrier against the unpleasing truth? Herein lies one of the truly remarkable features of the Turner essay, and the real source of its endurance: its ability to lend itself so easily to widely divergent interpretations.

The vagueness of key terms like *frontier* (and *closing*) frustrated historians' attempts to verify or refute Turner, but this ambiguity also made his thesis able to accommodate a variety of imputed meanings with highly emotional content. Not only could Turner's multivalent thesis speak to those, like Roosevelt, who lamented the loss of the frontier and sought its substitutes; it also suggested to a generation of younger, more collectivist-inclined intellectuals, such as Walter Weyl or John Dewey, that the frontier past was a source of American cultural pathology and needed to be jettisoned posthaste.[41] As for Professor Turner himself, he seemed to be genuinely of more than one mind on the matter.

If Turner was not ready to suggest any new departures, others were less reluctant. In the same year that Turner gave his paper in Chicago, the sociologist Lester Frank Ward, in his book *The Psychic Factors of Civilization*, attempted to face the problem of fashioning "original social ideals and social adjustments" as directly and vigorously as possible. Ward, too, had the great retrospective theme of the Columbian observance and its implications for the meaning of America itself very much in mind when writing *Psychic Factors*. He had composed the book "wholly within the quadricentennial year of [America's] discovery and published [it] in that of the great Columbian Exposition" and regarded the book as "consecrated to the cause of social progress and mental enlightenment" on the soil of "America, the experimental ground of civilization."[42] If the essential thrust of Turner's explorations had been murky at best, Ward's message by contrast seemed to be crystal clear. *Psychic Factors* concluded with a blunt assertion that brushed aside all of Turner's reservations and ambivalences, offering a quintessential consolidationist vision of America's future:

> The individual has reigned long enough. The day has come for society to take its affairs into its own hands and shape its own destinies. . . . [Society] should imagine itself an individual, with all the interests of an individual, and becoming fully *conscious* of these interests it should pursue them with the same indomitable *will* with which the individual pursues his interests. Not only this, it must be guided, as he is guided, by the social *intellect*, armed with all the knowledge that all individuals combined, with so great labor, zeal, and talent have placed in its possession, constituting the social intelligence.
>
> Sociocracy will differ from all other forms of government that have been devised.[43]

Such enthusiastic remarks suggest a great deal of common ground with Edward Bellamy. Indeed, Ward was very much taken with *Looking Backward*, which he called "a sugar-coated bomb," the reading of which led him to become active in a Commonwealth Club formed in Washington to further Nationalist ideas.[44] In fact, *Psychic Factors* was largely a distillation into more concise and readily accessible form of arguments and perspectives already put forward at greater length in Ward's encyclopedic two-volume study *Dynamic Sociology* (1883), which antedated *Looking Backward* by a half-decade.

*Dynamic Sociology* is surely one of the most remarkable unread books in our intellectual history—a pioneering work occupying virtually unknown and widely disdained intellectual territory. Ward toiled on this tome for at least fourteen years, working in virtual isolation and painstakingly devoting virtually every spare moment in his life to it, finally going deeply into debt to publish it largely at his own expense, even as he labored daily at a variety of bureaucratic positions in the federal civil service. The final product reflected this long and somewhat private gestation. An idiosyncratic, irrepressibly expansive work, given to flights of grandiosity and self-importance, a steady flow of neologisms (of which *sociocracy* is but the best known), a preoccupation with the formulation of taxonomic schemata, and a rebarbarative, amateurish literary style, it bore all the audacious marks of the brilliant autodidact who produced it. Half cosmic philosopher and half naturalist, Ward was hardly a model for what professional sociology was to become; yet he would nonetheless turn out to be, by general consent, the founding father of the sociological discipline in the United States, a thinker whose work, whatever its limitations may have been, set the discipline's initial agenda and limned many of its most recurrent problematical aspects.

Then and now, too, he has his admirers. Many of Ward's most vocal enthusiasts have been twentieth-century liberals, such as the historian Henry Steele Commager, who accord him a place of honor in the story of the intellectual origins of the welfare state, lauding him as a staunch opponent of the "social Darwinism" of Herbert Spencer and William Graham Sumner and as a prescient advocate for the positive contributions to be made by an activist government.[45] There is considerable justification for this view of him as a precursor to the energetic governmental conceptions of Progressives and New Dealers. Certainly, his notion of a sociocracy, in which the practice of government itself would rest "directly upon the science of sociology," which in turn permits the employment of disciplined mind as a powerful force for reshaping the social and natural worlds, points to the use of trained experts in economics, political science, and social policy to plan and administer vigorous and active central governments. To begin reading in his sprawling work, however, is in many respects to be transported into a vanished intellectual world—a Victorian universe of discourse awash in all-encompassing synthetic visions of cosmic evolution, moral philosophy, and speculative world history in the grand manner, modeled on works penned by the likes of John Fiske, Auguste Comte, or Herbert Spencer, a world light-years removed from the narrowly focused practices of professionalized modern social science that had become well-established by the early decades of the twentieth century. During Ward's lifetime the full articulation and compartmentalization of the intellectual disciplines and their languages, one of the defining features of professionalization, came to pass. Ward was not part of that movement, however.[46] Whatever his hopes and claims for a science of society may have been, the example supplied by those Victorian polymathic synthesists, who claimed all knowledge for their own, remained dearest to his heart. Hence, the sobriquet "the American Aristotle" that his admirers have sometimes pinned on Ward, though surely extravagant, nevertheless captures something genuine about the man, who was not only a wide-ranging social philosopher but an accomplished botanist and paleontologist as well.

Ward's is one of the more unusual and impressive lives in the annals of American scholarship. It would be hard to think of a scholar of comparable distinction who started life under less propitious circumstances and battled more adversities to achieve so much. To begin with, Ward had to overcome the most formidable enemy of all, the poverty and disadvantages of his own upbringing. Born in Joliet, Illinois, in 1841, the last of ten children in a wandering, footloose family, Ward experienced firsthand the restlessness that Turner had identified with the life of the West, moving several times during his youth as his father's needs dictated. His formal schooling was scrappy at best, and he was often required to contribute to the family income through part-time mill work or farm labor. Somehow, though, drawing on sources that will remain mysterious, Lester acquired an iron determination to better his lot in life, along with a conviction that education was the key to such self-betterment.

It is not hard to guess that a large part of Ward's motivation derived from a burning desire to escape these hard-scrabble origins. He was not held back by attachment to family. In particular, it is evident that he felt no affection for his parents, a fact that may well have been behind his rejection, in *Dynamic Sociology*, of the Old Testament requirement of filial piety, a precept he deeply resented, since "children are usually brought into the world through an act performed purely for the gratification of a sensual desire on the part of the parents" and therefore "the child could be under no possible obligation to the parents for any supposed sacrifices."[47] Such cut-and-dried unsentimentality certainly marks his surprisingly cut-and-dried autobiographical assertions, made late in life, that "I never took any interest in genealogy" and "I have cared little for my ancestors, except in a biological sense." For this visionary, who had in common with Edward Bellamy a mind "trimmed toward the future rather than the past," nothing was more unpleasant than looking backward. By the same token, a Darwinian belief in the boundless malleability of organisms was pleasingly complementary to his own hopes for liberation from a defining milieu he despised.[48]

That liberation would depend, he believed, not on the impersonal operations of the natural world but on the firm resolution of Ward's own will. Just as revealing, then, was his admission that "I have always had a horror of degeneracy, the proof of which in certain individuals, families, and even communities is manifest." He linked that horror with his contempt for the world to which he most feared being consigned: "Pride of ancestry is a mark of degeneracy."[49] Such a passage indicates how well he had absorbed the classic Protestant and republican fears of declension, of plunging hopelessly into sin and corruption. It was not a falling short of his father's standard that he feared, however, but the loss of willpower, the failure of moral sufficiency, that would hold him back him from the herculean effort needed to improve his way of life. His task would require of him the single-minded strength of the self-made man, who could not take the time for, or the risk of, backward glances. Whatever his view of individualism in the realm of social ideas, his personal commitment was to a self-propelled equal-opportunity Jacksonian and Emersonian egalitarianism, in which a man ought to get just as far in life as his abilities and his tenacity would take him—no less and no more. From this commitment arose his keen resentment of all hereditary rank, social hierarchy, and arrogations of both—a resentment further fueled by his own manifest lack of any such advantages upon entering life's race.

Ward's diary, which he wrote in French as a self-improvement exercise, is revealing in this respect, reminiscent in many ways of the famous diary kept by William Byrd II, another American frontier provincial who feared the specter of degeneracy.[50] Ward's diary is in the main a tedious, unreflective document, serving largely as a record of his struggles to educate himself through a relentless self-imposed program of study, including daily readings in Greek and Latin: Herodotus, Xenophon, the New Testament, Virgil, Cicero, and others. Yet the diary leaves two strong cumulative impressions: first, his Franklinian determination to make every minute count toward his rise in the world, which he always believed education would accomplish; and second, paradoxically, the depth and warmth of his attachment to his "sweet girl" (and, later, wife) Lizzie, whom he remembers with intense love and gratitude in nearly every entry. The satisfactions of love seem not to war with his intense ambition and at times even supersede it: "My sweet wife and I live together in great happiness. It is sweet love which sustains us beneath all our troubles and in all our poverty. It is better to live with her in poverty than to be surrounded by pomp and riches but without companionship, without a wife."[51] Even his effusive and often quite moving professions of love, however, sometimes betray an anxiety and a sense that, in love as in education, one must constantly redouble one's efforts—as when Ward remarks, during a period of separation, that "it sometimes seems to me that I must make admissions in my journal of my immutable love, either to myself or to some other person, as a witness of its sincerity."[52] No New England Puritan divine ever spoke more evocatively of the gnawing fear of falling away and of being thereby found unworthy of life's prizes.

There is no way of knowing what outlet, if any, Ward's large ambitions might have found had not the Civil War intervened. In August 1862, drifting and without sufficient funds to continue his education, the twenty-one-year-old Ward finally enlisted as a private in the 141st Regiment of the Pennsylvania Volunteers. It would prove a momentous decision, marking his entrance not only into the Union army but into the institutional web of a nationalizing America, wherein he could finally leave his old way of life. Ward's commitment to the Union cause was fierce, as was his emotional identification with fellow self-made Illinoisan Abraham Lincoln and his sharp hatred of the South, which he condemned as the "Kingdom of Satan."[53] That ferocity was only reinforced by his own serious wound suffered in action at the battle of Chancellorsville in May 1863, which took him out of the fighting; by the death from battlefield wounds of his beloved brother Erastus, the only family member for whom he had ever cared; and, close on the heels of Erastus's death, the assassination of Lincoln. Even after the Union triumph, Ward continued to urge that punitive measures be taken against the rebel southerners, "ineffable scoundrels who have grasped at [the nation's] throat and stabbed at its heart," and he generally enthusiastically supported the Radical Republican agenda.[54]

Ward was discharged from the army in November 1864 and soon, like many other veterans, began to look for a government position in Washington, hoping that his military record would translate into employment from a grateful U.S. government. After several months of frantic efforts, including a letter of appeal to Lincoln himself, his persistence finally paid off, and Ward landed a clerkship in the Treasury Department. The U.S. government would provide a livelihood and home for him for the next four decades. He was also able to continue his formal education, enrolling in night classes at Columbian College (forerunner to George Washington University) to work toward bachelor of arts, bachelor of laws, and master of arts degrees. Fortunately for Ward, federal employment in the postbellum years became a magnet for other fertile and vigorous minds, many of them also Civil War veterans, who found a home in the growing number of Washington government bureaus involved in systematic empirical scientific and social research. Ward's federal colleagues included capable and talented men such as the noted explorer (and fellow Illinoisan) Major John Wesley Powell, director of the Bureau of American Ethnology and the U.S. Geological and Geographical Survey; Carroll D. Wright of the Bureau of Labor; Francis A. Walker, director of the Bureau of Statistics, commissioner of Indian Affairs, and supervisor of the 1870 census; and geologist Clarence King, Powell's predecessor at the Geological Survey. As Washington also became home to a proliferation of philosophical, scientific, and debating societies, Ward was able to participate in an increasingly stimulating network of intellectual exchange, wherein he was eager to make his mark. Feeling insufficiently challenged by his clerical work at the Treasury, Ward began writing an enormous book (the beginnings of what would become *Dynamic Sociology*) called "The Great Panacea," an ode to the virtues of education as a tool of far-reaching social reform.

Eventually Powell became impressed by Ward's immense energies and talents and took him under his wing. Their professional relationship blossomed in 1875, when Powell invited Ward to join a botanical survey in Utah and then to help prepare a paleobotanical collection for the 1876 Centennial Exposition in Philadelphia. This work fired Ward's interest in the possibility of a scientific career within government employ. It eventually led to Ward's appointment by Powell in 1881 to join him at the Geological Survey, whose mission was to explore and map the entirety of the nation's physical domain, with a particular eye toward the assessment, exploitation, and conservation of natural resources; the classification of public lands; and the publication of survey results and maps. In addition to being the provider of Ward's employment, Powell became even more important as an intellectual influence and example. A forceful early advocate of the rational, disinterested, scientifically regulated exploitation of the nation's natural resources, Powell provided Ward with a concrete example of how the grand reorganization of society itself might proceed—and the role that an activist, scientifically informed central government might play in the making of that new order.[55]

Ward's sociological studies were deeply informed by this web of Washingtonian influences, as his dedication of *Dynamic Sociology* to Powell indicates. There was another influence always in the background, however: the formidable Herbert Spencer, whose work Ward had been studying with great care and interest for many years. Ward generally did his best writing when polemical passion moved him, and Spencer's work stirred his creative animosities like none other. It is not hard to see why. To begin with, there was much similarity between the two men's ambition to construct a grand evolutionary synthesis, even if Ward had to play David to the Englishman's Goliath. Where such similarities of intention exist, the differences that emerge may become all the more bitter.[56] Ward emphatically shared Spencer's evolutionary perspectives. But Spencer's most fundamental contentions—that biological evolution and social evolution were merely two aspects of the same process and, furthermore, that the attempts of men to interfere in the spontaneous playing out of these natural laws, particularly by instituting universal education and a powerful positive state, could only bring harm and social regression—were deeply offensive to Ward. A man whose entire life had been devoted to the possibility of bettering himself through the persistent exercise of his will and intelligence, Ward could never have accepted the complacency and hopelessness he detected beneath the slogan of laissez faire. Nor could he take so negative a view of an education that he had struggled so valiantly to obtain and that he believed to be the world's greatest hope for radical improvement. He was not likely to speak ill of the potentialities of positive government because the federal science bureaucracy had been his cherished ticket out of a dreaded life of rural poverty and into a meaningful life of productive and engaged intellectual activity.

Ward still had to deal with contradictions in his developing thought system, problems not unlike the dilemmas posed by Mr. Barton's sermon in *Looking Backward*. Ward's growing Darwinian convictions, mixed though they were with Lamarckian holdovers, reinforced his sense that human nature, like anything else in Nature, is profoundly conditioned by the full range of environmental forces. Yet that conviction was decisively at odds with his firm belief that the individual could shape his own destiny. "Man has risen by dint of his own efforts and activities. The nature of human progress has been the theme of much discussion, and the extreme scientific view seems to negative [*sic*] not only all praise or blame but all hope of success on the part of man himself in trying to accelerate his advancement or improve his condition. The very law of evolution threatens to destroy hope and paralyze effort. Science applied to man becomes a gospel of inaction."[57] How, then, could one hold onto the precious notion of individual striving—the very sense of freedom that had allowed Lester Ward to rise in the world—while accepting the modes of causality that his full embrace of science implied?

Ward's answer was to insist upon a disjunction between the biological realm and the social realm. As he neatly formulated the distinction, "The environment transforms the animal, while man transforms the environment."[58] Human intelligence and the capacity for purposive action were themselves products of biological evolution; hence, the most logical way of following the evolutionary principle was, paradoxically, to resolve to submit no longer to the blind authority and wasteful practices of Nature. "We are told to let things alone and allow nature to take its course. But has intelligent man ever done this? Is not civilization itself with all that it had accomplished the result of man's not letting things alone, and of his not letting nature take its course?"[59] Accordingly, Ward distinguished between those elements of sociology that were passive, dealing with objective social-structural characteristics, and those that were active, taking into their purview directives conceived and initiated by the creative mental capabilities of the human being as subject. Ward thereby established a distinction between two sources of social change, or social dynamics: there was the "genetic," which signified the unconscious and undirected play of social forces, resembling the Spencerian model; and there was the "telic," which signified the introduction of purposefulness, of human intention and direction, in short, of teleology—a property that a Darwinian view of untrammeled Nature most emphatically could no longer endorse.[60]

Such distinctions implied two entirely different understandings of what sociology was to be. The genetic emphasis pointed toward sociology as "discovery" (what he would later call "pure" sociology), an external and structural sociology unconcerned with conscious purposeful action. The telic emphasis pointed toward sociology as an instrument of "politics," as social reform—"applied" sociology, whose ultimate aim resembled Ward's sociocracy.[61] Ward clearly understood the distinction between these approaches to sociology, but he did not seem to feel them to be mutually exclusive.[62] His "answer," then, was less a solution than it was a restatement of the problem: a vehement assertion of the disjunctions between the biological and the social, or between the genetic and the telic, without supplying a plausible explanation of how and why such seeming dualisms might connect and coexist within an underlying monistic framework. The road from the individual to the social remained enveloped in fog. This problem arises partly because of the crudity of Ward's psychology. Ward saw the ultimate driving force behind all social action and social change to be "feelings," by which he meant not merely emotions but, more fundamentally, the elemental subjective facts of sensation and the resultant subjective states of pleasure and pain. A true Benthamite (or proto-behaviorist) in this respect, he argued that happiness was the only proper goal of human life, and happiness was to be defined in terms of the "excess of pleasure, or enjoyment, over pain, or discomfort."[63] All other goals were subordinate, then, to the satisfaction of desire and the maximization of pleasure: such drives, with the intellect's role in channeling them, formed the ultimate source of energy for the principle of "telesis." The "problem of social science" was merely to perform that role in the most comprehensive manner possible—to "point out in what way the most complete and universal satisfaction of human desires can be attained."[64] Ward was an Epicurean; he disdained self-denial and branded asceticism a concealed form of egoism, "dangerous to health and destructive of happiness and of progress."[65]

The subjective meaning of these desires, however, is entirely different from their meaning taken in the larger context of Nature, and there is poignancy in that fact. To put it in Ward's language, "The object of Nature is function, while the object of man is happiness." Nature itself is "utterly indifferent to both pleasure and pain" and coldly regards a trait or behavior with an eye only toward its contribution to the survivability of the species.[66] The subjective feelings that drive humans to consume food are addressed to the satisfaction of a complex of desires, but from the perspective of Nature, any such satisfaction is epiphenomenal, beside the point. To cite another example (one that also indicates Ward's moral radicalism for his time), there is no direct link between the feelings inducing men and women to engage in sexual intercourse and the procreative function that such acts perform in the preservation of the species—the latter of which constitutes Nature's sole interest in the matter.[67] In the courtroom drama of organic survival, Nature, the hanging judge, appraises organismic features and futures not according to human feelings but according to its own functional calculus. The process of natural selection merely ensures a coordination (not an identity) of the two, for feelings cannot long survive if their pursuit and satisfaction conflict with a viable natural function.

But coordination of feeling and function, of subjective psychology and Nature, is not the same as bridging the antagonistic distance between them. A persistent alienation of the isolated human subject, of the radical individual, is implicit in the very psychological structure of his sensations and yearnings, as Ward understood them. Such feelings stand always in incommensurable relation with the vastness of Nature, which the individual experiences, like the lovers in Matthew Arnold's "Dover Beach," as "a darkling plain / Swept with confused alarms of struggle and flight, / Where ignorant armies clash by night."[68] In that sense, Ward's Darwinian premises saw to it that he would diverge dramatically from any transcendentalist vestiges of his predecessors; the notion of mystical correspondence, of finding in the phenomenology of Nature the emblematic reflections of one's own inner world, could not have been more alien. Nature was no longer a spectacle to be admired or a force to be adored and followed; it was, at best, an enormous repository of partially formed materials, rich but disorganized, more or less stolid and inert, when not dangerous and inhuman, awaiting the hand of *homo faber* to be converted into something fine and useful. At worst, man and nature were perpetually at war, but even in that view, Ward felt the time had arrived for man to push to victory and take over the reins of his existence. If Nature in the past could thwart the heart's desire through the pitiless instruments of natural selection, the "social action" of human intellect now could turn the tables on Nature, refashioning it to satisfy that once-denied desire. "In so far as man has progressed at all, he has done so by gaining little by little the mastery in this struggle with the iron law of nature. . . . Every artificial form that serves a human purpose, is a triumph of mind over the physical forces of nature in ceaseless and aimless competition. In the social world it is human institutions,—religion, government, law, marriage, customs,—that have been thought out and adopted to restrain the unbridled individualism that has always menaced society."[69]

That last mention of unbridled individualism and restraint suggests, ever so slightly, an element of social discipline (what Ward called social friction) in the dynamics of these institutions, an element that seems, at first blush, to be at odds with a frankly hedonistic philosophy devoted to the notion that "satisfaction of desire" is the "sole theme" of human life.[70] But the discrepancy was only apparent, Ward believed, since he saw society subsisting upon the basis of a kind of calculated social contract, instituted to secure a greater happiness in combination than would be possible in atomistic isolation.[71] Society itself was (he admitted) "only an idea," an entity that "exists only for the individual," a means and not an end. One must keep firmly in mind that when social reformers talk about reforming society, they are not "so simple as literally to personify society and conceive it endowed with wants and passions." Instead, they should be taken to mean by "improvement of society" only "such modifications in its constitution and structure as will in their opinion result in ameliorating the condition of the individual members."[72] It was strictly a matter of utilitarian expediency for us to combine—united we stand, divided we fall—in the battle against Nature; hewing to the laissez-faire gospel of competition merely perpetuated the shocking wastefulness of Nature's genesis, in contrast to the great things to be expected from man's telesis. Unlike Aristotle and Comte, Ward did not believe man to be an inherently social animal, but that was so much the worse for Nature, for whose prodigal and inefficient ways he had surprisingly scant regard: "Nature is first to be observed, but, having been learned, the laws of nature become the property and servants of man, and he is not to imitate the methods by which nature accomplishes results, but must direct the forces of nature into channels of his own advantage, and utilize for his own good all the powers of the universe."[73]

Here, then, was the agenda of telesis, pure and simple. The use of so many singular pronouns, and of the singular noun *man*, obscures an important question: how is it that the individualized desires driving social change can become translated or canalized into broadly social instruments, which can be spoken of as if they were wielded by a single person? If society is a fiction, emphatically not to be personified, and if the satisfaction of individual desire is still the central theme of human life, how are we to understand Ward's appeal (in the very same pages) that society "should imagine itself an individual," guided "by the social *intellect*"? How do we effect a coordination of stubbornly distinct sensibilities so smooth and seamless as to present the aspect of a single individuality? Partly by the use of an active government, answered Ward, arguing by organic analogy: the state represents "the organ of social consciousness" and "the servant of the [social] will of its members in the same way that the brain is the servant of the animal will."[74] As yet, this relationship was only partially developed. Only after "the mind of society" came "to stand to the social organism in somewhat the relation that the individual mind stands to the individual organism" could "any fully developed art of government" be expected to appear."[75] A truly social intellect would require "the universal diffusion of the maximum amount of the most important knowledge." Universal education, then, Ward's "great panacea," would be the ultimate solution to the problem of discordant individual desires, which had hitherto rendered the "social will" little more than "a mass of conflicting desires which largely neutralize one another."[76] It was inconceivable to him that a properly educated populace might still be riven with endless and irresolvable conflicting interests, for education perfected desire by specifying its proper objects. The true basis for the world's ongoing conflict is not inequality of condition but inequality of access to information.[77] Education must be socialized, which amounts to "the complete social appropriation of individual achievement which has civilized the world."[78]

The word "appropriation" might seem to suggest the presence of Marx here, but Ward was very far from being a thoroughgoing socialist, Marxian or otherwise, despite the accusations of his detractors. Although Ward thought the ideological premises of competitive individualism to be wrongheaded and outmoded, it did not follow that he believed in working toward an equality of condition in society. The beauty of a system of universal education was that it substituted inequalities founded in an individual's nature for inequalities built around the accidents of one's origins. It enabled worthy persons of even the most indifferent social background to rise in the world and stride on an equal footing with the well-born; it ensured that those who were inferior in all respects but birth would not have a place of social eminence waiting for them upon attaining their majority.[79] Universal education would be the great meritocratic equalizer in the world to come; it would be, in a sense, a substitute for the Turnerian frontier in providing a fresh start for people (like Ward) who were not fortunate in their birth. Ward perhaps most cogently expressed the differences between sociocracy and its alternatives in his *Outlines of Sociology* (1897):

1. Individualism has created artificial inequalities.
2. Socialism seeks to create artificial equalities.
3. Sociocracy recognizes natural inequalities and aims to abolish artificial inequalities.
4. Individualism confers benefits on those only who have the ability to obtain them, by superior power, cunning, intelligence, or the accident of position.
5. Socialism would confer the same benefits on all alike, and aims to secure equality of fruition.
6. Sociocracy would confer benefits in strict proportion to merit, but insists upon *equality of opportunity* as the only means of determining the degree of merit.[80]

The personal subtext in such a view hardly needs to be highlighted. Ward's own life was a virtual ode to the self-made man; he was rightfully proud of his own surmounting of obstacles, he fervently believed in the "efficacy of effort," and he thought his efforts deserved to be proportionately rewarded.[81] Such a vision perhaps also reflects, in inverse form, the conditions Ward observed and experienced in a corrupt and patronage-ridden civil service, in which Ward had elected to seek his advancement by accumulating college degrees rather than by dirtying his hands and abandoning his scruples.[82] It should be conceded, however, that such a vision hardly abolished all competitive individualism, whatever Ward may have believed to the contrary, for it is inconceivable that the constant frenzied scramble for position produced in a completely fluid and meritocratic social order would produce conditions of effortless social harmony.[83] Ward did not want to abolish the individual in favor of the social; he wanted to preserve the Jacksonian (and Turnerian) virtue of boundlessness in an increasingly bounded world. A reformed Washington civil service might serve as a model for his new vision of a socialized frontier, wherein individual desire would be gratified beyond its most extravagant dreams.

There is nearly as much to be said in criticism of this view as of Bellamy's. The conviction that the social world, because it was man's creation, could be made amenable to the deepest needs of every person, rested in part upon an almost unbelievably simpleminded understanding of human psychology, which crudely equated psychic forces with physical forces.[84] Ward, so stingingly relentless in his verbal prosecution of Spencer and Sumner, was surprisingly vague in filling in the contours of his own vision and in offering specific procedures and reforms that might begin to implement it, often falling back upon the general authority of science. What, for example, was social intellect? What would be an example of it in action? Ward provided two examples in *Psychic Factors*, neither of which suggested that democracy had very much to do with social intellect. First, he enthused over the fact that legislative bodies have come to delegate much of their work to specialized committees, which are "carefully chosen with reference to their known fitness for the different subjects intrusted to them." These committees "really *deliberate*," they "investigate the questions before them, hear testimony and petitions, and weigh evidence for and against every proposed measure." This process, he said without irony, "is truly scientific and leads to the discovery of the principles involved."[85] The second example is of the increasing tendency of "various bureaus of government" in the executive branch to formulate far-reaching legislative proposals that the legislature, which "recognizes the wisdom of such recommendations," enacts into law. This legislation, too, "is in a true sense scientific."[86]

Ward evidently saw no intrinsic contradiction between such ingenuous scientism and the Jacksonian tenets he esteemed, perhaps because for him science was, by its nature, democratic and uncontroversial: it was disinterested; it constituted a fair-minded form of knowledge before which all stood equal; and it respected neither precedent nor authority, but only talent and demonstrable truth. Small wonder that a man so ashamed of his origins would be attracted to the allure of science, in whose meritocratic womb (and by the aid of whose environmentalist premises) he could be born again, the equal of Henry Adams.[87] The obvious problem posed by sociocracy, however, was how to reconcile democratic values with the growing political and cultural authority of accredited experts. This was not a question Ward felt it necessary to address, except to assert that a sufficiently broad and deep universal education would take care of the difficulty by ensuring that an enlightened populace would approve the arguments of science. To invoke universal education as a great panacea, however, was to invoke a deus ex machina, from a practical standpoint, since the day of such mass education lay far in the future. The practical question was, What ways of applying social intelligence to the urgent problems of a disorganized society could be put to work now, taking the state of the citizenry as it is?

That question inevitably cut against the Jacksonian grain of a transitional figure like Ward, for it opened the way to a Whiggish benevolent authority, now vested with the authority of science, poised over the wayward and ignorant many—a supervisory wisdom that would nudge them in the right direction and, if necessary, keep them in line. Ward believed that such prescriptive leadership, particularly in matters of morality, was soon to become a mere atavism, a form of social friction, an onerous check on individual human creativity—necessary, perhaps, in an earlier time but presently to be superseded by scientific knowledge that would remove the frictions of socially imposed precepts and laws and thus further "the moral progress of the world."[88] Such optimism was not shared by Ward's disciple Edward Alsworth Ross, however, whose 1901 book *Social Control*, by its very title, began to mark a subtle departure from Ward's assumption that the fulfillment of individual desire was the fundamental datum, initiating energy, and sine qua non of social existence. Such a development was not a complete departure from the spirit of Ward, however. It emerged easily from the tension between pure and applied sociology and between the aggregating and the anarchic impulses that Ward had been attempting to hold together. Yet there was a difference between social intelligence, serving the needs of individual desire by guiding it toward the most complete satisfaction, and social structure, which was thought to have shaped, altered, and redefined that desire in accordance with its own panoramic logic—a logic that might someday stand, like the old incommensurability of Nature, at a impassable remove from the primal fecundity of the individual impulse. The subordination of the private self, which Bellamy had so readily accepted, decisively altered the balance between individual and society in a way that Ward, despite his frequent resounding words in support of collectivism, in the end found he could never entirely accept.[89]

The liberalism of Ward was not the only evidence that postbellum conceptions of American society were tending, however incompletely, in the direction of consolidation. There was also a more conservative strain that also envisioned social unification as the proper object of social and political thought. This movement drew its principal intellectual inspiration from German sources, especially the magisterial philosophical system of Hegel, with its singular formulation of the way that the interplay of opposites led to a complex synthetic unity. Of course, that influence can be partly attributed to the fact that so many Americans completed their education at the German universities, breeding ground of the Ph.D. octopus and so many other structures that would become characteristic of the American research university. Many of the Teutonic prejudices and assumptions that Herbert Baxter Adams so forcefully advocated, and against which Frederick Jackson Turner had so understandably rebelled, naturally came across the waters with the techniques and research programs of the Göttingen seminar.

Given Hegel's emphasis upon the organic, evolutionary nature of the modern nation-state as an expression of *Geist* in its transcendentally sanctioned world-historical march toward concrete realization, Hegelian political and social thought easily found a place for itself in the wake of the American Civil War, as part of the growing interest in images of national coalescence. Hegel himself lived and wrote during years of exasperating political disunion in the Germanic world and was deeply affected by the Napoleonic incursions into German territory. Consequently, his intense devotion to the idea of the state as a comprehensive social institution arose from a patriotic desire, similar to that evoked in his contemporaries Johann Gottfried Herder and Johann Gottlieb Fichte, to promote a more potent and coherent German political entity.[90] He was struggling, in short, with problems of political and social cohesion very like those facing his later American adherents.

Moreover, Hegel's trademark conceptual tool, the dialectic, could have particularly valuable applications for postbellum American nationalists, who sought to bind the wounds left by the country's bitter conflict, redefining the terms of opposition in complementary, even conciliatory terms as the historically inevitable clash of sharp opposites—a horrendous clash, to be sure, but one nevertheless resulting in a richer and more harmonious synthetic unity. Whitman, who greatly admired Hegel ("Only Hegel is fit for America—is large enough and free enough") used a dialectical strategy to account for, and ultimately affirm, the horrible rending of the body politic he had witnessed.[91] Recall, for example, his belief, cited above, that the war of attempted secession was a conflict "between the passions and paradoxes of one and the same identity—perhaps the only terms on which that identity could really become fused, homogeneous, and lasting."[92] A more elaborate version of the same strategy was offered by members of the St. Louis Philosophical Society, founded in January 1866 by a small group of Hegel's most devoted American disciples, including William Torrey Harris, Henry C. Brockmeyer, and Denton Snider.[93] Fond of applying the classic Hegelian scheme of thesis, antithesis, and synthesis to nearly any phenomenon or process that interested them, the St. Louis Hegelians settled easily into a view of the Civil War as a dialectical collision between the southern position of "abstract right" and the northern position of "abstract morality"; the result, they believed, would be the emergence of a synthetic "ethical state" superior to either of its predecessors.[94] Abraham Lincoln was transformed in their eyes into a grand world-historical figure, the savior of the American nation-state, transcendent synthesizer of conflicting moral principles into a greater and more enduring melding of formerly contradictory elements.[95]

For all its seeming ethereality, the St. Louis movement emerged from the cauldron of Civil War–era Missouri, a fact that caused its members to read Hegel's pronouncements with a special sense of urgency.[96] No state in the Union had been more bitterly divided, not only by the war but by the years of sectional controversy preceding it. Though officially Unionist in its affiliation, Missouri was a slave state and a hotbed of Confederate sympathizers, and the repeated clashes of Unionist and Confederate factions on the state's soil, eventually degenerating into guerrilla warfare and banditry of Hobbesian proportions, brought Missouri frighteningly close to complete anarchy.[97] As William Torrey Harris watched this carnage from the relative safety of St. Louis—a city deeply divided in its loyalties but with its divisions largely suppressed by the presence of Federal armed forces—he found comfort and hope in clinging to the near-religious conviction that he was witnessing a necessary process unfolding, one that surely would eventuate in a deeper and more enduring national union.[98] The dialectic offered an alternative way of comprehending seeming historical setbacks. Under the "quieting and soothing effect" of the Hegelian idealist Weltanschauung, he saw that "the collisions and petty details of terrestrial affairs seem to fall away, and one gazes, as it were, into their eternal archetypes, and sees the essence of the conflict, the problem reduced to its lowest terms."[99] Small wonder that for him and his colleagues the concept of the state would represent a beacon of social cohesion and purposefulness in a roiling sea of troubles.

The state was the central figure in their compulsively grandiose formulae, the ultimate point of convergence for the panoply of historical forces wending their way toward ultimate unity. It fell to Denton Snider, the group's most prolific writer, to produce the most substantial explication of their social thought. He portrayed the state in highly personalistic, psychological terms, using figures and language strikingly reminiscent of both Ward and Bellamy in their own efforts to recruit the energies of individualism for the cause of a higher solidarity. The state, he declared, was to be thought of as a person, an entity possessing Will; indeed, "we may deem it a Will, distinct, working in its sphere, according to its own law." With such a conception, "we reach down to its fundamental psychical trait, and thus bring it back to the human Self, which also has Will, and correlates with the same."[100] State and Self were indistinguishable in the end, for "Government is the process of the Ego as actual, and is for all Egos, not simply for one." Such a corporate understanding of human self-realization seemed to leave little room for the older American notion of the individual's hard separateness and imprescriptible natural rights—certainly not when "Government is the very Self of man made real, made a true entity, which otherwise would be unreal, untrue, having no objective validity in the world."[101]

The social thought of the St. Louis group was never likely to take Gilded Age America by storm. But their lofty idealism, corporatism, and insistence upon the inculcation of prescriptive values were indicative of what they would have liked to think of as the Zeitgeist, for such perspectives would be shared by postbellum thinkers in a variety of disciplines. In particular, their emphasis upon the state as a principle of coherence would find especially distinct echoes and collateral support in the burgeoning new discipline of political science. The similarities emerge with particular clarity in the career of John W. Burgess, who as creator and director of the School of Political Science at Columbia University (founded in 1880) can be regarded as one of the founding fathers of the discipline in America.

The agenda of political science was, in the beginning, shaped by the very same factors that so powerfully influenced the St. Louisans: a heavy indebtedness to German social, political, and historical thought and a preoccupation with the political and social convulsions of the American Civil War and its aftermath. Small wonder, then, that the attention of the earliest professional political scientists would be so resolutely fixed upon the goal of cohesion and that the paradigmatic unified state would be regarded as their fundamental object of inquiry. The temper of early political science was intensely and insistently nationalistic, thoroughly hostile to secession and sectionalism, and deeply suspicious of the appeal to "popular sovereignty"; hence its most prominent exponents were most likely to be either northerners, or southerners of Unionist affinity, such as Burgess or his younger contemporary Woodrow Wilson.[102] The crisis of the Union presented a supreme test case for the nascent discipline, for that bloody clash was precisely the sort of debacle a science of politics might be expected to avert in the future by providing an intellectual foundation upon which a more substantial and enduring unity might be erected. In Burgess's case, the importance of the Civil War in precipitating such patterns of thought could hardly have been more personal, for Burgess was destined to feel that national rupture more acutely than most. His story is worth relating in some detail.

Born in Tennessee in 1844 into a family of politically active Whigs, Burgess was a southerner through and through, albeit of firmly Unionist principles. The image of the Old South fixed in his mind was decidedly picturesque and romantic, suggestive of the moonlight-and-magnolias school of postbellum southern literature. All in all, he took a rather benign view of his boyhood in what he was pleased to call the "medieval period of American history." The South, he felt, had been entirely misunderstood by the North, which regarded slavery "too much in the nature of crime" and the plantation aristocrats "too much as arrogant, overbearing, and violent men." Indeed, the "slaves themselves," he asserted, "did not, as a rule, feel their lot to be a hard one." The picture of antebellum slavery described in *Uncle Tom's Cabin* was "a gross exaggeration."[103]

True to the legacy of his Whig nationalism, however, Burgess's indulgent account of antebellum southern folkways did not translate into sympathy for secession. Like Lincoln, though with the added benefit of sober hindsight, he regarded the integrity of the national union as a far more important desideratum than the visions and fears proffered by extremists, North or South. He had watched and listened in his youth as moderate Whigs like his father had labored, to no avail, to persuade their fire-eating friends that secession would prove disastrous even to the slaveholders' own interests. He saw how the question of secession tore apart the social fabric of the world he had known, pitting neighbors against neighbors. Unionists became particularly vulnerable to persecution in the months between secession and the Union occupation of Tennessee in the spring of 1862. The horrifying sight of his fellow Tennesseans hanged from the limbs of trees for the crime of "loyalty to the Union as created and preserved in the Constitution" left an enduring impression upon young Burgess, convincing him not only of "the folly of indulging the passions of anger and hate in the solution of public questions" but also of the general depravity of "the mass of men."[104] Burgess's family history was a case study in the sad fate of southern Whiggery.

Such experiences by themselves might have been enough to sour him for good on popular sovereignty, but far worse was to come. In September 1861, Burgess tried to begin his collegiate studies at Cumberland College in the small town of Lebanon, in north-central Tennessee. By February of the following year, with the defeated Confederate forces in the region retreating toward Murfreesboro, he decided to return home, threading his way southward through the disheveled, chaotic Rebel lines. Home did not prove a safe harbor for him, however. Vengeful secessionists who knew of the Burgess family sentiments had marked young Burgess for persecution.[105] When a heavily armed Confederate trooper arrived one day in June to impress young Burgess into the Rebel army, he and his father fended off the man at gunpoint, and within a few minutes Burgess was galloping away on horseback, headed for the safety of Federal lines. After a desperate, blood-curdling nighttime sprint across the battlefield at Shiloh, he arrived at Federal headquarters in Jackson, whereupon his horse dropped dead of exhaustion.

Trouble, however, continued to pursue him. At the provost marshal's suggestion, Burgess immediately enlisted in the Federal army. Attached to a Missouri regiment, he worked for a month in January 1863, under the most hideous physical conditions imaginable, to repair the railroad in a swampy region between the forks of the Obion River, while fending off Confederate attackers. During a stormy night of sentinel duty, as he kept watch over the hellish landscape he was forced to listen in terror to the cries of mutilated animals and the shrieks and groans of wounded and dying soldiers. It was a night "awful beyond description," which remained "a hideous nightmare" in Burgess's memory for the rest of his life.

Unlikely as it might seem, however, this descent into hell planted the seeds of his distinguished later career as a political scientist:

> It was, however, in the midst of this frightful experience that the first suggestion of my life's work came to me. As I strained my eyes to peer into the darkness and my ears to perceive the first sounds of an approaching enemy, I found myself murmuring to myself: "Is it not possible for man, a being of reason, created in the image of God, to solve the problems of his existence by the power of reason and without recourse to the destructive means of physical violence?" And I then registered the vow in heaven that if a kind Providence would deliver me alive from the perils of the existing war, I would devote my life to teaching men how to live by reason and compromise instead of by bloodshed and destruction.[106]

In the most immediate and palpable way imaginable, then, these experiences of war had provided Burgess with a scholarly agenda. That sense of calling was only heightened by Burgess's subsequent stint as a Federal quartermaster in Nashville, where he witnessed the shattered lives of many old acquaintances and felt their murderous hostility toward him—for they now regarded him as a loathsome traitor to his region and to the sacred concept of states' rights.[107] The price paid for national disunity had turned out to be enormous, and it was increasing.

By 1864 Burgess began to make good on his epiphanic call. He enrolled that fall at Amherst College and, upon graduating, taught at Knox College in Illinois. In 1871 Burgess undertook the inevitable academic trek to Germany, all the while searching for clues to the problem of a rational basis for political cohesion. The time of his arrival proved especially fortuitous, for he appeared at the very moment when a consolidated, powerful German nation-state had at long last, after many false starts, become a formidable reality, and had demonstrated how formidable it was by smashing the French army in the Franco-Prussian War. Burgess made sure he was in Berlin to witness the "grand entrée" of the victorious returning troops. This Germanic replay of the 1865 Grand Review (which Burgess had also witnessed firsthand) affected him far more deeply, he claimed, than his exposure to German political and social thought. It marked the beginning of Burgess's lifelong obsession with the exemplary potential of German institutions:

> It was more to us to see the power of the new Germany make its triumphal entrance into the new imperial capital than to have heard a few lectures which we would have only partially understood. It gave us a more correct conception of the new Germany than we could ever have obtained from the reading of books or the hearing of lectures and addresses. It was the most magnificent manifestation of power which the world had ever furnished. I had seen the march of the Grand Army of the Republic through Washington six years before, and in me, as an American who had taken part in the battle for the Union, this roused far deeper feeling; but as a manifestation of power, I had never, and have never, seen anything to equal this march of the victorious German army, led by the newly made emperor and the royal and princely heads of all the States of the German Union.[108]

Triumphing over disunity, the Germans were showing the world the greatness that national consolidation could bring. The lesson was not lost on a rapt Burgess.

Indeed, only nine years later, still very much mindful of his Civil War vow, Burgess would begin to assemble the School of Political Science at Columbia University. The view of political life he set forth in that context was oriented toward the Germanic conception of the state as exemplary instrument for the rational resolution of social and political discord.[109] Over some three decades, until his retirement in 1912, he built what was arguably the most distinguished political science department in the country while controlling access to the most important journal in the field (*Political Science Quarterly*). He himself produced several highly influential and widely used texts in the field, most notably *Political Science and Comparative Constitutional Law* (1890), along with numerous other contributions to the scholarly literature in history, politics, and law.[110]

The breadth of those interests bespoke the vastness of the mission that early political science took upon itself—an ambition fueled for Burgess by his two unforgettable experiences: political incoherence in his own land, and political potency among the victoriously marching Germans. A bedrock element of Burgess's political thought was its profound commitment to a nationalism that warmly embraced the unifying concept of the "modern national popular state" as a necessary and desirable social formation, "a moral conception of the highest order," the "most perfectly and undisputedly sovereign organization of the state which the world has yet attained," an important step upward on the long historical ladder toward a world-encompassing accord and coordination of individual forces.[111] The state, wrote Burgess (in language redolent of Hegel) was "the product of the progressive revelation of the human reason through history," the gradual growth of the subjective into the objective, the slow refinement of the clash of individual wills into a perfectly coordinated form of human organization, "the realization of the universal in man."[112]

As such, the state could claim divine sanction for itself and point to the quality of sovereignty as its very essence; the state was merely the people in their organized sovereignty. For Burgess, the definition of such sovereignty could not be constrained or restricted: sovereignty meant nothing less than "original, absolute, unlimited, universal power over the individual subject and over all associations of subjects." Such an absolutist view of sovereignty was inevitable and indispensable, he thought, for the alternative was an unacceptably flexible formulation of the linchpin concept in modern political thought: "Power cannot be sovereign if it be limited; that which imposes the limitation is sovereign; and not until we reach the power which is unlimited, or only self-limited, have we attained sovereignty. . . . Of course, the state may abuse its unlimited power over the individual, but this is never to be presumed. [The state] is the human organ least likely to do wrong, and, therefore, we must hold to the principle that the state can do no wrong."[113]

Such a discussion seemed to recall the endless eighteenth-century British scrupling over the indivisibility of sovereignty, but that was not the least of its perplexing overtones. Burgess was well aware how such an assertion might carry alarming implications for Americans who treasured their sacred Anglo-American heritage of imprescriptible rights and strict limitations upon political power. This was precisely the point where continental contextualism and Declaration of Independence liberalism began to seem incompatible. He was therefore at great pains to distinguish his conception of the state, as a more or less abstract or transcendent expression of the nation as a cohesive whole, from that of the government, which was merely the particular agency created by the state at any given time to implement its directives. While the government might abuse and abort individual liberties, the state would not do so; on the contrary, "The more completely and really sovereign the state is, the truer and securer is the liberty of the individual."[114] In effect, Burgess defined the state as a distilled and disembodied national essence, like a Platonic *eidos*, in which existing governments might participate to a greater or lesser degree but which they could hope only to express imperfectly. The traditional American concern with the preservation of individual liberty could be respected so long as the intellectual distinction between state and government was scrupulously maintained.

Such semantic distinctions as that between *state* and *government* even provided him a critical escape hatch by defining out of existence the specter of state tyranny. Such were the uses of idealism.[115] But if Burgess can be understood as a philosophical idealist, in many respects, by making the idea of the state logically and ontologically prior to its empirical manifestations, he can with equal justice be called a pioneering antiformalist.[116] He argued, for example, that the U.S. Constitution, far from expressing eternal verities of political thought and abstract standards of justice, instead ought to be understood primarily as a historical and sociological artifact, an "interpretation of American society," an organic and adaptive response to the needs of a particular people at a particular time.[117] The replacement of the Articles of Confederation by the Constitution, he felt, merely reflected the growing force of national cohesion, the consolidation of the older, more localized republican consciousness into the broader and more encompassing framework appropriate to a modern nation. The older values had become superseded by the imperatives of nationalism, as surely as the various and variegated uniforms worn by the state militias in 1861 had yielded, by the time of the 1865 Grand Review, to the standardized blue uniforms of the national army.[118] The Civil War itself had been a part of "the plan of universal history," directed toward the ultimate goods of "emancipation and nationalization" in a United States that was "lagging in the march of modern civilization" due to the inhibiting anachronisms of "Slavery and 'State sovereignty.'"[119]

Similar challenges to pieties in the traditional American civic repertoire also followed. Burgess greatly esteemed Abraham Lincoln, not only because of Burgess's long-standing Unionist sentiments, but also because of Lincoln's clear and firm enunciation of the principle that the Union was logically and historically prior to the states, a principle resoundingly consonant with Burgess's own nationalism. He did not share Lincoln's devotion to the Declaration of Independence, however, a document to which Lincoln recurred again and again as the *fons et origo* of the American political experiment but for which Burgess had little regard. Burgess firmly rejected, for example, the notion that political societies were founded in any meaningful sense upon a social contract or popular assent.[120] As he pointed out, the belief that such an agreement could serve as "the starting-point in the evolution of the state" already presupposes "a highly developed state-life," in which "the idea of the state, with all its attributes, is consciously present in the minds of the individuals proposing to constitute the state"—conditions that "are attained only after the state has made several periods of its history." Instead, Burgess saw the state as product of "the gradual and continuous development of human society, out of a grossly imperfect beginning . . . towards a perfect and universal organization of mankind[,] . . . the gradual realization, in human institutions, of the universal principles of human nature, and the gradual subordination of the individual side of that nature to the universal side."[121]

The doctrine of the individual's inalienable natural rights, too, which held a conspicuous place in the declaration's argument, Burgess found "utterly impracticable and barren" as well as "unscientific, erroneous, and harmful."[122] The notion of *any* rights was inconceivable and unintelligible without the social entity from which they might arise, within which they would have meaning, and by means of which their legitimacy might be ensured. "There never was, and there never can be, any liberty upon this earth and among human beings outside of state organization. . . . Mankind acquires liberty through civilization. Liberty is as truly a creation of the state as is government."[123] For Burgess, liberty, in a word, was always and inevitably grounded in a corporate reality, inconceivable and unsustainable without reference to, and deference for, the social entity that produced and supported it. Like Edmund Burke, Burgess saw the rights some men deem to be natural and abstract as the precious and fragile accretion of many centuries of customary usage and law.

Such a corporate, anti-individualistic, historicist, and relativist understanding of liberty might, ironically, have been far more congenial to southerners like Jefferson Davis or George Fitzhugh than to northerners like Abraham Lincoln. Indeed, the patent racialism in Burgess's work that has dismayed many of his admirers was utterly consistent with his emphatic stress upon the primacy of the national unit, for a consensual and indivisible state-entity such as he envisioned would have required an almost completely homogeneous social composition to function properly.[124] Most likely, however, neither belligerent party would have felt very comfortable with Burgess's irreverent postbellum reading of their country's sacred declaration. As with the St. Louis Hegelians, Burgess's attachment to the notions of individual rights and popular sovereignty was equivocal, too deeply affected by his experience of the Civil War for him to endorse them unqualifiedly; he felt that it was precisely those popular freedoms, expressed in freestanding or excessive form, that had led the United States into the calamities of secession and anarchy. Just as the Christian understanding of liberty directed men and women toward conformity to the will of God, so the corporate understanding of liberty directed them toward conformity with the will of the nation and toward thereby recognizing the indivisible sovereignty of the state, which was posited to be the creator and sustainer of their freedoms. Were our society to regress toward a system "in which the sovereignty of the state was less and less perfectly developed," we would find "the liberty of the individual more and more uncertain and insecure, until at last the barbarism of individualism would begin to appear."[125] Like Bellamy, Ward, and the St. Louis Hegelians, Burgess saw individualism not as liberty but as a pit of iniquity, the Hobbesian war of all against all. Liberty, rightly understood, presumed a well-regulated social and political order.

It was ironic that the Civil War, among other things a pitched battle over the proper understanding of the Declaration of Independence—was it to be a magisterial nation-creating document, asserting the primacy of natural rights and making equality a bedrock and binding American principle? or was it a more narrowly focused brief for small-scale self-governance, with an explanation of the prior conditions for political separation?—should have given rise to a political science that regarded the most burning theoretical issues of the conflict as irrelevant, and the fighting words that had animated the revolution as intellectually obsolete. Yet the causes of this reversal of opinion were not hard to detect. The idea of the state as a great and historically inevitable instrument of advancing social cohesion not only addressed itself consolingly to an America that seemed to be careening toward sectional, ethnic, and class fragmentation. It also offered scholars an appealingly coherent focus of study that appeared to combine the conceptual fixity of idealism with the potential applications of empirical research. Hence, the postbellum idea of the state was an odd combination of the descriptive and the normative; it was partly an account of the way things actually were and partly a proclamation of what they ought to become.[126]

Burgess's central distinction between state and government, which plays off that odd combination, could easily begin to look like a shell game, in which any and all imperfections and malfeasances wrought by real existing states were facilely slipped into the sublunary category of government; thus the Platonic purity and sovereignty of the state could be preserved. Such a semantic tactic tended inevitably to render the state more and more hazy and metaphysical, able to maintain its purity precisely by its cloistered remoteness from experience. Formulation of that distinction also made it possible for Burgess to sustain, without fear of self-contradiction, a more traditional American commitment to individual liberty and laissez-faire—a commitment that seemed, at first blush, strikingly at odds with his statism. The key move in his strategy was to assign individual liberties to the realm of the state, where they could stand as vigilant and inviolable protections against the ever-present potential depredations of particular governments, which too often fell victim to the pathologies of tyranny, majoritarianism, venality, party politics, dema-goguery, and all the other tendencies of popular government.

High regard for individual liberty did not, however, translate into affection for democracy. Indeed, perhaps as a residue of his Whiggish background and Civil War experiences, Burgess nearly always evinced a deep suspicion of American democratic politics and of the sort of people it bred; "the active men," he sniffed, were "as a rule, that quarter of the electorate pecuniarily interested in the liquor saloons, the gambling-houses, the brothels, and in the schemes of organized labor," men "without any public sense" who were merely "bound together by class interest."[127] The saving salt in the American system was the Supreme Court, the most aristocratic branch of the federal government, valuable because of its faithfulness to the Constitution, its inde-pendence from the winds of popular sentiment, and its adherence to a rational and disinterested standard of justice.[128]

There were, then, significant tensions at work in Burgess's thought, ten-sions born of the fact that he—in ways very like Turner, Ward, and the St. Louis Hegelians—could not quite bring himself to accept the full implications of his own intellectual innovations. In particular, the supple antiformalism and empiricism inherent in his "sociological" understanding of the Constitution and of the origins of rights and liberties stood in stark contrast to his granite insistence upon the metaphysical reality of the idea of the state, the omega point of social evolution, an elusive entity whose existence stood both logically and ontologically prior to that of real governments. Clearly Burgess had little use for reference to absolutes grounded in unchanging Nature, but at the same time he was not enough of an antiformalist to abandon the teleological habits of thought that his Hegelianism had imparted to him—the sense that the succession of institutions in human history had indubitable structure and meaning. His distinction between state and government concealed the weight of a profound ambivalence: the same Teutonophile who worshiped at the altar of unlimited state sovereignty and extolled the virtues of an imperial Germany in its moment of triumph over the French also greatly feared the power of governments and praised the American system for providing protections against the influence of just such power.

Foreign relations presented him with a particularly vexing problem. Bur-gess was so transfixed by his vision of the national state as "the *ultima Thule* of political history" that he had tended to think of states as if they were space col-onies, freestanding units of analysis sufficient unto themselves when founded upon the proper constitutional basis.[129] This tendency, however, while an understandable outgrowth of his search for cohesion and unity, rendered him unable to get a firm grip on the transformations of American foreign policy occurring in his time, and those changes brought his ambivalences into the open, leaving him deeply confused and progressively embittered. His model of a state did not take sufficient account of the diplomatic and international dynamics, the embeddedness and entanglement in an unreliable outside world from which states are called into being and from which they derive much of their coherence and function.

The Spanish-American War marked, for him, a sinister development in the history of the United States. Not only did it prove "disastrous to American political civilization" by bringing the corruptions of nakedly imperial rule to American life and causing a fatal separation of Americans into two separate categories, "citizens and subjects," but it also led to a grotesque "exaggeration of government at the expense of liberty," which showed no signs of abating in the 1920s, when he began his memoirs.[130] The march of liberty in American history had reversed itself, and "now there remains hardly an individual immunity against governmental power which may not be set aside by government, at its own will and discretion, with or without reason, as government itself may determine."[131] A careful reader will notice, however, that Burgess himself, in his single most important work, justified the "imposition of Teutonic order on unorganized, disorganized, or savage people for the sake of their own civilization and their incorporation in the world society." This statement, he acknowledged, not only justified "the colonial system of the British Empire especially" but confirmed that the Teutonic states had a "great world-duty," a "manifest mission," to "interven[e] in the affairs of unorganized or insufficiently organized populations."[132] It was not clear why these imperatives of imperial noblesse oblige should not be applicable to Americans operating in the Caribbean and Asia.

If the Spanish-American War represented to Burgess the sowing of the first seeds of ruin, then the First World War was the bitter fruition. At first the war drew upon Burgess's warm and long-standing German affinities—personal, intellectual, and institutional. Above all, perhaps, he was influenced by a worldview that made him dogmatically certain of where the currents of history were carrying things. "History and ethnology," he had frequently and fervently asserted, "teach us that the Teutonic nations are the political nations of the modern era," "the great modern State builders," the pioneers of human progress to whom "the duty has fallen . . . of organizing the world politically."[133] Although his writings during the war were characterized by scholarly distance and evenhandedness, such statements marked him, as well as others of known or suspected pro-German sympathy, as a potential target for reprisals, which in Burgess's case included the abrupt and high-handed rescinding of an important contract to publish an abridged version of *Political Science and Comparative Constitutional Law*.[134]

At the moment the United States entered the war on the Allied side, Burgess felt the bottom fall out of his vision of a rational and normative political science, the life's mission to which he had felt called on that rainy, desolate night of sentry duty in Civil War Tennessee and to which his subsequent career had been devoted. That feeling could only grow, as he watched his beloved country fall not only into an anti-German war but under the sway of anti-German propaganda, much of it generated and orchestrated by the administration of his old political science colleague Woodrow Wilson. On "the sixth day of April, 1917," as he related in his memoirs, "with one grievous blow this vision was dispelled and my life's work brought down in irretrievable ruin all about me."[135] The great advocate of nationalism in theory had become a victim of nationalism in fact. His tendency to conflate Germany and America as emerging paragons of the modern state had received a rude shock. The confident believer in history's necessary track had found its locomotive bearing down on him instead.

Irretrievable ruin: surely there is an air of querulousness and self-dramatizing overstatement in this image, and that same dank atmosphere, at once despairing and defensive, often drifted into Burgess's unfinished and posthumously published memoirs. He mulishly clung to the very end to his precious distinction between state and government, as a defense against the charge of statism or Prussianism and as a way of fending off any sense of responsibility for the results he so vehemently deplored. He complained with considerable energy of what he saw as repeated misunderstandings and careless or willful misreadings by his critics, who persisted in misrepresenting his magnum opus as "the 'Leviathan' of modern political science" and its author as "the monster of political philosophy." Such criticisms clearly exasperated and wounded him, since he regarded himself as a friend to liberty; with a pathos tinged by vanity, he brooded that "I do not feel that [the *Political Science*] has ever been completely understood anywhere, although it was translated by competent linguists into German, French, Italian, Spanish, and Japanese."[136] Perhaps that was so. But his long, and exceptionally cogent, attempt to answer his critics one last time in the pages of his memoirs only showed that he had never really grasped what *they* were getting at either—that the idealist conception of the state to which Burgess was so deeply committed, even if it could be shown to be entirely innocent of malevolence or Hobbesianism, was irrelevant to an understanding of, and transformation of, American political reality.[137] By the pragmatic standard, which Burgess had only partly embraced but which was far more congenial to the coming generation of American political scientists, sociologists, and historians, any concept that could not be held accountable for the results it produced was a concept that was literally inconsequential. By that standard, there was no longer any need even to speak of Burgess's state.

So Burgess and his work drifted into the obscurity in which they languish today.[138] When he is remembered, he is generally classified as a postbellum conservative; it is certainly the case that, along with his faith in the omnicompetence of the state, he also advocated a largely laissez-faire government, a position that counted as conservative in his time. But the conservative designation (depending upon how one defines that term) may be only partly accurate. By discarding the notion of natural rights, or any other metasocial bulwark for individual freedom, Burgess was also entrusting the safekeeping of all such liberties to the authority of the social and historical matrix in which they originated. Such cultural organicism might indeed seem compatible, in some respects, with the temper of Burkean conservatism, but its antitraditionalism more closely resembled the historicism and social constructivism of Burgess's fellow Hegelian Karl Marx. The entire history of the evolving state, argued Burgess, was a succession of "fictions," "makeshifts," and "temporary supports," ranging from the mythology of divine revelation and of the God-given authority of priests and kings, to the countermonarchical myths of natural rights and social compacts. Each fiction, after having done its work successfully, had been properly demystified and "swept away." But now humankind had come to the moment when the mature nation-state was at last able to "take care of itself" without mythological props and to stand on its own rational foundation as "the realization of the universal in man."[139]

There were revolutionary choices implicit in this account, with immense implications for the coherence-seeking tendency in postbellum American intellectual life that Burgess exemplified. Their full significance seemed to elude Burgess, however, ensconced safely and comfortably within the fortified Hegelian categories he regarded as unassailable, and firmly, if paradoxically, committed to the doctrines of laissez-faire and limited government. His own private agony, in retrospect, was rather like that of the cautious revolutionary who endorses bold slogans but holds back from bold actions and eventually finds himself detested both by Jacobins in the van and by legitimists in the rear. The logic of demystification was not so easily stilled, however. Burgess's agonies were the stigmata of an innovator reluctant to yield to the full implications of his innovations. Yet the pattern thus set was not entirely idiosyncratic. In ways strikingly parallel to Turner, Ward, and the St. Louis Hegelians, Burgess proved an ambivalent consolidator whose ambivalences were characteristic of a transitional figure.

As Daniel Rodgers has nicely put it, Burgess was "an architect of the idea of the absolute, unlimited State, who found himself appalled at the idea that the State might take its powers seriously. . . . [He was] a devotee of the idea of the State who found the real thing deeply unnerving."[140] Ever since the personal and social terror of his Civil War experiences, he had been driven by a desire to find or create social and political cohesion, the kind he had found so tantalizingly figured in the Germanic notions of the state. He seemed not to have thought beyond that conviction, however, or to have taken into account the dangers of cohesion. A neat semantic distinction between state and government offered no shred of protection outside the seminar room. Nor did the essentially conservative Burgess reflect that the consolidation of the state as the self-conscious realization of rational, universal man might imply that the state should *do* something with its sovereignty, rather than sit back and passively observe. For his Progressive successors, practical and activist men and women imbued with the spirit of public service, that latter terminus became their starting point.

# 5

## The Search for Disinterestedness

It was difficult to dispatch convincingly the very individualistic premises challenged by the new postbellum order. The drive to formulate more comprehensive visions of social cohesion was too persistent and too pervasive to be easily derailed or deterred, however. If a thinker like Burgess resorted to an ungainly dualism wherein the analytical concept of a perfectly cohesive and authoritative state served only as an idealist fig leaf covering the chaotic, laissez-faire imperatives of actual government, there were other, more adventurous analysts willing to dispense with such devices altogether and follow the logic of cohesion and social embeddedness wherever it led. These Progressive intellectuals shared a belief in the fundamentally social etiology of entities, qualities, and principles that might in former times have claimed their ultimate ground in Nature or God. In his derogation of the concept of natural rights as a fiction, Burgess had already begun to reach toward such a belief in a halting and partial way. The emerging model of consolidation, however, was increasingly accompanied by a more thoroughgoing "socialization of mind," an assertion of the social, relative, accretional, and evolutionary character of such fundamental concepts as law, rights, and morality. This was not just a reorientation of thought toward social ends. It was a bold assertion of thought's ineluctably social origins. Such reconceiving represented a stunning reversal of the antebellum Emersonian claim that society was nothing more than "a joint-stock company," to which naturally free and independent individuals should steadfastly refuse to surrender their liberty.

On the contrary, in an age of incorporation and interdependence, all social reality was beginning to resemble a joint-stock company, in which no individual was less than fully vested. Postbellum and fin-de-siècle thinkers accordingly came to regard the self not as a hard, well-defined object endowed with objective rational capabilities and imprescriptible natural rights, but as a more or less plastic expression of intersecting social and cultural forces, a permeable entity with indistinct boundaries and a fundamentally adaptive nature. One could turn to any number of influential thinkers from that period, men and women who might otherwise differ in important ways—Edward A. Ross, Lester Frank Ward, George Herbert Mead, Thorstein Veblen, Richard Ely, William James, Washington Gladden, William Graham Sumner, Mary Parker Follett, Charles Sanders Peirce, Josiah Royce, Walter Rauschenbusch, G. Stanley Hall, Albion Small, Jane Addams, Charles Horton Cooley, Oliver Wendell Holmes, James Harvey Robinson, Charles A. Beard, James Mark Baldwin, John Dewey—and nevertheless find them in substantial agreement with all or most of that formulation. The loose intellectual movement that Morton White called a "revolt against formalism," a movement that stood at the heart of Progressive social thought, also challenged the concept of the separate, efficacious, bourgeois, classical-liberal self in all its manifestations: psychological, social, moral, religious, economic, legal, and political.[1]

That there was a necessary connection between the rejection of the notion of permanent and universal intelligible forms and the questioning of permanent and efficacious selfhood was not immediately apparent. Indeed, nearly all of White's antiformalists saw their work as profoundly empowering, rescuing intellect from the dead hand of obsolete deductive categories and releasing it into a dynamic and experimental relationship with a fluid reality. Certainly the jurisprudence of Oliver Wendell Holmes, Jr., the philosophical writings of William James and John Dewey, the social criticism of Thorstein Veblen, and the historical thought of Charles Beard and James Harvey Robinson all seemed to embody fresh and liberatory elements: a disdain for abstract and disembodied ideals; a respect for the precise details of concrete human experience; a reverence for the experimental methods of modern science, with a faith in their applicability to human phenomena; a conviction that the apprehension of truth is not the passive absorption of static essences but a continuous adaptive process requiring the active participation of the ordering intellect; and an insistence that thinkers engage in concrete problem solving rather than the fruitless (and untestable) posturings of metaphysical speculation. Such thinkers were a world apart from the formulaic dualism, originating in the influence of German idealism, that had hardened the arteries of nineteenth-century American academic philosophy into the debility George Santayana diagnosed as "the genteel tradition." Here, instead, were minds that seemed to break free of all disingenuous gentility and stale parlor dualisms to allow American voices to speak at last in open and confidently American accents. Their achievement would seem to represent the triumph of the Emersonian intellectual project, if "the heart of American pragmatism," as Hilary Putnam has written, was "the supremacy of the agent point of view."[2]

Only a partial application of the antiformalist agenda could vindicate such Emersonian accents, however. Something important had been sacrificed in the apostolic succession. By applying a combination of historicism and cultural organicism to comprehend the complex interdependency of social phenomena, these thinkers had greatly invigorated the realm of ideas, casting doubt upon the applicability of rigidly formal, universal, abstract, deductive, or legalistic structures of thought and substituting for them a pragmatic or instrumental standard of truth, clearly modeled upon the ever-shifting dynamics of Darwinian natural science. But consistency required that the same combination of influences be turned back on thought itself and point out that the same multiplicity of historical and cultural influences conditioned the would-be autonomous self. If laws, institutions, and ideas were formations adaptive to the peculiar requirements of their time and place, so too was the would-be heroic intellectual embedded in the very structures of time, space, culture, and history that he had insisted upon imputing to others. Antiformalist premises eliminated any Archimedean place to stand. As James Kloppenberg has pointed out in his recent study of Progressive intellectuals, coming to terms with this conundrum meant a frank acceptance of epistemological uncertainty, a recognition of the inevitably social, pragmatic, and contingent character of all knowledge.[3] The price paid for such uncertainty, however, for such acceptance of the individual intellect's fallibility, was increasing social embeddedness and dependency. More specifically, it meant subjecting one's particular perspectives, one's genius, to the scrutiny and ultimate judgment of specialized communities of inquiry—professionalized, disinterested "communities of the competent" that were to serve as validating agencies for the determination of what could stand as scientific truth. Truth was not only socially contingent; it was, increasingly, socially defined by the procedural reality of peer review, a procedure extending laterally into social space and forward indefinitely in time, a web of synchrony and diachrony—a corporate, social substitute for an Archimedean point.[4]

This effort went much further than Burgess or Ward had been able to go, but it did not eliminate all of the tensions or vestigial notions with which they struggled. One thinks again of Turner, whose commitment to the scientific professionalization of historical writing warred with his esteem for the erstwhile adventurer Ulysses, and with the Sturm und Drang of his own bouts with writing. Few resisted the corporate tendency more valiantly and held out more stubbornly for the Emersonian model of heroic intellect than William James. When asked to join the American Philosophical Association (APA) in 1901, James refused, defiantly declaring that "the philosopher is a lone beast dwelling in his individual burrow."[5] For better or worse, however, a distillation of the psychology of self-sacrifice and disinterested service that James would adumbrate nine years later in his great essay on the "moral equivalent of war" came a good deal closer to describing the requirements of a modern "culture of inquiry"; and in the end, James acquiesced and joined the APA.[6] James's hesitation is as important as his acquiescence. James was devoted to the epistemological model of science, though, and as his sometime Harvard colleague Charles S. Peirce understood (perhaps better than he), the growing dominance of science would involve not the triumph of the individualistic lone-wolf intellect, but a yielding of individual authority to an increasingly cohesive, corporate, professionalized locus of authority—a yielding that, whatever its distinctive premises and its empowering objectives, was in the end not unlike the self-yielding exacted by a religious or military vocation.

The term *disinterested*, which is, significantly, so frequently misunderstood and misused in our own time, carried a powerfully ethical, almost religious weight in Progressive social thought, for no word was freighted with more negative weight in the vocabulary of Progressivism than the noun *interests*. A favorite epithet hurled here and there by the era's muckraking journalists (and the modern descendant of the civic-humanist and Harringtonian bugbear of "the monied interests"), "the Interests" not only stood for the specific venality of Standard Oil and the other "trusts" or for other self-interested organized political pressure groups. In a deeper sense it came to stand, in a vague but compelling way, for the pernicious values of individualism, particularism, self-seeking, and growing structural inequality. It stood for everything that threatened to corrupt the great American experiment in political democracy, everything that thwarted the Progressive dream of a restored social integrity, of a centralized, consolidated, and cooperative commonwealth.[7] So disinterestedness stood for a contrasting vision of hope that promoted and reinforced its version of Christian self-sacrificial values in public life: common subjection to the rule of the common good. But it also meant an unsullied ideal of theoretical and practical expertise, to be conscientiously, impartially, and selflessly administered by an enlightened "new middle class" trained in the burgeoning new research universities, the nation's new factories of the scientific and action-oriented knowledge needed to produce a just and rationally ordered public realm. Such a new middle class would not be imprisoned by the shortsighted pursuit of self-interest or the false individualism of classical-liberal economics; it would instead be bound by the self-regulating and rational autonomy of professional organizations and the uncorrupted social altruism of those trained to identify the public interest and pursue the common weal. Contrary to the rhetoric about "warfare" between science and religion, the two had in common their stress upon the singular virtue of disinterestedness. Progressive intellectuals believed this same virtue could reform and redefine the arena of politics, thereby reviving the civic-humanist notion of a res publica adapted to the conditions of modern industrial polity and society and thereby successfully addressing the same pathologies of American individualism that had bedeviled Whitman and Bellamy.[8]

The confluence of religion, science, and politics emerged distinctly in the generation of political economists who formed the American Economic Association (AEA) in 1885, and particularly in the works and person of a figure like Richard Ely, the AEA's first secretary. During his postgraduate studies in Heidelberg during the 1870s, Ely had come under the influence of Karl Knies and the German historical school of economics; this led him to reject the classical liberalism that had long dominated the field and to embrace instead the relativity and mutability of economic truth.[9] Like Bellamy, he was drawn toward the ideal of the commonweal, of social solidarity, wholeness, and reconciliation, rather than Marxian inevitable class conflict. Men, in his view, had formed themselves in "a social and industrial organism, whose numberless parts are in infinite variety of manner interdependent. Infinite interrelations! Infinite interdependence!" Yet the economist was not to be a mere passive observer and recorder of clashing autonomous forces but a creative analyst and forger of ethical norms called to direct the ongoing "social growth of mankind." As Ely remarked in the statement of principles he wrote for the AEA, "We regard the state as an agency whose positive assistance is one of the indispensable conditions of human progress." The conflict raging between labor and capital could only be solved, moreover, by "the united efforts of church, state, and science."[10]

Ely's triple endorsement of science, government, and religion suggests how growing confidence in the disciplined methods of natural science and the remedial power of government were so often linked (as they were in his case) to the furtherance of Protestant ethical imperatives. The early sociological profession in America was overwhelmingly dominated by Protestant clergymen, ex-clergymen, offspring of clergymen, and seminary students, all of whom had been attracted to the field of sociology as a potent new means of advancing the evangelistic mission of their faith.[11] For example, Albion Small, founding chairman of the sociology department at the University of Chicago, founding editor of the *American Journal of Sociology*, president of the American Sociological Society, and the first occupant of an American university chair in sociology, regarded his discipline as "a science . . . of God's image," "a moral philosophy conscious of its task"—and that task was nothing less than "an approximation of the ideal of social life contained in the Gospels." Social science was "the holiest sacrament open to men," devoted to "laying the individualistic superstition" and to ensuring that human experience was not seen as an "affair of aggregated monads." Instead, Small asserted, "we live, move and have our being as members one of another." Here was the logic of the fundamental Christian injunction, "Whoso would save his life must lose it," now dressed not in military garb but in the language of sociology.[12]

For those liberal Protestants who still held passionately to the essential spirit of the gospel but could no longer accept the strict and literal authority of Scripture or of traditional creeds and dogma, it made sense to rescue and reinvigorate the gospel by socializing it, by recasting its self-sacrificial ethical imperatives to address the needs of a modern, interdependent society.[13] This strategy had ample forerunners in the American Protestant past, which was well furnished with efforts to realize a new Zion through creation of a sanctified worldly order. Never before, however, had the proponents of such holy experiments been so willing to neutralize or negate the gospel's individual and otherworldly thrust by insisting upon its translation into strictly social terms. Such emphasis upon social and structural considerations had the effect of downplaying, sometimes to the vanishing point, the traditional evangelical concern with the moral accountability before God of every individual soul. The reinforcing combination of social Christianity and social science not only contributed in crucial ways to a climate of anti-individualism, but it led many to regard the very concept of personal responsibility as an "unhelpful" way to think about "the social causation of untoward behavior."[14] Such thinking was perhaps most notably offered by Walter Rauschenbusch, the most subtle and intellectually penetrating of the proponents of a social gospel, who argued in 1907 that "we have the possibility of so directing religious energy by scientific knowledge that a comprehensive and continuous reconstruction of social life in the name of God is within the bounds of human possibility."[15] Church, state, and science had a common standard of disinterestedness, a devotion to higher, transpersonal ends.

The ends might be transpersonal, but they were not transcendental, at least not in any Emersonian sense. Disinterestedness, properly understood, was firmly grounded in the concrete collective life of human society. Such was the contention of Charles Peirce, who devoted much of his professional energy to a rigorous investigation of the logic of the sciences. That inquiry led him to assert that truth necessarily relies upon social validation.[16] The search for truth was inevitably bound up in the conditions of human beings' limited and social nature; hence, there was no more ardent foe of individualism than Peirce. "The individual man," he argued, writing in the Columbian Exposition year of 1893, "since his separate existence is manifested only by ignorance and error, so far as he is anything apart from his fellows, and from what he and they are to be, is only a negation." Though congruent in some respects with the contemporaneous reflections of Turner and Ward, Peirce's view suggested a far more radical communitarianism. Reality itself, he argued, "depends on the ultimate decision of the community," since "the very origin of the conception of reality shows that this conception essentially involves the notion of a COMMUNITY, without definite limits, and capable of a definite increase of knowledge." Independent thought has "only a potential existence, dependent on the future thought of the community."[17]

> When we come to the great principle of continuity and see how all is fluid and every point directly partakes the being of every other, it will appear that *individualism and falsity are one and the same.* Meantime, we know that man is not whole as long as he is single, that he is essentially a possible member of society. Especially, one man's experience is nothing if it stands alone. . . . Individual action is a means and not our end. . . . We are all putting our shoulders to the wheel for an end that none of us can catch more than a glimpse at—that which the generations are working out.[18]

The pursuit of science, no less than the pursuit of social solidarity, held up an ideal of self-overcoming. The logic of scientific inquiry requires "that our interests . . . must not stop at our own fate," for logic is "rooted in the social principle"; its "great principle" is "self-surrender." Because there is "a residuum of error in every individual's opinions," individual thoughts must submit themselves to the test of consensus and time. That self-sacrifice, Peirce added, must be genuine, heartfelt, and complete; it is not enough for "the self . . . to lie low for the sake of an ultimate triumph." Such covert pursuit of individualism while clad in the sheep's clothing of self-negation can never be permitted to be "the governing purpose."[19] Religion, too, Peirce believed to be potentially a powerful force of social reconstruction through self-sacrifice. Declaiming in Bellamyesque martial accents, he called upon religion to be "sworn in as a regiment of that great army that takes life in hand, with all its delights, in grimmest fight to put down the principle of self-seeking, and to make the principle of love triumphant."[20]

Such a radical view was not without its countervailing tensions, however, which should not be passed over. There is considerable irony in the fact that Peirce, who argued so strenuously for the inevitable social consecration of the offerings of any thinker, was in his own life an isolated, outcast misfit of a man who could not hold onto a university position and who never managed to become accepted into the very sort of community of inquiry he so ardently championed.[21] That fact lends a hidden pathos to his reflection that civilization is "the process whereby man with all his miserable littlenesses, becomes gradually more and more inbued with the spirit of God."[22] His social marginality apparently made him feel all the more keenly the yearning to belong, to be connected, even though (or perhaps because) his willful personality and stubbornly maverick ways—in short, his own incurable individualism—perhaps ensured such connectedness could never be securely achieved in his own life.

His case recalls the shrewd observations of his younger contemporary Jane Addams, who acknowledged that profound subjective needs as much as objective conditions lay behind the creation of social settlements like her own Hull-House. Addams felt that educated and cultivated young middle-class people (especially educated young women like herself) were oppressed by an overwhelming sense of "uselessness," of disconnection from the real pulsating life of the "great mass of humanity" (the "race-life," as she called it). Social service was for them an opportunity to recover true social connection, a connectedness modeled upon "the wonderful fellowship [and] true democracy of the early Church." The subjective need for settlements demonstrated that the "solidarity of the human race" was not only an ethical imperative but a psychological and spiritual one too, since no strictly individual salvation was possible. A settlement united people like "a thousand voices singing the Hallelujah Chorus in Handel's 'Messiah,'" their differences "lost in the unity of purpose and in the fact that they are all human voices lifted by a high human motive."[23]

Addams's internal struggle, then, echoed the disparity, in Peirce's experience, between a consensual understanding of truth and a disassociated, radically separated social existence: the gnawing sense of personal disconnection that, for them and others, quietly and subjectively fueled the self-transcending spirit of social science and social Christianity alike. Some elements in Addams's struggle were more distinctly her own, however, and therefore carry their own significance. They reflected the problems faced by an altruistic and reform-minded woman attempting to negotiate the territory between the public (and male) realm of equality and the private (and female) realm of difference, while respecting the legitimacy of both. Like other nineteenth-century feminists active in public reform movements, Addams often justified women's public role as a necessary extension of their private domestic responsibilities, particularly their role as inculcators, guardians, and trustees of their families' moral sensibilities.[24] In arguing for the extension to women of the right to vote, a quintessential mark of public and civic equality, Addams began by conceding that woman's duty "within the walls of her own home" was, and would continue to be, her "paramount obligation"; but she then went on to argue that the conditions of modern society had made it "necessary that woman shall extend her sense of responsibility to many things outside of her own home if she would continue to preserve the home in its entirety."[25] Such a position was rather different from the gender neutrality sought by, for example, the pioneering feminist educator M. Carey Thomas, founding dean and later president of Bryn Mawr College.[26] In Addams's view, women needed to become a force in the public realm in order to rule properly over their entrusted private domain. Such a position attempted to keep faith with the separate-spheres vision of Catharine Beecher and, before that, the postrevolutionary concept of Republican motherhood, even as it was challenging the male monopoly of the public sphere in practice.[27]

Addams's efforts at Hull-House, and the more general settlement movement it exemplified, perfectly mirrored this complicated task. The idea was to have young, idealistic, educated, and reform-oriented men and women come to live in houses situated in poor, urban working-class and immigrant areas, where they would provide the needy residents with practical help, training in life skills, and intellectual and moral uplift.[28] It was as if the prospective benefits of home-as-haven were being expanded outward, as settlement houses would progressively bring the confusion and brutality of the dissociated urban world under control within the gentle, protective confines of these model habitations of calm, grace, intelligence, and order. At its most grandiose, the settlement movement almost seemed aimed toward the progressive domestication of the world, by combining the nurturant maternal conscience of the loving layperson with the rational and disinterested research techniques of the emerging new social science clerisy—the two sides, as it were, of disinterestedness.[29] As Addams was also candid enough to admit, however, Hull-House was also designed to address the psychological needs of intellectuals like herself (and women like herself) who were dogged by the sense that they were separated from "the great mass of humanity," a feature that sharply distinguished Addams's motives from the standard Whig-Protestant missionary rhetoric (although the settlement movement frequently suffered from some of the same tendencies toward social-controlling paternalism).[30] Both features, in any event, promoted the same goal: a sense of connectedness, of solidarity, of being "at home" in modern urban society, forsaking self to blend together in one mighty hallelujah chorus whose unity and power prefigured the solidarity of the human race.

The domesticizing thrust in Addams's thought was further evidenced by her relative disinclination to use military metaphors for solidarity (the lyrics of "Onward Christian Soldiers" notwithstanding). Her autobiographical account of the metanoia that she said had turned her toward the establishment of Hull-House is revealing in this regard. Addams's biographer Allen F. Davis is probably right in claiming that Addams had greatly embellished the story in her retelling for dramatic effect, engaging in the sort of mythmaking and self-creation that all autobiographers are tempted by.[31] Still, her choice of dramatic effects is highly indicative in itself. She had attended a bullfight in Madrid in April 1888, during a period of aimless European travel, and had found herself, to the horror of her companions, sitting calmly through the killing of five bulls and "many more horses," taking in that primal and bloody gladiatorial spectacle in cool fascination. Later, however, she recoiled from her act with a sense of self-loathing and disgust at "the entire moral situation" this episode had revealed in her. She reproached herself with the thought that, though she was always making grand plans for her life, in the end she always deferred them indefinitely and instead chose to be a spectator to the senseless cruelties of life, "tied to the tail of the veriest ox-cart of self-seeking." But that would henceforth change, she decided; she returned to Chicago and energetically launched into the foundation of Hull-House with her dear friend and longtime companion Ellen Gates Starr.

Though a psychoanalytic reading of this story virtually leaps off the page, it also suggests something far more important: Addams wanted to present the settlement-home idea of solidarity and self-transcendence as a direct challenge and civilizing antidote to the primal impulses of a violent and predatory world. Seven years before William James's essay on the moral equivalent of war, Addams was already speaking of the need for a "moral substitute for war."[32] Here too for her, as in other matters, the distinctive moral vision she attributed to women was of crucial importance. The pacifism with which she increasingly became identified, especially after the beginning of the First World War, was securely linked to her feminism. It was women, she argued, whose nurturant capacity—the "maternal affection and solicitude in woman's remembering heart"—gave them a special role in the preservation of life and the establishment of settled communities, of settlements. The extension of suffrage to women, she trusted, would serve as a purifying, domesticating force to counterbalance the violent, chaotic, coarsened hearts of the men who ruled. The outbreak of a world war had made the need for this impulse more imperative.[33] "As women we are the custodians of the life of the ages," she wrote in 1915, the year of the disastrous Gallipoli campaign and the sinking of the *Lusitania*, "and we will no longer consent to its reckless destruction."[34] Whatever the validity of her gender characterizations, two other things about Addams's views are well clarified by them: the virtues of self-sacrifice, self-transcendence, and social solidarity were virtues only if they were harnessed to a true public purpose; and she would no longer trust the nation-state to articulate that purpose. "In celebrations of selfless male action in wartime," Jean Elshtain has rightly written, "Addams sees a centuries-old trail of tears."[35] But Addams was not the only one. The trail she saw was the same flow that Bret Harte had glimpsed on a still postbellum night, moving silently and steadily down the emptiness of a darkened Pennsylvania Avenue.

------

No one articulated the political implications of the Progressive creed of social solidarity and disinterestedness more comprehensively than Herbert Croly, critic and founding editor of *The New Republic*. While Addams, true to her view of the feminine mind, tended to be at her best when she was most concrete and particular, Croly was comfortable with a far-ranging consideration of highly abstract philosophical issues. If Addams's combination of Protestant Christianity, feminism, and pacifism led her to suspect the nation-state, Croly, who had been christened shortly after birth into the religion of humanity by his ardently Comtean parents, was more willing to trust in the blessings of consolidation.[36] Indeed, his landmark opus, *The Promise of American Life* (1909), addressed nearly every important issue raised by the postbellum transformation of American life: nationalization, economic consolidation, specialization, labor unions, the influence of business corporations, the relationship of federal to state and local governments, foreign policy, reform movements, and many other such matters. Croly is perhaps best known for his assertion that under modern social and economic conditions it had become necessary to use "Hamiltonian means" (a vigorous national government) to achieve "Jeffersonian ends" (the preservation of democratic values). All these considerations, however, were related at bottom to a new conception of the individual, with which Croly intended to sweep away the outmoded model of the "pioneer" that had dominated previous American social thought.

Croly, then, had little good to say about the character traits that Frederick

Jackson Turner identified with the frontier legacy: the economic and social individualism ("licensed selfishness") that Croly associated with the political vision of Thomas Jefferson, traits epitomized in his mind by the unruly western Democrats of the antebellum era. It is significant, however, that for all his concurrence in the anti-individualist currents of thought in his times, Croly did not wish to abandon the word *individualism* (or, as he sometimes preferred to say, *individuality*) but rather to redefine it. Perhaps it was because Croly addressed political and social issues, in which he was likely to be read by a broad spectrum of readers, that he felt the need to rehabilitate the word rather than proscribe it. Whatever the reasons, and whatever confusions he introduced by his own vocabulary—for he himself felt free to use *individualism* in either sense—there was perhaps no writer before or since who has employed the word *disinterested* with greater frequency or forced it to bear a more critical argumentative weight.

In the economic realm, Croly felt, individualism had become particularly disastrous and self-negating: "The popular enjoyment of practically unrestricted economic opportunities is precisely the condition which makes for individual bondage."[37] The reason for this was simple: the economic system as presently constituted compromised a man as much in his success as in his failure, for the system's emphasis upon "acquisitive motives" forced all men into a common mold, namely, that of cash value. Yet that, Croly argued, is not really what individuality is all about. "The truth is," he continued, "that individuality cannot be dissociated from the pursuit of a disinterested object." Such a man distinguishes himself by the excellence of his work, for any disinterested achievement has "unequivocal social value," since it "reunites [the individual] with his fellows." Such reunification could have boundless ramifications; by thus making himself an individual (as Croly defined the word), he "made an essential contribution to national fulfillment."[38] By the same token, the coalescence of the nation as fact and idea would enable the fullest possible individual development: "The individual American will never obtain a sufficiently complete chance of self-expression, until the American nation has earnestly undertaken and measurably achieved the realization of its collective purpose." Any success in "the achievement of the national purpose will contribute positively to the liberation of the individual."[39]

As those last words imply, Croly's *Promise* was a brief for national consolidation, firmly committed to the curtailment of sectional antagonisms and the reorganization of state and local authority, all in favor of a powerful central government. Nationalism was a sine qua non: "No permanent good," he asserted, "can come to the individual and society except through the preservation and development of the existing system of nationalized states."[40] Croly, then, saw the problem of nationalism in continuum with the problem of individualism. He was alarmed at the "vast incoherent mass of the American people" and feared the country was "falling into definite social groups, which restrict and define the mental outlook and social experience of their members." Here he was not only concerned with what we might today call the Balkanization of American politics; he was also concerned with the perils of a social disaggregation wrought by specialization and extreme division of labor. The task of nationalizing was much the same as the one faced by those who would rescue and reintegrate the separate self: the creation of "a conscious social ideal" to take the place of a lost and outdated "instinctive homogeneity" based upon religious and ethnic uniformity, which it was neither possible nor desirable to recover.[41] Nevertheless, Croly believed that "in one way or another such solidarity must be restored."[42] Croly did not oppose specialization per se, but he did believe that only within a national structure that created "special niches" where each individual could exercise his talents disinterestedly could there be any real individual self-realization. Recurring to one of the oldest tropes in political thought, the analogy at the center of Plato's *Republic*, Croly declared that the individual was "a nation in miniature," while the nation was "an enlarged individual . . . in whose life every individual should find some particular but essential function."[43]

Croly's survey of the history of American political thought underscored his nationalist sympathies. The Hamilton-Jefferson conflict during the Washington administration was the starting point in this account. In Croly's eyes, Hamilton's "constructive" nationalism made him a "finer man" and "sounder thinker and statesman" than Thomas Jefferson, whom Croly thought an "amiable enthusiast" for democracy at best and a dangerous purveyor of "intellectual superficiality and insincerity" at worst.[44] Although Jefferson was resoundingly correct in insisting that his country was "nothing, if not a democracy," his impoverished definition of democracy was "tantamount to extreme individualism," a form of social organization designed strictly for "the greatest satisfaction of its individual members" and to guard at all costs against the growth of a strong central government.[45] Jefferson's logical successor, Andrew Jackson, was an unmitigated disaster, destroying a salutary national institution (the Bank of the United States) and replacing an honest class of public-spirited officials with partisan cronies and spoilsmen. The popular orators of the "Jacksonian Democratic tradition" followed in the Jeffersonian line, mouthing a similar version of individualism that had "not the remotest conception" of a "gallant and exclusive devotion to some disinterested, and perhaps unpopular moral, intellectual, or technical purpose."[46] Senator Stephen A. Douglas stood firmly in this tradition through his championing of the antinational concept of "popular sovereignty," a notion that would make the democratic principle "equivalent to utter national incoherence and irresponsibility."[47] The most recent spokesman for this Jeffersonian tradition had been the benighted William Jennings Bryan, a man born "a few generations too late" and devoted to "anti-nationalist" and "Jacksonian" prejudices, which included "dislike of organization and of the faith in expert skill, in specialized training, and in large personal opportunities and responsibilities which are implied by a trust in organization." Such backwardness had decisively "disqualified him for effective leadership of the party of reform."[48]

Croly's political heroes, on the other hand, tended to be nationalists above all else, beginning with the paradigmatic example of Hamilton. Adequate examples taken from American history were few and far between, however, an indication of the tight grip in which, he believed, populistic and antinational conceptions of democracy held American political thinking. The desert of post-Jeffersonian nineteenth-century statesmanship was relieved only by the extraordinary figure of Abraham Lincoln, the savior nationalist par excellence. Lincoln won his debates with Douglas, and thereby Croly's fervent admiration, because in embracing the national ideal he also embraced the highest democratic ideal and therefore demonstrated the ultimate compatibility of the two. Although a western man, and often depicted as the quintessential Man of the People, Lincoln was "vastly more and better" than the milieu he had come out of, Croly asserted; he was in fact "an example of high and disinterested intellectual culture."[49] He "had made for himself a second nature, compact of insight and loving-kindness," a Christlike magnanimity that rose above the petty individualism of his time and place. He had also come into a profound sense of humility, which had imbued him with "the most fruitful and the most universal of all religious ideas."[50] Small wonder that Croly compared Lincoln's selflessness to the selflessness of St. Francis of Assisi, who was supposed (as Croly must surely have known) to have experienced the miracle of the stigmata at his death.[51] The great national martyr had found the highest fulfillment by making himself "the individual instrument whereby an essential and salutary national purpose was fulfilled."[52] Moreover, the qualities of "intelligence, humanity, magnanimity, and humility" he embodied were precisely the virtues Americans need to become better democrats—and "just the qualities which Americans are prevented by their individualistic practice and tradition from attaining or properly valuing."[53]

The one hopeful sign on the immediate horizon was the vigorous nationalist who had recently come out of Lincoln's party, which Croly called "the party of national responsibility." Although conceding that Theodore Roosevelt's accomplishments had been limited, Croly nevertheless praised him for yoking the cause of reform to "the national idea." Indeed, he fancied Roosevelt a "Thor wielding with power and effect a sledge-hammer in the cause of national righteousness." Through mighty and enlightened efforts to produce a "nationalization of reform," Roosevelt had proposed to use a powerful federal government to make America "a more complete democracy in organization and practice"; thus his "devotion both to the national and to the democratic ideas," a prerequisite for political wisdom in Croly's eyes, was "thorough-going and absolute." In contrast to the Jeffersonian-Jacksonian-Bryanite antipathy to the authority of scientifically trained experts, Roosevelt endeavored to give such men "a better opportunity to serve the public," not only by appointing them to public office but by giving them the administrative machinery that would enable them to use their abilities effectively."[54]

We know that Roosevelt, having just left the presidency, read *The Promise of American Life* with great appreciation. We do not know whether it had any significant influence upon the vision put forward in Roosevelt's famous 1910 "New Nationalism" address at Osawatomie, Kansas, aside from providing Roosevelt with the speech's title.[55] In the opinion of most Roosevelt scholars, the influence probably ran the other way. In a sense, though, it matters very little who influenced whom, for the conjunction of the two works gives evidence of a shared outlook. The speech evidenced the degree to which Roosevelt had succeeded in giving practical political expression to at least part of the same creed of disinterestedness Croly and his other intellectual contemporaries had attempted to articulate, albeit with precisely the martial accents that Addams disdained.

To begin with, Roosevelt sounded the mystic chords of memory by invoking the Civil War as the source and standard of national solidarity. We all now stand in awe, he intoned, of "the valor and the disinterestedness and the love of the right[,] . . . the sincerity [and] self-devotion" shown by those who fought in the war. To the veterans of the Grand Army of the Republic, "the republic owes its all"; because of them we belong "not to one of a dozen little squabbling commonwealths" but to a consolidated nation, "the mightiest nation upon which the sun shines." Theirs was a pattern to be emulated. This meant that "in civil life" Americans should be governed by "what [they] fought for in the Civil War," that civil life should be carried on in "the spirit in which the army was carried on." That meant one thing above all else: "We must," he declared, "drive the special interests out of politics." Our government, both federal and local, must be freed from the interests' "sinister influence or control," and the only plausible guarantor of the public interest was a strong and independent central government. As a political and economic consolidationist, Roosevelt had long ago decided that industrial combination was the result of imperative economic laws and that a powerful national state was best situated to correct the abuses and regulate the problems caused by such combination. Although he recognized the inequities of the present system, he repudiated open class conflict as a means of addressing them, and he raised instead an ideal of solidarity and class reconciliation along with an inner transformation. The proper remedial legislation or administrative organization would not accomplish anything unless it were accompanied by a transformation of heart on the individual level, "a genuine and permanent moral awakening" that would make Americans just as disinterestedly devoted to the duties of citizenship as members of the Grand Army were to the duties of war.[56]

Roosevelt was hitting all the right notes, harmonizing religious and nationalist sentiment with the call to transcend "interestedness." Even so, there would be something inescapably odd in the spectacle of Jane Addams and Herbert Croly crusading for a Bullmoose presidency in 1912, as both did. No one stood more vehemently for classically Victorian, individualistic, and masculine conceptions of moral character and moral responsibility than Theodore Roosevelt. He managed to embody in his person all the scattered connotations of the word *virtue*: a conflation of the moralistic Victorian notion of virtue as propriety and restraint, with the more active and classical-republican notion of public virtue—and, not least, with the insistently masculine and martial Machiavellian connotations of *virtù*.[57] An economic and political consolidationist he may have been, but as Edmund Morris has remarked, Roosevelt's favorite adjective was *manly* and his favorite pronoun was *I*.[58] The legendary saga of Roosevelt's boisterous and swaggering life, from his Wild West sojourns to his nocturnal anticorruption patrols as New York police commissioner to his hyped Rough Rider career and his periodic sanguinary hunting expeditions, not to mention his famed advocacy of big sticks, suggested something more complicated, and split-minded, than the steady and progressive consolidationist Croly wanted to find in him. Despite his social consciousness, Roosevelt was convinced that a man's ultimate development occurred through times of testing and ordeal, through triumphant exposure to solitary extremity and life-threatening conflict, through the agon of "the strenuous life." Indeed, Roosevelt's 1922 book by that name used as its epigraph the same poem, Tennyson's "Ulysses," that had spoken so eloquently to the divided heart of Frederick Jackson Turner.[59] Its similar use suggests a similar division of mind. Perhaps Roosevelt, in his own odd and unreflective way, was trying to act out the conflicting premises at the heart of Progressivism, linking its attraction to antiformalism and its assertion of our world's essentially social, corporate, and fluid nature with its activism, its desire to unleash the power of personal agency upon a plastic world.

The failure of the Progressive party's 1912 campaign did nothing to dim Herbert Croly's admiration for Roosevelt; indeed, if anything, his distaste for Wilsonian progressivism, with its persistent Jeffersonian echoes, made TR's star shine all the brighter in his eyes. If *Progressive Democracy* (1914), based upon his 1913 Godkin lectures at Harvard, was partly a valentine to Roosevelt, it was also partly a poison-pen letter to Wilson. But *Progressive Democracy* also built in significant ways upon the argument of *Promise*. If *Promise* had emphasized the division between Hamiltonian and Jeffersonian political philosophy, *Progressive Democracy*, while building upon that framework, also gravitated toward a slightly different dichotomy, highly suggestive of the opposition between the formalist and the antiformalist. From the revolution onward, he said, Americans had been divided between two different views of the sources of political authority: a view that placed its faith in the people, and another that profoundly suspected the people and instead rested authority in the formal and procedural safeguards of the Constitution. It was time, Croly argued, to throw off the artificial constraints of the latter and yield to the fresh insights offered by the former. His call for faith alluded to the classic Christian opposition between law and spirit; a genuine democracy with faith in its people would naturally become "progressive and ascendant," while one without such faith would cling to "some specific formulation of a supposedly or temporarily righteous Law."[60] Moreover, the fulfillment of Croly's vision of progressive democracy was a faith that, "like the faith of St. Paul, finds its consummation in a love which is . . . a spiritual expression of the mystical unity of human nature." Yet such a faith would also lead to a reordered, post-economic society in which each member would be able to realize fully his individuality without the distortions of soul wrought by an outmoded system burdened by competition and legalism.[61]

Although Theodore Roosevelt liked *Progressive Democracy* a great deal, even (modestly) consenting to review it in *The Outlook*, the book never enjoyed the wide readership and influence of *Promise*, and it has since been largely forgotten.[62] But two features of this later formulation of Croly's views are especially worthy of note here. First, there is its strong embrace of pragmatism, particularly evident in his condemnation of the formalist tendency to adopt rules and laws as if they were "sacred words . . . deposited in the ark of the covenant," and his preference for a frankly experimentalist and instrumentalist approach to ideas.[63] In this regard, and in his discussions of educational reform, he clearly demonstrates the growing influence upon him of the pragmatism of both William James and John Dewey.

Second, there is the degree to which Croly had begun exploring the possible link between expanded social consciousness and self-realization, rather than setting the two up as implacable opposites. A surprising number of young American intellectuals were exploring the same possibility at the same time. "We are an uprooted people," Walter Lippmann declared, for example, in *Drift and Mastery* (1914), because "the absence of central authority has disorganized our souls."[64] An even more vivid and memorable characterization came the following year from the deft pen of literary critic Van Wyck Brooks, whose manifesto *America's Coming-of-Age* (1915) was a passionate call for cultural consolidation and the "formation of a social ideal." Brooks compared contemporary America to "a vast Sargasso Sea—a prodigious welter of unconscious life, swept by ground-swells of half-conscious emotion[,] . . . a welter of life that has not been worked into an organism." What was wanted was "to leave behind the old Yankee self-assertion and self-sufficiency, to work together, think together, feel together, to believe so fervently in the quality of standards that we delight in prostrating our work and our thoughts before them." Yet Brooks did not see such togetherness as sacrificial self-denial. Indeed, only by creating such an "intimate feeling" of social connection and correspondence between the works of intellect and the needs of the public realm could America reinstate the "right, free, disinterested" qualities that allowed "personality" to flourish.[65]

*Personality* was a key term for Brooks, as for his friend Randolph Bourne, and its meaning to them requires some explanation. Contrary to the idea, now commonplace, that personality is an ensemble of superficial appearances designed to charm others and thereby manipulate them, both men saw the realization of personality as a process of achieving the full blossoming and fruition of one's deepest potentialities, which only occurred when the proper conditions of social existence were first provided.[66] Both writers tended to speak in liberatory accents, seeing the imprisoning constraints and genteel evasions of late Victorian culture as the proximate obstacle to personality's fulfillment. The end toward which their critiques of American culture were directed, however, was not mere individual liberation but personal fulfillment within a revitalized social structure—a structure in which, as Bourne wrote in 1916, "all our idealisms" will offer "future social goals in which all can participate, the good life of personality lived in the environment of the Beloved Community."[67] To be personal was not at all incompatible with being disinterested, but the latter was entirely different from being impersonal;

indeed, Brooks argued that one "cannot have personality . . . so long as the end of society is an impersonal end like the accumulation of money."[68] Such a formulation echoed and built upon Croly's and suggested that it might indeed be possible to square the circle of the individualist versus collectivist antagonism, while reconciling the claims of full democracy with the claims of free intellect.

Brooks and Bourne, then, sought the achievement of personality and individuality through social reconstruction; such reconciliation of opposites would also be the essential task at the heart of the social thought of John Dewey.[69] Dewey's early involvement with Hegelianism seemed to have fixed in him at the outset of his career a keen appreciation for the social, associative element in human self-realization. That orientation did not change as Dewey moved from idealism and embraced a more experimental, pragmatic, and Darwinian epistemology that he felt could more effectively address the problems of a modern consolidated society and economy. In *The School and Society*, for example, he argued that, when schools perform their proper role in a democracy, "individualism and socialism are at one," because such a society thrives and is "true to itself" only in "being true to the full growth of all the individuals who make it up."[70] Indeed, as Robert Westbrook has insisted in his recent biography, Dewey fairly consistently—though not invariably—attempted to link his frank recognition of modern society's essentially corporate, interdependent, and consolidated character with his determined espousal of a radically participatory democratic polity and his stress upon enabling the full growth of personality in those comprising that society.[71]

Dewey's fullest and most important effort to present a systematic understanding of the proper relationship between the individual and modern society was embodied in his conception of the Great Community, put forward in *The Public and Its Problems* (1927). The Great Community stood in stark contrast to the Great Society (a term he had taken from Graham Wallas), by which Dewey meant merely the end product of the various technological and industrial revolutions that had produced the complex, consolidated, impersonal, and interdependent modern industrial world. Dewey did not advocate repeal of the Great Society and its changes and the return to a simple *Gemeinschaftlich* social order, but he insisted that the Great Society's genesis had pitilessly destroyed older forms of political and social association without providing a substitute "public" adequate to human needs. As he put it, the Great Society "invaded and partially disintegrated the small communities of former times without generating a Great Community," thereby leaving "the Public" in eclipse.[72] Mere aggregated collective action does not in and of itself, he insisted, constitute a public. It takes a perception of common interest, a high degree of conscious moral and intellectual association, and flexible and comprehensive networks of communication to accomplish that. Perhaps it would not be misleading, particularly in light of Dewey's Darwinian epistemology, for us to envision the problem in organismic terms, as the predicament of a person whose central nervous system is utterly out of phase with, and unable accurately to register or control, the feelings and movements of his or her body. One might compare it to the anxious vertigo of a Julian West, who arrived in paradise imprisoned by nineteenth-century cognitive and empirical barriers that at first prevented him from grasping the reality of the new world before him.

Dewey saw no contradiction between the pursuit of a more disciplined and intelligently controlled social and economic order, the rising authority of social science, and the imperatives of democracy. Democracy was to him "the idea of community life itself," the human associative need and tendency brought to its fullest logical extension, its highest perfection. Its success depended, again, upon a free and rapid flow of information and communication, for these were the lifeblood of the continual formation and reformation of the public and its will. Nor did Dewey see any imperative of Great Society consolidation that prevented the revitalization of local, settled "neighborly" communities, which were where the freest "flow of social intelligence" occurred, and hence where "democracy must begin."[73] Moreover, genuine democracy meant "an alignment with science," for science alone could serve as a completely disinterested public standard—nonhierarchical by its nature and, under the proper conditions, equally available to all.[74] The Great Community was a grand synthetic ideal, linking science, democracy, and self-realization in a reconciliation of modern means of production and organization with older forms of human association, mutatis mutandis.

This vision of a Great Community left no doubt that the self was profoundly social, and especially so in a time when, as Dewey later wrote in *Individualism, Old and New* (1930), "the United States has steadily moved from an earlier pioneer individualism to a condition of dominant corporateness."[75] The problems of the dissociated self, the "lost individual," could best be addressed not by individual therapy or adjustment but by first reforming our conception of the individual:

For the idea that the outward scene is chaotic because of the machine, which is a principle of chaos, and that it will remain so until individuals reinstate wholeness within themselves, simply reverses the true state of things. The outward scene, if not fully organized, is relatively so in the corporateness which the machine and its technology have produced; the inner man is the jungle which can be subdued to order only as the forces of organization at work in externals are reflected in corresponding patterns of thought, imagination, and emotion. The sick cannot heal themselves by means of their disease, and disintegrated individuals can achieve unity only as the dominant energies of community life are incorporated to form their minds.[76]

It was an "unreal question" to ask, as the now-discredited social-contract theorists had, how individuals went about banding together in societies and groups, for "an individual cannot be opposed to the association of which he is an integral part nor can the association be set against its integrated members."[77] Those who propose that individuals should try to reverse, for example, the disintegration of family life and sexual morality by their own "personal volition" (or "inner check") merely "profess faith in moral magic," since the social realities that led to the disintegration are what created the problem, and they cannot be willed away.[78] Instead, individuals needed to "refind themselves" by bringing their ideas and ideals "into harmony with the realities of the age in which they act"—in short, to consciously socialize their identities and form themselves into a new kind of revitalized public.[79]

There were multifold ambiguities beneath the surface of this argument, for Dewey had asserted far more than he demonstrated and never ventured very far into the thickets of specific, practical, political questions. Contending that the "individual" and the "social" defined and interpenetrated each other, Dewey sharply distinguished between the false individualism of natural rights, social-contract theory, laissez-faire economics, the Turner thesis, and the "money culture," and the genuine individualism that placed the individual in full, conscious, and sustaining relationship to the great social forces operating in a consolidated society. But Dewey's vision of the "new individualism" and how it would be concretely realized was vague and indistinct. What did it really mean for the larger "forces of organization at work in externals" to be "reflected in corresponding patterns of thought, imagination, and emotion"? How, specifically, could such patterns be created and propagated? What would the new individualism look like? To that last question, his answer was, "I do not see how it can be described until more progress has been made in its production."[80] To be sure, his pragmatism virtually dictated such an open-ended and experimentalist response. Beyond getting rid of all vestiges of the "old" individualism, however, Dewey had few concrete suggestions as to how the progress he advocated might be realized, other than the discouraging suggestion that his Great Community would be exceedingly difficult, perhaps even impossible, to create.[81]

Indeed, his discussion of the subject in *The Public and Its Problems* often lapsed into abstractions, even misty idealisms, despite his pragmatic, instrumentalist convictions. Dewey seemed to be projecting disembodied guiding standards or ideals (individuality, democracy, science, the Public, or the Great Community) that did not rise from the web of existing social realities but were the product of his projective moral vision and were supplied as prospective social goals, prescriptive and teleological in all but name. Quite irrespective of the continuously self-questioning scientific method he so insistently championed, the images of prospective social democracy he repeatedly proposed could harden into slogans or absolutes, little different in that respect from their deposed formalist forerunners.[82] Perhaps the abstractness for which Dewey's writing is so frequently criticized is, then, more than a stylistic consideration. Some of the uses (or untoward effects) of abstraction lie precisely in its ability both to enlarge and to obscure the precise objects of one's speech and leave a very wide berth for contingency—the very characteristics that led Tocqueville to link the use of abstract language with democratic societies.[83]

There was another aspect of the reconciliation of society and the individual that Dewey did not concretely address, however, one that goes ultimately to the potential conflict between democracy and the authority of intellect that he was so anxious to allay. Was there an inevitable gulf between scientific knowledge and the forces that actually moved citizens in a democracy? Between the authority of disciplined mind and the vox populi? Everything hinged for Dewey on the possibility of decisively answering that question in the negative. Though Dewey, like other Progressives, had high ambitions for social science, he was equally adamant that the experts not become a clerisy or self-vaunting aristocracy, and that even the most recondite social knowledge must be "indissolubly wedded to the art of full and moving communication."[84] If there were such a gap, then scientific knowledge would become nothing more than an instrument of elite domination, and democracy nothing more than a windswept plain of ignorant, manipulable passion.

Dewey himself seemed, through the sheer power of his own example, to make his conciliatory, antidualistic claims plausible. He embodied a surprisingly poised balance between popular-democratic and elite-scientific perspectives and, moreover, managed to balance the brand of sacrificial Christian disinterestedness in which he had begun his career, with the post-Christian secular disinterestedness that characterized the scientific ethos.[85] Yet his 1922 *New Republic* essay, "The American Intellectual Frontier," indicated he knew his culture might find such a balance difficult to sustain. Looking at the religious crusade against evolutionary theory, which would culminate three years later in the Scopes trial, Dewey argued that such deplorable antiscientific prejudice was a product of the frontier mentality—but so too were many of the best, most democratic elements in American society. William Jennings Bryan "is a typical democratic figure," Dewey observed; "there is no gainsaying that proposition." Bryan's mediocrity was understandable, since "democracy by nature puts a premium on mediocrity." Yet Bryan and his followers also spoke, Dewey insisted, for much of what was most morally admirable in American society: "The church-going classes, those who have come under the influence of evangelical Christianity . . . form the backbone of philanthropic social interest, of social reform through political action, of pacifism, of popular education. They embody and express the spirit of kindly goodwill towards classes which are at an economic disadvantage and towards other nations. . . . It has been the element responsive to appeals for the square deal and more nearly equal opportunities for all."[86] As he pleaded with his fellow intellectuals to take the Bryanites more seriously, Dewey understood that more was at stake here than the separation of Populism from Progressivism. The example of Bryan, and the contempt gleefully heaped upon him by the urban intellectuals like Mencken, Croly, and Brooks, also marked the ongoing separation of democratic sentiment from free intellectual inquiry, something Dewey could not view without the deepest concern.

The key link between science and democracy in the Deweyan perspective, then, was the concept of the public as an ideal point of convergence and interaction, and in that respect, his project represented a culmination of Progressive thought. To be sure, Dewey defined the public in his own way. Rather than relating it to disinterestedness, he preferred a less moralistic and affect-related, more purely operational definition of the public: it was the aggregation of all individuals "affected by the indirect consequences of transactions to such an extent that it is deemed necessary to have those consequences systematically cared for." But the implications were the same. For him the state was the institutional expression of the public and not merely, as in the pluralist understanding, a referee or broker among competing interests. Without the distinctive assumption of a public interest, which could be articulated through institutions of political democracy and clarified through the disinterested resources of scientific intelligence, the essential moral core of the Progressive strain of political and social thought would collapse. There had to be something called a public, and it had to have an identifiable interest, distinguishable from any individual interests of its constituent elements. Social science was needed to reveal that interest and somehow, whether authoritatively or democratically, to persuade the citizen that the public interest was also his own.

By the time that Dewey published *The Public and Its Problems*, however, the general notion of a public interest was already crumbling under the force of concentrated assault by a younger generation of "democratic realists," both inside and outside the academy. In retrospect, it is clear that the progressive attack upon interest, though saturated with moral energy, was also riven with internal contradictions. Croly's disdain for law reflected the influence of Charles Beard's revolutionary study of the economic origins of the U.S. Constitution, arguably the most influential single work of Progressive historiography, which shocked many Americans by contending that the men at the Philadelphia Convention which drafted the Constitution were, "with a few exceptions, immediately, directly, and personally interested in, and derived economic advantage from, the establishment of the new system."[87] Though Beard professed respect for the framers' hardheaded realism, there could be no doubt that his argument, making a classic antiformalist move, was also meant to demystify them and the sacred Constitution and to rattle public complacency about the givenness of American political institutions by showing the concrete and self-interested social forces from which they emerged. If the founding of the American political system, which had traditionally been mythologized as a supremely Olympian act of political wisdom and prudential disinterestedness, could be seen as a fundamentally interested act, then what act in the American political past could pass muster? How, indeed, could any deed be upheld in the court of disinterestedness? Was there still sufficient cognitive and social space for the ideal of disinterestedness once the Pandora's box of multitudinous interests had been opened and set loose upon the world of ideas? Or had Beard's own slashing forays against Victorian piety recoiled upon the dignity of thought itself and made appealing to disinterestedness incongruous without self-contradiction or bad conscience?

After the First World War, the insurgency would include Walter Lippmann as a visible member and, in the 1920s, an intellectual dueling partner to John Dewey. Such a development was not without its ironies. There was no more eloquent and penetrating argument for the disinterested scientific ideal as a solid basis for cultural authority in a postreligious democratic era than Lippmann's *Drift and Mastery* (1914), a book whose title contained the bywords for the stark alternatives facing the era. Lippmann's restless intelligence, alert to the flow of events, however, quickly moved beyond the confines of that youthful production. In the wake of the First World War's many disappointments for Progressives, particularly the Wilson administration's heavy-handed use of domestic propaganda and curtailment of civil liberties to impose univo-cal public support for the war effort, Lippmann's view of democratic gover-nance and its connection with the ethos of science changed dramatically. In *Public Opinion* (1922), Lippmann argued that, because citizens in a modern mass democracy made decisions strictly on the basis of stereotypes, experts would have to control and adjust the flow of information to the public in order to keep the "pictures in their heads" in line with realities that only a few could properly understand. The wartime propaganda emanating from the Creel Committee had taught Lippmann how frighteningly plastic and manipulable public opinion was; the only sensible answer was to attempt to achieve rational mastery over the problem.

By 1925 Lippmann had gone further, with the briefer, more astringent book *The Phantom Public*. Not only was it inconceivable, he argued, that the average voter was capable of governance, but there was really no such thing as the public. What was called the public was a "phantom"; to the extent that there was a genuine and effective public, it was "merely those persons who are interested in an affair." As for the claims of expertise, even these began to be circumscribed; the important distinction was not between experts and ama-teurs but between "insiders" and "outsiders," those with firsthand knowledge and those without. Men were thereby "denied the fraudulent support of the fiction that they are agents of a common purpose. They are regarded as agents of special purposes, without pretense and without embarrassment. They must live in a world with men who have other special purposes. The adjustments which must be made *are* society. . . . When men take a position in respect to the purposes of others they are acting as a public."[88] Lippmann's naturalistic vision of the public realm was more Madisonian than Christian, little more than an immense and complex congeries of clashing interests.

Dewey meant *The Public and Its Problems* partly as a direct and respectful attempt to answer Lippmann's mounting pessimism (and growing influence). It valiantly clung to the belief that the public was no phantom but something quite real, though currently "in eclipse." The chief problems of "the public" revolved around the current lack of shared symbols ("intellectual instrumen-talities for the formation of an organized public," in Deweyese) and inade-quate communication of the "numerous, tough and subtle" bonds "which hold men together in action," whether or not they are conscious of it.[89] In the same year, however, Lippmann wrote that "the more or less unconscious and unplanned activities of businessmen are for once more novel, more daring and in a sense more revolutionary, than the theories of the progressives."[90] Few more deliberately insulting rebukes to Deweyan intelligence and the Deweyan democratic faith could be imagined.

By 1929, Lippmann's post-Progressive reaction had deepened even further and had borne fruit in his *Preface to Morals* (1929), which became a best-seller and a Book-of-the-Month Club selection. It echoed and restated the great theme Lippmann had been building upon for a decade and a half: the erosion of traditional forms of authority by the "acids of modernity." It had become impossible to live within the old religious orthodoxies; there was no going back. It was also proving intolerable to live without them, however, since the substitutes for religion so far had proved woefully inadequate. Even the cultural authority of science had now been called into question for Lippmann, partly by the relativism of Einsteinian physics (Darwinism was now, he asserted, "out-moded"), which presented man with a bewildering physical universe even more incommensurable with his inner life than Henry Adams could have imagined, and partly through a growing awareness of science's inherent limitations.[91] Citing Charles Peirce's work on the social constitution of scientific truth, Lippmann drew a devastating conclusion: "When we say that something has been 'explained' by science, we really mean only that our own curiosity is satisfied." As it advances, we see that scientific explanation "does not yield a certain picture of anything which can be taken naively as a representation of reality," but only "provisional dramatizations which are soon dissolved by the progress of science itself." Therefore a religion of "scientific materialism has nothing in it, except the pretension that it is a true account of the world"; scientific explanations "cannot give men such a clue to the plan of existence as they find in popular religion."[92] A prolegomenon to morals could begin by ruling out any scientific discovery of moral principles.

All that was left, believed Lippmann, with all other supports teetering, was a highly ascetic understanding of the principle of disinterestedness itself—attached not to "nature" or "super-nature" but to "human nature," to a doctrine of "humanism" arising not from science but from the phenomenology of human life and directed toward the purification and discipline of the individual will.[93] The "ideal of disinterestedness," he asserted, is "inevitable in the modern world," for only it can "untangle the moral confusion of the age." Disinterestedness in fact was the still-living "core of high religion," the "central insight of the teachers of wisdom" such as Jesus, Buddha, and Confucius. Such disinterestedness was equally present in science; indeed, "pure science is high religion incarnate," and one of the greatest services of science was its service as a school of disinterestedness, which "matures the human character" and teaches us, as Bertrand Russell put it, not to regard "our desires, tastes, and interests as affording a key to the understanding of the world."[94] The modern world seemed to teach men that emancipation from the old authorities meant they could at last pursue their passions without restraint and thereby achieve happiness. The lesson Lippmann taught was the opposite, however; we needed to learn to detach ourselves, not only from the tyranny of public opinion, but from the force of our own desires—even deep, highly personal longings in the intimate recesses of marriage and sexual relations.

Disinterestedness, detachment, asceticism, discipline, and (not least) disillusion were the guiding spirits of the *Preface*. The book owed much to the ethical spirit of Spinoza, whom Lippmann frequently quoted, but perhaps more immediately, it showed the influence of his old Harvard teachers George Santayana and Irving Babbitt: the unillusioned naturalism and stoicism of the former and the antidemocratic and self-disciplined mien of both. Lippmann had come a long way from his days as a habitué of Mabel Dodge's Greenwich Village salon, an editor of Herbert Croly's *New Republic*, an apostle of progressive mastery, and a believer in the malleability of human nature. Santayana admired the book, but not without reservation. Perhaps because of his own eerily detached disposition, he instantly recognized what was missing from Lippmann's high religion of science: any sense of meaningful involvement in, or connection to, the social world. The pure intellect would become "divorced . . . from [human] affairs and morality"; a disinterested love would become "divorced as far as possible from human objects." Other reviewers offered similar assessments: as one remarked, the nominally Jewish Lippmann had proffered a disinterestedness that "surrenders that sense of 'being together with others' so essential in all Hebraic history," a strange directive to come from a writer presumably laying the groundwork for a sustainable modern morality. Indeed, Lippmann's ascetic ideal at times sounded more reminiscent of Nietzsche's Zarathustra than Rauschenbusch or Croly or Peirce; disinterestedness was "a mountain track which the many are likely in the future as in the past to find cold, bleak, and bare." Nevertheless, the ideal man must "take the world as it comes, and within himself remain quite unperturbed. . . . He would face pain with fortitude, for he would have put it away from the inner chambers of his soul. Fear would not haunt him."[95]

Such heroic accents contrasted strikingly with the anti-individualistic, self-sacrificial ethos that writers from Ely to Dewey had hoped a standard of disinterestedness might promote. Like them, too, he wrote from a combination of social concern and personal need. Like them, Lippmann consciously sought to replicate and sustain certain elements of the Christian faith under modern circumstances, but the elements he wished to sustain were quite different. In particular, he did not share their acute hunger for social connection. If his predecessors had sought a postsupernatural religion that would socialize Christ's teachings and immanentize his kingdom, Lippmann sought to individualize those same notions and to reopen thereby the possibility of a purely individual transcendence. When citing St. Paul as a great ascetic who spoke of "the law of his members warring against the law of his mind" and of "bringing his body into subjection" in the service of the "spirit," Lippmann chose to ignore Paul's image of the church as the body of Christ, the indispensable corporate expression of Christian life. Even self-renunciation for Lippmann served the larger purpose not of affirming his inevitable entanglement in a greater social web, but of heightening his sense of individual self-control: an ideal more Stoic than Christian or Jewish. Judging from the testimony of Lippmann's biographer and others who have written about his personal life, his apotheosis of disinterest was at least in part an attempt at philosophical rationalization and moral cover for the kind of disposition Lippmann already had: supremely detached, disconnected, independent, and emotionally chilly. Santayana, who knew Lippmann well and shared a few of the same tendencies, once remarked, "Genuine detachment presupposes attachment. What can it signify for you to say that you renounce everything, if as yet you have loved nothing?"[96] Perhaps Lippmann had the disinterestedness of an intellectual saint, but that very detachment made him prone to emotional stinginess and monstrous acts of betrayal.[97]

Most relevant to the present purpose, however, Lippmann had taken hold of a moral ideal—disinterestedness—originally meant to foster social cohesion and social consciousness in a post-Christian era and had shown how the unfolding of its logic might lead only to further dissociation and further disconnection. By mercilessly smashing the Progressive notion of the public into its constituent elements, he opened the way to a post-Progressive conception of politics as a "realistic" process of effectively brokering an openly interest-based pluralism. Such politics ultimately had no higher conception of the public interest than, as in the subtitle of Harold Lasswell's 1936 book *Politics*, who gets what, when, and how—or E. E. Schattschneider's dry observation that public policy was merely "the result of 'effective demands' upon the government," or Thurman Arnold's jaundiced conclusion that public debate over matters of political principle or value was little more than the play of useful mythologies and "magic words."[98]

Ideas of "the public interest" or of a consolidated and unified national community did not suddenly expire. They continued and comprised one of the intellectual strains in the tangled history of the New Deal, visible, for example, in the National Recovery Administration, the Civilian Conservation Corps, or President Franklin Roosevelt's frequent invocation of the analogue of warfare—the ultimate unifying, self-transcending clarion call, which had worked so memorably in 1861–65.[99] Lippmann himself eventually changed his thinking entirely in reaction to the rise of totalitarianism in Europe and his growing fears about the consequences of New Deal collectivism; he become an exponent of a "public philosophy" based upon something he called a "higher law."[100] For Lippmann, the antiformalist revolt and the search for order had both come up morally empty-handed, and that indicated a move in the direction of older verities. It remained to be seen, however, whether such long-abandoned Archimedean points were now recoverable.

---

There were other powerful and outspoken voices of dissent in the intellectual world of the 1920s and 1930s quarreling with the optimistic premises of Deweyan progressivism: the antidemocratic gibes of H. L. Mencken; the bleak disenchantment of Joseph Wood Krutch; the anti-industrial, anticonsolidationist regionalism of the Nashville Agrarians; and the romantic revolutionary appeal of the American Communists. A rebuke that carried especially stinging force was offered by theologian Reinhold Niebuhr. Niebuhr was a liberal Protestant of progressive sympathies, a comrade of Dewey's in Norman Thomas's Socialist party, and a man imbued with the values of the social gospel who spoke directly from Dewey's own intellectual and moral tradition. With his explosive book *Moral Man and Immoral Society* (1932), however, Niebuhr declared independence from the conventional progressive wisdom and began to stake a position for himself as a perpetual critic of what he regarded as progressives' and liberals' naive assumptions about human nature and the requirements of social reform. From the very first pages, it was clear the book would be in part a direct assault upon the era's most prominent progressive "educators and moralists," specifically including Dewey himself. By the third page Niebuhr was already quoting Dewey: "What stands in the way (of a planned economy) is a lot of outworn traditions, moth-eaten slogans, and catchwords. . . . We shall only make a real beginning in intelligent thought when we cease mouthing platitudes."[101] Then Niebuhr replied: Dewey's analysis was "so platitudinous that it rather betrays the confusion of an analyst who has no clear counsels about the way to overcome social inertia."[102] Niebuhr gave notice that he was not going to be taken in by Deweyan crypto-idealism.

At bottom, Niebuhr was quarreling with the progressives' belief in the near-complete plasticity of human nature.[103] The assurance of such plasticity was the essential antiformalist element in an optimistic belief in progress, for it translated what had formerly been regarded as inherent defects of sinful human nature into remediable flaws, reversible by a better-understood, more intelligently controlled process of nurturance and socialization. Such was (and is) the source of reformers' attraction to social or cultural determinisms, for what is socially generated can presumably be socially undone once the deus ex machina of intelligent intervention can somehow be seated in the director's chair. But Niebuhr was having none of this. The supposedly outdated orthodox Christian understanding of man—as a fallen creature who through his free choice became alienated from God and tainted by sin in his innermost being and was therefore incapable of redeeming himself by his own unaided efforts—seemed to Niebuhr a far more accurate description of modern man's condition than the fantasies of progressives and liberals who envisioned the glorious coming of the kingdom through the application of human intelligence. For him, there was a definite, essential human nature, and it was largely selfish, irrational, and incorrigible. By 1939, his political and social convictions having coalesced into the neoorthodox theology so often linked with his name, Niebuhr remarked that "liberalism" was little more than "faith in man" exemplifying "that perversion of the will, that betrayal of divine trust, which is called sin."[104]

Even more specifically, Niebuhr was taking direct aim at the Deweyan assumption that, because man is a fundamentally social being, his nature can (and should) be progressively enhanced by being brought into closer harmony with the social contexts in which he operates—that, as Dewey had put it, the "lost individual" will "refind" inner wholeness not in trying to recover religious faith, but only by "subduing" himself to "the forces of organization at work in externals."[105] No, responded Niebuhr; the opposite result was far more likely. Men have little enough goodness in their natures, taken one by one, as God will ultimately judge them. What meager tendencies they have toward disinterestedness and goodness, however, were almost certain to be erased by their association with others. Contrary to the logic of socialization, people behaved even worse in groups, any groups, than they did taken singly. Therefore, Niebuhr asserted, there needed to be a radical disjunction between the moral standards of individual behavior and of social behavior. To miss that fact was to commit a grievous and highly consequential error. Even if man's sinful individual nature were reformable—a dubious proposition to begin with—there was no comparable way of reforming the behavior of groups, whose very raison d'être ensured that they merely amplified the individual sins of their members into a harder, more powerful, more remorseless, and more resistant form of collective sinfulness.

By attacking the premises of the social and perfectible nature of man, Niebuhr brought nearly every important element of the Progressive worldview into question. Progressive social reformers who offered visions of individual self-transcendence through harmonious, cohesive, and inclusive social arrangements failed to grasp "the brutal character of the behavior of all human collectives, and the power of self-interest and collective egoism in all inter-group relations." Liberal Protestants who had fallen for the illusion that "all social relations are being brought progressively under 'the law of Christ'" were suffering from profound moral confusion, since they could not see that the inequitable social arrangements in modern industrial society were en-forced by coercion and would have to be overturned by the same means. As for the ideal of scientific disinterestedness, assuming such a thing was even possi-ble in a world permeated by self-interestedness, its "cool objectivity" would be insufficient to provide the "morale" needed to undertake the dangerous task of "social struggle." We live in a world dominated by irrationality and self-interested, partial perspectives; in such a world, only the right kind of "emo-tionally potent oversimplifications" could galvanize an aggrieved group into effective action. Dewey had argued that "with a little more time, a little more adequate moral and social pedagogy and a generally higher development of human intelligence," social problems could be decisively solved. Niebuhr scoffed at such optimism, ignoring as it did the degree to which sheer irra-tionality, selfishness, and the entrenched economic interests of the dominant classes dictated the social arrangements of humankind. "Our contemporary culture," he concluded, "fails to realize the power, extent and persistence of group egoism in human relations." As bad as men were individually, in groups they were incomparably, frighteningly worse.[106]

Niebuhr, then, had drawn his own conclusions about the relative primacy of interests, as opposed to the faint possibility of disinterestedness, in all collec-tive relationships; in the tensive space between the small world of individual morality and the large world of power politics, there appeared to be little room for the notion of a Great Community or even a public interest. On the contrary, the ideal of complete social solidarity was a dangerous chimera, for "society is in a perpetual state of war" between different, equally self-interested groups; the only way a society can sustain itself as a coherent entity is by the coercive power of its dominant members or classes, who then go on to "invent romantic and moral interpretations of the facts."[107] The peace thus gained, though, will always be unjust in some respect and will last only so long as the underdogs are unable to challenge it (and then impose another unjust peace). This is not to say that moral factors had no influence in human history, only that they could never be trusted sufficiently to check the effects of man's ingrained collective propensities. Only power can counter power, and power, said Niebuhr (citing Henry Adams), is poison, no matter who wields it. Therefore the exercise of power was always morally dangerous but also mor-ally necessary—and that necessity might well entail willingness to resort to violence or revolution in some instances. The only solution to this problem of disjunction was "a frank dualism in morals," which would distinguish sharply between the behavior expected of individuals and that expected of groups. "The selfishness of human communities must be regarded as an inevitability," he believed, and it can be countered "only by competing assertions of interest"; yet the needs of political strategy do not lessen the requirement of "the strictest individual moral discipline and the most uncompromising idealism" enjoined upon us as individuals.[108] To employ the parlance of the gospels, Niebuhr seemed to be saying, Be ye wise as serpents in collective affairs and harmless as doves in your individual dealings. To apply the rules of one to the conditions of the other was to commit a grave moral and tactical error.

In no area of human endeavor was that error more grave than in the complex of issues relating to nationalism. Here too, Niebuhr broke with a strain of progressive thought stretching back through Croly and Roosevelt to Bellamy, and before him to the Grand Review. For the better part of seven decades the immense possibilities of coordinated, collective action had enthralled the imaginations of American social thinkers, and the highest and most complete embodiment of those possibilities was the idea of the national community itself. The First World War, however, had left Niebuhr's enthusiasm for the nation deeply scarred. One of his earliest articles, appearing in the *Atlantic*, bore the indicative title, "The Nation's Crime against the Individual." Niebuhr there contended that modern warfare cheats the individual soldier who sacrifices his life for his country, for the soldier is drawn by the great disinterested virtues of loyalty and courage, but the nation, being nothing but an agency of crass self-interest, could do nothing to "hallow his sacrifices." Its crime lay in its claiming "a life of eternal significance for ends that have no eternal value."[109] In *Moral Man* he formulated this paradox unforgettably: "Patriotism transmutes individual unselfishness into national egoism." It is the unselfishness of individuals that "makes for the selfishness of nations"; that is why "the hope of solving the larger social problems of mankind, merely by extending the social sympathies of individuals, is so vain."[110]

Indeed, by the time he wrote *Moral Man*, his conviction had hardened to the point that he baldly asserted that "hypocrisy" was "the most significant moral characteristic of a nation."[111] It was precisely the ability of nations to harness together the valiant and the venal, to provide an outlet for the individual's "combination of unselfishness and vicarious selfishness," that gave such force to national egoism, a force that "neither religious nor rational idealism can ever completely check." The prophets of "a more perfect social intelligence" guiding the operations of a national community were never more misguided than here, for the "perennial weakness of the moral life in individuals is simply raised to the *n*th degree in national life."[112] In any event, nations really only coalesced into "full self-consciousness" when they were in "vivid, usually bellicose, juxtaposition to other nations"—that is to say, when they were at war. The rest of the time, the average citizen had little reason to look beyond the circles of immediate community and local circumstance. The moment swords are drawn, however, the simple patriot convinces himself that the nation protects his way of life and embodies all of society and civilization; meanwhile the politicians go to work manipulating such feelings shamelessly for the state's benefit. Those whose "religious or rational culture" made them reluctant to issue nakedly chauvinistic appeals instead undertake to clothe them in "the attributes of universality"—and become thereby "the worst liars of war-time."[113]

Such harsh words against universalism may well be directed toward the diplomacy of Woodrow Wilson. Certainly one of the chief factors shaping Niebuhr's tough-minded view of international relations was his own profound disillusionment over the postwar collapse of Wilsonian idealism, which Niebuhr himself had supported despite his German roots and sympathies. The result was an inveterate suspicion of all idealistic professions in diplomacy and an assumption of dark, unacknowledged motives driving human affairs. In particular, Niebuhr's analysis of international and intranational relationships was very much in the jaundiced, unillusioned, demystifying spirit of Beard, whose work in the economic interpretation of history Niebuhr admired and drew upon in *Moral Man*, along with his growing awareness of and respect for Marx and Marxism. One of the general themes of *Moral Man* was Niebuhr's palpable contempt for the stupidity and arrogance of idealistic middle-class reformers, who saw the world as their moral classroom and attempted to impose their "canons of individual morality" upon all social classes. The "educational philosophy of Professor John Dewey," he sniffed, was hopelessly "bound by middle-class perspectives," for it ignored the fact that there was but one real obstacle to a more rational and just society: "the interests of the powerful and dominant groups, who profit from the present system of society."[114] A term like *the public interest* was a typical sentimental smokescreen used by middle-class progressive reformers to conceal the class interests bound up in their reform agenda. Niebuhr stopped short of calling such men capitalist stooges, but he might as well have.

There was a generous measure of intellectual pretentiousness in this: the more-hard-boiled-than-thou middle-class seminary professor (and former pastor of a solidly middle-class suburban church) lecturing his fellow middle-class professors in the differences between the middle-class mind and "the proletarian mind," about the latter of which he appeared to know little beyond his reading of Marx, Lenin, and Trotsky.[115] This flourish reminds us, however, that *Moral Man and Immoral Society* ought to be read, at least in part, as an artifact of the Great Depression, culturally of a piece with Mike Gold's *Jews without Money* (1930), Lincoln Steffens's *Autobiography* (1931), John Chamberlain's *Farewell to Reform* (1932), and the radical, anticapitalist pamphlet *Culture and Crisis*, which grew from the endorsement by fifty-three American artists and intellectuals of the Foster-Ford Communist party ticket in the 1932 presidential election. Niebuhr's impatience with high-minded progressive gradualism and his exploratory praise for Marxian revolutionism surely derived, to a large extent, from the moral and material urgencies of that historical moment, but it had less immediate antecedents as well. Niebuhr's reservations about the social gospel, theological liberalism, the progressive vision of human perfectibility, and the search for the kingdom's realization on earth had been growing for many years, and those misgivings about Progressivism formed the core of the neoorthodoxy that he and his theologian brother Richard began to formulate in the 1930s.[116]

It would be a distortion merely to say Niebuhr was revolting against the social gospel, however, for he was also carrying on its mission and the more general mission of social Christianity, albeit under far more challenging and morally chastened strictures. Indeed, it is impossible to understand Niebuhr's intricately balanced, ambivalent, paradoxical, and even self-contradictory thought without taking into account the ideological complexion of the social gospel and theological liberalism against which (and within which) he was reacting. By insisting upon the inherent fallenness of human nature, the sinfulness of all social structures, and the disjunction between individual and social morality, Niebuhr did not somehow exempt Christians from the responsibility for progressive social action and from the responsibility to realize Christian ideals in history. On the contrary, Christians were being told to remove their rose-colored glasses, to take a long and realistic look at the world's wicked and irredeemable ways, and to recognize that to be socially efficacious they would have to be willing to play the game by the world's rules and therefore descend into the mire and muck of real human relations, foreswearing all hope of the earthly kingdom and all hope of keeping perfectly clean hands. In a word, the effective pursuit of righteousness would inevitably implicate them in sin and imperfection; yet the Christian faith called its adherents to nothing less than a life of perfection. Niebuhr adamantly refused to blink or to dilute either side of that formulation.

If Niebuhr seemed to elude all the usual categories, that fact was reflected in the kind of intellectual role he embodied. Niebuhr had a passion for criticism. He staked for himself an independent position within the progressive-liberal ranks: part free-ranging critical and corrective intellect, part prophetic scourge and gadfly. Like Socrates' *daimonion*, he was more gifted at saying no to dangerous half-truths than at offering direct prescriptions, which made him something of an inveterate intellectual counterpuncher. On one hand, he would lambast conservatives when they used the assertion of God's transcendence to justify their unwillingness to address themselves to systemic social injustice; on the other hand, he would berate progressives for their naive belief in individual or social perfectibility and their squeamish inability to apply "realistic" thinking to human affairs. This critical process occasionally involved setting up rather one-sided straw men who had been created expressly to be knocked down. As Richard Fox has pointed out, in practical terms the "chastened" progressivism that Niebuhr advocated, in which the utopian omega point was envisioned, perhaps approached asymptotically, but never quite reached, was not very different from Dewey's own formulation—or, Fox might have added, from Rauschenbusch's.[117] Where Niebuhr did embody a striking difference was in distancing himself from the ideal of what Richard Kirkendall has called the "service intellectuals," the kind of authoritative, university-trained, specialized, scientific professionals whose practical, problem-solving expertise played so significant a governmental role in the progressive (and then the New Deal) years. Although Niebuhr was certainly a public intellectual with a sober and realistic bent, such a role would have been anathema to him. Like Randolph Bourne, Niebuhr felt certain that intellect would be corrupted by being placed in service to poisonous power; better to be detached than to risk such contamination. The role he evolved for himself was an odd combination of national pastor-moralist and detached modernist intellectual.

The thrust of *Moral Man and Immoral Society* posed a genuine personal dilemma for an intellectual like Niebuhr. The momentum of the argument seemed to point ineluctably toward increasingly hard-boiled political involvement; anything less amounted to complicity with the status quo. To become further enmeshed in public affairs, however, was to surrender the yearning to be morally pure and, instead, to yield oneself to all the sins and difficulties of power politics—including the sacrifice of a disinterested search for truth in favor of the "emotionally potent oversimplifications" necessary to mobilize social change. The thoroughly chastened, fastidiously self-critical turn of mind fostered by Niebuhr's increasingly neoorthodox outlook, with its profound awareness of the fatal partiality of all human perspectives, was ill suited to the sloganeering rough-and-tumble of the public arena. Niebuhr would either have to accept an intellectual *kenosis*, a crucifixion on the cross of partiality, in becoming a political activist, or he could withdraw further from the arena, into a more theological, above-the-fray detachment where he could explore moral issues without the sinful entanglements of commitment. In the end, there really was no alternative for him but the latter, and his subsequent work, beginning with *Reflections on the End of an Era* (1934), reveals an increasingly theological and increasingly individual-oriented cast.

The posture of detachment was not one Niebuhr could follow consistently, for it conflicted with his engagé predilections. It comported well with Niebuhr's restlessly independent mind, however, and seemed to follow logically from his deeply skeptical view of all allegiance to groups. The orthodox Christian understanding of human nature was in no wise progressive, and Niebuhr regarded as extremely dangerous all attempts to overcome the sinful burden of selfhood through the delusion of solidarity. A Kierkegaardian Protestant, he preferred to meet his God in solitude. In a sense, then, his own "high religion" could be as isolating and individualized as Lippmann's, in light of Niebuhr's sustained, almost programmatic suspicion of the creedal, dogmatic, confessional, and traditional elements that help make religion socially cohesive. The price paid for rigorous self-critical honesty was a studied distrust of the snares of social bonds, which meant a limited, highly provisional recognition of the social dimension of faith—seemingly an odd position for a proponent of social Christianity and teacher of social ethics. "Trust no man," he later wrote, for "there is no form of human goodness which cannot be and will not be corrupted."[118] Yet Niebuhr was not cynical; he placed this realistic view of the sinfulness of groups and individuals in permanent tension with the ideal force of sacrificial love, arguing for a necessary dialectic of justice and love, with each serving as balance and corrective to the other. Even so, Niebuhr seemed, in a way that recalls the Whitmanian chasm between self and nation, to be creating an affective chasm between the commandment to love one's neighbor and the commandment to love God.

Arguably, Jesus' teaching in the Gospels had always presented that very difficulty. It had summarized the teaching of the law and the prophets in those same two great universalistic love-commandments.[119] The Apostle Paul, although the great institutionalizer of early Christianity, was too consumed by eschatological expectancy to have had much patience with what Reinhold's brother Richard would call "the social sources of denominationalism." Some of the same impatience and perhaps a similar sense of impending crisis probably kept Reinhold from settling comfortably into the role of institution-building pastor at his suburban Detroit church and drove him instead to become a restless and prophetic national figure. Still, the social dimension of religious life, the full recognition that the church must be embodied in and realized through the life of particular moral communities embedded in particular social, economic, and ethnic settings seemed strangely missing from Niebuhr's work and continued to be ignored or underemphasized as his thought developed. Instead, he was increasingly preoccupied with the complexity, depth, contradictoriness, and prospects of the self; therefore such themes as the individual basis of sin, the possibility of individual transcendence, and the "radical freedom" of the self became more and more prominent.

In one of his later books, *The Self and the Dramas of History* (1955), Niebuhr offered his own capsule history of the shifting relationship between the individual and the community; he also underscored his enduring suspicion of the latter and his reasons for insisting upon "the self's freedom and its discontinuity with the coherences and structures of the temporal world."[120] The modern technological and political order had precipitated an unprecedented and bewildering tension between the individual and the community, for modern civilization had "emancipated the individual from his organic ties to the community," even as its consolidating tendencies had "given the community a greater cohesion and intensity" than had ever been possible in an agrarian society. This tension gave rise to "a struggle in the soul of each individual" between a heightened sense of individual destiny and a heightened sense of collective dependency—Niebuhr's formulation of the quintessential antiformalist dilemma. This struggle translated into a moral dilemma, pitting conscience as an independent, individual moral sense against the more modern, psychosocial, historicist, and antiformalist view of conscience as "the pressure of the community upon the individual." Although Niebuhr affirmed that moral judgment actually involved a tension between the two, he clearly leaned toward the former conception. He pointed to the times when "the individual is embarrassed by the morally mediocre standards of the community" and the individual rises "to an heroic defiance of the community and thus refute[s] all simple 'social' interpretations of conscience."[121]

Niebuhr did not balk at reaffirming the biblical ideal of being saved through being lost, of transcendence through submission, and of a high disinterestedness. The self, he argued, "can only realize itself by endlessly being drawn out of itself into larger ends." Although the community may serve as such an end "provisionally," however, it "can not be so ultimately" because the community's greater scope is more than counteracted by its greater entanglement in "the necessities of nature." It was inevitable that the "moral sense of the community" be at "a lower level than that of the individual," for the community's summum bonum was "a wise self-interest," not an unlimited self-sacrificial love. In short, "the individual must have a higher end than the community." In the discussion that followed, Niebuhr showed how thoroughly he had thought through and beyond the conclusions of those who had grappled with the same issue. For Whitman, in modern society "an explicit act of the will" was required for the individual to be "delivered from preoccupation with himself," and such an act was "beyond the moral competence" of most individuals. For Bellamy, the "forces of cohesion in an organic society" could be helpful in "drawing individuals out of the narrow prison of their self-concern." For Jane Addams, the need for such cohesion could be demonstrated by a comparison of "the spiritual health of a peasant mother" with "the malaise from which sophisticated cosmopolitans suffer." For Dewey, "the isolated individual, lost in an anonymous mass, was rather a sorry fulfillment of the hopes of the nineteenth century. . . . His situation was too untenable to be long maintained." For Lippmann, that situation "was challenged by overt forms of collectivism and by further technical developments which added mass communications to other technical forms of cohesion."[122]

The lonely individual tended "to become identified with his community so that its pride and prestige become his own." That, Niebuhr believed, was why the "pride of national and racial communities" was so attractive to precisely those individuals suffering from powerful feelings of unhappiness and personal frustration. That, he believed, was why modern liberal societies had a particular attraction to the cohesion offered by the national ideal, even when it involved "disavowals of individual liberty" and "worship of the community." That was why the French Revolution eventuated in Napoleon and why "national loyalty" came so quickly to take on "religious dimensions" in a country that had "only recently celebrated the emancipation of the individual." To describe the climactic expression of this tendency, Niebuhr used a word that, though very familiar in 1955, was as yet almost unknown in 1932: *totalitarianism*. That word not only gave a name to the tendency but it marked the transforming distance that was to be traveled, from the intellectual world of the 1920s and early 1930s to the very different environment of two or three decades later.

The names Hitler and Stalin suffice to describe the proximate cause of that transformation, and Niebuhr saw a connection between those men's rise to power and the errors inherent in the modern understanding of human nature. Although he conceded that the totalitarian movements of Nazism and Communism had complex social roots, he was certain that they were fueled by "the spiritual embarrassment of the individual in a technical society." Nazism sought to make individuals renounce "their individual dignity and freedom" in order to reestablish the "simple communal cohesion of a primitive society." Marxism, even without taking into account its brutal Stalinist variant, sought to make the community "the source and end for individual existence," subjecting the individual mind to the tyranny of a Rousseauean "general will." To be sure, Niebuhr was still enough of a social gospeler, socialist, and antiformalist to declare without hesitation that the individualistic philosophy underlying laissez-faire bourgeois liberalism was philosophically and morally insufficient. Still "it was even more intolerable to force the individual to find the final end of his existence in the community (whether conceived in nationalistic or pseudo-international terms)."[123] If forced to choose between the totalitarianism of a thinker like Auguste Comte and the libertarianism of a John Stuart Mill, Niebuhr would choose the latter. Fortunately, he felt, those were not the only choices. There was still a living remnant of biblical Christianity available, holding up a "frame of meaning" inherent in the Christ revelation that was entirely independent of community or secularism.[124]

Niebuhr was proposing a purified biblical understanding of an utterly transcendent God and an imperfect man, an understanding that had been stripped of its historical accretion of dogmatic and institutional barnacles as well as obsolete assumptions about the divinity and literal veracity of Scripture. In a sense, this quest to renew, recover, or reconstruct the church according to its true and essential nature had always been the heart of Protestant theory and practice, from Luther to Rauschenbusch. As some of Niebuhr's Roman Catholic critics pointed out, however, his was really an "as-if" orthodoxy, an extrapolation and adaptation from orthodoxy of what he deemed to be its permanently valid principles, as opposed to its historical accidents. This was a large claim, which was founded in the end upon nothing more substantial than Niebuhr's own authority. Niebuhr was fundamentally a liberal in his free approach to questions of Scripture, sacraments, creeds, and institutions; in his view of the divinity of Jesus Christ, the Trinity, the Virgin Birth, Heaven and Hell, and the supernatural in general; and in his willingness to adapt such mythic constructs as original sin into liberal practice in order to give sobriety and a sense of limitation to an otherwise unreflective progressive triumphalism.

Niebuhr refused to accept the authority of churches (particularly of Rome) on the grounds that such attribution elevated "an historic institution into a trans-historic reality," which was an act of presumption and effrontery. In a sense, it was the same objection he had to all social authority: its tendency to make absolute moral claims for itself against the wishes and judgments of the individual. One could feel the force of his criticism and yet ask, Why was the solitary, fallible, historically-bound, and shifting judgment of a Reinhold Niebuhr preferable? This point Niebuhr could not answer, except to say that he was merely following in the Reformation tradition of the "priesthood of believers."[125] Yet his real reasons perhaps had more to do with an ingrained uneasiness, both personal and intellectual, with any social sources of authority, ecclesiastical or secular. That this represented a reversal of the intellectual current that had been building since the Civil War is manifest. If institutional and social authority could not be supported by a disinterested standard of science or faith, if indeed the fact of self-interest lay coiled serpentlike around the heart of every social entity, then a detached, individual inquiry became the only semblance of an independent road left. Niebuhr had already begun in 1932 to sketch some of the contours of such a neoindividualistic perspective. The crucial push, however, would come from ideas and events he and other American thinkers would encounter in the ensuing years—ideas and events summed up by the word *totalitarianism*.

# 6

## Totalitarianism: The Mind in Exile

The history of ideas is, in large measure, the history of words. For that reason, it is worth recalling that the word *totalitarian*, which would come to stand for our era's political and social *summum malum*, did not exist until the early years of the twentieth century. It has been applied retrospectively, and a little promiscuously, to any more or less comprehensive social order, such as the imaginary polity of Plato's *Republic* or the organization of the Roman Catholic church, but such uses are in truth anachronistic.[1] *Totalitarianism* was a distinctive word, called into usage by and for distinctive circumstances; it became a considerable influence in reciprocally shaping those circumstances by shaping the way they were perceived. Its origins are, to some extent, obscure, like the origins of most words, and its meaning, like the meaning of any other powerful emotionally and politically charged abstraction, has been shifting and often indistinct. Yet one point seems clear: at the time of its coinage, the word did not carry the chilling connotations it eventually acquired. Indeed, in its earliest consistent usage, in the political discourse of early twentieth-century Italy, it appears to have been a word of utopian scope and power, offering an attractive and plausible vision of coordination, solidarity, and efficiency to revive a dissociated, dysfunctional society.[2] In that context *totalitarianism* apotheosized the consolidating, centralizing, integrative tendencies that had figured so prominently in the social thought of postbellum America. By the same token, the word's rapid descent into opprobrium also marked the descent of precisely the consolidated utopian ideal it was meant to denote, and its gradual replacement by more sober, limited, equilibrist, pluralist, and procedural views of the American social and political order. When utopia began to look like dystopia, *Looking Backward* was destined to be replaced by *Nineteen Eighty-Four*.

The language of Giovanni Gentile, the court philosopher of Italian Fascism, and his disciple Benito Mussolini subserved the rendering of a profoundly cohesive society, knit together in ways more deeply satisfying than could ever be hoped for from a decaying and decadent liberal order.[3] Their observations about human nature seemed roughly in line with the cultural organicism and historicism that had been the hallmark of the "revolt against formalism" in American social thought; at the same time, they incorporated the same yearning for disinterestedness and self-transcendence that had inspired so many American social thinkers in the wake of the Civil War. Gentile decisively rejected the classical-liberal, bourgeois understanding of the solitary self; the individual "was not an atom," because the "concept of society" was always "immanent in the concept of an individual." Fascism merely made that embeddedness explicit:

> *L'uomo del fascismo* is an individual who is at once nation and fatherland, the moral law which binds . . . individuals and generations . . . [to] an objective will that transcends the particular individual and elevates him to conscious membership in a spiritual community. . . . Liberalism negated the state in the interest of the particular individual; Fascism reaffirms the state as the true reality of the individual. . . . Fascism is totalitarian and the Fascist state, the synthesis and unity of all values, interprets, develops, and gives power to every aspect of the life of the people. . . . The nation as state is an ethical reality.[4]

*Lo stato totalitario*, a term Mussolini employed in speeches, was properly descriptive of the centrally organized political and economic order he hoped to fashion through the agency of the corporate state and the force of his own leadership.

It hardly seems surprising, then, that so many pragmatically oriented American liberals were initially fascinated by Mussolini; there is less scandal in that fact than there might seem at first glance. Mussolini seemed to be addressing himself boldly and vigorously to precisely the same problem of fostering social cohesion and social consciousness that so bedeviled industrial American society and that so preoccupied the postbellum advocates of consolidation. Indeed, that integrative thrust presents itself vividly in the very image of the fasces itself. Pragmatists who endorsed the experimental approach to social reform were not likely to make an a priori condemnation of a thinker whose aims were so consonant with their own. Horace Kallen was deeply impressed by Mussolini's experimentalism and hoped his efforts might prove "a fruitful endeavour after the good life." Charles Beard saw Fascism as "an amazing experiment . . . in reconciling individualism and socialism, politics and technology." Perhaps the most indicative comments were those of Herbert Croly. Although he acknowledged the dangerous aspects of Mussolini's rule, Croly saw in Fascism a powerful movement that had "substituted movement for stagnation, purposive behavior for drifting, and visions of a great future for collective pettiness and discouragement."[5] The use of such affirmative words as *movement*, *purpose*, and *visions*—no less than the negative *pettiness*, which recalled one's higher calling to self-sacrifice and disinterestedness, or *drift*, which was surely meant to echo Lippmann's influential dichotomy—was not to be taken lightly. It indicated that, allowing for cultural differences too myriad to enumerate, Croly could see many of his own intentions for America being mirrored in the Italian experiment.

Too much can be made of this pragmatic enthusiasm, which had little practical effect and in any event faded rapidly by 1930 as Mussolini's brutality, evident long before his invasion of Ethiopia in 1935, became impossible to ignore. The point is not that Croly and his like were somehow cryptofascists, though one might fairly accuse them of naivete. Rather, the concept of the totalitarian state was designed to address the same problems that American writers since Bellamy had been addressing—problems of disorganization, disconnectedness, and dissociation characteristic of the industrial age—and the concept proceeded from and was consistent with many of the same explicit premises about human nature and human needs that had already been embraced by American progressives and antiformalists. Small wonder that, particularly during the 1920s, they should have been listening and watching attentively as Mussolini set about the task of integrating a recalcitrant Italian society and recasting it into a coherent organismic unity.

It did not take long, however, for *lo stato totalitario* to become a term of condemnation, gathering the other dictatorial movements of its time under its rubric. Hitler's ascension to power in 1933, full of oratory about the virtues of *der totale Staat*, allowed German efficiency to put into brutal practice what Mussolini had fantasized: insisting upon the complete primacy of the national state, superseding all autonomous operations of the economy and the independent authority of all lesser groups and individuals, establishing unchallenged single-party rule, and liberally and systematically employing violence and propaganda to further the consolidation of power in the hands of the state. The rise of Hitler crystallized the fundamental sense of totalitarianism; within weeks, journalistic and scholarly writers alike had begun to speak in ominous tones of Hitler's progress toward a "totalitarian state," a National Socialist "revolution" that would "go uncompromisingly forward until it embraces the totality of the German people in every phase of activity."[6] Just as significant was a growing tendency to group all the new dictatorships of the time under the rubric of a single term. Writing in 1935, Oswald Garrison Villard saw no reason to differentiate between the practices of Communists, Fascists, and Nazis. Although lingering pro-Communist sympathies during the years of the Popular Front delayed broader acceptance of that formula, by the late 1930s, and particularly after the 1939 Hitler-Stalin pact, *totalitarianism* seemed the inevitable term to describe just that similarity. By 1939, Dewey, Sidney Hook, Horace Kallen, and other liberal intellectuals proclaimed that the "totalitarian idea" was in control of Germany, Russia, Italy, Japan, and Spain.[7] Although the outlines of the concept were sometimes difficult to delineate with precision, it was widely understood as a more or less coherent political and moral philosophy and as an aggressive rival to the values and practices of American democracy.[8]

The advent of totalitarian regimes, then, seemed to pose a direct challenge to the ideas and institutions of the Western democracies. It caused American political and social thinkers to take stock of the virtues of their own system. There was no unanimity in the American intellectual response to that challenge, however; indeed, much of the debate that ensued seemed to use the concept as a vehicle for perpetuating older debates, a new skin for old wine.

Edward Purcell has usefully grouped the responses into two broad categories. First, there were the "absolutists," men such as Lippmann (now converted to a belief in "higher law"), Niebuhr, Robert Maynard Hutchins, and a variety of Roman Catholic and neo-Thomistic thinkers and natural-law advocates. They contended that the rise of totalitarianism was the inevitable fruit of the antiformalist project itself, which entailed abandonment of any absolute moral standards grounded in nature, revelation, or tradition as well as a negation of the independent dignity and moral responsibility of the individual. On the other hand were the "relativists," a who's who of liberal intellectuals led and epitomized by John Dewey, who saw in the rise of totalitarianism a challenge to the all-important liberal principle of freedom of inquiry and a dangerous and antiscientific fixation upon closed, fixed, and rigid patterns of thought—upon the very absolutes that the antiformalist revolt had been initiated to combat. Philosophical absolutism, Dewey had long believed, inevitably translated into political absolutism, whereas philosophical pragmatism substituted the disinterested authority of science for the interested authority of men and thereby translated politically into individual freedom and democracy. Far from challenging antiformalist premises, to his mind the rise of totalitarianism was confirming and justifying them. In short, the debate between the two sides pitted a perceived need for absolute and prescriptive standards against a perceived danger in all absolute and prescriptive standards.[9]

There was a certain blindness or provinciality to both sides of this debate, with each side attempting to score points by pinning the totalitarian label upon the other side's premises. The absolutists pointed to the way that assumptions about the plastic and social character of the individual, the "cults" of skepticism and scientism, and the primacy of the state as embodiment of directive intelligence paved the way, as Robert Hutchins put it, "from the man of good will to Hitler." The Deweyans, reeling at the prospect of their intellectual liberties being curtailed by natural-law dogmatists, reacted by invoking the mind-controlling features of totalitarian regimes and by asking, to use Dewey's words, "who is to determine the definite truths" that the absolutists were demanding. Only science, Dewey concluded, could answer that question in a nonauthoritarian way acceptable to the sensibilities of modern democrats. As he observed in *Freedom and Culture* (1939), those who complained that the "decay of former theological beliefs" had made it easy for German totalitarianism to triumph were begging the question; the problem was the theological cast of mind itself, which demanded the security of absolute truths. If that cast of mind could only be removed and be replaced by a recognition of the universal cultural authority of science, the result would be "a new morale," "new desires and new ends," a culture that was "so free in itself that it conceives and begets political freedom" as its inevitable consequence.[10]

One could readily see the flaws of either side's position, as they talked past one another. In light of an obvious cultural dissensus on the constitution of natural law, Hutchins had indeed evaded an important question by failing to say *whose* authority would identify absolutes; since it was precisely the disappearance of authority in a relativistic world that was at stake for the absolutists, this omission was crucial (though its disclosure might have made them even more forensically vulnerable). By the same token, however, Dewey continued to put an inordinate weight upon the possibilities of a "common faith" built upon the disinterested authority of science and to wax vague and impractical about the concrete political means by which his new culture would be realized. Their personal faults and demerits aside, the two were illustrating the fundamental antinomies that arise in all discussions of the tension between negative and positive liberty. Could there be a form of genuine social cohesion that did not involve the imposition of moral authority? Conversely, could there be a commitment to genuine individual liberty that did not have to forgo all efforts to achieve moral community and coherence on something more than the barest procedural grounds?

The word *totalitarianism* had become a general bogeyman and debating trump card—a horror compared to whose darkness the glories of American democracy would achieve sharper definition and appear all the more radiant. Neither side, however, was yet exploring the word's meaning on its own terms in a serious and nonpolemical way. What was missing was an explanation, grounded not in ideas but in concrete realities, of why certain modern societies "went" totalitarian. What, for example, were the social and psychological sources of totalitarianism? What sort of people, what sort of social and cultural structures, and what sort of belief systems and character traits gave rise to or were engendered by the totalitarian phenomenon? What human needs did totalitarian movements satisfy? Although American thinkers had formed opinions on these subjects, it would remain for an extraordinary group of outsiders, men and women whose lives had come within close range of totalitarian institutions, to become their most compelling and influential explicators. The most influential theoreticians of totalitarianism had one thing in common: nearly all were writing about something from which they themselves had fled. In a sense, therefore, their perspective was no less partial, but it had an urgency, grounded in personal experience, that their American hosts could scarcely have matched. Indeed, the refugees from totalitarianism had been shaped by a whole set of highly distinctive cultural circumstances, which differed profoundly from the characteristic experiences of American progressives. Since this distinctive set of experiences defined the nature of their contribution, it deserves our close attention.

---

No single event in this century altered the landscape of American intellectual life more than the massive immigration during the 1930s and the early 1940s of a gifted generation of continental, mostly German-speaking intellectuals fleeing from Nazism and Fascism. This intellectual migration was one of the most extraordinary cultural transfers in modern history. Trained in the world's finest educational institutions, these refugees brought to the United States a dauntingly high standard for intellectual endeavor and made impressive contributions to nearly every field imaginable. There were political and social thinkers Hannah Arendt, Leo Strauss, Karl Wittfogel, Herbert Marcuse, Franz Neumann, Leo Lowenthal, Eric Voegelin, Hans Morgenthau, Theodor Adorno, Paul Lazarsfeld, and Erich Fromm; psychologists and psychoanalysts Wolfgang Koehler, Kurt Lewin, Erik Erikson, Bruno Bettelheim, Wilhelm

Reich, Heinz Hartmann, and Karen Horney; theologian Paul Tillich; writers Thomas Mann and Bertolt Brecht; architects Ludwig Mies van der Rohe and Walter Gropius; artists Hans Hofmann and Josef Albers; musicians Arnold Schoenberg, Paul Hindemith, and Kurt Weill; filmmakers Otto Preminger, Fritz Lang, and Billy Wilder; distinguished scholars Hajo Holborn, Felix Gilbert, Paul Oskar Kristeller, Erwin Panofsky, Werner Jaeger, Erich Auerbach, and Leo Spitzer; and an astonishing number of gifted scientists, of whom the physicists Albert Einstein, Hans Bethe, Leo Szilard, and Edward Teller are merely the best known. Even this brief list barely begins to suggest how impressive was the array of imported intellect, for it necessarily omits the many distinguished scholars who happen to be little known outside their disciplines. Nor can it take notice of the considerable number of gifted individuals whose brilliance did not survive the transatlantic journey—the unfortunates who were, for a variety of reasons, unable to carve out a suitable niche for themselves in American intellectual life.[11]

Clearly their arrival was a great windfall for the cultural life of the United States. As Walter W. S. Cook of the New York University Institute of Fine Arts, who recruited such notable refugee scholars as Erwin Panofsky, Walter Friedlander, and Karl Lehmann, quipped, "Hitler is my best friend; he shakes the tree and I collect the apples."[12] The dynamics of intellectual migration and cultural transfer are, however, complex. They involve subtle asymmetries of transmission and reception, perception and misperception, resistance and adaptation. Transplanted ideas and thinkers are always subject to the stresses of translation: of transposition in space, time, language, culture, and circumstance. Such stresses certainly affected the Hitler-era refugee intellectuals to a greater or lesser extent, depending upon their field of endeavor. The most successful, in general, were working in disciplines employing universal, abstract, metacultural languages, such as mathematics and the natural sciences. The least successful were those whose work had been closely tied to the particularities of the German tongue, such as novelists and dramatists. Social and political thought stood somewhere in the middle ground. Though susceptible to a high degree of abstract formulation and analysis, it was also unavoidably bound to the usages, expectations, and experiences arising from a particular cultural and intellectual milieu.[13]

The German refugees did not find an effortless fit with American life, for reasons both personal and intellectual. For one thing, they encountered structures of thought quite different from those to which they were accustomed. The political scientist Franz Neumann, whose *Behemoth* (1942) was among the first efforts to examine the structure of the National Socialist regime, wrote with perceptiveness and candor about this problem. The Germans had been "bred in the veneration of theory and history" and trained to feel nothing but "contempt for empiricism and pragmatism" and for the entire Anglo-American philosophical tradition from Locke to Dewey. In America, they entered a "diametrically opposed intellectual climate: optimistic, empirically oriented, a-historical, but also self-righteous."[14] These remarks echo earlier observations of the Russian émigré Pitirim Sorokin, who saw American sociology as a reform-oriented practical discipline marked by its "quantitative and empirical character," while European sociology involved "an analytical elaboration of concepts and definitions[,] . . . a philosophical and epistemological polishing of words."[15] Both descriptions suggest a clash of cultures, with a nod, inherent in Neumann's mention of American "self-righteousness," toward the still-powerful influence of American Protestantism.

Behind the difference in ideas was a profound difference in experiences. Most of the refugee intellectuals fit a particular profile as German Jews of a secular background. Born as outsiders in their own society, they had come of age intellectually in the polarized, politically unsettled, hothouse environment of Weimar and had personally experienced the coming to power of Hitler and the collapse of German civilization. They differed in one crucial way from the overwhelming majority of previous European-American immigrants: they were exiles. It was not the pull of opportunity but the push of terror that motivated them.

As writers and intellectuals, they were drawn to reflect upon their loss, to unpack the full significance of their stories. Indeed, that subject threatened to overwhelm all others for them. The difficulties that beset their lives were more complicated than merely an adjustment to a different culture, a different language, and a different workplace—formidable though these obstacles were by themselves. "Being an exile," émigré Henry Pachter wrote, "is not a matter of needing a passport; it is a state of mind."[16] The experience of exile united the most disparate thinkers in a bond of shared psychological and social displacement.

Even those fortunate enough to escape the worst deprivations of emigration felt inalterably scarred by it. One of the most plaintive evocations of this condition was penned by Theodor Adorno, in his *Minima Moralia* (subtitled, significantly, *Reflections from Damaged Life*): "Every intellectual in emigration is, without exception, mutilated, and does well to acknowledge it to himself. . . . He lives in an environment that must remain incomprehensible to him. . . . He is always astray." Even the most innocent pleasures of an earlier life have vanished for him: "There is nothing innocuous left. The little pleasures . . . directly serve their diametrical opposite. Even the blossoming tree lies the moment its bloom is seen without the shadow of terror." The space that naturally exists between men has become a yawning abyss: "Sociability itself connives at injustice by pretending that in this chill world we can still talk to each other." The theme of alienation is sounded again: "For the intellectual, inviolable isolation is now the only way of showing some measure of solidarity. All collaboration, all the human worth of social mixing and participation, merely masks a tacit acceptance of inhumanity. It is the sufferings of men that should be shared: the smallest step towards their pleasures is one towards the hardening of their pains."[17] The sense of marginality that had been a painful fact in Germany had hardened, in exile, into a powerfully bleak worldview.

The title of *exile* was not without its romantic appeal as a self-appellation for American intellectuals; Malcolm Cowley appropriated it for his influential self-dramatizing memoir of the Twenties, *Exile's Return*. The expatriate intellectuals of the 1920s, Cowley asserted, had already been uprooted in spirit at home long before they uprooted the flesh by emigration. When the exiles returned, "there was nowhere else to go" but to New York, "the homeland of the uprooted," the modern city par excellence where "nobody seemed to have parents."[18] There was a world of difference, however, between this largely chosen marginality and voluntary departure (and return) of Americans, and the enforced marginality and involuntary departure of Germans and Italians. The refugees came to embody Karl Mannheim's dream of free-floating intellect (*freischwebende Intelligenz*)—but only by being stripped of all customary forms of social connection. The independence of the solitary self had become a source of dread; yet fear of the snares of false connectedness, as embodied in the Fascist appeals to solidarity, was even greater.

That fear is an unmistakable presence in one of the first influential books dealing with the social sources of totalitarianism: Erich Fromm's *Escape from Freedom* (1941), which reached an enormous American popular audience, going through five printings during the war years. The history of man, for Fromm, was the history of growing individuation and freedom, along with growing alienation. "The worst of all pains," he argued, was the pain of "complete aloneness and doubt." Along with man's progressive mastery of Nature has come "growing isolation, insecurity, and thereby growing doubt concerning . . . the meaning of one's life." When the socioeconomic conditions of life fail to support man's "active solidarity with all men," man's freedom becomes an unbearable burden; life becomes meaningless. Modern man had become free of all his ancient external ties, but such freedom has only resulted in "a panicky flight from freedom into new ties or . . . complete indifference." Modern man believes himself free because he is no longer under the absolute authority of the church, the state, or conscience, but rather "the anonymous authority of common sense and public opinion." He is mistaken, however, if he thinks this is freedom. "We have become automatons," Fromm cried, "who live under the illusion of being self-willing individuals." Modern man "lives in a world to which he has lost genuine relatedness and in which everybody and everything has become instrumentalized, where he has become part of the machine that his hands have built. He thinks, feels, and wills, what he believes he is supposed to think, feel, and will." His loss of identity makes it all the more imperative to conform, for "one can be sure of oneself only if one lives up to the expectations of others." Otherwise we risk the loss of our very sanity.[19]

As an early member of the Frankfurt Institut für Sozialforschung, Fromm was enamored of the Frankfurt school's attempt to use Freudian conceptions of psychosexuality to interpret political and historical developments. A great admirer of Marx's Paris manuscripts that had only recently been discovered, Fromm began to employ some of the early Marx's key concepts—albeit in somewhat diffuse and poetic terms and generally without identifying their origins. Totalitarianism thrived because of the lonely individual's "tendency to give up the independence of one's own own individual self and to fuse one's self with somebody or something outside of oneself in order to acquire the strength which the individual self is lacking."[20] Authoritarianism seems to offer an attractive source of such "secondary bonds," and the psychological prerequisite for an authoritarian regime, he believed, was sadomasochism. The individual's "unbearable feeling of aloneness and powerlessness," his alienation from self and from the world, let him into the comforting structure of domination and enabled him to escape from freedom. "The frightened individual," he asserted, "seeks for somebody or something to tie his self to; he cannot bear to be his own individual self any longer." Both the sadist and the masochist are driven by the need to transcend selfhood through a coercive symbiosis, to obliterate the uncertainty and anxiety that are the concomitants of freedom.[21]

Fromm was writing at one of the darkest moments in the history of modern Europe. With Hitler by then in uncontested control of the European continent, the need to account for the sources of his extraordinary power had become an obsession for all the refugee scholars. *Escape from Freedom* was meant to be just such an account. Modern man's aching psychological distress, his inauthentic automatonlike existence, his sadomasochistic ambivalence, his frantic search for meaning in self-abnegating political and social movements: surely, Fromm felt, these were the ultimate sources of the Fascist and Nazi appeal, whatever the epiphenomenal political and economic histories might tell us. How else could one explain that "millions in Germany were as eager to surrender their freedom as their fathers were to fight for it"?[22] Hitler's authoritarian ideology both reflected the aberrant psychological tensions afflicting his followers and provided a solution of sorts for them, a palliative that absorbed the tensions enough to make life endurable. The multitude of modern men could no longer be counted on to pass their lives in quiet desperation, for the "despair of the human automaton is fertile soil for the political purposes of Fascism."[23] The totalitarian enemy was not an exotic and faraway foe. It was as near as our own unexamined impulses.

If the exilic element in Fromm's thought made it distinctive, even more did its long historical background. He was born and raised in one of the greatest and most ancient of German cities. Then, as now, Frankfurt was a crossroads municipality, established since the time of Charlemagne as a major commercial center. Located on the Main near its juncture with the Rhine, Frankfurt stood at the center of Europe, a hub of busy trade and transportation routes. It was also generally near the center of the history of German politics and ideas. In Frankfurt the *Kurfürsten* met in the old city hall, the *Römer*, to elect the emperor. Some three centuries later, it was the birthplace of Goethe, symbol of the tenuous Western and Enlightened strain in the German intellectual tradition. Nearly a century after Goethe's birth, in the fateful year of 1848, a convention of idealistic German liberals assembled in the venerable oval-topped *Paulskirche*, meaning to create a democratic, liberal, and united Germany. Their effort failed, a fact whose fateful significance would be painfully clear a century later. Like Weimar, Goethe's adopted city, Frankfurt would stand for certain cherished Western liberal ideals—and for the impediments to their realization in German politics.[24]

Jews had a particularly large stake in those liberal ideals. They had been excluded from participation in Christian European society for many centuries, confined to the squalor and isolation of ghetto life, and subjected to medieval restrictions upon their rights of residency, movement, occupation, and citizenship. The Enlightenment commitment to secularism, the rights of man, and the abolition of irrational dogma had promised to change that; hence one of the leading figures of the German Enlightenment was Moses Mendelssohn, whose emancipatory agenda included not only full political rights for Jews but a Jewish willingness to undertake full integration and assimilation into the German mainstream.[25] Editor, with Lessing and Nicolai, of the *Allgemeine deutsche Bibliothek* and translator of the Torah into German, the gentle and courtly Mendelssohn came, in his person as much as in his work, to symbolize the desirability of synthesizing those two worlds that had been so painfully separate for so long. His example was followed by the growing German-

Jewish bourgeoisie, which found the Goethean ideal of *Bildung* particularly congenial to Jewish habits of diligent study. Indeed, as Jacob Katz has observed, they began to think of the pursuit of *Bildung* as an essential component of Jewish identity, which they actually pursued more zealously than their Gentile counterparts—partly out of intellectual propensity and partly as a path to overcome social discrimination.[26]

In 1900, the year Fromm was born, Frankfurt was a vibrant center for the German-Jewish bourgeoisie. The city's commercial vitality had made it a magnet for Jewish enterprise ever since the Middle Ages, and with the advent of an increasingly industrial, money-based economy in the post-Napoleonic years, the opportunities for and influence of Jews in the city's life had increased dramatically. The city became the financial capital of Germany; perhaps the most famous product of its *Judengasse*, though by no means the only one, was the Rothschild banking family, which used its power to ensure the establishment and protection of Jewish civil rights in the city.[27] Though Jews never made up much more than a tenth of the population, they exerted a considerable influence upon city affairs. The generation born at the turn of the century, which could presume the economic and social benefits conferred by emancipation, could entertain admission to the universities and the professions, to the arts and the sciences, to the full pursuit of *Bildung*.

In many respects, however, this comfortable assimilation was more apparent than real. Frankfurt Jews had been forced to battle for their citizenship more than once, and their municipal influence was in fact a double-edged sword, for it also gave their detractors a weapon to use against them. As elsewhere in Germany, the liberation of Jewish energies from long confinement, and their immersion in the mainstream of German cultural and social life, disturbed the Gentile majority, which was not prepared for such formidable competition from those it was pleased to regard as its social inferiors. Contrary to appearances, the German Jews were not really becoming assimilated into German society; they were not even assimilated fully into the emerging German professional middle class. Instead, they were a group unto themselves, a parallel subculture "which happened to conform to the German middle class in certain of its characteristics," in Jacob Katz's words, but in fact remained tantalizingly and frustratingly on the fringes of Gentile acceptance. The headlong rush toward assimilation, a development that had, in essence, taken place within the astonishingly short span between 1780 and 1870—a mere three generations—left the Jews without a heritage to fall back on. They were trapped between past and future, between ghetto Jewry and high Gentility, not clearly part of either, and cast into a vertiginous ambiguity. Theirs was a social marginality heightened, not alleviated, by prosperity. It was as if the closer they came to Gentile society, the more insurmountable the remaining distance became, and the more impassable was the road back.[28]

The generation of the Frankfurt school thinkers, then, came into possession of a mixed legacy: a materially comfortable existence fraught with hidden dangers and subliminal precariousness. They were firmly grounded in the postemancipatory, liberal Enlightenment ethos that their parents' and grandparents' generations had so ardently espoused. The reigning household gods were the ideals of *Bildung*, optimism about the power of human reason, confidence in the autonomy of the individual, belief that self-cultivation and the acquisition of knowledge inevitably bore moral and spiritual benefits, and hope that the differences separating Jew and Christian would be erased as mankind ascended to the higher common ground of universal humanism. For the sons and daughters of emancipation, that faith was held a little more tenuously, more ambivalently. They resented the tense and artificial role playing, the constant anxiety about living up to Gentile expectations, and the price that their parents' generation paid for assimilation.[29]

The younger intellectuals, then, were unrepresentative of German Jews in general. These were the deracinated, well-educated, cosmopolitan, cultivated young, the third-generation product of the drive for assimilation. Within the Frankfurt school alone, the biographical profiles of the principals are strikingly similar. With only a few exceptions, they were of Jewish descent, born into haute bourgeois families, their fathers being either successful businessmen or professionals.[30] Despite their privileged background, however, a persistent sense of Jewish apartness—raised to an extreme by its having become an apartness from Jewry as well—took its toll on them as well, even in the relative freedom of Weimar. The attraction of Marxism, its salvific potential, derived from the same source. Erich Fromm put it eloquently in his remembrance of boyhood:

> Probably the immediate reason for [my early] absorption by the idea of peace and internationalism is to be found in the situation in which I found myself: a Jewish boy in a Christian environment, experiencing small episodes of anti-Semitism but, more importantly, a feeling of strangeness and of clannishness on both sides. I disliked clannishness, maybe all the more so because I had an overwhelming wish to transcend the emotional isolation of a lonely, pampered boy; what could be more exciting and beautiful to me than the prophetic vision of universal brotherhood and peace?[31]

What better way to overcome the pain of estrangement than to seek a universal higher ground, from whose vantage point the differences that separate human beings would shrink into insignificance?

Fromm's feelings of loneliness at that age were perhaps heightened by the fact that, unlike most of the other Frankfurt school intellectuals, he was raised in a orthodox household. Even more significant, however, were the internal dynamics of that household. As the only child of a troubled marriage between an emotionally distant wine-merchant father and an overprotective mother with grandiose musical ambitions for her son, Fromm grew up as an "unbearable, neurotic child," painfully conscious of his parents' antipathies, both desirous and wary of acceptance by his remote father and his smothering mother.[32] Such a background was unlikely to produce a writer who sentimentalized middle-class family life or revered the Wilhelmian pattern of patriarchal domestic authority.

Instead, young Fromm found refuge and exhilaration in his reading of the Hebrew Scriptures, particularly the prophetic books of Isaiah, Amos, and Hosea, which thrilled him with their apocalyptic promise of the "end of days," of the nations beating their swords into plowshares, and of the earth "full of the knowledge of the Lord, as the waters cover the sea." A craving for such ultimate reconciliation and reintegration, as well as a desire for rebellion against the world of his businessman father, led Fromm (in German the surname means *devout* or *pious*) to form an early ambition to become a rabbi and to apply himself energetically to Talmudic studies with a succession of teachers, including Gershom Scholem, the great scholar of the Kabala.[33] Still, Fromm was deeply convinced that all orthodoxies and all group loyalties could be treacherous and devouring. This conviction, fed by his horrified reaction to the irrational carnage of the First World War, led him to "wish to understand the irrationality of human mass behavior" and made him "deeply suspicious of all official ideologies and declarations."[34]

The tug of secular modernity was as powerful for Fromm as for many other young orthodox Jews. When he went to college at Frankfurt and Heidelberg he studied sociology and psychology and became friendly with students and faculty alike who were thoroughly secular in their outlook. Fromm was increasingly torn between the pull of his orthodox heritage and the lure of the secular perspectives to which he was being exposed, and the strength of his faith began to falter. First he sought compromise. He wrote a doctoral dissertation at Heidelberg under Alfred Weber that compared the psychological structures associated with Karaites and Chassidim with those of modern Reform Jews; it was an obvious attempt to reconcile conflicting worlds. Fromm also began visiting a sanatorium run by the orthodox analyst Freida

Reichmann, who was experimenting with a unique combination of Freud and Torah (which skeptics called "Torah-peutic" treatment); Leo Lowenthal also visited the same sanatorium. In the end, as Scholem recalled, this attempt to meld orthodoxy and therapeutic modernism merely resulted in the triumph of the latter. It was like the sort of marriage counseling that merely eases the client's way into divorce, for all but one of the analysands "had their Orthodox Judaism analyzed away."[35] Nevertheless, Fromm's stubborn struggle against the orthodoxy in which he was raised imparted an enduring cast to his thinking, for although he would draw heavily upon the work of Marx and Freud, he adamantly resisted any attempt to confine himself to orthodox interpretations of those thinkers—or any other intellectual or institutional orthodoxy. He would always be a bit of an intellectual loner.

The pain of separateness was not peculiar to the orthodox-raised individual like Fromm; a strikingly similar pattern can be detected in the boyhood reminiscences of the secularly reared Theodor Adorno. As the only child of a wealthy, highly assimilated Jewish wine merchant and his Italian-Catholic wife, Adorno also experienced a pampered, high-bourgeois childhood in Wilhelmian Frankfurt. His mother had given up a promising singing career to marry, and in compensation she poured her considerable energies into the rearing of her beloved "Teddie." He was extraordinarily precocious musically and intellectually. His mother's constant attentions—in marked contrast to the authoritarian remoteness of his Central European father—made him naturally prefer her world of musical parlors and refined drawing rooms to his father's world of commerce, which he quickly came to regard with suspicion and fear. Such feelings no doubt also extended to his father's person. The solicitous warmth of his childhood home would be the standard against which his future experiences in the greater world would be judged—and fall short.[36]

By all accounts, the mature Adorno was an arrogant man, yet he also had a relatively unguarded and childlike nature, which was constantly assailed by forces threatening to overwhelm it.[37] His searing autobiographical fragment in *Minima Moralia* called "The Bad Comrade" ("Der bose Kamerad," an allusion to the popular song "Der gute Kamerad," which was used by the Nazis), offers a graphic picture of the agonizing separateness Adorno experienced in his youth:

In a real sense, I ought to be able to deduce Fascism from the memories of my childhood. As a conqueror dispatches envoys to the remotest provinces, Fascism had sent its advance guard there long before it marched in: my schoolfellows. . . . I felt with such excessive clarity the force of the horror towards which they were straining, that all subsequent happiness seemed revocable, borrowed. The outbreak of the Third Reich did, it is true, surprise my political judgment, but not my unconscious fear. So closely had all the motifs of permanent catastrophe brushed me, so deeply were the warning signs of the German awakening burned into me, that I recognized them all in the features of Hitler's dictatorship: and it often seemed to my foolish terror as if the total State had been invented expressly against me, to inflict upon me after all those things from which, in my childhood, its primeval form, I had been temporarily dispensed. . . . Now that they, officials and recruits, have stepped out of my dream and dispossessed me of my past life and my language, I no longer need to dream of them. In Fascism the nightmare of childhood has come true.[38]

In Adorno's case, a remarkably gifted and abnormally sheltered sensibility collided with an ugly social reality, resulting in paralyzing visions of mounting and helpless terror.

For the radical intellectuals associated with the journal *Weltbühne* or with the Frankfurt Institut, assimilation as a solution to the problem of Jewish marginality held limited promise. They did not wish to trade their Jewish identity for a "Christian-German" one; rather, they wished to be done with both, so that all Germans could transcend the outdated and illegitimate categories that separated them. Hence the appeal of Marxian universalism, radical secularism, and Enlightenment ideals. In the Marxian vision, differences of ethnicity, nationality, and religion were reduced to insignificance, subsumed under the more transcendent distinction of class, which was also fated to eventual historical extinction. In the best Hegelian manner, the differences between German and Jewish identities would best be reconciled by being transcended.[39]

The disappointing political showing of Marxism in the years after the First World War, however, forced these hopes into quietistic channels. The growing interest in Hegel was but one manifestation of a more general response to the crisis of Marxism in the West. When the Spartacist uprising failed, when the Social Democrats betrayed the Marxist vision, and when the German Communist party fell under the control of Moscow, intellectuals were faced, like the early Christians, with stark choices: either abandon the faith or find another means to carry it on, and another eschatology consistent with those means. Since the proletariat had refused to play its historically appointed role and had left the radical thrust of Marxism without a plausible protagonist, how could that radical thrust be preserved? The answer was to perpetuate the Marxian resistance as philosophical struggle, a symbolic and inner battle that would not be subject to the vagaries and betrayals of praxis. The new Marxism would not press for a revolution in the outer world but, rather, a rethinking of the entire tradition, "with the dual hope," Martin Jay put it, "of explaining past errors and preparing for future action." Ironically, the independent inherited wealth and ease of the Frankfurt school thinkers, the fruits of capitalism, allowed them to pursue such an independent course; otherwise, they might have been forced to choose between one or the other of the unsatisfactory practical roads that they had avoided. It was not leisure, however, but the thwarting of radical praxis, the permanent displacement of the spiritually isolated, that shaped their thought. They were already in exile before Hitler.[40]

There was nothing in the American intellectual life of the time comparable to the characteristic Frankfurt school approach. It can be understood only in reference to the history of Marxism in Europe and to the revival of "metaphysical idealism," which began, in the wreckage of revolutionary hopes after World War I, with Georg Lukacs's *History and Class Consciousness* and Karl Korsch's *Marxism and Philosophy*. These writers deemphasized the progressive optimism and scientific pretensions of the later Marx and revivified the Hegelian elements in Marx that had been ignored. The concept of alienation, especially as elaborated in Marx's Paris manuscripts, was crucial to them.[41] But they also tried to fuse their Marxism with a newer strain of modernist thought: Freudian psychoanalysis. Indeed, the attempt to integrate psychoanalysis and Marxism as the two thought systems that offered the preeminent radical critiques of modern bourgeois civilization made the Frankfurt Institut distinctive. At bottom, the allegiance to Marx was stronger, for although Freud was admired for his remorseless dissection of the human condition in modern times, his nineteenth-century biological-mechanist assumptions made him fall victim to a form of "false consciousness": the psychologistic belief that the consciousness can be understood separately from the society that shapes it. "The divergence of the individual and society," Adorno declared, was "essentially of social origin" and was "first of all to be explained in social terms."[42] Hence, it was not surprising that members of the institute would be attracted to social psychology, which provided a way of explaining the intersection between the individual psyche and the social conditions that created it. It was not surprising, either, that when Fromm joined the institute, he was made head of the social psychology section.[43]

Also adding to this distinctiveness was the intellectual cohesiveness of the institute. Despite the wide range of the authors' interests, the institute writings taken as a whole add up to a remarkably unified view of the world: a comprehensive assault, which they called "Critical Theory," upon the culture of modern capitalist society. This intellectual cohesiveness was all the more remarkable because Critical Theory was a theory without tenets; in fact, it repeatedly asserted its programmatic opposition to any and all programmatic systems of thought. It was not a set of doctrines but a series of self-consciously critical analyses of other thinkers, a never-ending dialectical exchange between thought and social reality. If this definition seems to lack specificity, that is no accident. Critical Theory made it possible for its practitioners to escape being pinned down to unsuccessful commitments—the fate that had befallen those who had put their faith in praxis. Indeed, Critical Theory involved a prolonged series of negations, since any point of view was partial and mediated and therefore had to be ruthlessly criticized from another, equally partial and mediated point of view. It was a combination of Hegelian dialectics and modern social thought but, lacking the progressive Hegelian developmental logic, structured itself as an endless series of intellectual crossfires. By preoccupying themselves with the study of culture, Critical Theorists could continue to claim revolutionary goals without endangering them in battle—and without falling into the trap of a devouring creedal or organizational orthodoxy.[44]

The essays presented in the institute's 1936 volume of studies on authority and the family were clearly a response to Hitler's rise, yet they typified the unity in diversity that was the institute's trademark. Subjects as diverse as the sexual attitudes of German doctors, unemployment, family law, and adolescence were treated in its pages. The theoretical material, however, presented in the work's three opening essays, was the most important. These essays, by Max Horkheimer, Fromm, and Herbert Marcuse, presented a unified view of the family, mindful of its role in Marxist thought as a mediating institution linking the material realities of the economic base with the ideological superstructure—a conduit through which the concrete needs of the former are translated into the legitimating ideas of the latter. In keeping with the cultural emphasis of Western Marxism, however, Horkheimer stressed how ideological patterns can be perpetuated even in spite of a decisive shift in the material basis of life. The current notions of the family, he believed, were an example of such an incongruity; under the conditions of late-capitalist society, the paternal authority of the nineteenth-century bourgeois had ceased to have an "objective" (that is, material) basis. Hence, the family was a source of pathology and no longer had the strength to withstand the all-encompassing power of modern society to shape human institutions to its ends. "The education of authoritarian characters," he wrote, "does not belong to transient appearance, but to a relatively lasting condition": that is, the bourgeois family's decline and its replacement by broader, more general forces as the agents of socialization.[45]

Erich Fromm's contribution touched upon some of the same themes, albeit from a slightly different perspective. As a Freudian-trained psychiatrist, Fromm was deeply committed to Freud's work and viewpoint, but as a Marxian socialist, he found ultimately unsatisfying Freud's neglect of the social and economic etiology of dysfunctional family relations. He was willing to accept the notion that a decline in the ego strength of modern men had something to do with their willingness to submit to authoritarian rule, and like Freud, he recognized that the willingness to submit and the desire to dominate were two sides of the same pathological coin. But the proper explanation of this pathology was woefully incomplete if grounded only in the examination of the individual psyche and the family background from which that psyche had emerged. The socioeconomic structures of a society had to be considered, for they inevitably produced certain characteristic psychological types. The distinctive responses to the challenges posed by those structures constituted the "social character" of a group, an expression of the way these external structures were internalized. The family's role in this process was crucial, for it was the "transmission belt" through which prevailing social-character traits were inculcated in individuals.[46]

Fromm's essay marks the group's first attempt to elaborate psychoanalytically the notion of "authoritarian personality," to which Adorno would turn after the Second World War. For Fromm, the authoritarian personality was based upon the sadomasochistic character (Freud's "anal" structure), which he saw as an inevitable result of a declining society founded upon patterns of hierarchy and dependency.[47] This type of individual was racked by simultaneously felt aggressive and submissive drives; fearful of his own sense of weakness, he characteristically reacted with a rigid, domineering attitude toward himself and a compulsion to control others. This ambivalence also played itself out politically in confused attitudes toward authority, just as in the patriarchal family. The sadomasochistic authoritarian was simultaneously driven to rebel against authority and to submit to it unquestioningly. Membership in a radical charismatic right-wing political movement promised relief from this tension, for it satisfied his need to submit even as it fulfilled his need to dominate. So, too, had adherence to the sort of rigid and archaic orthodoxy from which Fromm had struggled to free himself. Indeed, it is not hard to find the personal element in Fromm's account of the authoritarian personality, since it represented the dangers of the very yearnings for connectedness and conciliation that Fromm himself understood so well.

The foregoing discussion should not be taken to imply that Fromm was always a member in good standing of the institute's inner circle. In fact, by the time *Escape from Freedom* appeared, Fromm had already been disassociated from the institute for two years, largely because even his gloomy prognosis for modernity was deemed insufficiently negative and his criticisms of Freud excessively revisionist according to the severe standards of Adorno, Horkheimer, and other core members.[48] In the years to come, Fromm, of course, resisted their orthodoxy and became a frequent target of their attacks, most notably in Marcuse's *Eros and Civilization* (1955), which attempted to rescue the "radical" Freud from the revisionists' deemphasis upon instinctual needs.[49] Despite intramural differences, however, the émigrés' visions of the challenges posed by modernity were strikingly similar and in striking contrast to the progressive and optimistic view that prevailed in America.

In the early years of emigration, the institute continued to be impressively unified in its interests and direction. The figure supplying this unity, however, was not the liberating spirit of Freud or Marx but the diabolical spirit of Hitler. "We were all possessed, so to speak, of the idea that we must beat Hitler and fascism," remarked Horkheimer's secretary, "and this brought us all together. We all felt we had a mission. . . . This mission really gave us a feeling of loyalty and belonging together."[50] Not only did the Nazi phenomenon unite the institution, giving a feeling of esprit de corps to an otherwise isolated and fearful band of displaced marginals, but it came to be the linchpin holding together the members' far-flung intellectual pursuits. The preconditions that make forms of total domination possible, and the various means by which they are carried out, became their central animating concern. Rather than an interest in politics, however, it was the control and mutation of consciousness, above all else, that they studied.

As in the case of Fromm, however, the concern that began with Hitler did not end with him. It rapidly extended to a consideration of the exiles' newly adopted home. If the Frankfurt refugees were haunted by the question, "How could it have happened?," they were equally haunted by the possibility that it might happen here. Fromm had already begun to wonder whether in a modern "mass society" like America, the most powerful forms of coercion and the most damaging deformations of consciousness and character are imposed not by the demonic likes of Hitler but in more indirect, intangible, but no less powerful, ways. Though writing from a distinctively European socialist intellectual tradition, Fromm had nevertheless begun sounding notes and touching upon sentiments that would seem oddly familiar, even venerable, to Americans.

---

What kind of self produced, and was produced by, modern capitalist society? One of the answers to that inquiry, and an important contribution to the emerging understanding of the totalitarian character, was *The Authoritarian Personality* (1951). This massive study, produced by Adorno and a group of collaborators, was part of a "Studies in Prejudice" series commissioned by the American Jewish Committee, which sought to discover the social-psychological sources of extreme prejudice—especially anti-Semitism—and to find ways of quantifying and measuring an individual's predisposition toward such prejudice. As a cooperative effort of specialists in such diverse fields as social theory, depth psychology, political sociology, clinical psychology, and projective testing, it was a model for interdisciplinary research in the social sciences. Combining the resources of the Berkeley Public Opinion Study with a subdued version of Critical Theory, the book seemed a fruitful combination of the former's empirical methods and the latter's theoretical sophistication.[51] As a project first begun in May 1944, at a time when Hitler still controlled continental Europe and the horrifying dimensions of the Final Solution were becoming more and more widely known, the questions it addressed were far from academic. For American Jews no less than European refugees, the etiology of Fascism and Nazism and its possibilities in an American context was an urgent problem.

The book's title conveyed its central conclusion. The rise of modern industrial society, the authors contended, had brought with it the rise of a new kind of human being: "an 'anthropological' species we call the authoritarian type of man," which threatened "to replace the individualistic and democratic type prevalent in the past century and a half of our civilization."[52] The study did not directly address the social, economic, or political origins of authoritarian movements; instead, it set out to demonstrate that, on the individual level, certain distinctive protofascist social and political attitudes could be regularly correlated with a particular psychological structure, and that this correlation could be discerned in any modern Western society. The implicit conclusion— in fact, an implicit premise—was that the barbarism that had arisen in Germany and Italy could, indeed, have easily arisen in the United States as well. The factors that made for a predisposition toward the assertion and acceptance of authoritarian rule could be found anywhere that the pathologies of modern society could be found. America too had a "fascist potential." This work, so eminently the product of émigré minds, also reflected a universalizing of émigré fears. It would, however, enjoy considerable influence in Americans' ongoing struggle to come to terms with the problems of autonomy and solidarity.

It also reflected the émigré influence in the specific texture of its ideas and indeed drew heavily upon work that these men had done long before they came to America. Adorno's description borrowed heavily from the work of his former Frankfurt colleagues, particularly Fromm's earlier exploration of "authoritarian-masochistic character" in the 1936 studies of authority and the family and then in *Escape from Freedom*. Like Fromm, Adorno closely followed Freud's account of the "anal erotic" character, a description that fits well what we know of the households in which Fromm and Adorno were reared.

The typical authoritarian personality grows up in a household ordered by a pervasive pattern of dominance and submission. The father is cold, distant, and domineering and implants in his child an agonizing dividedness of mind. (The émigré psychiatrist Erik Erikson elaborated similarly upon this vision of punitive German paternal authority in an influential essay on the origins of the National Socialists' popular appeal.)[53] On one hand, the child experiences an overwhelming need to please, at whatever cost, a cruel and unappeasable father and thereby gain some small measure of the self-esteem he so desperately desires; this makes him eager to submit to paternal authority and creates the habit of such submissiveness.

On the other hand, the child feels an equally powerful resentment of the father's authority, a need to rebel that must be forcibly suppressed, since any attempt at rebellion is sure to be thwarted by the father's cruel power. Part of the hostility toward the father is transformed, by reaction formation, into love. But part of that hostility remains untransformed, and the individual must find a suitable substitute for the father as an object of his hatred. It is this psychological need that the attitudes and behaviors characteristic of ethnocentrism, stereotypy, and hatred of outgroups, including Jews, blacks, and Asians, fulfill in the individual's psychic economy.[54] Therein, the authors believed, lay the origins of extreme prejudice. The authoritarian character had the following traits: "a mechanical surrender to conventional values; blind submission to authority together with blind hatred of all opponents and outsiders; anti-introspectiveness; rigid stereotyped thinking; a penchant for superstition; vilification, half-moralistic and half-cynical, of human nature; projectivity."[55]

*The Authoritarian Personality* quickly made its mark upon postwar American intellectual life, both inside and outside the social sciences, everywhere inspiring intense interest and controversy. It was the sort of book whose influence far exceeded the number of individuals who read it cover to cover, for that was a formidable undertaking. Its thousand pages fairly bristled with the imposing apparatus of empirical social-scientific research: endless tables, statistics, lengthy quotations from interviews, elaborate typologies, and technical terminology. As critics of the book's methodology were quick to see, however, its theoretical component, for which Adorno bore chief responsibility, utterly dominated the empirical research; the endless tables and quotations merely served to illustrate conclusions that had already been arrived at well in advance. Adorno himself admitted this, openly acknowledging the primacy of theory in the study: "We never regarded the theory simply as a set of hypotheses but in some sense as standing on its own two feet, and therefore did not intend to prove or disprove the theory through our findings."[56]

Despite the extensive contributions of Adorno's coauthors, the substantive core of the book may be regarded as a product of Adorno's sensibility, edited for American consumption.[57] Actually, a true empirical study could hardly have been more unlikely and more unrepresentative of Adorno's work. Like his colleague Franz Neumann, he had been shaped by a theoretical and philosophical tradition very different from, and very much at odds with, the practical-minded experimentalism he encountered in American exile. The bewilderment experienced by many American readers of *The Authoritarian Personality*, however, had to do specifically with its unacknowledged debt to an established and sophisticated Marxist intellectual tradition which simply did not exist in the United States. Throughout its American years, the institute went to some lengths to disguise its Marxian orientation, prudently altering its vocabulary to avoid inflaming American sensibilities (which in turn incurred the wrath of their more candid radical brethren). In his American career, Adorno traveled incognito, reserving his truest sentiments for the relative privacy of the German language. He regarded each of his works in exile as a "message in a bottle," a fragile vessel set forth uncertainly into the turbulent sea of the present, in the hope that it might someday be recovered by more sympathetic hands.[58]

If the perceived ubiquity of authoritarian personalities in modern America made Adorno anxious, the spectacle of American mass culture filled him and Horkheimer with horrified fascination. It was not that they had never encountered such modern popular culture at home. The years of the Weimar Republic were, in fact, halcyon days for German popular film, theater, photomontage, phonograph recordings, radio, typography, advertising, sports, and all the modern organs of publicity, and Adorno made no secret of his distaste for such "Broadway methods on the Kurfürstendamm."[59] As the comparison implies, however, he saw America as the great exemplar of such methods, the fatherland of what he and Horkheimer would call "the culture industry." Their contempt for commercial popular culture stemmed from more than snobbery; they needed to make sense somehow of the failure of the proletariat to perform its historically appointed role, and the stupefying effects of mass culture seemed a likely culprit. They distracted the working class and diverted its insurgent energies from the overthrow of existing oppressions. As Lowenthal wrote in an essay that enjoyed great influence in the United States, "Wherever revolutionary tendencies show a timid head, they are mitigated and cut short by a false fulfillment of wish-dreams, like wealth, adventure, passionate love, power and sensationalism in general." As the Austrian Paul Lazarsfeld put it with characteristic bluntness, his fellow émigrés saw jazz and the radio day-time serials as "opiates of the people."[60]

Adorno, to be sure, did not resort to such shopworn, vulgar-Marxist jargon, but his and Horkheimer's view of the "culture industry"—which they observed at close range when they moved the institute to Los Angeles—was much the same. They preferred the term *culture industry* to *mass culture* because the latter expression implied a spontaneous welling up of mass senti-ment, when in fact the artifacts of mass culture were nothing but commodities pressed upon the consuming public from above, consciously wrought not for their expressive meaning but for their exchange value. Cultural commodities became instruments of "false consciousness"; even their claim to be nothing but relaxing entertainment did not save them from that sinister accusation, for by distracting the mass consumer from an unsparing contemplation of his social and economic situation and by dulling his awareness of his inchoate needs, they served as essential props for the status quo. Moreover, the culture industry's productions did not even satisfy the needs that they claimed to address. It "piously claims to be guided by its customers and to supply them with what they ask for," but in reality it "not so much adapts to the reactions of its customers as it counterfeits them" and "drills them in their attitudes," forcing them to accept a "pseudo-individuality" as if it were the real thing. These proud and up-to-date productions of modernity were in fact regressive and debilitating.[61]

Their assessment of mass culture, however, was only a small part of a vaster and more sweeping critique of modernity that Adorno and Horkheimer were quietly evolving during the war years. The English-speaking world was largely unaware of the nature of this critique until 1972, when the wartime work *Dialektik der Aufklärung* was finally published in English translation as *Dialec-tic of Enlightenment*.[62] Adorno and Horkheimer rejected the conventional progressive historiography that classed the Enlightenment as an unequivocal good in the evolution of human consciousness. Instead, they argued, in a phrase that has since become famous, that "Enlightenment is totalitarian." By this they meant that the enlightened belief that everything can be illuminated and manipulated by the power of instrumental reason led ineluctably to the belief that everything can be administered or reconstituted—and thereby to the horror of "the administered world," in which all reality is a "delusional system." The Baconian drive for the domination of Nature led to a parallel attempt to control the human world as well. The ideology of progress had led to barbarism, and modern science had become a tool of enslavement rather than a tool of liberation. In this post-Nietzschean world, the enslavement was not restricted to dictatorships, the usual recipients of the epithet "totalitarian"; it was just as pervasive in the "democratic" countries of the West, where the all-embracing power of the culture industry had nearly buried the possibility of independent critical thought beneath an enormous refuse heap of commodified artifacts and reified minds.

It was an astonishing book—not least for having been written on American soil during the heat of the Second World War. That fact gives some insight into how distant the men felt from their surroundings, how completely and hermetically they had closed off their genuine intellectual life. In that connection, *Dialectic of Enlightenment*'s discussion of anti-Semitism is indicative, once again recalling how inescapably grounded in the trauma of personal displacements their perceptions were. In "the administered world" of Enlightenment dream (the world that Herbert Marcuse would later dub "one-dimensional"), the Jew was the last bastion of resistance, they argued, to the all-encompassing instrumental-rational order, a stubborn reservoir of "otherness," of nonconformity, nonadjustment, and nonadaptation. Yet it hardly needs saying that the archetypal Jew they were describing was not the Jew of historical reality, whose life was embedded in centuries of Jewish texts, traditions, and cultural practices. Instead, it was Adorno's projection onto the universal fiction of "the Jew" of his own self-conception as a permanent exile. "Homeland," he declared, "is the state of having escaped." With these words he thought to rescue himself from the corrupt form into which a totalitarian, all-demanding modernity had transformed the very idea of homeland. He also affirmed, however, the separateness that, by the iron whim of fate, had become the lot of him and his fellow refugees—a state that, in the end, he found preferable to the fear of betrayal inherent in all attachment and connectedness. In the end, there was no solidarity but in separateness, and there was nothing left in this world to revere except the independent critical intelligence. "Thought honors itself," he declared, "by defending what is damned as nihilism." It was as if he had adopted Emerson's dictum from "Self-Reliance" that "nothing is at last sacred but the integrity of your own mind," transposed it into a minor key, and banged it out in a defiant fortissimo.[63]

---

Hannah Arendt most emphatically did not share the Marxism and Freudianism of the Frankfurt intellectuals, but she shared their unhappy childhoods, their social background, and their flight from Hitler. Like them, she produced scholarship that told her own story, projected onto the vast screen of world history. As personal as such an enterprise may have been, there was little in it that was hers alone. The work in which Arendt managed to project herself most spectacularly was her monumental tome *The Origins of Totalitarianism* (1951), which certainly ranks as one of the most influential works of the postwar era in the United States. Writing in a self-consciously epic style, which strode purposefully through the rubble of modern history with hardly a glance toward the more mundane factual disputes of conventional historians, Arendt produced a kind of Nietzschean history, an account of modern times that illuminated the darkness by the light of generalizing thunderbolts. Disdainful of the usual way historians constructed plausible links of influence and causation, Arendt specialized in grand leaps of the imagination, which carried her across the globe in her quest for the ideational pieces that, she believed, finally fit into the totalitarianism of her time. Alternately stimulated and irritated by her intellectual boldness, historians and political scientists have been grappling with *The Origins of Totalitarianism* and the concepts to which it gave classic expression ever since, but few have denied its significance. As recently as 1985, one American historian called it "the political masterpiece of the postwar era."[64]

At the bottom of her argument was the premise that totalitarianism was "a novel form of government," unprecedented in human history, which differed from the "other forms of political oppression known to us such as despotism, tyranny, and dictatorship."[65] It was the burden of the *Origins* to show how this new political species came to be, and to make the texture of life under its regime vividly clear to Western readers. In the latter aim, the *Origins* was successful beyond anything that could have been expected of a writer who was still learning the English language. Indeed, the book's third section, devoted to an imaginative exploration of fully realized totalitarian regimes (especially as manifested in the quintessential totalitarian institution, the concentration camp), is an unforgettable evocation of a hell where nothing is unthinkable, where an inside-out logic based upon the twin compulsions of terror and ideology usurps the very world of common sense. When historians pointed out, as they invariably did, that life in the camps did not follow the lines of Arendt's analysis, she remained unruffled. For Arendt, in whom the intellectual habits of philosophical idealism were deeply ingrained, the totalitarian world depicted in her book bore the same relationship to fact that the Platonic *eidos* did to that which embodied it; or, as Judith Shklar nicely put it, "the totalitarian world was a philosophical nightmare of which the actuality of the camps was the expression."[66] For Arendt, the *idea* of totalitarianism, grounded as it was in the crisis of Western philosophy after Nietzsche, was more real than any particular (and partial) concrete expression of it. An awareness of this aspect of her thinking, which amounts to a modified idealism, helps illuminate the unorthodox manner by which her argument proceeds in the *Origins*.

The origins of totalitarianism, for Arendt, lay deep within the changing structure of bourgeois European civilization. The nineteenth century, she believed, had seen a crumbling of the old class hierarchy and a deterioration of the European nation-state system, both of which liberated powerful and unfocused social energies, as in nuclear fission. The disappearance of class structures turned the people into undifferentiated masses, uprooted from tradition and yearning for the structure and support that political movements offered. The weakening of the nation-state system, she argued, had been intimately tied to the pattern of imperialist exploitation into which all the great European powers had been drawn by "the political emancipation of the bourgeoisie." Imperial adventures gave legitimacy to the corruptions of racialist thinking and spurred the pursuit of economic expansion as an end in itself, without the concomitant creation of authentic political and social institutions; instead, the colonial masses were ruled by Kafkaesque administrative bureaucracies. Imperialism and the decline of the nation-state also gave impetus to the "tribal nationalisms"—diametrically opposed, in her view, from older nationalisms—of Pan-Germanism and Pan-Slavism, mass movements that filled the void left by the withering nation.

All of these developments spelled particular trouble for the Jews of Europe; indeed, Arendt, like Adorno, did not think the scapegoating of Jews in modern times was some accident or aberration. Jews had achieved their high status in eighteenth-century Europe, she argued, by serving as court financiers and counselors; both the decline of the nation-state and the growth of imperial enterprise meant that the Jews had lost the function they formerly performed. Hence they became highly vulnerable, the ideal target for the unfocused resentments and hatreds generated in the masses by the rise of industrial capitalism. To Arendt, the resurgence of anti-Semitism in nineteenth-century Europe played a key role in the crystallization of totalitarianism.

The discontent of the masses was central to Arendt's argument, and she leaned heavily (although she did not acknowledge the source) upon the earlier work of her fellow refugee Emil Lederer, whose posthumously published work *The State of the Masses* (1940), edited for publication by Hans Speier, was one of the earliest attempts to account for the common social basis of Nazism and Fascism. Though a socialist by political sentiment, Lederer argued that it was the breakdown of the social class system in modern Europe that had created mobs of undifferentiated individuals eager to be yoked into the false sense of community provided by totalitarian regimes. To Lederer, this meant that the Marxian dream of classless egalitarianism would in fact result in horror; the demise of social classes would mean the demise of any semblance of individual liberty. The state had to accept, even encourage, individualism and social conflict, for "social struggle" was "the great agent of life and what we might term progress."[67]

Arendt took the argument further. The modern world by its very nature conspired, in a variety of ways, to render the mass man superfluous. With superfluity came a host of other privative states: homelessness, statelessness, loneliness, rootlessness, and selflessness, each adding another dimension to the individual's nightmarish experience of weightlessness and displacement. World War I added to the weakening of all political and social structures and created a permanent refugee population of millions—the very embodiment of the human superfluity toward which the Bourgeois Century had been tending, and a rich resource for the ruthless manipulators who would fashion totalitarian movements. The superfluity of displaced persons prefigured the superfluity of the concentration-camp inmates, for their statelessness and homelessness were but one image of the loneliness that beset mass man, "the experience of not belonging to the world at all, which is among the most radical and desperate experiences of man."[68] It was not hard to see in her expressions the experiences of a woman who had been imprisoned and then had spent eighteen months as a "stateless person," fleeing Germany first to Prague, then to Geneva, then to Paris, and then, after being held in a Vichy internment camp, to the United States.[69]

That "radical and desperate" experience remained in Arendt's thought, leaving her with a bitter skepticism toward Enlightenment universalism as a solution for "the Jewish problem": "I arrived at the conclusion which I always, at the time, expressed to myself in one sentence, a sentence which clarified it to me: 'When one is attacked as a Jew, one must defend oneself *as a Jew*.' Not as a German, not as a world-citizen, not as an upholder of the Rights of Man."[70] She also rejected the entire assimilationist enterprise as misbegotten, unsuccessful, and craven. Better, she thought, to be a self-conscious pariah, to accept the outcast status that had ever been the lot of European Jewry, than to abandon solidarity with one's own and pant after general approbation. The parvenus who longed for nothing so much as Gentile acceptance were, at bottom, ashamed of their Jewishness; they wished to be accepted in spite of their Jewishness, as exceptions to the rule. They were willing to go to any length to prove that they did not feel the conflicting tugs of dual loyalty. They wanted to be as solidly bourgeois as their Gentile counterparts—an unworthy, unheroic desire, in her eyes. Pariahs and parvenus: these were the Jews' stark alternatives, as she saw them.

Her experience of displacement informed many of her other works on politics, albeit often only as a shadow in the background. For example, her enthusiasm for the republicanism of the Aristotelian *polis*, although typical of the classically trained German intellectual's adoration of all things Greek, also bespoke her intense conviction that the threat of totalitarian regimes set the agenda for modern political thought, and that in a decentralized participatory polity, in which the possibilities of citizenship and political action were fully realized, there would be no homelessness, rootlessness, or loneliness. Arendt was especially drawn to the idea of spontaneously organized workers' councils (soviets), such as those advocated by her heroine Rosa Luxemburg, as well as to the New England town meetings or the kibbutz. Again and again, the image of self-realization through participation in political life, the Aristotelian dictum that man is a political animal who fulfills his nature only by action in the *polis*, recurred in her work.[71] For Arendt, as for all genuine republicans, there could be no higher title than citizen.

There was, however, a strong element of sheer romanticism in her esteem for the participatory polity, as if it were a compensatory fantasy of some early lost love-object, some form of social connectedness that could never be replaced. For all that she extolled intense citizenship and localism in the abstract, she was stubbornly aloof and guarded in her own life. Her bristling independence was already clearly visible in her twenties. When she visited Palestine as a Youth Aliyah worker in 1935, partly to see the kibbutzim in action, she took an intense dislike to what she saw: "I knew even then . . . that one could not live there. 'Rule by your neighbors,' that is of course what it finally amounts to."[72] Thus did she dismiss an earnest attempt to realize concretely many of her most cherished social, political, and economic ideals. During her years in America she was rarely involved in practical politics of any sort. There was a puzzling gap between her ideals and the principles she actually lived by—a contradiction that would have been less troubling had it not issued from one whose motto was "We must think what we are doing." But recognition of the gap is essential to a full understanding of her, for no less important than the celebratory image of the *polis* was the image of the Jewish intellectual as a proud pariah—the very antithesis of citizenship. Her reaction to the kibbutzim showed that Arendt conceived of her Jewish identity not in terms of shared practices, language, and worldview but as "an act of personal defiance[,] . . . a personal fact, not a communal way of living."[73] Arendt was a self-willed pariah who cherished an ideal of citizenship she would never try to realize.

Part of the explanation for this seeming paradox lay in her attraction to elements in the conservative critique of mass society, which in turn informed her (and Lederer's) understanding of totalitarianism. The influence of Martin Heidegger upon her thinking was a channel for this influence, for Heidegger stood squarely in the tradition of German romanticism, reviling industrialization, technological innovation, and mass communications.[74] Germany's relationship to the West, and hence to the ends and means of Enlightenment, had always been at best complicated, equivocal, and often openly hostile. German romantic thinkers of the nineteenth century felt nothing but disdain for the shallow positivism, materialism, mechanism, "objectivity," universalism, meliorism, urbanism, liberalism, and optimism that had swept Western Europe. In place of these ideas, men like Wilhelm Mueller, Friedrich Schleiermacher, and Johann Gottlieb Fichte conjured a pastoral vision of community life as a living organism, a naturally evolved *Volk* mystically bound together by the spiritual richness of kinship and tradition—not by the chimera of reason or by the universal rights of bourgeois individualist man.[75]

The critique of mass society emerged from the same sources. Although elements can be detected even as far back in European history as the ancient Roman diatribes against the influence of the many, or the disdainful speeches that Shakespeare put into the mouth of his Coriolanus, it was not until the nineteenth century, when economic and political revolution rocked the foundations of ecclesiastical authority and feudal tradition, that the scatterings of patrician or aristocratic lament begin to coalesce into a more or less coherent vision. The critique proposed that modern societies have evolved to the point that their inhabitants are best understood as particles in a centrally organized mass aggregation, rather than as members of smaller, traditional, less centrally directed groups with shifting, overlapping affiliations woven together in a complex and evolving pattern of social interaction. In the words of Robert Nisbet, the new organization of society constituted "a landscape inhabited by atomized individuals rather than by organically connected groups interposing themselves between individual and state."[76]

The consequences and implications of this change in social organization had been far reaching. Rather than bringing unambiguous progress, the movement toward greater democracy, urbanization, and industrialization had produced acute social disintegration and anomie by reducing men and women to interchangeable ciphers, floating free of the anchoring bonds of kin and tradition. Unfortunately, however, the decline of authentic forms of community did not also result in a decline of the human need for these things. The result was their replacement by pseudoauthority and *Ersatzgemeinschaften*—phony, vulgar, desperate, or dangerous stopgap substitutes for the supports once supplied by tradition. Even Marx, who extolled the masses as a positive revolutionary force, had only contempt for the unorganized and unclass-conscious *Lumpenproletariat*, the ultimate product of modern social dissolution.

Marx himself, however, was no mass-society theorist. As its antimodern overtones imply, the concept of mass society originated in conservative reaction—initially, reaction to the ominous implications of the French Revolution. Not only Tocqueville—whose principal ideas, one should remember, were already firmly fixed well before his journey to America—but Joseph de Maistre and Vicomte de Bonald, as well as Briton Edmund Burke, found in the revolution's extreme passion for social leveling a disturbing portent of the sinister forces egalitarian modernity might really be unleashing upon the world, the revolution's Enlightenment-tutored apologists notwithstanding. In these early stages, as well as in the writings of Jakob Burckhardt, Gustave Le Bon, and José Ortega y Gasset, the theory had been employed to defend, however ineffectively, what remained of older values against the intrusions and depredations of the many, to prevent the vulgar and unprincipled passions of the mob from overwhelming the few islands of intellectual and moral refinement and discernment.

With the emergence of Hitler, however, whose rise to power could in some respects have been scripted from Le Bon's classic study *The Crowd* (1895), the theory attracted advocates of an entirely different character than ever before. It began to be espoused by left-wing radicals and liberals, the very sort of thinkers for whom it might otherwise be assumed that the French Revolution had constituted the most promising event of modern times. Although such thinkers had little in common with Old World aristocrats, ultramontanes, partisans of the ancien régime, and social organicists, as Germans they were naturally heir to their people's uneasiness with bourgeois democratic institutions—an uneasiness that, after all, both a monarchist and a Marxist can, for quite different reasons, agree upon.

Intellectuals on the Left now also saw in the specter of mass society a dangerous social potential for unparalleled forms of domination, as Hitler had just made vivid by his success in imposing his authority upon the German populace. Moreover, they feared that the extension of culture to the masses might result not in the uplifting of the masses but in the degradation of culture. This meant the devaluation of all that they, as intellectuals, most deeply cherished, and it meant that culture could easily become used as a tool of domination over the very stuff of consciousness itself. By 1940 Karl Mannheim, whose own Marxian sympathies precluded a frankly conservative position, danced around an elitist stance without actually enunciating it: "The crisis in culture in liberal-democratic society is due, in the first place, to the fact that the social processes, which previously favored the development of the creative elites, now have the opposite effect, i.e., have become obstacles to the forming of elites because wider sections of the population under unfavorable conditions take an active part in cultural activities."[77] Mannheim was describing, ever so gently and diplomatically, a shift that would have profound implications not only for his own time but even more for the status of intellectuals in the postwar liberal democracies. Quite simply, he was arguing that under the conditions of a mass society, the participation of wider sections of the population in the culture could well turn out to be inimical to the interests of intellectuals. Here was yet another compelling reason for the intellectual to stay independent, detached, and free-floating and to reconsider the very conceptions of personal autonomy that Bellamy and many other American postbellum social thinkers had tried to supersede.

The rise of Hitler, then, stimulated the analytical use of the concept of mass society, just as it stimulated the use of the idea of totalitarianism. Indeed, the two concepts were closely related and in some versions were nearly identical. They rose to preeminence together, in response to the twentieth century's turbulent political and social history. Both notions were first and most clearly articulated by Europeans and clearly connected by Germans—especially the German-Jewish refugees who had suddenly felt their identity fixed in the crosshairs of history and felt themselves the target of the mob from which they had hoped for revolution instead. Edward Shils has rightly credited the establishing of mass-society theory on the Left to the general influence of the Frankfurt school émigrés; however, what he said of them was largely true of the very different Hannah Arendt:

> The synthesis of [contemporary mass-society theory] took place in the quasi-Marxist assessments of the regime of National Socialist Germany. The disintegrative influence of capitalism and urban life had left man alone and helpless. To protect himself, he fled into the arms of the all-absorbing totalitarian party. Thus the *coup d'etat* of Louis Napoleon of December, 1851, and the *Machtergreifung* of March, 1933, became the prototypical events of modern society, and the society of the Weimar Republic was declared to be the characteristic pattern of modern society in preparation for its natural culmination.[78]

For the refugee intellectuals, their personal experience had ramifications beyond the merely personal: it was emblematic of a fearsome new era in human history. A pessimistic and even, in some respects, antimodern metahistory had begun to take the place of the progressive vision that had animated the scions of the Enlightenment, including Marx. A radical distrust, far deeper and far more sweeping than the ironist musings of Niebuhr, lay at the heart of the haunted legacy that the Weimar refugees would bring to American soil.[79] None of it boded well for a revitalized vision of large-scale social and political solidarity or of a more socially connected conception of intellect.

---

"The truth," Arendt declared in *The Origins of Totalitarianism*, "is that the masses grew out of the fragments of a highly atomized society whose competitive structure and concomitant loneliness of the individual had been held in check only through membership in a class." As the nation-state lost its viability—one of Arendt's more curious historical assertions, to be sure, given the persistence of nationalism in modern European history—and as the old class system began to crumble inexorably, the way was prepared for political and social disaster. "Totalitarianism," she claimed, "became this century's curse only because it so terrifyingly took care of its problems." Indeed, totalitarianism's insatiable drive "to make men superfluous" merely reflected "the experience of modern masses of their superfluity on an overcrowded earth."[80]

Totalitarianism, then, was far more than a political phenomenon. It had, even for the resolutely antipsychological Arendt, a psychological dimension. In her revised 1958 edition of the *Origins*, she appended to the conclusion a lengthy meditation upon the subject of loneliness, examining its fundamental role in the fashioning of totalitarian movements. Beneath its abstractions, the passage vibrates with the power of personal conviction:

> Loneliness, the common ground for terror, the essence of totalitarian government, and for ideology or logicality, the preparation of its executioners and victims, is closely connected with uprootedness and superfluousness which have been the curse of modern masses since the beginning of the industrial revolution and have become acute with the rise of imperialism at the end of the last century and the break-down of political institutions and social traditions in our own time. To be uprooted means to have no place in the world, recognized and guaranteed by others; to be superfluous means not to belong to the world at all. . . . What prepared men for totalitarian domination in the non-totalitarian world is the fact that loneliness, once a borderline experience usually suffered in certain marginal social conditions like old age, has become an everyday experience of the evergrowing masses of our century. The merciless process into which totalitarianism drives and organizes the masses looks like a suicidal escape from this reality[,] . . . a last support in a world where nobody is reliable and nothing can be relied upon.[81]

A world in which nobody is reliable and nothing can be relied upon; a world cursed by uprootedness and superfluity; a world in which loneliness formed the sole common denominator of human experience: this was a world that Arendt knew intimately. This was the world she thought especially prone to totalitarian solutions, the world against which her cherished vision of the civic-humanist *polis*, with its heightened sense of community and its active, self-realized citizenry, came to serve as a spiritual counter. If her republicanism was fantasy, then it was at least compensatory fantasy—a luminous shield with which she tried to fend off the darkness that threatened to envelop her. She loved to quote Martin Luther on the way that totalitarian thinking comes to dominate the mind of the lonely and isolated man; such a one, Luther said, "always deduces one thing from the other and thinks everything to the worst."[82]

Yet Luther's words seem even more applicable to the theorist of totalitarianism herself, who thought the condition of modern man to its archetypal worst, even as she chose, contradictorily, simultaneously to exalt both the role of citizen and the state of pariahdom. Her account of the superfluousness of the modern man could have served as a description of the desperate struggle of the outcast Jew to survive or the proud refugee intellectual to gain a hearing in a hostile world. Yet her remarks are also oddly reminiscent of Bellamy's struggles, and of Julian West's pilgrimage from the grotto of his individualistic underground sleeping chamber to his self-overcoming transformation in solidaritist Boston. Arendt well understood the lures of collective identity, knowing that its achievement could lift the weight of loneliness and offer a final solution to the burdens of selfhood. And she understood, in a way Bellamy could not, the dangers of final solutions.

Not that there were no indigenous American voices warning against the dangers of a Leviathan state or a devouring totalistic social order in the years before the Second World War. Republican reactions to the New Deal sounded this theme repeatedly, as did the crusty libertarian editor Albert Jay Nock, author of the 1935 book *Our Enemy, the State*. So too, in his own way, did a writer like Sinclair Lewis, from the social satire of his earliest serious works, *Main Street* (1920) and *Babbitt* (1922), to the 1935 novel *It Can't Happen Here*, which depicted the rise to power of a popular American fascist movement. The evolving perspectives of Niebuhr and Lippmann, too, clearly betokened a similar fear of social tyranny. It took the émigré voices from the maelstrom of Europe, however, to give impetus and intellectual focus to such thoughts, particularly in the years after the Second World War, when émigré insights seemed increasingly germane to the concerns of postwar American intellectuals.

When Carl J. Friedrich organized an important conference on totalitarianism, held in Boston in 1953 under the auspices of the American Academy of Arts and Sciences, it was not surprising that so many of the participants were Hitler-era refugees, among them Arendt, Erik Erikson, Karl Deutsch, Marie Jahoda, Sigmund Neumann, Else Frenkel-Brunswik (Adorno's collaborator on *The Authoritarian Personality*), Alexander Gerschenkron, Waldemar Gurian, and Leo Lowenthal. Also in attendance were Harold Lasswell, who had done work on the authoritarianism of the German working class, and David Riesman, a close friend of both Friedrich and Erich Fromm; invited, but unable to attend, were Fromm and Reinhold Niebuhr.[83] Mention of Fromm and Niebuhr underscores the convergence of European emigrants and American ironists. Even stronger evidence came from the conference's keynote speaker, American diplomat George F. Kennan, whose remarks left no doubt of his own embrace of the totalitarianism theory, as a way of capturing the ironies that had transformed the dreams of progress into the calamities of the modern world.

Most important for our purposes, however, Kennan saw profound domestic implications raised by the theory and practice of totalitarianism, and he used the address to call attention to them. The old American progressive faith was now cast in an exceedingly dark light by the recent experience of Europe. "Woe to any of us," he warned, with Niebuhrian irony reverberating in his voice, "if [Americans] yield to the leveling influences of the perfectionist, to utopian dreams of progress and equality, to the glorification of conformity in tongue or outlook that . . . have gone before the disasters of totalitarian triumph." Yet Kennan did not rule out that unpleasant possibility. The "purgatory of totalitarianism," he asserted, in tones resonant with the words of Arendt, Adorno, and Fromm, may be easier for the human soul to abide than "a liberal chaos from which the sense of community is absent and in which freedom means only the sense of being lost and lonely and helpless."[84]

He well understood Arendt's assertion that totalitarianism's attraction flowed precisely from the way it "took care" of this century's problems. At the same time, though, his fear of a mad, despairing lunge into totalitarian solidarity had not caused him to lose all sense of the opposite peril or to embrace a purely libertarian ethos. Like a latter-day Whig moralist, he sought the balance of ordered liberty, not "only a freedom *from* something," but "a freedom *to* something." Indeed, totalitarianism is least likely to arise "when the framework of individual obligation is firmest, and where certain forms of restraint are not highly developed."[85] As he wrote in another context, a recovery of the "spiritual distinction" and "clarity of purpose" of American national life was wanted.[86] The Cold War, as he had declared in his famous 1947 "Mr. X" article in *Foreign Affairs*, had proved a fair "test of national quality" assigned us by "a Providence" that was enjoining upon the American people the obligation of "pulling themselves together and accepting the responsibilities of moral and political leadership."[87] If the United States was to defeat the Soviet Union, it would best do so partly by its patient containment of aggression, but even more by its example.

One might have wished that Kennan had elaborated upon the precise nature of the nation's distinction, purpose, or quality, or its responsibilities. In the end, however, it probably would have made little difference. Kennan was seeking something like a reprise of the Grand Review—not literally but insofar as the Grand Review symbolized the hope that the quest for solidarity and connectedness could crystallize around a grand national purpose, which could be an occasion for individual self-transcendence. But American political thought in the wake of the war was running in a very different direction. Writers like Robert Dahl, Sidney Verba, Gabriel Almond, Edward Shils, James Coleman, Daniel Boorstin, and (not least) Reinhold Niebuhr were making a convincing case that American pluralism itself was a "normative concept," a kind of golden mean between Left and Right authoritarianism— the true and only liberal antithesis to totalitarianism.[88] What might have seemed a purely political paradigm also had its psychological counterparts. Kennan's fellow conferee Erik Erikson had already, in his *Childhood and Society* (1951), praised the looseness and fluidity of the "democratic" American family, whose occasional chaotic excesses and tendencies toward "momism" were much to be preferred to the highly structured, patriarchal, and authoritative domestic institutions of Germans and Russians, which were seedbeds of totalitarianism.[89] Erikson's conference paper followed similar lines, distinguishing between a desirable ideal of psychic "wholeness," a healthy pluralistic inner state that gave respectful hearing to the full range of psychological needs, and an undesirable quest for "totality," which sought to make the psychic economy subservient to some single end—the psychological equivalent, so to speak, of *Gleichschaltung*, or a consolidated command economy.[90]

It was one thing, however, to proclaim pluralism as totalitarianism's proper antidote and quite another to look to pluralism for the sort of clear, crisp articulation of shared goals that Kennan was seeking. The practical effect of totalitarianism theory was not a desire to rethink the proper relationship among community, nationhood, and selfhood, as Kennan's remarks seemed to call for, but an invigorated commitment to the protection of the endangered self against the depredations of society. Theories of totalitarianism and mass society had elevated the long-standing American concern with conformity into the more general specter of total institutions, with the potential for total control, total manipulation, and total submission. The proper answer to these seemed to be an affirmation of the freedom and integrity of the self.

The most philosophically extreme of such affirmations came in the postwar vogue of existentialism, which had its roots in Kierkegaard's rejection of Hegelian "absolutism" and emphasized man's radically self-creating nature. It was equally indicative that émigré Freudians like Erikson and Heinz Hartmann elected to concentrate their own efforts upon a clarification and elaboration of Freud's late work in ego psychology, and that Erikson left his mark on American psychological and social thought with a "life-cycle" theory that provided a kind of bildungsroman formula, a self-development story, for the ego's struggle toward greater wisdom and integrity.[91] The enormous popularity of Jungian analytical psychology in the postwar years also suggested the same defiant orientation toward individuation and transcendence rather than adjustment to one's embeddedness in a mass society.[92] In an odd and quite unexpected way, the wheel seemed to have come full circle in postwar America, back to the full embrace of a version of the Emersonian individualism of a century before—whoso would be a man (or, increasingly, a woman) must be a nonconformist. But if it was Emersonianism, it would have to be Emersonianism with a distinct difference.

# 7

## Guardians of the Self

Nothing quite like the Grand Review took place at the end of the Second World War. The logistics of demobilization from an immense overseas war precluded it. There was no lack of popular enthusiasm, however, when the Japanese capitulation was announced early in the morning on Monday, August 14, 1945. "The country," effused the ubiquitous *Life*, in whose pages some of the most unforgettable images of that pinnacle moment would be recorded, "went on the biggest spree in American history."[1] For once *Life* spoke without exaggeration. From New York to San Francisco the crowds turned out in force. In staid Salt Lake City, thousands snake-danced in a pouring rain, while in Indianapolis celebrants formed a chain parade of horn-tooting automobiles. In Washington, at the gates of the White House a beleaguered force of MPs struggled to keep the exultant throngs from swarming onto the grounds. In Times Square, leather-lunged nightclubbers poured onto the streets and raised such an ungodly din as to rouse the entire Tenderloin District; it was, said one awed witness, like "ten New Year's Eves rolled into one." Sailors in San Francisco went on a veritable riot, commandeering trolley cars, setting huge bonfires, and helping themselves to the contents of liquor stores. By noon of Tuesday morning, the streets of New York's garment district were already five inches deep in confetti, shredded office memos, dismembered phone books, and yards and yards of discarded remnants. In

Little Italy the fire escapes were festooned with flags and bunting and jammed with onlookers. Marines in San Francisco let off steam by reenacting the Mt. Suribachi flag-raising on the tops of cars, while civilians gleefully bombed the sidewalks with potted plants hurled from windows. Conscientious journalists everywhere noted an epidemic of public kisses, which "ran the osculatory gamut from mob-assault upon a single man or woman to indiscriminate chain-kissing."[2]

The end of conflict of course meant even more to those in uniform, especially those who had seen combat overseas and yearned for the safety and familiarity of home. GIs on the last battlefront in the Pacific theater bellowed and whooped for joy, pounded one another's backs, fired colored flares and tracers into the air, careened wildly honking jeeps through the dusty streets of Manila, and broke out specially reserved caches of hoarded whiskey. The weary troops departing the European theater breathed an extended sigh of relief as they began the long journey home, for they would not have to endure transfer to the Pacific theater followed by the unprecedented horrors of an invasion of Japan. Instead, they could look forward to the enervating boredom of a tedious passage home, packed aboard such capacious leviathans as the grey-painted British liner *Queen Mary*, which displaced over 80,000 tons and embarked some 15,000 men and women. These cramped veterans, too, would eventually have their moment of epiphany, especially if they were lucky enough to arrive in New York harbor. The deck of a ship passing through the narrows and steaming into New York Bay offered an unforgettable sight: the distant towers of Manhattan coming into view, little by little, rising from the sea mist like the majestic, uncanny apparitions of a fabled land.[3]

No sight could have been more ripe with symbolism for the returning American GIs. They had, after all, seen with their own eyes what their countrymen knew only secondhand: the appalling devastation this war had inflicted upon the face and heart of Europe. Many had walked the charred and rubble-strewn streets of Berlin, Frankfurt, or any number of other venerable cities whose ancient names once conjured only exotic images in the minds of Americans. A few had seen firsthand the mass graves of Jews murdered at Dachau and Buchenwald. There could be no greater contrast to those gruesome, unspeakable memories than the splendid spectacle they now saw rising before them. "Untouched by the war the men had left behind them," the Manhattan skyline "stood there metal-clad, steel-ribbed, glass-shrouded, colossal and romantic—everything that America seemed to represent in a world of loss and ruin."[4]

Never did New York seem more alluring, more powerful, more full of promise; never did its swaggering, gaudy style seem more daringly heroic, a confident affirmation hurled into the face of despair—an affirmation that much of the world now badly needed to hear and see. In that respect, too, the distant tapering silhouette of its Empire State Building, rising in splendid solitude, symbolized the unequivocal ascendancy of the United States to a principal position among the nations of the earth—even if the word *empire* was rather jarring to traditional American moral and geopolitical sensibilities. The American future never looked brighter for the nation, for the city, and for the men and women streaming off those arriving ships and scattering across the face of the continent. They could hardly wait to begin their private lives again, having been lucky enough to win a reprieve, for the time being at least, from the voracious demands of history.

Even amid popping corks, flying kisses, and freshly restarted lives, however, there were indications that this moment of glory was freighted with irony and anxiety. Triumph had its considerable price, declared *Time* in its August 20 issue: "More fearful responsibilities, more crucial liabilities rested on the victors even than on the vanquished." Victory's aftershock opened a curious split-mindedness, a dividedness of heart, and an ambivalence that had partly to do with the way that the conflict had been so speedily concluded by the use of previously secret nuclear weapons of unimaginable power against Japanese civilians. "The greatest and most terrible of wars ended, this week," observed *Time*'s unidentified editorialist—the writer was James Agee—"in the echoes of an enormous event—an event so much more enormous that, relative to it, the war itself shrank to minor significance. The knowledge of victory was as charged with sorrow and doubt as with joy and gratitude." Agee had instantly grasped the challenge the bomb's very existence presented to the progressive creed: "With the controlled splitting of the atom, humanity, already profoundly perplexed and disunified, was brought inescapably into a new age in which all thoughts and things were split—and far from controlled. . . . The power of good and of evil bordered alike on the infinite—with this further, terrible split in the fact: that upon a people already so nearly drowned in materialism even in peacetime, the good uses of the power might easily bring disaster as prodigious as the evil."[5] The words appeared in print on August 20, a somber reminder amid the mountains of confetti, a mere six days after peace terms were reached.

Returning GIs did not, perhaps, share precisely these sentiments. Many experienced split thoughts too, however, because they were coming back to such a prosperous and unscathed country—indeed, a country that had gotten huge benefits from the war. Their personal experience of radical disjunction was captured memorably in Sloan Wilson's quintessential title of the 1950s, *The Man in the Gray Flannel Suit*.[6] Although the book's title quickly became synonymous with the faceless and interchangeable white-collar "organization men" who were supposed to populate the large business corporations of the time, Wilson's novel actually had a quite different focus. Its protagonist, Tom Rath, was in fact not a typical organization man but the personal assistant to a kindly and offbeat boss, and he worked in a highly flexible, interesting, creative job. What haunted Tom Rath most was not the sterility and conformity of his work world or even the incessant nagging of his socially ambitious wife, but the absurd disjunction between the life he was now living and the time he had spent as a soldier in Italy. During the war he had personally killed seventeen men, and now he could not shake the memories of the time he stabbed a man to death, feeling a sharp and savage pleasure course through him with the act, or of the time he accidentally killed his best friend with a hand grenade. Nor could he forget about Maria, the Italian girl with whom he had lived and whom he had left behind, pregnant with his child. There was no one he could talk to about these things. His anguish and cynicism are apparent in his reflections on the meaning of it all:

> They ought to begin wars with a course in basic training and end them with a course in basic forgetting. The trick is to learn to believe that it's a disconnected world, a lunatic world, where what is true now was not true then; where Thou Shalt Not Kill and the fact that one has killed a great many men mean nothing, absolutely nothing, for now is the time to raise legitimate children, and make money, and dress properly, and be kind to one's wife, and admire one's boss, and learn not to worry, and think of oneself as what? That makes no difference, he thought—I'm just a man in a gray flannel suit. . . . I will keep my gray flannel suit spotless. I will have a sense of humor. I will have guts—I am not the type to start crying now.[7]

Hence, for Tom Rath anyway, the proverbial grey flannel suit was not a badge of resigned white-collar conformity; rather, it represented the cloak of denial beneath which the postwar world hid while it went on with its work. A disconnected world meant that all truths and intimacies were compartmentalized, provisional, and revokable; that civilization was but a thin veneer; and that the disjunction between the inner and the outer life had to be nearly complete. How could the people who had not been there possibly understand the experiences of those who had?

---

An extreme example of the disjunction Rath was talking about emerged with the full disclosure, at the end of the war, of the existence and appalling extent of the Nazi concentration camps. Most Americans got their first concrete knowledge of the camps from the ghastly newsreels shown in American theaters of the camps liberated by Eisenhower's armies. Detailed accounts about the unprecedented scope and murderous brutality of the camps had been filtering out of continental Europe for years before the war's end, however, and indeed, a handful of Jewish leaders had tried without success to press the Roosevelt administration to move more vigorously against these crimes.[8] Inevitably, there was keen and growing interest among concerned psychologists and social scientists in the effects of such total and systematic brutalization upon the individuals subjected to it. It is perhaps not surprising that the German émigré intellectuals stood in the forefront of such investigations. In particular, a 1943 article by the psychiatrist Bruno Bettelheim, entitled "Individual and Mass Behavior in Extreme Situations," had an enormous influence in setting the terms for subsequent discussion of the psychopathology of the camps—and, by extension, of all similarly closed, total social organizations, of which the Hitlerite camp became an ideal type. Originally appearing in an obscure professional psychiatric journal, the article achieved prominence when it was reprinted in Dwight Macdonald's influential magazine *politics*.[9]

Bettelheim's article carried such weight for a number of reasons. It had the ring of personal authenticity because Bettelheim (unlike most of the other refugee intellectuals) had spent a year in the camps, first Dachau and then Buchenwald, before being released and making his way to the United States in 1939, and he drew freely and effectively upon his personal observations. Perhaps more important in accounting for the article's influence, however, was its conceptualization of the concentration camp as a social system, an ideal type of a total institution; this suggested the possibility that the camps might fruitfully be viewed in a continuum with other similar social environments. Bettelheim's conclusions, too, were disturbing in their implications. The camp inmates, he asserted, were prone to an extreme form of infantile regression, and the older inmates tended over time to adapt themselves, to an astonishing degree, to the perspectives and values of their oppressors—exemplifying what would today be called the "Stockholm syndrome," or "identification with the aggressor." Shocking as such behavior was, it perfectly illustrated Bettelheim's understanding of what made such "adjustment" possible. What was required was a "splitting of personality," in which the inmate convinces himself that "these horrible and degrading experiences somehow did not happen to 'him' as a subject, but only to 'him' as an object." Splitting off an inmate-self that was "unreal," the inmate did not need to hold *that* self accountable to any higher moral standard; he could say, without any sense of untruth or dissembling, "What I am doing here, or what is happening to me, does not count at all; here everything is permissible as long and insofar as it contributes to helping me survive in the camp."[10] The "real" self could be buried or held aloof and apart, inviolate, while the "social" self went through the motions of life in an unspeakably degraded situation.

Bettelheim's nightmarish insights were further amplified at Columbia University by Leo Lowenthal in a 1944 lecture based upon the first accounts of what had been transpiring in the camps since Hitler's implementation of the Final Solution. The lecture was later published in *Commentary* (it had been turned down by the *American Journal of Sociology*, for lack of sufficient empirical data!) under the title "Terror's Atomization of Man," as the second installment in a series called "The Crisis of the Individual." The totalitarian terror of the camps, Lowenthal asserted, could disintegrate the individual personality and obliterate all social bonds and all potential for authentic human loyalty or solidarity, producing a radically isolated, subhuman, animalistic type of man who is willing to do whatever the Gestapo requires, no matter how heinous the act or contemptible the betrayal.[11] The Bettelheim article, and his subsequent book *The Informed Heart: Autonomy in a Mass Age* (1960), which placed his interpretation of the camps in the context of a larger critique of mass society, found other points of resonance as well. Hannah Arendt, for example, drew upon his work (along with the work of David Rousset) for her crucial description of the camps in *The Origins of Totalitarianism*. Although she always disdained the use of Freudian categories, she strongly shared Bettelheim's conviction of the profoundly consciousness-bending power of totalitarian rule.[12]

Some of the other uses to which Bettelheim's work was put went much further afield, indicating not only the power of his work but the riveting and continuing intellectual effects of the idea of the camps. Stanley Elkins's influential and controversial 1959 study *Slavery* may serve as an example. Elkins attempted to apply Bettelheim's description of the social psychology of camps to the psychology of enslaved black people in the United States, and thereby to explain perceived differences between the characteristic personalities of North American and Latin American slaves. The former were said to exhibit the so-called Sambo personality—a childlike, indolent, submissive, dependent, fawning relationship to their all-powerful masters—while the Latin slaves showed few if any signs of such Samboism. Elkins speculated that this regional difference flowed from the rigorously closed features of the North American plantation system, which stood in marked contrast to the more open social and political institutions in which Spanish and Portugese slavery were embedded. The North American plantations, he believed, resembled Nazi concentration camps. "Both were closed systems," he remarked, "from which all standards based on prior connections had been effectively detached," and both therefore produced similarly infantilized inhabitants. The Latin American slaves, however, benefited from the existence of countervailing autonomous institutions, such as the Roman Catholic church, which blunted the exclusivity of the master's authority and provided alternative psychological resources for the formation of an independent personal identity.[13] The North American system, however, because it was closed, claimed both body and soul in all but a few exceptional cases.[14]

An even more startling social application of the concentration-camp model, drawing upon Bettelheim's work in *The Informed Heart*, came four years after Elkins, in Betty Friedan's book *The Feminine Mystique*. Friedan devoted an entire chapter, entitled "Progressive Dehumanization: The Comfortable Concentration Camp," to an extended comparison of the lot of the American suburban middle-class housewife to the experiences of Dachau's tortured, emaciated inmates. Beginning by noting the alarming passivity of the younger generation of postwar Americans, Friedan found the explanation in the frustrations of the middle-class mother, who tended, because of the lack of any creative outlets for her energies, to absorb her children into her own world. Thanks to the effects of "the feminine mystique," the woman's development is arrested "at an infantile level," and such infantilism will cause her to seek "fulfillment" strictly as a wife and mother. But she will suffer from "increasingly severe pathology, both physiological and emotional" as a result of this choice, and her motherhood will be "increasingly pathological," marked by a compulsion toward "vicarious living," thus making it impossible for her children to achieve "human selfhood."[15] It is urgent, she continued,

> to understand how the very condition of being a housewife can create a sense of emptiness, non-existence, nothingness, in women. . . . The women who "adjust" as housewives, who grow up wanting to be "just a housewife," are in as much danger as the millions who walked to their own death in the concentration camps—and the millions more who refused to believe that the concentration camps existed. . . . [Isn't the housewife's] house in reality a comfortable concentration camp? Have not women who live in the image of the feminine mystique trapped themselves within the narrow walls of their homes? . . . They have become dependent, passive, childlike; they have given up their adult frame of reference to live at the lower human level of food and things. . . . They are suffering a slow death of mind and spirit.[16]

By adjusting herself to the comfortable concentration camp, the American woman accepts an infantilized state and denies her "adult human identity";

she "turns away from individual identity to become an anonymous biological robot in a docile mass."[17]

The parallel was overdrawn, even outrageous; but Friedan did not make the comparison merely for dramatic or rhetorical effect, but on what she believed were substantive grounds. Nor was her argument based exclusively on idiosyncratic or impressionistic sources; instead, she found considerable support for many of her conclusions in works of the most respected figures in the mainstream of contemporary social science, including David Riesman, Erich Fromm, Erik Erikson, and Bruno Bettelheim. While this does not automatically validate her assertions, it does tell us something about the position of the camps in the landscape of the postwar social imagination. Her use of the camp model could build, as did Elkins's, upon a pervasive American postwar fascination with, and fear of, total institutions or closed social systems—with totalitarianism, hard and soft. The camp image was not only a representation of a particular set of institutions used under particular historical circumstances; it was an archetypal symbol of all that was most threatening about the postwar world: its tendency to subjugate the individual to the social whole or otherwise to make genuine individuality dangerous, undesirable, superfluous, or impossible. The idea of the camps became a kind of defining prototype for those fears.

The only antidote to such domination was a reassertion of personal autonomy. Friedan concluded her examination of the camp model with a story taken from Bettelheim. A group of naked prisoners were being led off by the SS to the gas chambers—men and women "no longer human," she remarked, but degraded to the point of being "merely docile robots." On learning that one of the women had been a dancer, the commanding officer, on a sadistic whim, ordered her to dance, and she complied. But as she danced, she edged toward him and, in a flash, seized his gun and shot him dead. Although she was immediately killed in turn, that moment of dancing had somehow freed her to be "once again a person" instead of a "nameless depersonalized prisoner." Her example, said Bettelheim, showed that "the old personality can be regained, its destruction undone, once we decide on our own that we wish to cease being units in a system." The dancer "threw off her real prison," because "she was willing to risk her life to achieve autonomy." For Friedan, the same moral, the same prescription, applied to the postwar American housewives; they must "refuse to be nameless, depersonalized, manipulated" and must instead "live their own lives again according to a self-chosen purpose."[18] Self-chosen: for them, as for the dehumanized inmates, the chief challenge was the recovery of the autonomous self.

These concerns can only be understood as reflecting widespread anxiety about the prospect of social tyranny in postwar America. That the camp metaphor occupied such a crucial place in this enormously influential book, whose significance in the postwar era probably exceeds even that of *Looking Backward* in its own; that the analogy could be so plausibly supported by the contemporary scholarly literature; and that it could be so effectively used as part of an intellectual battering ram directed at barriers to women's exercise of autonomy: these say a great deal about the place that images of devouring totalism and of the endangered self occupied in the economy of the postwar American imagination. The multifaceted complex of issues raised by the Cold War caused these images to be experienced in an especially intensified form, particularly for intellectuals who were actively involved in defending the autonomy of intellectual life and resisting the totalistic demands of both McCarthyism and Stalinism. Certain specific fears still smoldered and flickered in the background of these works: fears of internal subversion by organized Communists, countered by fears of internal tyranny at the hands of authoritarian anti-Communists; fears of a militant totalitarianism abroad, pitted against fears of a totalitarian potential from within. Even innocuous or respectable features of social existence came into question. If the mass man of Hannah Arendt's *Origins of Totalitarianism* was a cipher, so too was the American white-collar corporate employee, whose total subservience to a new "Social Ethic" at work and at home was memorably described by *Fortune* journalist William S. Whyte in *The Organization Man* (1956). If the American public was shocked by accounts of the victims of chilling North Korean brainwashing techniques, Vance Packard's exposé of mass advertising techniques in *The Hidden Persuaders* (1957) raised doubts about the degree to which the American public itself was immune from psychological manipulation.

In an outpouring of similarly influential works, from Packard's *The Status Seekers* to Herman Wouk's *The Caine Mutiny*, Eric Hoffer's *The True Believer*, David Riesman's *The Lonely Crowd*, John Kenneth Galbraith's *The Affluent Society*, C. Wright Mills's *White Collar*, and Daniel Boorstin's *The Image*, many elements of a singular indictment recurred. Americans, who had formerly prided themselves on their stubborn independence and devotion to the work ethic, had succumbed to a collectivism of the mind, a dangerous susceptibility to the mass appeals of advertising and media, a deification of organizational life, and a social ethic that relinquished personal integrity and authenticity and instead enshrined as the American Way the bland and anxious conformism of the new white-collar personality-selling occupations, as well as the leisure- and consumption-oriented lifestyle of the sprawling new American suburbs. Totalitarianism, it seemed, could come in two varieties: hard and soft. Americans, even as they were passionately engaged in containing the spread of the former, were helplessly surrendering to the deformations of the latter, a soft tyranny that, like Baudelaire's devil, could control Americans by convincing them it did not exist. Imprisoned in an inner emptiness even as it outwardly enjoyed an unprecedented wealth, America resembled, from this standpoint, a mass society without a mob, a totalitarianism without overt coercion.

Tocqueville, too, had envisioned a tyranny that was no less powerful for being noncoercive and whose power was "absolute, minute, regular, provident, and mild." It would, he said, be like the authority of a parent

> if, like that authority, its object was to prepare men for manhood; but it seeks, on the contrary, to keep them in perpetual childhood. . . . Thus it every day renders the exercise of the free agency of man less useful and less frequent; it circumscribes the will within a narrower range and gradually robs a man of all the uses of himself. The principle of equality has prepared men for these things; it has disposed men to endure them and often to look on them as benefits. . . . Such a power does not destroy but it prevents existence; it does not tyrannize, but it compresses, enervates, extinguishes, and stupefies a people, till each nation is reduced to nothing better than a flock of timid and industrious animals of which the government is the shepherd.[19]

For Tocqueville, too, the transformation of adults into children was at the heart of this modern type of soft tyranny. The second volume of *Democracy in America* concluded with an urgent plea that men recognize and affirm their own liberty, since "it depends upon themselves whether the principle of equality is to lead them to servitude or freedom."[20]

It was fitting, then, that the postwar period saw an extraordinary rebirth of interest in Tocqueville, especially the *Democracy*, which had fallen out of print but was newly popularized by an edition published in 1945 by Alfred A. Knopf. Hard as it is to imagine today, Tocqueville had been a negligible influence upon American thinkers in the years between the Civil War and World War II. Yet the reason for this relative eclipse is not difficult to identify. The ebulliently progressive and consolidating spirit of American social thought in those years was at odds with the Frenchman's complex, skeptical view of the coming world of centralized mass democracy. The rise of Hitler and Stalin, however, and the chastening of American progressive hopes also altered Tocqueville's standing and stimulated a fresh assessment of his oeuvre. The advent of European totalitarianism and the efforts of émigré intellectuals to understand it caused "a seedbed [to come] into existence in which Tocquevillean ideas could take root."[21] Indeed, Tocqueville's stress upon social egalitarianism as the modern phenomenon par excellence, particularly as he presented it in the more abstract and theoretical second volume of the *Democracy*, offered a master interpretation of modernity and of American society's vanguard (but not exceptional) place in that history.

In so doing, it offered an alternative to Marx. Where Marx's understanding of history had been progressive and teleological, Tocqueville's was more complex and equivocal, though he claimed to see the hand of Providence working in the great process of social leveling that was producing the democratic societies of the future. The endless pursuit of equality that Tocqueville saw as the great driving force of modernity had undoubtedly had favorable material consequences for the many. But it also would produce an endless restlessness and dissatisfaction, even in the midst of the most profligate prosperity. The class division and class consciousness that Marx had seen as the dialectical engine of historical development were replaced in the Tocquevillean view by a general equality of condition, a dissolving of class and caste into a homogeneous and undifferentiated social order marked by the ceaseless struggle for status in a society lacking established marks of distinction. Where Marx had envisioned a progressive concentration of power, status, and wealth in the hands of the ascendant capitalists, leading to an inevitable proletarian revolution and establishment of the classless society, Tocqueville saw a gradual diffusion of power, status, and wealth, a great historical movement toward a general state of rough equality. Such a vision was a plausible complement to the theories of modernization that enjoyed such a vogue in the postwar years, notably in the influential works of Walt W. Rostow and Daniel Lerner, although containing a strain of irony or pessimism largely missing from the modernization theorists.[22]

---

No work of the 1950s showed Tocqueville's influence more palpably, or better exemplified the way that the new postwar perspectives began to affect the interpretation of American society, than David Riesman's *The Lonely Crowd*. Indeed, its evocative title suggested the combination of spiritual malaise and massified social conditions, of inner emptiness and excessive outward conformity, that was at the heart of both refugee social thought and 1950s American social criticism. Written in a lively, accessible style and drawing on a vast variety of materials and disciplines to support its contentions, *The Lonely Crowd* probably had an even greater influence upon humanists and other nonspecialist readers than upon those within the sociological guild. Lionel Trilling, for example, read it with the greatest admiration and envy, feeling that Riesman had, with the help of his collaborators Nathan Glazer and Reuel Denney, produced a magisterial study that was also a work of literature—

superior, indeed, in nearly every way to the novels of the day for its keenness and perspicacity.[23]

A measure of its general influence was the fact of Riesman's appearance on the cover of *Time* magazine, the first sociologist ever to be so recognized. Henry Luce's publications were the most powerful image purveyors of the era, a veritable fountain of shared national imagery; hence, an appearance on *Time*'s cover secured one a place in the national iconography. For many years the content of those covers tended to reflect the fixed ideas of *Time*'s founding spirit. Luce was a man of exceedingly strong opinions and intensely nationalistic views, but he was also a man shrewd enough to understand that a successful popular magazine must give the public mood its due.[24] Hence *Time*'s cover for the issue of September 27, 1954, was respectfully given over to the countenance of a decidedly un-Lucean figure: a sober, unillusioned, greying, tweedy, lawyerly, bespectacled liberal sociologist from the University of Chicago—a certifiable Fifties "egghead," if there ever was one, and the author of a decidedly un-Lucean book.

The cover did more than just recognize Riesman, however; it put him forward as a heroic sage. (Whatever it did, *Time* was certainly not going to do it halfway.) The caption asked, with an undertone of perplexity and urgency, What is the American Character?, and the cover art deftly limned some of the disturbing possibilities Riesman had provided. Behind and beneath Riesman's head stretched an enormous sea of anonymous human heads, perhaps the herdlike audience for some unspecified mass-cultural spectacle. Rising from the crowd, in the middle ground, were two crisscrossing striated beams of light, upon each of which stood a man. The first man, dressed in a dark Victorian suit and wearing long, bushy, nineteenth-century sideburns, seemed to stride briskly and purposefully away from the reader, oblivious to all but his quest, a giant gyroscope strapped to his back. The second man, dressed in a light-colored suit, was a more modern, twentieth-century man, perhaps a salesman; he was facing in the opposite direction. Following the conventions of graphic design, the second man faced forward, into the magazine and into the future, by facing to the reader's right; by facing left, the other man faced backward, into the spine and into the past. The second man extended his left arm in an extravagant posture of beckoning friendliness, while to his back was strapped a small radar dish, a device mysteriously integral to his designs. Meanwhile, in the near foreground, social scientist Riesman gazed forward coolly and disinterestedly, his back turned to both men and to the mob.[25]

Certainly this cover art spoke volumes about the rising status of intellectuals in America, and so too did the accompanying article and photographs. As Steven Weiland has pointed out, *Time* intended to present Riesman as "the model American intellectual," a heroic example of the prototypical "autonomous man" celebrated by *The Lonely Crowd*.[26] The article and photographs thus not only summarized the findings of *The Lonely Crowd* but provided glimpses into the life of such an exemplary man. In a biographical sidebar entitled "An Autonomous Man," we are told about him. "Author David Riesman tries to be an autonomous man," we are told, "and many of his friends think that he achieves a high degree of success." We watch while Riesman and his wife and children rehearse Mozart chamber music together. We are told that he has a large Chicago house with two servants and owns a Vermont dairy farm; that he plays "vigorous, competent, year-round tennis"; that he is "interested in his clothes and his food"; that he "keeps a good wine cellar"; that he drinks "orange juice mixed with soda"; and that (to show a trace of the common touch) he "likes movies," so long as they are not "message movies." This ode to Riesman's impeccably tasteful, well-rounded, well-tempered, vibrant existence was so lavish as to be embarrassing. A thoughtful social scientist had been turned into mere grist for the journalistic mill.

Nevertheless, if *Time* had to choose "the" American intellectual of the mid-1950s—and it is in the iconographic nature of such magazines to do such things—it could hardly have done better. The portrait of modern American society presented in *The Lonely Crowd* was so compelling that, four years after the book's initial 1950 publication, it was still being read by many people and discussed by many more. Four years after his book's publication, Riesman would still be current enough to make the cover of one of the nation's leading current affairs weeklies.[27] Although *The Lonely Crowd* was coauthored with Nathan Glazer and Reuel Denney, in the end it bore Riesman's unmistakable intellectual stamp in the suppleness, clarity, and unsolemnity of its style; in the amazingly catholic reading in the social sciences and humanities it drew upon; in the intuitive leaps and worldly savvy of its social and cultural observations; and in the remarkable agility with which it deployed an eclectic armory of concepts. As an intellectual who seemed to be equally comfortable working inside the university, like a thoroughbred academic man, or outside it, like the legendary *Partisan Review* writers of New York, Riesman seemed to span the variegated possibilities of American intellectual life. These qualities were not only a function of Riesman's unusually capacious and versatile mind and the special advantages inherent in his patrician Philadelphia upbringing. They were also a product of a protracted vocational search, which brought him to the discipline of sociology very late in his life.[28] As he recently wrote, he and his collaborators were, for better or worse, "under-socialized as sociologists," by which he meant not only that they were not professional sociologists. In his own case, he had neither a Ph.D. in any field nor substantial formal sociological training.[29]

That vocational search led him on a circuitous route, though he always excelled at whatever he did. After majoring in chemistry at Harvard, he graduated from Harvard law school, clerked for Supreme Court Justice Louis Brandeis, worked as a trial lawyer in Boston, taught law at the University of Buffalo, worked in the New York district attorney's office, and during World War II was employed as a "contract termination manager" for the Sperry Gyroscope Company. In 1946, at the age of thirty-seven, after undergoing several years of psychoanalysis under Erich Fromm[30] and after amassing an impressive fund of practical experience in American legal, academic, and corporate cultures, he accepted a position as an assistant professor on the social-science faculty of the University of Chicago, at a time when Chicago's faculty was abundantly endowed with both established and rising stars of the sociological firmament—Edward Shils, Milton Singer, Everett Hughes, Lloyd Warner, Robert Redfield, Daniel Bell, Barrington Moore, Morris Janowitz, and Philip Rieff, among others. Riesman had turned down two offers of college presidencies to become an untenured assistant professor, mainly because he wanted the kind of "colleagueship" that would help him to "educate myself more fully in the social sciences."[31] A mere four years later, he would be one of the most famous sociologists in the world.

*The Lonely Crowd* was a certifiable event in American intellectual and cultural history, a book of both importance and significance, if these rough synonyms may be distinguished from one another, as it is sometimes useful to do, by reference to their etymological roots. *The Lonely Crowd* was intrinsically important in its contributions to American intellectual life; it imported or carried into American social thought a brilliant and endlessly suggestive perspective on the social psychology of the burgeoning new professional-managerial middle class, and the ways in which that social psychology might represent a dramatic departure from previous American precedents. Unlike the narrow empirical studies so characteristic of Riesman's contemporaries, it stands squarely in the rich sociological tradition of the early masters, like Max Weber, Georg Simmel, Emile Durkheim, and Tocqueville, who saw their work as part and parcel of the Western philosophical and literary tradition. Moreover, it is a book that still seems strikingly fresh and relevant even after over forty years, for it anticipates so many of the most salient themes in subsequent social and political analysis.[32]

Its significance, however—the cultural meanings that its appearance and reception in the postwar era signify—lay elsewhere. The deep resonances it elicited in the minds of the American reading public suggest that, aside from the innovative content of its arguments, it was also a sign of the times. As H. Stuart Hughes nicely put it, *The Lonely Crowd* "both reflected and stimulated a mood of national soul-searching" in the 1950s. Hence, the often disturbing image of themselves that contemporary Americans discovered in its pages did not deter them from taking Riesman's critique seriously and from appropriating the book's irresistible taxonomy of "inner-directed" and "other-directed" modal personalities to account for their dissatisfaction with the changing character of their neighbors, their colleagues, and perhaps even themselves.[33] The book's great public success, then, and the resultant recognition embodied in the *Time* cover, was yet another indication of a subterranean stream of doubt that ran beneath the triumphant surface of postwar American culture.

*The Lonely Crowd* was above all else a study of "social character"—the modes of psychological conformity that a society inculcates in its members and by which it holds together. As such, the book was far from alone in its time, since similar "culture and personality" studies, which attempted to connect individual psychology with the distinctive practices of a given culture, had proliferated during and after the Second World War, produced by such writers as Fromm, Margaret Mead, Ruth Benedict, Geoffrey Gorer, Karen Horney, and Abram Kardiner.[34] What was distinctive about *The Lonely Crowd*, however, and what made for its wide readership, were the personality typologies it introduced and the dynamic element in its argument. Riesman asserted that the social character of Americans had changed dramatically since the nineteenth century from inner-directed personality types, self-reliant souls who navigated through life by relying doggedly upon principles inculcated early in life, especially by parents, to other-directed types, who were brought up to look to external cues from others—not only their parents but their peers, their co-workers, their co-professionals, the mass media, and so forth—as a guide to proper behavior and beliefs.[35] Riesman best expressed the difference between the two types by navigational analogy, comparing the mechanism of inner-direction to the self-contained gyroscope—shades of Sperry Gyroscope—and that of other-direction to radar, which takes its measure of the world by sending out electromagnetic pulses and attending carefully to what comes back.[36] Thus *Time*'s cover artist chose to depict these modal personalities not only in period dress with characteristic gestures, but with their indispensable tool of social navigation readily at hand.

Both types differed significantly from the tradition-directed person who had preceded them, a type whose characteristics were generated by older, tradition-bound, static, highly ascriptive social orders wherein the individual stood in a well-defined functional and status relationship to the rest of the group. (Significantly, the tradition-directed man was not depicted on the *Time* cover.) The tradition-directed person stood on the "before" side of all the classic sociological dualisms: status versus contract (Maine), *Gemeinschaft* versus *Gesellschaft* (Tönnies), mechanical solidarity versus organic solidarity (Durkheim), feudalism versus capitalism (Marx), communal relationships versus associative relationships (Weber), primary versus secondary groups (Cooley). Individuality was kept to a minimum in the tradition-directed order; correctness of behavior rather than inward disposition were emphasized, and the characteristic weapon of social sanction was shame or expulsion.[37]

With inner-direction, however, we are in the emerging capitalist world, where flux is the only constant, where strictly behavioral norms are undermined, and where, therefore, parents must psychologically equip their children to find their own way, like intrepid explorers venturing into unstable and unpredictable environments. Hence the appropriateness of the metaphorical gyroscope as the navigational tool.[38] Ideally, the inner-directed family instilled within the souls of its children a "rigid though highly individualized character," which could be a kind of internal substitute for the comprehensive traditional social systems modern life had left behind, using guilt rather than shame as its sanctioning mechanism. In Riesman's description, the inner-directed personality resembled the personality type of Freudian psychoanalytic theory, largely by virtue of Freud's emphasis upon the introjections of parental (and especially paternal) ideals and authority to form the powerful, and highly compulsive, superego.[39] Inner-direction was suggestive, too, of Max Weber's quintessential pioneering capitalist, a character type whose accumulating and rationalizing discipline flowed from, or was crucially supported by, the internal restraints of the Protestant ethic.[40]

Inner-direction was appropriate to the era of capitalist expansion. In a production-oriented age ruled by a psychology of scarcity, the force of productive labor was concentrated on conquering "the hardness of the material," work and play were severely differentiated, and pleasure was a "sideshow," a fleeting escape from care that principally served to refresh an individual for a return to life's battle. Like self-propelled economic monads, inner-directed persons relied upon "the invisible hand" to provide social coordination for their actions, which meant that in day-to-day social existence they asked for, and gave, little quarter. The tendency of a society in which inner-direction was dominant was "to protect the individual against the others at the price of leaving him vulnerable to himself." This tendency had its positive aspects, for it relieved the individual of the oppressive requirement to meet the standards of others; but it also left that same individual vulnerable to the searing wounds of his or her own self-criticism. Life was a continual struggle for self-approval, in which even the achievement of one's goals did not relieve the burden of striving, for "mere behavioral conformity cannot meet the characterological ideal."[41] Salvation, so to speak, was not achieved by works but by faith alone.

With the national economic transformation, commencing just after the turn of the century, from a production- and extraction-oriented economy into a consumption-oriented one, the need for a different kind of person and a different mode of conformity soon became manifest. Inner-direction was rapidly becoming outmoded. Instead of the hardness of the material, the crucial tasks of work now increasingly revolved around the softness of men; therein lay the great opportunity and challenge for the ambitious and upwardly mobile. This change flowed not only from the manipulative demands of a consumption-driven national economy, as exemplified in the bevy of skilled and alluring advertisers and other such siren songsters that came to national prominence in the 1920s.[42] It also flowed from the often intense demands created by the increasingly interpersonal and bureaucratic patterns of office work, the professions, and even industrial labor, characteristic of a less freewheeling, increasingly corporate and monopolistic phase of capitalism.[43] The new industries arising in the United States would rely on higher levels of formal education in the work force; they would be built around "techniques of communication and control," relating to both the morale and the efficiency of employees as well as to the demands of the marketplace; and hence there would be unprecedented uses for "men whose tool is symbolism and whose aim is some observable response from people"—a group, in short, rather like that which has sometimes been designated by the imprecise term *the new class*.[44]

Riesman vivified this transformation from inner-direction to other-direction through a set of his own dualisms, often quite as witty as they were revealing: From Morality to Morale, From Craft Skill to Manipulative Skill, From Free Trade to Fair Trade, From the Bank Account to the Expense Account, From the Wheat Bowl to the Salad Bowl, and From the Invisible Hand to the Glad Hand.[45] All these changes can be correlated, as was true for the previous two types, with changes in family and child-rearing practices. In the "other-directed round of life," the severe internal discipline of the inner-directed family unit is largely abandoned, since the rigidity of the inner-directed character had become irrelevant, even a liability, in a brave and fluid new world of consumer-oriented abundance and people-oriented work. (Accordingly, the more appropriate psychological model for socialization is not that of the patriarchal Freud but the more fluid and interpersonal emphases of the American psychiatrist Harry Stack Sullivan.) The parents must learn to accept a supporting, or at best costarring, role in the drama of their children's formation, for the child's peer group had became "much more important to the child." Well-informed, progressive-minded parents readily accepted this demotion; indeed, the principal reason they would be likely to intervene authoritatively in their child's affairs is "not so much about his violation of inner standards as about his failure to be popular or otherwise to manage his relations with these other children."[46]

For Riesman, these priorities both acknowledged and furthered the gestation of a new kind of child, the product of a dense new network of socialization forces whose immense aggregate impact often left parents feeling like nervous bystanders. Unlike their inner-directed predecessors, such children looked to "their contemporaries" as "the source of direction for the individual—either those known directly or those with whom they are indirectly acquainted, through friends and through the mass media."[47] Their individual worth, the appropriateness of their behavior, the acceptability of their tastes, and so on were all judged, in the end, by "a jury of their peers"; hence, there was good reason to have one's radar in good operating order. In that peer group, contemporaries competed against one another to achieve "marginal differentiation" even as they appealed to one another for approbation—a paradoxical combination of the sociable and the unsociable that Riesman labeled "antagonistic cooperation."[48] As Riesman repeatedly emphasized, the mass media played a critical role in this characterological transformation. "Increasingly," Riesman observed, "relations with the outer world and with oneself are mediated by the flow of mass communications"; this statement, it should be remembered, was made when television broadcasting was still in its infancy.[49]

The consequences of that mediation were especially striking in the business of child rearing. Children were now "bombarded by radio and comics from the moment [they] can listen and just barely read." Such exposure not only began the child's absorption into a distinctive peer culture but initiated the socially important task of training him or her as a consumer. Consumer taste became a crucial part of the other-directed child's social equipment, virtually a substitute for etiquette in easing one's way into the group and allowing one to grasp the "socialization of consumer preferences" which was so indispensable to membership in good standing. (Are Chevys to be preferred to Fords? McDonald's to Burger King? Coca-Cola to Pepsi? As anyone with school-age children knows, the answers to these inconsequential questions might be very consequential indeed.) Riesman also looked closely at the attributes of children's stories, always an important agency of character formation and socialization, and there too he saw change. Instead of the quintessentially inner-directed story "The Little Engine That Could," other-directed parents were reading to their children stories like "Tootle the Engine," a "cautionary tale" in which the adventurous young engine Tootle lands in trouble because of his unwillingness to "stay on the tracks" with the other engines, as his instructors have repeatedly warned him to do. Riesman also supplied the following example, which is not quite so tongue-in-cheek as it may first seem:

> We may mark the change by citing an old nursery rhyme: "This little pig went to market; / This little pig stayed at home. / This little pig had roast beef; / This little pig had none. / This little pig went wee-wee-wee / All the way home." The rhyme may be taken as a paradigm of individuation and unsocialized behavior among children of an earlier era. Today, however, all little pigs go to market; none stay home; all have roast beef, if any do; and all say "we-we."[50]

The new other-directed sensibility, then, was most clearly visible in children growing up under the new dispensation; it was not quite so evident in their parents, who must dwell in the twilight zone of transition. Even adults who in effect accepted the other-directed regime still held conscious convictions acquired under the auspices of inner-direction, and contemporary social institutions also still reflected an admixture of these convictions. Nevertheless, the characterological shift was no less real for these ambiguities:

> The parents, harking back as they do in their character structures to an earlier era, are themselves competitive—more overtly so than the children. Much of our ideology—free enterprise, individualism, and all the rest—remains competitive and is handed down by parents, teachers, and the mass media. At the same time there has been an enormous ideological shift favoring submission to the group, a shift whose decisiveness is concealed by the persistence of the older ideological patterns. The peer-group becomes the measure of all things; the individual has few defenses the group cannot batter down.[51]

This is a far cry, indeed, from Dewey's image, a mere two decades before, of the "inner man" as a "jungle" needing to be "subdued to order."[52]

In the wake of Hitler and Stalin and other modern despots who sought to subdue to order the individual psychology, such sentiments could take on genuinely sinister overtones—though nothing could have been further from Dewey's resolutely antitotalitarian mind. It was precisely the stubborn jungle of the independent self that so many cultural critics of the postwar era were anxious to preserve.[53]

---

Other-direction, then, did not seem an acceptable resting place for the American character. All the postwar social critics seemed to agree about that. Thus

Riesman elected, in the concluding pages of *The Lonely Crowd*, to put forward "autonomy" as an alternative to inner- and other-direction. In so doing, he rather abruptly transposed the discussion into a different key—a more fluid, more optimistic, less deterministic key whose tonic was one of the fundamental concepts of classical liberalism. There is some reason to wonder, however, whether such a reappropriation was really possible for Riesman. A brief excursus into the history of the concept of autonomy may help illuminate the grounds of this problem.

Although *autonomy* is an ancient Greek word, it designates the largely modern idea of the individual's moral self-governance.[54] This understanding of autonomy can be understood as a product of the Reformation's freeing of the individual conscience, although even the Lutheran notion of "the priesthood of the believer" presumed ultimate obedience to God, not an individual's empowerment to do-as-thou-wilt. In Immanuel Kant's view, too, autonomy was really a fairly rigorously circumscribed concept. It stood for the capacity of a rational being to subject himself or herself to self-generated—but rational, and therefore universal—laws. Kant was just as dissatisfied as was Riesman with the compulsive quality of much of what passed for morality; autonomy was for him truly "the basis of the dignity of both human nature and every rational nature."[55] He even contrasted *autonomy* with *heteronomy*, a word that could be almost exactly translated as "other-direction."

Autonomy, however, actually entailed the enormous responsibility of imaginatively legislating for the rest of humanity by the terms of the famous categorical imperative "Act only according to that maxim by which you can at the same time will that it should become a universal law."[56] In that sense, the autonomous person was no more free to create his or her own values than was Luther, or Sophocles' Antigone. Such a standard arguably made the concept of freedom more meaningful, however, especially in a world still glowing in the contented early Enlightenment belief in a lawful universe. Yes, the will was subject to the law, "but subject in such a way that it must be regarded also as self-legislative and *only for this reason* as being subject to the law (of which it can regard itself as the author)."[57] Autonomy is thus also distinguished from mere self-indulgence or appetitive license; instead of being governed—that is, directed—by religious precepts, by the traditional *nomoi*, or by whims, appetites, and other compulsive forces within and without, one could declare one's independence and become the constitutional monarch of one's own soul. That constitution, though, was not easily amended.

In retrospect, we are likely to see Kant's formulations as one of the most impressive efforts in a brave *arrière-garde* effort to save rules of morality from the terrors of an entirely individual, "emotivist" standard—no standard at all, really, since it cannot refer persuasively to anything outside itself. Utilitarianism, too, was involved in the same fight, putting forward the principle of utility as a practical teleological substitute for divinely sanctioned moral principles. But neither was able to hold back the antinomian tide that would be so powerfully embodied in Nietzsche.[58] A wild and vital experience of radical freedom swept in, demolishing rational authority in the process. "The price paid for liberation from what appeared to be the external authority of traditional morality," writes Alasdair MacIntyre, "was the loss of any authoritative content from the would-be moral utterances of the autonomous agent." The moral agent in his radical freedom "spoke unconstrained by the externalities of divine law, natural teleology, or hierarchical authority; but why should anyone else now listen to him?"[59] The marketplace of moral ideas had become a consumer's paradise, but many of the goods were of questionable value.

One can see this development as both the culmination and the failure of what MacIntyre calls "the Enlightenment project of providing [the autonomous moral agent] with a secular, rational justification for his moral allegiances."[60] It was "Nietzsche's historic achievement to understand more clearly than any other philosopher . . . that what purported to be appeals to objectivity were in fact expressions of subjective will."[61] The "death of God"—the death of an ultimate external authority—is both a cause and a consequence of this unmasking. Yet it is important to remember that, at roughly the same moment in Western intellectual history, "the Enlightenment project" was in the process of erecting another, entirely different, self-negating criticism, arising from the new antiformalist disciplines of social science. As Robert Nisbet has pointed out, the nineteenth century witnessed a reorientation of social thought that was, in many respects, as momentous as that which the Enlightenment originated:

In widening areas of thought in the nineteenth century we see rationalist individualism (kept alive, of course, most impressively by the utilitarians, whose doctrines provide negative relief for so many sociological concepts) assailed by theories resting upon a reassertion of tradition, theories that would have been as repugnant to a Descartes or a Bacon as to a Locke or a Rousseau. We see the historic premise of the innate stability of the individual challenged by a new social psychology that derived personality from the close contexts of society and that made alienation the price of man's release from these contexts. Instead of the Age of Reason's cherished natural order, it is now the institutional order—community, kinship, social class—that forms the point of departure for social philosophers as widely separated in their views as Coleridge, Marx, and Tocqueville. From the eighteenth century's generally optimistic vision of popular sovereignty we pass to nineteenth century premonitions of the tyranny that may lie in popular democracy when its institutional and traditional limits are broken through. And finally, even the idea of progress is given a new statement: one resting not upon release from community and tradition but upon a kind of craving for new forms of moral and social community.[62]

In other words, at the same time Nietzsche disdainfully pushed aside the dream of rational autonomy in favor of a naked subjectivism, a sociological antiformalism was pulling the rug out from under it, asserting the binding irrational force of its master concepts, which transformed the autonomous actor back into an inescapably social and heteronomous creature. While individuals were more and more freely urged to declare their independence from norms, the assertion that norms were ultimately indispensable to any kind of social order seemed more and more persuasive.[63]

Such were the problems, noted in chapter 5, that beset the antiformalist revolt, but they also bring us back to the questions raised earlier about *The Lonely Crowd*. By taking up the cudgel for autonomy, was Riesman not only battling the recent past of American intellectual history and what he and others saw as the current social and cultural tendencies of postwar America, but also disregarding the very structural presuppositions of his discipline and skipping by the mounting evidence that autonomy was, at best, a problematic ideal? Was he, in a sense, writing an antisociological work of sociology by creating powerful typologies of social character and then exhorting the reader to cast them aside? If the norms embodied in social character are to be a genuine prerequisite for social cohesion, then how could one pick and choose which ones to obey? by what standard?[64]

So far as the text of *The Lonely Crowd* is concerned, the answers to these questions are elusive, since the discussion of autonomy is not nearly so concrete and well-developed as what precedes it. This deficiency became a factor influencing the book's critical reception. While many reviewers lauded the book, some rather pointedly exempted the ending, which was precisely the part of the book in which Riesman put forward the ideal of autonomy. *Commonweal*'s reviewer, for example, called the book "one of the most penetrating and comprehensive views of the twentieth century urban American you're likely to find," but with a "disappointing happy ending."[65] The *New Yorker*'s critic believed the book was admirably "spirited," beautifully written, and "full of sharp and disturbing conclusions," but that its "chief weakness is its ending, which leaves us entirely up in the air, uncertain of where we go next."[66] Perhaps one reviewer's happy ending is another's uncertainty, but it seems more likely that the ending's vagueness lent itself to a variety of very different reactions.

Riesman himself later acknowledged this fault in the book. It would have been hard for him not to, since as he remarked in the 1961 preface to *The Lonely Crowd*, "most articulate readers of *The Lonely Crowd* . . . tended to regard inner-direction and autonomy as much the same thing." He believed that "the confusion between autonomy and inner-direction that many readers fell into reflects our own inability to make the idea of autonomy a more vivid and less formal one—to give it content, as inner-direction gained content because the concept called to mind many historical exemplars available to everyone's experience."[67] In an article published in early 1990, he went further, acknowledging that "the notion of autonomy was rather thinly sketched" and that "as it was interpreted by many readers, it proved to be at best an ambiguous and at worst a harmful ideal"; it "strengthened the cult of candor" and gave rise to "a new hypocrisy" in which "we disguised even from ourselves our virtuous selves, our impulses of caring and concern toward others."[68] It became, in short, a sanction for a kind of low-grade Nietzschean individualism. It negated the categories of compulsion but without supplying a sufficient philosophical basis for moral freedom.

Some of the most penetrating critiques of the book in the years after its publication were offered by historians, who quarreled with Riesman's claim of a characterological shift.[69] Notably, David Potter disputed the validity of Riesman's cultural generalizations, arguing in a 1962 essay that, like the generalizations of Frederick Jackson Turner and others before him, Riesman's were extrapolated exclusively from male experience.[70] Women, Potter argued, had always been made overwhelmingly other-directed by virtue of their experience of motherhood and of dependency, which caused their acute attunement to "the moods and interests of others" to take precedence over the search for autonomy. Such a criticism seemed somewhat at odds with the success of *The Feminine Mystique*, however, published the following year, which offered a different, insistently gender-neutral perspective on autonomy and charged, moreover, that the household regime perpetuated by the feminine mystique was creating a deplorable softness of character in American boys and girls alike.

Such confusion was perhaps reflected in *The Lonely Crowd*'s own mixed judgment about the relative merits of inner- and other-direction. When looking at the matter from a strictly developmental standpoint, Riesman was likely to suggest that other-direction was more advanced than inner-direction and, therefore, would more easily evolve into a state of autonomy. For example, "other-direction gives men a sensitivity and rapidity of movement which under prevailing American institutions provide a large opportunity to explore the resources of character[,] . . . and these suggest [to him] at least the possibility of an organic development of autonomy out of other-direction."[71]

This optimism, so characteristic of the book's section on autonomy, had much to do with some of the specific features of autonomy that the book identified. To deal with the problem of other-directed "false personalization" in the workplace ("the spurious and effortful glad hand"), he recommended a general "de-personalizing" of work, so that other-directed workers would be able to save their precious "emotional reserves" for use in play—play having become "the sphere for the development of skill and competence in the art of living."[72] Therefore, "competence in play" was precisely what was wanted for the transition to autonomy. This training in competence was heavily oriented toward consumership, the development of taste, the discovery of fun and fulfilling leisure pursuits (through the assistance of "avocational counselors"), and the liberation of fantasy. (One is reminded of *Time*'s sidebar portrait of the autonomous man as, above all, a discerning consumer.) For example, he suggested "the creation of model consumer economies among children," offering a description of a "world's fair for children" that was eerily reminiscent of the economic system depicted in Bellamy's *Looking Backward*:

> A group of advertisers . . . might issue scrip money to groups of children, allowing them to patronize some central store—a kind of everyday world's fair—where a variety of "luxury" goods ranging from rare foods to musical instruments would be available for their purchase. At this "point of sale" there would stand market researchers, able and willing to help children make their selection but having no particularly frightening charisma or overbearing charm or any interest on the employers' side in pushing one thing rather than another. These "experiment stations" might become the source of revealing information about what happens to childhood taste when it is given a free track away from the taste gradients and "reasons," as well as freedom from the financial hobbles of a given peer-group. In precisely such situations children might find the opportunity to criticize and reshape in their own minds the values of objects. In the "free store" they would find private alcoves where they might enjoy books and music, candy and comics, in some privacy.[73]

This remarkable passage, which is perhaps the most specific exemplification of autonomy in the book, suggests several things about Riesman's conception. First, autonomy is well modeled for him in a classical-liberal market situation, but a market in which consumer choices have been artificially purged of all adulterations, such as needs, advertising, sales pressure, peers—and reasons.

The buyer is not a Kantian will or even a Freudian ego, but a kind of unmoved mover/connoisseur whose freedom lies precisely in his or her imperviousness to external influences. Yet Riesman also believed there was political value in such experiments. "Market research," he remarked, "has for many years seemed to me one of the most promising channels for democratic control of our economy," since market researchers "can be employed to find out not so much what people want but what with liberated fantasy they might want."[74]

In short, Riesman's conception of autonomy turns out to have been an empty or, at best, negative concept, since it negates whatever is compulsory in his other characterological types without supplying anything tangible to take its place. He made no effort to struggle with the paradoxes of autonomy that Kant so painstakingly addressed. His vision of a radically unconditioned self was remarkably benign; there is no Nietzschean abyss or heroic amoralism anywhere to be seen. To repeat a point that must be frequently stressed about *The Lonely Crowd*, it assumed that economic abundance was here to stay and that the problems of production had been solved; therefore, the conflicts that typified a scarcity economy would no longer be a significant factor in Americans' lives.[75]

Indeed, it is no wonder that readers who followed the book's argument to the point where autonomy is introduced became badly confused. In the first three-fourths of the book, Riesman presented a chilling (if humorously related) story of the embattled individual whose very socialization was yoked to the consumption preferences of his peers, and of a society that had corrupted the meaning of its governmental institutions into "politics as an object of consumption."[76] Just as important, if much more difficult to pin down, was the tone of that portion of his account, which often suggested (albeit without stating) an ironic, even Veblenian disdain for his subject. In the case of Veblen, his peculiar literary style is crucial to his meaning, since its severe, defamiliarizing detachment conveys a mocking and supercilious undercurrent that is all the more effective for being unstated.[77] Riesman and his collaborators are far less consistent in, and exert less control over, the messages conveyed by their stylistic choices, but the following passage may be taken as one of many possible instances when a Veblenian undercurrent appears:

> Business is supposed to be fun. . . . The demand to have fun is one that the inner-directed businessman never faced. He could afford to be properly gloomy and grim. The shortening of hours . . . has extended the requirements for office sociability largely in the top management of business, government, and academic life. Here people spend long hours in the company of their office peer-group. Their lunches are long; their golf

games longer still. Much time in the office itself is also spent in sociability: exchanging office gossip ("conferences"), making good-will tours ("inspection"), talking to salesmen and joshing secretaries ("morale"). In fact, depleting the expense account can serve as an almost limitless occupational therapy for men who, out of a tradition of hard work, a dislike of their wives, a lingering asceticism, and an anxiety about their antagonistic cooperators, still feel that they must put in a good day's work at the office. But, of course . . . this kind of sociability, carrying so much workaday freight, was [not] free or sociable.[78]

It is hard to disentangle the satirical from the descriptive in such a passage; that is part of its charm. The satire is carried by the very way the scene is observed and narrated, by the observer's implicit distancing of himself from all that he is observing. It recalls the comic stance of social-observation stylists that Kenneth Lynn called "the style of a gentleman," a pose that conveys to the reader, in detailed but mildly amused prose, one's superiority to one's subject—a subject, moreover, for whom the author wants to make certain he will not be mistaken. It is a style, therefore, especially useful in a fluid social world like Addisonian London or colonial America—or Riesman's own upwardly mobile 1950s.[79]

The comparison of Veblen's view with the modus operandi of *The Lonely Crowd*, however, would surely elicit a howl of protest from Riesman, and not without reason. He has often taken great pains to stress explicitly his abhorrence of elitism, his distaste for those critics who snobbishly stigmatize popular culture and popular tastes, and his serious intellectual and conceptual differences with Veblen.[80] All of that is readily granted, but the problem remains: does the style, intentionally or not, communicate a distaste for other-directedness that clashes with the explicit disclaimers? Was *The Lonely Crowd* a book moving, like surf waters, in two different directions at once? If so, is the force of its incoming waves enfeebled by the great power of its undertow, so that the reader is not propelled joyfully forward into the direction of autonomous consumption but is instead pulled backward, into a nostalgic yearning for inner-direction?

The answer cannot be simple. To be sure, the book sometimes genuinely attempts a tone of ethnography, an air of scientific neutrality; but then that may unexpectedly give way to a strong suggestion of moral critique. Too many pages pass an unfavorable judgment upon the other-directed, whether explicitly or implicitly, and the cumulative effect is too unrelievedly negative to be entirely disposed of by Riesman's claim that he was trying to "develop a view of society which accepts rather than rejects new potentialities for leisure, human sympathy, and abundance."[81] Even the book's most ardent admirers admitted the problem. No one cheered *The Lonely Crowd* more loudly than Lionel Trilling, who called it "one of the most important books about America to have been published" as well as "one of the most interesting books that I have ever read." Trilling mused after reading it that sociology was perhaps "taking over from literature one of literature's most characteristic functions, the investigation and criticism of morals and manners," for Riesman had shown he could write "with a sense of social actuality which Scott Fitzgerald might have envied." This was almost unimaginably high praise, coming from such a high priest of the literary imagination. Nonetheless Trilling tempered his praise in one important respect, observing that "Mr. Riesman remarks that he has found it almost impossible to make a comparison of the two forms of character-direction without making inner-direction seem the more attractive. I don't agree with Mr. Riesman that the preference is a mere prejudice which we must guard against. . . . It is still inner-direction that must seem the more fully human, even in its excess."[82]

Hence, it is hardly surprising that many readers were inclined to agree with Trilling and to find the central part of the book—the invidious contrast between inner- and other-direction—was the only part that really spoke to them, or the only part they heard.[83] Thus, they read *The Lonely Crowd* selectively, conflating inner-direction and autonomy and ignoring Riesman's utopian-consumerist flights of fancy. That central opposition between inner- and other-direction spoke powerfully to a long-standing repertoire of Americans' most enduring fears. The British scholar Rupert Wilkinson has recently argued that four fears have been especially characteristic of Americans: the fear of "being owned," the fear of "falling apart," the fear of "falling away," and the fear of "winding down."[84] The first relates precisely to the loss of independence and autonomy; the second, to the dissolution of the community into egoism and chaos; the third, to the specter of moral and spiritual decline; and the fourth, to the loss of personal and economic dynamism and the competitive spirit. These fears are also related to one another as polarities: the first against the second, and the third against the fourth. All but the second are powerfully present in *The Lonely Crowd*.

---

*The Lonely Crowd*, then, presented yet another facet of the ironist turn in American thought after World War II. Its debt to Tocqueville was considerable, not only for the many quotations from *Democracy in America* scattered through its pages, but for the tenor and content of its conclusions, which also borrowed heavily from the Tocquevillean treasury. Even more significant, however, was the very personal influence that refugees from Hitler, steeped in the traditions of European social thought and powerfully affected by the pathologies of their history, had upon Riesman. In different but complementary ways, Arendt, Fromm, Adorno, and Lowenthal all left their intellectual mark on the premises and conclusions of *The Lonely Crowd*.

Riesman came by his interest in German culture early in life, for his German-Jewish father was one of the most respected physicians in the Philadelphia of his day. His interest flourished in college, however, when Riesman became friendly with Carl Friedrich, a German émigré of the 1920s (and future analyst of totalitarianism) who was then an instructor in the department of government at Harvard. Riesman quickly adopted Friedrich as his mentor, a relationship that eventually blossomed into a close friendship. In 1933 the two shared expenses in buying an old farmhouse and pasturage in southern Vermont, where they frequently spent weekends. Through his close friendship with Friedrich, Riesman was able to meet many of the German refugee intellectuals that had begun to trickle into the United States. Even if he had not been an intellectual of German-Jewish descent with broad, cosmopolitan sympathies, Riesman would likely have been greatly moved by the plight of the refugee scholars. Eventually, during the late 1930s and early 1940s, Riesman and Friedrich organized and directed a program designed to resettle refugee intellectuals and lawyers into American positions.[85]

Riesman's interests in the refugees, however, extended further than a merely humanitarian concern for their exiled and vulnerable position. He became intensely drawn to their ideas. Like many of his generation, he had been brought up to believe that all "real culture lay in Europe" and hence was thrilled to have the opportunity to absorb that culture directly from the source.[86] He had been influenced by his mother, Eleanor, an elegant, highly cultivated Bryn Mawr graduate with a keen interest in the European intellectual avant-garde, including Freud, Thomas Mann, and, above all, Oswald Spengler, whose romantic pessimism she wholeheartedly shared.[87] Perhaps his long-standing sympathetic interest in German culture, not to mention his own heritage and the particular interests he inherited from his mother, made him unusually sympathetic to Continental perspectives. Paradoxically, his lack of formal sociological training freed him from intellectual bondage to standard American sociological practice and made him open to the fresh winds blowing in from abroad, where sociology had always remained closely related to the humanistic disciplines.

Especially important to Riesman, both personally and intellectually, was his contact with Erich Fromm. The author of *Escape from Freedom* served as both teacher and psychoanalyst to Riesman, and the effect of Frommian ideas was abundantly in evidence in much of Riesman's work, especially *The Lonely Crowd*. Above all else, the concept of social character, so central to *The Lonely Crowd*'s argument, was taken from Fromm's effort to harness psychoanalytic insights for social explanation. Like Fromm, Riesman rejected an orthodox application of Freudian libido theory and instead argued that fundamental character types, or "modal" personalities, had to be explained as a function of social and economic conditions. Like Fromm, he "historicized" Freud by treating the Freudian man—the inner-directed man—as a particular response to the particular social and economic conditions of post-Reformation, pre-socialist Western man. *The Lonely Crowd* cited Fromm's explication of social character at length: "In order that any society may function well, its members must acquire the kind of character which makes them *want* to act in the way they *have* to act as members of the society. . . . They have to *desire* what objectively is *necessary* for them to do. *Outer force* is replaced by *inner compulsion*, and by the particular kind of human energy which is channeled into character traits."[88] As Riesman put it on the first page of *The Lonely Crowd*, the other-directed man, "the middle-class urban American of today," no longer internalizes adult authority à la Freud, but is rather "a product of his peers," to whom he conforms not only in his overt behavior but in "the very quality of his feeling." Yet, Riesman added, "paradoxically, he remains a lonely member of the crowd because he never comes really close to the others or to himself." Riesman's other-directed man clearly resembles Fromm's lost and alienated modern man, bereft of tradition and yearning for authority. Both types have lost the fundamental core of consistency that makes for healthy individuation; both risk ceding their inmost selves to social forces that care little for the integrity of the individual.[89]

Fromm was not the only Central European refugee thinker whose influence would be apparent in *The Lonely Crowd*. Riesman had drawn explicitly upon work by the Institute of Social Research and Paul Lazarsfeld's Bureau of Applied Social Research dealing with mass media and their influence upon audiences.[90] He had also been taken with Leo Lowenthal's article "Biographies in Popular Magazines," published under Lazarsfeld's auspices, in which Lowenthal's content analysis of popular culture led him to posit a shift from "heroes of production" to "heroes of consumption" in American popular consciousness—a change that mirrored the overall shift in character structure that economic and social change was causing. At Riesman's request, Lowenthal read *The Lonely Crowd* in draft. In fact, though, Lowenthal saw his own thinking so faithfully mirrored in *The Lonely Crowd* that he criticized it only for the narrowness with which it applied its findings. The book's "observations on the development of character types in American society," he remarked, "may well turn out to be a description of a secular trend of modern industrial society as a whole." Because Riesman, like most American scholars of the time, was unfamiliar with the entire body of the Frankfurt school's work, he was unaware of the larger structure of ideas from which Lowenthal's remarks derived. Many of Riesman's criticisms of modern American life, however—its "false personalization," its transformation of all of human life's elements into commodities for consumption—faithfully echoed theirs.[91]

It is hardly surprising, then, to discover what a keen interest Riesman also took in the work of Hannah Arendt, another thinker who emphasized the radical disjunction between the twentieth century and all earlier centuries, and who had also found in the weakness of modern man's character structure a source of political and social unfreedom. Even though *The Lonely Crowd* was published a full year before *The Origins of Totalitarianism*, the former bears the impress of the latter, for Riesman had carefully read Arendt's book in manuscript during the summer of 1949. The long, generously detailed letters that he wrote Arendt that summer in commentary upon the draft leave no doubt of how deeply his encounter with the *Origins* had affected him.

Indeed, even before that summer, Riesman had already fallen under the spell of Arendt's work, having read with admiration her pre-*Origins* articles in *Partisan Review* and other periodicals on race, nationalism, and power. In 1947, when Riesman was teaching at the University of Chicago, he tried to persuade Milton Singer, then chair of the social sciences staff, to hire Arendt to teach there.[92] As *The Lonely Crowd* took shape in his mind, he pleaded with Arendt to consider contributing a historical section for the book, as he felt that "to understand what has changed politically and characterologically requires a kind of historical analysis and comparison which only you are capable of making."[93] Although Arendt declined the offer, their intellectual relationship continued.

He shared outlines and memorandums on the project, and she responded with surprising admiration, given her usual disdain for social scientists. She found his account of other-directedness frighteningly persuasive; "what shocks me most in your description, which is so extremely convincing . . . because of the inescapable consistency of this whole approach to life, is that these phenomena indeed arise here [in America] simply out of society, without as it were anybody doing anything about it." Arendt had the greatest regard for Tocqueville, and she too was convinced that Riesman was describing something new in the world, "a being lost in the world which is similar to the . . . situation of my mass-man in Europe." The American people exhibited the most advanced form of this new characterological trend; "in Europe," she remarked, mass men "had not yet time to develop definite character structure" to the extent Americans had done. In America, "the other-directed type actually and sincerely believes in the 'other,' because he represents to him the ideal man. . . . It is as though Americans have liquidated the old belief in original sin and, precisely because they no longer believe in the sinfulness of man, come to the conclusion that they, every single one of them in his non-admitted privacy of a probably intolerable anxiety, is the only sinner."[94]

As for Riesman, his reading of *The Origins of Totalitarianism* only heightened his enthusiasm for Arendt's approach and insights. Indeed, his comments in correspondence leave little doubt of how much the other-directed man owed, both in sociological and psychological terms, to Arendt's mass man. After reading the first one and one-half chapters, he wrote, "I have the feeling that nobody understands our times so well as you, that nobody has such an extraordinarily acute sense of what has *changed*." A week later, he wrote "I am simply overwhelmed by your vision. . . . I think now you have really touched genius." Some two months later: "I feel you have accomplished a great work of the human spirit in making sense of the world. . . . There is no excitement in . . . any other historian I can think of, of modern times, to compare with your own work." After finishing the book—with, he remarked, the regret one feels at the conclusion of "a great book,"—he wrote her again, confessing "that your work haunts me and that I think of it all the time." So concerned was Riesman with seeing to it that Arendt's *Origins* received a respectful reception that he himself wrote an unusually long and highly favorable review of the book for *Commentary* (where his coauthor Nathan Glazer was assistant editor).[95]

What haunted Riesman in Arendt's work, above all else, was the same thing that haunted him in Fromm's work: the image of a collectivism so complete that it could only be hinted at by words like *conformity*, and so deep that it penetrated beyond overt expression of opinions to the very recesses of consciousness itself. Riesman, however, lacked the antimodern and conservative biases of so many critics of mass society, even those of the Left; he sought to use the critique of mass society rather as John Stuart Mill did, to promote libertarian rather than conservative (or revolutionary) ends. Part of the immense audience for *The Lonely Crowd* was composed of liberal intellectuals who found that the work addressed two of their principal anxieties. Given the environment of the Cold War, which was conceived as a struggle of civilizations in which ideas were conceived as weapons, the pressures upon intellectuals to dedicate their energies to national purposes became more intense than ever; witness the proliferation of state-required loyalty oaths, which many intellectuals regarded as an infringement upon the always fragile prerogatives of academic freedom. They were acutely anxious about the popular support for a demogogue like Senator Joseph McCarthy, who repeatedly questioned the loyalty of freethinking intellectuals. Such academics experienced vividly the conflict between the autonomous (or inner-directed?) man who had the courage to go his own way, and the other-directed man who cravenly strove to reflect the public consensus and who, therefore, willingly signed the loyalty oath and carefully tailored his views.

Riesman hoped, however, to appropriate the categories of mass-society theory without being forced to fully accept either its premises or its conclusions. That was easier said than done. The social basis of mass society, as well as of the totalitarianism into which it degenerated, was evident enough in the democratic West—as, indeed, had been pointed out by the leading proponents of those theories. The logic of the theory separated a full-blown totalitarianism from the massifying tendencies of the liberal-democratic West by only the most fragile of membranes. The mass-society theorists' pessimism did not go down easily with Riesman, and so *The Lonely Crowd* also contains liberal-progressive countercurrents—as, for example, in its utopian vision of an autonomous man who would transcend all the limitations of inner- and other-direction, of all internal and external coercions. These countercurrents coexist uneasily with the book's strain of Continental pessimism. Two visions of the world seemed to compete for his conscience.[96]

Nowhere is this clearer than in his introduction of the autonomous man, who resembled nothing so much as a social scientist or some other Mannheimian "free-floating" intellectual.[97] Having begun with the assumption that all societies depend upon some form of compulsion (whether originating in tradition, child rearing, or "a jury of one's peers") to hang together, Riesman had no plausible basis for proclaiming a social ideal that had somehow liberated itself from those same basic social forces. How could a comprehensive and relentlessly structural explanation of modern American society suddenly yield, at the crucial moment of its argument, to the leaven of individual initiative? Had Riesman succumbed to a revival of American uplift, an appeal to the progressivism that he and his postwar generation had been at such pains to reject? Had he failed to see how the overpoweringly gloomy logic of the German refugees' conceptions made a liberal answer problematical?

---

Riesman was not the only important American intellectual of the postwar period whose concerns were focused by the provocative ideas of German refugee intellectuals. Daniel Bell, editor of *The New Leader* during the war years, worked closely with the Frankfurt school émigrés, serving as a consultant to a 1944 study of anti-Semitism that the Institute of Social Research had organized. The study found an alarming rise in anti-Semitism among working-class Americans, including trade unionists. Its findings impressed Bell, who had been developing deep reservations about the devolution of organized labor into a "new proletariat" comprised of "lumpen" elements with "sadistic, macabre" traits.[98] The work of Erich Fromm, particularly *Escape from Freedom*, and the institute's earlier studies of authority and the family seemed to provide a plausible explanation of this phenomenon.[99] In 1944, Bell wrote an essay, "The Grass Roots of American Jew-Hatred," that used the work of Fromm and the other, more orthodox institute authors for this purpose.[100]

Despite Germany's persecution of Jews, Bell felt certain that "the country where anti-Semitism can emerge in the most violent shape and unabated fury is the United States." The American industrial worker, he felt, "is less immune to the fascist virus than the European worker." Bell based these perceptions on his growing conviction that the United States had the world's most advanced mass society. In a letter written in 1945 to his friend Lewis Corey, Bell revealed how deeply his thinking had become indebted to the mass-society theory expounded by Fromm:

> I think the great lesson of fascism as a social and political movement is the importance of *masses* and the manipulation of *masses*. . . . My hunch is that fascism was accepted by those who rejected classes and the older class system, by those, whether they were workers, intellectuals, lumpen elements etc who did not want to belong to any class and who accepted fascism as a movement against *all* classes. In the United States where we do have, psychologically, a classless society, I feel that a revolutionary fascist movement will have more chance of winning over the working class than any other.

It was precisely the *perceived* classlessness of American society, then, and the alienation of its members from the former order, that made the United States so vulnerable to fascist movements—a vulnerability that Bell saw exemplified even in a "progressive" movement like Populism. Following Fromm, Bell identified a sadomasochistic character structure, created by the "aggressive and competitive world" of capitalism, which predisposed Americans to resentment and political discontent and made them susceptible to demagogic and violent mass movements.[101]

A decade later, Bell edited a collection called *The New American Right*, containing essays by Bell, Riesman, Glazer, Seymour Martin Lipset, Richard Hofstadter, Peter Viereck, and Talcott Parsons. Obviously inspired by the McCarthy phenomenon, *The New American Right* elaborated upon many of the very themes that Bell and Riesman had already begun to adumbrate. All of the essays expressed a profound distrust and fear of the dangerous potential to be found in mass movements. The "lower a person is in socio-economic status or educational attainment," declared Lipset, "the more likely he is to support McCarthy, favor restrictions on civil liberties, and back a 'get tough' policy with the Communist states." The dissolution of society in America into a perceived classlessness, along with the tensions incident to capitalism, gave rise to an especially keen form of "status anxiety," a disorientation arising in any mass society but exacerbated in postwar America by the plentiful prospects for upward mobility.[102] Much of the right-wing and McCarthyite political ferment of those years was explained not by the time-honored competition of interests that political thinkers since Madison had stressed, but by the quest for status—for a sure and solid "place" in an amorphous social order.

One of *The New American Right*'s contributors, Richard Hofstadter, drew upon a different aspect of the refugee legacy: the studies of authoritarianism that Adorno and Horkheimer had published five years earlier. Hofstadter, a former Marxist who was fascinated and amused by the strange passions that had so often animated American political history, seized upon Adorno's Weimarian description of the authoritarian personality to provide his own social-psychological diagnosis of the McCarthyite-Populist Right.[103] Borrowing the term *pseudoconservative* from Adorno's study to describe the new rightists, Hofstadter found them suffering from an "enormous hostility to authority, which cannot be admitted to consciousness"; such inner tension "calls forth a massive overcompensation which is manifest in the form of extravagant submissiveness to strong power." The pseudoconservatives could not be called authentic conservatives because such fanatics were motivated by "a profound if largely unconscious hatred of our society and its ways"—a hatred for which *The Authoritarian Personality* provided the "clinical evidence."[104] Pseudoconservatism was a product of the "rootlessness" of American life, resulting in a "scramble for status" and a "peculiar search for secure identity"; America was a country full of people who "do not know who they are or what they are or what they belong to or what belongs to them."[105] Because of the pervasiveness of mass media, the slumbering lumpen had begun to take an interest in politics—indeed, had transformed it into a clash of "projective rationalizations" into which they invested their craving for status. "Mass communications," he sighed, "had aroused the mass man" and provided targets for his inchoate discontent. Given the continual crises afflicting postwar America, particularly in matters of foreign policy and internal security, as well as the two decades of liberal-Democratic hegemony since 1932, there were plenty of convenient targets for pseudoconservative wrath and envy.[106]

In his famous essay "The Paranoid Style in American Politics," published in

November 1964—not coincidentally, the very month that Lyndon Johnson crushed the presidential aspirations of the "radical right" Republican candidate, Arizona senator Barry Goldwater—he again drew from *The Authoritarian Personality* for his central terminology. Indeed, "The Paranoid Style" offered an explanation that was, like *The Authoritarian Personality* itself, far more psychological than the essays in *The New American Right*. In a discussion of those high in fascist potential, Adorno had identified a personality syndrome he called "the crank," who had "an affinity to psychosis"—indeed, who was "paranoid." Such people "build up a spurious inner world, often approaching delusion, emphatically set against outer reality." These types "are likely to form sects" in order "to confirm to each other their pseudoreality," associations built upon "ideas of conspiracy," such as the Jews' "quest for world domination," as rendered in the Protocols of the Elders of Zion.[107] The classic paranoid-stylists of American political history—the anti-Masons, anti-Catholics, nativists, anti-Semites, McCarthyites, John Birchers, and so on—partook of precisely these traits, Hofstadter believed. "History *is* a conspiracy" for them, "set in motion by demonic forces of almost transcendental power, and what is felt to be needed to defeat it is not the usual methods of political give-and-take, but an all-out crusade. The paranoid spokesman sees the fate of this conspiracy in apocalyptic terms—he traffics in the birth and death of whole worlds, whole political orders, whole systems of human values."[108] In the end, however, Hofstadter had to confess that it was the style, not the content, of the paranoids' ideas that most disturbed him: "Nothing entirely prevents a sound issue from being advocated in the paranoid style, and it is admittedly impossible to settle the merits of an argument because we think we hear in its presentation the characteristic paranoid accents. Style had to do with the way in which ideas are believed and advocated rather than with the truth or falsity of their content."[109]

There was an illiberal and ad hominem element in this critique, an a priori refusal to take seriously the extremists' thoughts, even though he also believed them to represent a not inconsiderable segment of popular sentiment. Paradoxically, a rigid anti-individualism could exist in easy symbiosis with idiosyncratic political lunacies, as Adorno's work appeared to demonstrate. But why, one wonders, did Hofstadter devote so much attention to them and to the wilder Populists like "Coin" Harvey, Ignatius Donnelly, and the assorted cranks and crazies that dwell on the fringes of a modern democratic polity? Part of the answer surely lies in Hofstadter's tendency, like his early hero H. L. Mencken, to batten upon the curiosities inhabiting the American political zoo and make a career of mocking them. He was, his friend Alfred Kazin remembered, "a derisive critic and parodist of every American Utopia and its wild prophets[,] . . . a creature suspended between gloom and fun."[110] He could and did play it both ways, deriding those prophets while disclaiming their significance. Kazin called him "a secret conservative" who shared Mencken's extreme distaste for the masses, a distaste that, in his case, rotated among amusement, contempt, and fear. As an intellectual who prided himself upon his critical independence, he was disturbed by the demotic anti-intellectualism that he believed to be endemic to American life and of which McCarthyism was only the most recent example.[111] He was only too aware that "the paranoid style" had enjoyed its "consummatory triumph" not in anti-intellectual America but in Germany, homeland of the very institutions, such as the modern research university, that he most honored.[112]

Hofstadter, then, shared his colleagues' fear of the discontents produced by a mass society in America; indeed, nothing was more striking about postwar American liberal intellectuals than their heightened tendency to distrust "the people." Our "populistic culture," he believed, ensured that we "lack a responsible elite with political and moral autonomy" and hence have no enlightened barrier against the winds of outrageous popular doctrines and delusions. The possible result was "a political climate in which the rational pursuit of our well-being and safety would become impossible."[113] The *ideological* character of right-wing fanaticism—its tendency to be dogmatic and uncivil—even more than the character of its arguments disqualified it from a serious hearing in an unillusioned, "post-ideological" age.[114] Hofstadter was also powerfully, even obsessively, alert, however, to the tendency of modern American life to produce such excesses, and the fragility of a demotic society's defenses against them.

A similar liberal distrust of the people became evident in the debate that raged during the 1950s over mass culture. Here, too, the image of a soft-core totalitarianism, which controlled other-directed men and women not by coercing them but by infiltrating and remolding their malleable consciousnesses, played an important part. The Frankfurt émigrés' critique of the culture industry, which had initially arisen in reaction to the mass culture of the Weimar and Hitler years and had gained added force during the refugees' years in Los Angeles, found fertile ground in the analysis of American popular culture. The absence of any substantial political radicalism in America seemed to confirm their guess that the American working-class audiences had been rendered even more suggestible and stupefied than European ones. With the postwar explosion in mass communications, including the advent of television, there was reason to wonder if an intellectual tyranny of the majority in a mass society would simply render serious intellectual productions superfluous.

A 1953 article by Dwight Macdonald called "A Theory of Mass Culture" would become the locus classicus of American mass-culture criticism, drawing upon the writings of Adorno, Horkheimer, and Lowenthal as well as American admirers of their work such as Clement Greenberg (who popularized the term *Kitsch* in America) and David Riesman. Macdonald also drew freely upon mass-society theory, expressed in his always clear and forceful prose. "The mass man is a solitary atom," he wrote, "uniform with and undifferentiated from thousands and millions of other atoms who go to make up 'the lonely crowd,' as David Riesman well calls American society." Mass men are "unable to express themselves as human beings because they are related to one another neither as individuals nor as members of communities . . . but only to something distant, abstract, nonhuman . . . [such as] a system of industrial production, a party, or a State." Hence, mass culture is expressly designed for such a society, which has "broken down the old barriers of class, tradition, [and] taste," offering instead a "homogenized" and homogenizing "commodity" that is carefully designed by the "Lords of *Kitsch*" to be sufficiently unchallenging so as to achieve maximum appeal. Mass culture "absolutely refuses to discriminate against, or between, anything or anybody." Hence mass culture "can never be any good."[115]

Mass culture represented a threat to the high culture that intellectuals esteemed, for a Gresham's law seemed to operate in the realm of culture as well as in economics: "bad stuff," Macdonald lamented, "drives out the good." Mass culture threatened high culture "by its sheer pervasiveness," by suffocating the audience for serious arts. It also threatened folk culture, which had traditionally stood at the opposite pole to high culture. The "spreading ooze" of mass culture, he argued, resulted in the debasement and usurpation of folk culture, which had been the "spontaneous, autochthonic expression of the people." Mass culture, however, is imposed from above, "fabricated by technicians hired by businessmen." The lords of *Kitsch* "exploit the cultural needs of the masses in order to make a profit and/or to maintain their class rule." Mass culture "breaks down the wall" that protected "the people's own institution," thereby "becoming an instrument of political domination."

One might have expected Macdonald to see mass culture as a byproduct of capitalism's exploitative and expropriative dynamic, but his indictment is more sweeping; it blames modern mass society and technology, independently of particular economic systems. Even the Soviet Union is "a land of Mass Culture," whose artifacts are also manufactured by "technicians employed by the ruling class." Indeed, Macdonald saw little hope for the revival of high culture "in a world dominated by the two great mass nations, U.S.A. and U.S.S.R., and becoming more industrialized, more massified all the time."

Nor did he dare hope that the sensibilities of the masses might be improved. They had already been "debauched by several generations" of *Kitsch* and had settled into "a narcotized acceptance of mass culture and of the commodities it sells as a substitute for . . . real life." Mass culture was indeed the new opiate of a hopelessly unrevolutionary and secular age.

Macdonald's attack brought the haute Weimar critique of mass culture into the mainstream of American thought, bridging the gap between the left-Hegelian intellectual preoccupations of the Frankfurt school's mandarin neo-Marxism and the soul-searching mood in some sectors of American society in the 1950s. The obsession with totalism, the terror instilled by the idea of total institutions imprisoning human individuality within strictures of total con-trol—in politics, in social organization, in culture, and in consciousness—ran like an Ariadne's thread through much of the most distinguished social and cultural criticism of the time, giving a philosophical and world-historical focus to a host of discontents that beset postwar America. But the message is not entirely separable from the messenger. The particular ways in which intellec-tuals conceive and render the social order is inseparable from their particular situation and concerns. The postwar period saw a dramatic refiguration of the role of intellect in American life, a change that, though largely positive, also had the paradoxical effect of breeding certain confusions and fears and perhaps magnifying their influence.

For Arendt, Adorno, and Fromm, as we have seen, the loneliness of the mass man mirrored the superfluousness and alienation of the exile. For Ameri-can thinkers, the disturbing postwar vision of totalism disclosed some of the anxieties and projections of the free-floating intellectual trying to find his way in a democratic social order. As Daniel Bell suggested in a 1946 article, "A Parable of Alienation," in tones that strongly recall Adorno's *Minima Moralia*, all avenues of praxis "exact [their] own conformities." Therefore, "all that is left," Bell observed, "is the hardness of alienation, the sense of otherness." The deracination that was said to be exacted by mass society was, in fact, epito-mized in the person of the principled intellectual who proposed to be that society's scourge and conscience. Like Hannah Arendt's citizen-pariah, Bell's intellectual is called upon "to point to the need of brotherhood" but never to acknowledge and accept that need in himself; "as he has been bred, he cannot today accept any embodiment of community as final. He can live only in permanent tension and as a permanent critic." Like other postwar intellectuals, Bell was breaking with a long procession of previous American intellectuals, stretching as far back as Bellamy, by presenting the yearning for social con-nectedness as a snare to be forsworn by all authentic critical intellects; for such was the price of truth-seeking. Instead, the paradigm for such intellects to Bell was the archetypal wandering Jew, whose life was "the image of the world's destiny."[116]

What Bell saw as a specific prescription for the intellectuals, Nathan Glazer, commenting upon Bell and several other writers in a 1947 *Commentary* article that built upon Bell's "A Parable of Alienation," saw as a generalized description of modern American society. Alienation appeared to be a systemic feature of "modern social organization as we know it." The war had marked "a revolutionary change in the psychological condition of man, reflected in the individual's feeling of isolation, homelessness, insecurity, restlessness, anxiety." As for Bell's image of Jew-as-alien, Glazer thought it only a more pronounced version of "the homelessness felt by all men in our great industrial society." The individual's intense need for connectedness was pathetically obsolete, since there was no longer any basis for community in the world. The chief task of social science in our time was the "theoretical construction of models of possible social organization" that would "enable the expression of such values as freedom and individualism."[117]

The concept of alienation even crept into the history of American immigration. The historian Oscar Handlin, in *The Uprooted*, his classic 1952 account of American immigration, resoundingly echoed Glazer's view, conflating the situation of modern man with the situation of displaced persons—and the meaning of America. "A time came," wrote Handlin in his account of the origins of European emigration, "for many men when the slow glacial shift of economic and social forces suddenly broke loose in some major upheaval that cast loose the human beings from their age-old setting. In an extreme form this was the experience of the immigrants. It was also in some degree the experience of all modern men." For emigration, wrote Handlin, was "the central experience of a great many human beings" in modern times; hence, "the history of immigration is a history of alienation and its consequences," and "America was the land of separated men." Newcomers to America "were on the way toward being Americans almost before they stepped off the boat, because their own experience of displacement had already introduced them to what was essential in the situation of Americans."[118] To be American was to be modern, floating free—and alienated.

Underlying this intellectual tendency to universalize alienation, it must be added, was a striking sense of alienation from the ordinary people. The Hungarian-born historian John Lukacs, who emigrated to the United States just after the Second World War, was struck by that fact and tells a revealing story about his observations. "Numerous American intellectuals and academics," he wrote in his autobiography, "kept telling me, early in my American years, that to understand America I ought to read the short story by

Shirley Jackson, 'The Lottery.'" This chilling story, originally published in the June 26, 1948, issue of *The New Yorker*, relates the yearly ritual stoning, by the citizens of an otherwise civilized New England community, of a randomly selected member of the community. The recommendation shocked Lukacs because he saw the story as "incarnating a hatred and fear of The People," even though it was being "devoured and admired by the people who were votaries of Liberalism"—an interpretation fully consistent with what we know of Jackson's intentions in writing the story.[119] A similar reaction might as easily have been elicited by such postwar productions as Arthur Miller's 1953 play *The Crucible* or the film *High Noon*, which contrasted heroic individualism to the cravenness of the many. Such images were a figuration of the intellectual's dilemma in a mass society. No wonder that so much of the period's social thought was directed toward the assertion of personal autonomy.

In asserting autonomy, however, social scientists were reaching back to the individualistic concepts that the consolidationist thinkers had been struggling to overcome or redefine. Indeed, the concerns that had stood at the heart of Tocqueville, Mill, and Emerson—the concerns animating nineteenth-century liberalism—were brought back to center stage in a work like *The Lonely Crowd*. Even so, they came back with a profound difference, lacking the assurance of a hard, clear-cut sense of individuality that Emerson had inherited from the eighteenth century. "Social science," wrote Riesman in the title essay of *Individualism Reconsidered*, had made us aware of "the extent to which individuals . . . are the creatures of their cultural conditioning."[120] That was not the only problem. Shirley Jackson's story memorably depicted the demonic mind-controlling menace and lurking savagery of a devouring culture. But her own tortured life, as Judy Oppenheimer has disclosed in a biography appropriately entitled *Private Demons*, reveals a veritable jungle of psychopathologies whose power crippled Jackson's efforts at autonomy and even her ability to write. Through years of depression, pills, and eventual descent into psychosis, however, the dream of autonomy remained steadfast. The last obsessive, pathetic words in Jackson's journal, written shortly before her premature death, eerily recall the same combination of desperate self-assertion and mocking nihilistic humor that had gripped the aging Mark Twain: "I am the captain of my fate I am the captain of my fate I am the captain of my fate. Laughter is possible laughter is possible laughter is possible."[121] Perhaps the dream of an unencumbered, autonomous self was no pearl, despite its great price.

To be sure, Riesman and his collaborators did not think they had composed a neoindividualist manifesto. In fact, they explicitly denied any such intention in the 1961 preface: "The authors of *The Lonely Crowd* are not conservatives harking back to a rugged individualism that was once a radical Emersonian ideal."[122] That they felt compelled to make such a denial, however, is as significant as the denial itself. So, too, is the fact that by 1969 the book had accumulated fifty pages of prefatory material, most of it devoted to corrections, amplifications, and explications designed to address readers' errors and misunderstandings. By the 1969 edition, Riesman indicated in his "cautionary preface" that in some respects he had come to regret the book's enormous influence. *The Lonely Crowd* had "entered the picture many Americans . . . have of ourselves," he averred, and as such, it had "contributed to the climate of criticism of our society and helped create or reaffirm a nihilistic outlook among a great many people who lay claim to moral or intellectual nonconformity."[123] More recently, he rued the fact that "individuals seeking to show that they were not 'other-directed,' that they were unconstrained by parents and peers found extravagant ways to flaunt their supposed authenticity."[124] Riesman has more than once asserted that he and his collaborators "had no expectation" that the book would appeal to a wide audience, but that assertion is hard to accept. It is belied not only by the book's fluid and witty expository style but by Riesman's own admission to Arendt in 1949 that he was "trying to organize [the book] in such shape that I can appeal to a wider audience than academic people."[125] Unfortunately, perhaps, he succeeded in doing just that.

Riesman's protestations, however, do point to one fact: the remarkable reception of *The Lonely Crowd* may have to be considered somewhat separately from its argument. If for no other reason than its inability to provide a convincing image of autonomy, the book lent itself rather easily to the very misinterpretations that Riesman lamented. The book's description of other-direction exercised a particularly fatal attraction upon educated Americans, as Cushing Strout, one of Riesman's admirers and defenders, observed: "The relish with which so many academics devoured these depressing images of American society reflects a blend of self-congratulatory relief for not having 'gone into trade' and self-accusing recognition of their own fate in the struggle for tenure and grants in the affluent 'multiversities.'"[126]

Still, however projective the various versions of mass society may have been, the question of the truth in Riesman's work remains. In a stimulating essay on *The Lonely Crowd*, the German sociologist Ralf Dahrendorf took up this issue and pointed to several important respects in which *The Lonely Crowd* seemed to miss the mark in its description of American life. First, it did not seem to Dahrendorf that there had been any significant decrease in the ambitiousness of Americans; "the belief that everybody might someday be a millionaire . . . has survived even the challenges of depression and New Deal as an ideology."

Second, "the death of the Protestant character" in America seemed to him an egregiously premature diagnosis, for "the importance of work, occupation, and individual advancement is still striking in the United States"; this disposition was symptomatic, in turn, of the continued dominance of inner-direction. In politics, the American system continued to thrive on uninhibited conflict, "both personal and ideological"; no tendency toward tepid consensus seemed to be evident.[127]

His final point was perhaps the most interesting, however, touching the tangled and complex relationship between thought and social reality. It was impossible, he acknowledged, to ignore the enormous popular appeal of books like *The Lonely Crowd*, *The Organization Man*, and *The Hidden Persuaders*, but it was far more difficult—and important—to ask what that popularity meant. Did it indicate that a decisive shift in American consciousness toward a collectivist, other-directed mentality was taking place? Or might it not have demonstrated exactly the opposite—that Americans, jealously guarding their personal liberties as ever, were becoming annoyed by the restrictions on their freedom exacted by the new consolidated, bureaucratic national order and were finding them difficult to accept? If America, wrote Dahrendorf in a neat parody by compression, had really become "a democracy without liberty at the mercy of the hidden persuaders of advertising, run by organization men for whom the Protestant ethic is but a distant myth, and made up of other-directed characters without any internal gyroscope of life," then why the intense public interest in such far-reaching social criticism? If Fromm was right in thinking that social character made people "desire what objectively is necessary for them to do," then why did there continue to be such profound anxiety over what the national character was becoming? Why did *The Lonely Crowd*, of which Yale University Press had initially printed only 1,500 copies, become a surprise bestseller, whose sales passed the half-million mark with the release of a paperback edition in 1954 and which continues to sell briskly to this day? Why, indeed, did the editors of *Time* put David Riesman's picture on their cover?

Perhaps *The Lonely Crowd* can be understood, in both its intentions and its effects, as a secular sermon in the hallowed American tradition of periodic intense self-scrutiny inaugurated by the New England Puritans. Perry Miller described the Puritan jeremiad as "the voice of a community bespeaking its apprehensions about itself"—apprehensions that revolved particularly around the horror of declension, of falling away from the founding ideals.[128] Use of the jeremiad implies not a hopelessly advanced case of sinfulness but something closer to the opposite—a highly developed watchfulness lest the standard of righteousness be so profoundly flouted as to incur divine wrath. In this case, the "sin" constituted an offense against the vestigial republican sensibility of Americans as much as against the Puritan-Protestant sentiment, for a surrender to total control, even in the attempt of other-directed individuals to adjust to the needs and demands of their peers, represented the surrender of an American's birthright—liberty.[129]

From that standpoint, the spate of anxious social criticism in the 1950s could also be taken as evidence of the stubborn persistence of the individualistic character traits that the authors claimed to see fading away and that they seemed to think worth affirming. In that respect, it appears that *The Lonely Crowd* may have mirrored its times exactly, turning out to be significant even in its ambivalences. "The whole history of ideas," declared the anthropologist Mary Douglas, "should be reviewed in the light of the power of social structures to generate symbols of their own."[130] Perhaps a suitably symbolic way of reading *The Lonely Crowd* would dwell less on its internal inconsistencies than on its cultural consistencies, the way in which its internal tensions were perhaps even more meaningful than its explicit argument, as a window onto the actual cultural task a book is performing. In any case, the social critics were not only prophets of totalist doom; they were also guardians of the self, of its integrity, autonomy, and resiliency. But they were, however inadvertently, reinforcing the very centrifugal, antiauthoritarian tendencies that had been the principal objects of earlier efforts at reform. In that way, the fear of totalism in American life helped give rise to its opposite: something perhaps resembling the very "liberal chaos" against which George Kennan had warned.

# 8

## The Hipster and the Organization Man

In its zeal to buttress the liberty of the lonely self and protect it against the threat of total absorption, *The Lonely Crowd*, along with much of the other trenchant social criticism of the 1950s, seemed to neglect the postbellum writers' insights into the social nature of the self. Like an army steeled for a frontal assault, it fixed its crosshairs upon the looming conformist threat, seemingly unaware that another formidable force—the antinomian, antiauthoritarian, and countercultural sensibility that is imprecisely associated with the 1960s—was fast approaching from the rear. John Dewey, however, by then in his late eighties, had already begun to feel such a neoindividualist movement building in the wake of the Second World War, and he most emphatically did not approve of it. Five years before *The Lonely Crowd* was published, Dewey offered his criticisms in his own contribution to *Commentary*'s "Crisis of the Individual" series, thereby questioning the very premise of the series. His article, "The Crisis in Human History: The Danger of the Retreat to Individualism" was less concerned about the endangered self than it was filled with misgivings about the current "swing back to magnification of something called *the individual*," and back to an outlook that ascribes "independent reality and ultimate value to the individual person alone."[1]

Such separation of "individual and associative aspects of the unitary human being" ran counter to everything Dewey stood for. The opposition between "individual" and "society," he insisted, a little impatiently, was a false one, which merely perpetuated the kind of "absolutist" thinking he cordially detested.[2] Dewey's position in this respect was not unprecedented. Tocqueville had asserted that tendencies toward extreme conformism and extreme individualism might in fact be complementary, polar expressions of a single modern condition. The very image of a "lonely crowd" pathology suggested that possibility, evoking a simultaneous need for greater connectedness and for greater independence. There was also increasing reason to wonder whether a modern consolidated, bureaucratic, nationalized social order could satisfy either need.

Perhaps the martial image misleads us in another way, by concealing the degree to which radicals of the Sixties were carrying out the implicit prescriptions of the Fifties. Indeed, the facile contrast frequently drawn between the Fifties and the Sixties—the former as a time of torpid complacency and conformity, the latter as a tumultuous era of cultural upheaval—shows how misleading such close-order periodizations can be, particularly in the history of ideas, which can unfold without a predictable relationship to major external events. The intellectual continuities between the two "decades," and over a far longer span of American history, were considerable. Specifically, whatever culture-shattering changes the tumultuous Sixties may have wrought, most were already clearly visible and astir in the supposedly stagnant preceding years: not only the growing predominance of the white-collar organization man, but also the frenzied neo-Whitmanian effusion of Allen Ginsberg's *Howl* (1956), the alienation cult movie *Rebel without a Cause* (1956), the hipster existentialism of Norman Mailer's "The White Negro" (1957), Jack Kerouac's romantic celebration of outcasts and wanderers *On the Road* (1957), or Paul Goodman's *Growing Up Absurd* (1960).[3] These works shared important elements of *The Lonely Crowd*'s vision of postwar American life; what made them different was their willingness to press its logic and implications in the direction of praxis, more directly and rudely than Riesman would ever have considered desirable or proper. Indeed, they often pressed their positions forward with a certain angry insouciance, like a child who taunts his imperfect parents by exposing their all-too-human uncertainties and ambivalences.

Norman Mailer, for example, mocked Riesman as "the professional liberal's liberal," anointed by "such intellectual deacons of the liberal body as Arthur M. Schlesinger, Jr., and Max Lerner"; but Mailer's vivid, if pervervid, vision of the postwar situation had a great deal in common with the musings of Riesman and the other guardians of the self—and none with Dewey's.[4] For Mailer, too, the imagery of totalitarianism was indispensable. The war, he thought, particularly the "psychic havoc" wrought by the bomb and the concentration camps, had held a telling mirror up to the horror of the contemporary human condition. "One could hardly maintain the courage to be individual," Mailer cried, during these "years of conformity and depression. . . . A stench of fear has come out of every pore of American life, and we suffer from a collective failure of nerve. The only courage . . . has been the isolated courage of isolated people."[5] Onto "this bleak scene" had come the hipster, the man who knows that, since it is our collective condition to live with "quick death by the State as *l'univers concentrationnaire*, or with a slow death by conformity," then there is only one authentic way left to live. One has "to divorce oneself from society, to exist without roots, to set out on that uncharted journey into the rebellious imperatives of the self." The social alternatives Mailer saw could not have been more stark: "One is Hip or one is Square (the alternative which each new generation coming into American life is beginning to feel), one is a rebel or one conforms, one is a frontiersman in the Wild West of American night life, or else a Square cell, trapped in the totalitarian tissues of American society, doomed willy-nilly to conform if one is to succeed." What was at stake was nothing less than "the liberation of the self from the Super-Ego of society." The "nihilism of Hip proposes as its final tendency that every social restraint and category be removed."[6]

All this would seem to mark Mailer's hipster as a kind of radical formalist, at least insofar as he asserts the primacy and efficacy of the self. In fact, the contrary is true. The hipster not only abstains from moral judgments, but he utterly disclaims any "recipe knowledge" regarding the chain of causation that flows from his actions. He does not possess a humanitarian sensibility. In fact, Mailer asserts, "Hip abdicates from any conventional moral responsibility because it would argue that the results of our actions are unforeseeable, and so we cannot know if we do good or bad." Indeed, the hipster is a kind of antiformalist: "Hip sees the context as generally dominating the man, dominating him because his character is less significant than the context in which he must function." Character, that great Victorian pillar, is actually an optical illusion or, at best, a "perpetually ambivalent and dynamic" concept, existing in "an absolute relativity [*sic*] where there are no truths other than the isolated truths of what each observer feels at each instant of his existence." So the completely unencumbered, isolated, solitary self, obedient above all else to its own inner promptings, is also, oddly, in thrall to a kind of fatalism. The hipster surrenders control over and responsibility for his own actions and "lives with death as immediate danger," the complete existential hero.[7]

This formulation overflows with quintessentially American tropes: the revolution, the frontier (Turner having been urbanized), the open road, the fear of being owned. More to the point, however, it shows how the fantasy of devouring totalism and the fantasy of an unencumbered self went together, standing in symbiosis, testimony to a continuing reliance upon an uncertain notion of individual autonomy—and an even more unsteady conception of the grounds (if any) for genuine social connectedness. But the abolition of repression was hardly Mailer's private project. A more philosophically sophisticated (if sometimes less intelligible) contribution to that end came from a Weimar refugee, Herbert Marcuse, a forbiddingly difficult scholar of Hegel and an early member of the Frankfurt group who became one of the most influential intellectual figures in the New Left. His *Eros and Civilization* (1955), a book based upon an ingenious transposition of Marxian concepts into the psychoanalytical realm—a characteristic Frankfurt school undertaking—attempted to transcend the inflexibly gloomy implications for man-in-civilization posited by Freud's *Civilization and Its Discontents*. Marcuse, too, was involved in completing the liberation of the self from its postindustrial social constraints.

The strategy was one of historicizing the phenomenon of repression in a way that Freud, with his emphasis upon the bedrock unchangeability of instinctual life, would surely not have countenanced. Just as the capitalist system ran on the "surplus value" that the capitalist expropriated from labor, so the system of bourgeois culture depended upon "surplus repression," whose historically transient existence Freud had mistaken for an unbendable absolute. In an affluent society that had solved the problem of production, such surplus repression no longer served a social purpose. Instead, the material cornucopia of postindustrial affluence offered the possibility of an entirely "non-repressive civilization," freeing human nature from the antinomies Freud had posited. Sexuality would be allowed virtually unlimited expression, and the multiform alienation of modern man would be thus overcome through immersion in the pleasure principle.[8]

*Eros and Civilization* was one of the few works by a Frankfurter—indeed, one of the few by any Marxist theorist—to try to limn the contours of utopia. As such, it was to find an eager readership among younger American students and intellectuals who were impatient with, among other things, the more severe orthodox Freudianism of their elders. The tone of the book was almost cheerful, full of an Emersonian sense of boundless possibility. By the time Marcuse published *One-Dimensional Man* (1964), however, he was no longer in any mood to accentuate the positive. Its dystopian vision of the modern world, parallel in broad outline to the indictment handed down by Adorno and Horkheimer in the little-known *Dialectic of Enlightenment*, saw the depredations of mass society now fully barring the way to utopia.[9] Even the prospect of sexual liberation proffered in *Eros and Civilization* had been captured and redirected by the unidimensional culture of monopoly capitalism; far from being liberating, sex had become trivial and narcotic, an example of what he called repressive desublimation.[10] Instead of offering a *promesse de bonheur*, it had become an agent in the service of false consciousness, a brand of "pseudo-liberation" that in fact presented an even more sturdy barrier to sustained critical thought than that of bourgeois moralism. In the nightmarish world of the modern West, in which positivism and instrumental rationality defined the very nature of reality, and in which a soft totalitarianism controlled human thought and action far more effectively than the coercive tyrannies of the past, all one could do was to practice a dogged resistance to the world as given. Marcuse called for "the great refusal," which entailed, first and last, a refusal to adjust to, or otherwise acquiesce in, a society that was "irrational as a whole." He punningly boasted that, unlike that exemplary American popular sage Dr. Norman Vincent Peale, his intellectual energies derived from "the power of negative thinking."[11] Yet the popularity of his work surely also owed much to the resurgence in the postwar generation of the temporarily submerged temper of Protestant social gospel reformism and utopian perfectionism—expressed, paradoxically, by a teacher who saw no further need for the Protestant ethic.

Marcuse's great refusal left little room for the limited and procedural freedoms offered by liberal democracy, and Marcuse did not hesitate to make plain his contempt for such "pseudo-democracy." His critique in this respect reflected the fascinating combination of conservative and radical influences that converged in his mandarin Marxism; it certainly does not appear to have derived in any significant way from his experience of American democracy. As Martin Jay has pointed out, the Marcusean ideas that "seemed so fresh to Americans in the 1960s" had in fact been "worked out in the pages of the [Institut's] *Zeitschrift* three decades before."[12] His intellectual outlook was so firmly fixed before emigration that his American years did not cause him to reconsider his dismissive view of liberal democracy, as it eventually did for some of his Frankfurt colleagues such as Fromm and Lowenthal. In Marcuse's vision of "totalitarian democracy," the distinction between the relative tolerance and freedom of expression offered in Western societies and the brutal suppressions exacted under Soviet rule was rendered nugatory:

> By virtue of the way it has organized its technological base, contemporary industrial society tends to be totalitarian. For "totalitarian" is not only a terroristic political coordination of society, but also a non-terroristic economic-technical coordination which operates through the manipulation of needs by vested interests. It thus precludes the emergence of an

effective opposition against the whole. Not only a specific form of government or party rule makes for totalitarianism, but also a specific system of production and distribution which may well be compatible with a "pluralism" of parties, newspapers, "countervailing powers," etc.[13]

The seeming tolerance of Western societies was illusory, for the total system could absorb dissent and defuse radical opposition without suppressing it, thus disabling incendiary speech even more effectively than mere coercion ever could. Western democracy substituted the tyranny of debased consciousness for the tyranny of secret police and concentration camps.

Like Mailer, who applied the word *totalitarian* promiscuously to every form of political and social constraint, Marcuse saw no reason to make much of a distinction between totalitarianism's hard or soft manifestations. He quoted approvingly the following words of Eugene Ionesco: "The world of the concentration camps . . . was not an exceptionally monstrous society. What we saw there was the image, and in a sense the quintessence, of the infernal society into which we are plunged every day."[14] The only small glimmer of hope he saw emerged from *deraciné* quarters not unlike those inhabited by the hipster: "the substratum of the outcasts and outsiders, the exploited and the persecuted of other races and other colors, the unemployed and the unemployable." Perhaps if intellectuals could strike an alliance with such people—"the most advanced consciousness of humanity" aligned with "its most exploited force"—there was a chance (though "nothing but a chance") of a radical change.

Marcuse was disappointingly unspecific about how a revolutionized society would be run, however, and what few specifics he did offer seemed like little more than revolutionary sloganeering or rehashes of naive Progressive ideals. For example, "technological rationality" was to be "the sole standard and guide in planning and developing the available resources of all," since "self-determination in the production and distribution of vital goods and services" was merely "a technical job." Centralized control was not to be abandoned; all that had to be established were "the preconditions for meaningful self-determination" in other realms of life.[15] Just how this was to be accomplished, how self-determination could be completely divorced from the means of production and distribution, was apparently a question too trivial to be addressed. Perhaps even more exasperating was his blithe willingness, as expressed in his infamous essay "Repressive Tolerance" (1965), to control speech and behavior deemed reactionary (in an Orwellian turn, he called this practice "discriminating tolerance").[16] How, in either case, would the necessary authority be constituted and legitimated? One could only wonder.

"Marcuse," one American historian has written, "hovered like a monad over the mind of the New Left."[17] Indeed, it is a nice question for the sociology of ideas whether his work's popularity—and the influence of radicals who brandished his work in their assault on modern American society—suggested that the one-dimensionality he envisioned was more easily overthrown than even he had suspected; or whether, on the contrary, it showed that even Marcuse's stern nihilism could be coopted by American society, thereby confirming his contentions in spades. Marcuse himself asserted the latter.[18] But one cannot plausibly argue that Marcuse's campus followers misunderstood him. Indeed, if there was any doubt of Marcuse's own sympathy for the radical student movements of the 1960s, he removed it with his *Essay on Liberation* (1969), which he dedicated to the "young militants" struggling against "the rules and regulations of a pseudo-democracy in a Free Orwellian World."[19] The essay appeared in the wake of the pinnacle year 1968, when student rebellions erupted all over the Western world, most notably in the United States, France, and Germany. Marcuse wanted to be certain to express his admiration for the praxis of these young rebels, like his militant former student Angela Davis.

---

Perhaps Marcuse's principal value in the present context lies not in his politics but in the way his efforts bespoke the simultaneous yearning for an extreme, nearly antinomian individualism with an equally powerful impulse toward social solidarity. At first glance, this combination appears paradoxical, since we are prone to place, as Bellamy did, the desire for autonomy and individual liberty in opposition to the desire for social solidarity. The paradox goes back at least as far as a thinker like Jean-Jacques Rousseau: how could the same man who produced the highly individualistic vision of the *Confessions* also produce the highly compulsory "totalitarian" republicanism of *The Social Contract*? Yet this conjunction of seeming opposites may be an increasingly characteristic perspective upon the modern, and American, condition, marked as it is by a liberation from the guideposts of traditional or authoritative institutions. Tocqueville, too, had insisted that a concurrent emphasis upon social equality and upon the potential boundlessness of the individual self would drive the members of a society toward both individualism and conformism, under the auspices of a growing centralization; and the two should not be seen necessarily as opposites.

An even more suggestive description and explanation of this pattern has been offered by Alasdair MacIntyre. Not only Mailer's hipster, MacIntyre would assert, but most men and women in modern Western societies are guided in their personal moral judgments by what he calls emotivism, the doctrine that moral evaluations ultimately represent nothing more than expressions of personal preference, attitude, or feeling. This would seem to promise a chronically disordered and anarchic world; yet the modern organizational world is easily able to accommodate such potentially disruptive moral subjectivism. It does so by requiring a split-mindedness, by demanding the sacrifice of the "conception of the whole human life," characteristic of traditional social orders. Instead, the modern social world is "bifurcated" into a "realm of the organizational" and a "realm of the personal," each operating by a different moral calculus. In the former realm, "ends are taken to be given, and are not available for rational scrutiny"; in the latter, "judgment and debate about values" occurs but is not amenable to rational resolution. There are constant debates in such bifurcated societies about "a supposed opposition between individualism and collectivism," but in fact, such debates are superficial. The crucial fact is one upon which the opposing parties agree: "namely that there are only two alternative modes of social life open to us, one in which the free and arbitrary choices of individuals are sovereign and one in which the bureaucracy is sovereign, precisely so that it may limit the free and arbitrary choices of individuals." In light of this "deep cultural agreement," the policy debates dominating the politics of modern societies tend to vacillate between "a freedom which is nothing but a lack of regulation of individual behavior" and "forms of collectivist control designed only to limit the anarchy of self-interest." In contemporary society, in short, bureaucracy and individualism are "partners as well as antagonists. . . . It is in the cultural climate of this bureaucratic individualism that the emotivist self is naturally at home."[20] The organization man and the hipster may be opposites, but in a deeper sense they are mutually defined, mutually enabling.

If one can grant the validity of this aerial view of the current social landscape, lofty enough to reveal the contours of the shared ground upon which seeming antagonists struggle, then the question that arises for projective social thought is one of envisioning alternative grounds, alternative landscapes—and thereby moving from the descriptive to the prescriptive. On this question, MacIntyre invokes a familiar but disturbing parallel to the declining years of the Roman Empire, a comparison favored by Henry Adams, when "men and women of good will turned aside from the task of shoring up the Roman *imperium*," preferring instead to construct "new forms of community within which the moral life could be sustained" despite the surrounding darkness and barbarism. "We too have reached that turning point," he declares, and our task is "the construction of local forms of community within which civility and the intellectual and moral life can be sustained through the new dark ages which are already upon us." In other words, the vast social achievement that has been designated by the term *consolidation* in these pages has itself become the central part of the problem, and its effects must be, somehow, reversed, counteracted, or failing all else, evaded. The reconstruction of community, of the possibility of social bodies mediating between the radical individual and the vast megastructures in which he or she is embedded, bodies in which genuine connectedness and genuine moral responsibility were once again possible, had become paramount in importance. In such communities, neither the organization man nor the hipster could any longer serve as characteristic or exemplary types.[21]

By recommending a turning away from the imperium, MacIntyre was asserting, in the tradition of Plato and Aristotle, the connection between a particular political regime or social order and a particular kind of soul. He was also implicitly rejecting one of the time-honored answers to the individualist-collectivist quarrel: the idea of the national community. It was an answer that had been ascendant in American life since the end of the Civil War and that had been vividly limned by Bellamy, crisply articulated by Croly and Roosevelt, and defended by Dewey; thereafter it was a staple of progressive and liberal political rhetoric. Perhaps its political high-water mark came in the presidency of Lyndon Johnson, who was committed, in both rhetoric and policy, to the conception of the nation as a community, even as a family, very much in contrast to the imagery of self-reliant frontier individualism favored by Senator Goldwater. His America, Johnson said, was to be "a united nation, divided neither by class nor by section nor by color, knowing no South or North, no East or West, but just one great America, free of malice and free of hate, and loving thy neighbor as thyself." We must "turn unity of interest into unity of purpose, and unity of goals into unity in the Great Society. . . . I see our Nation as a free and generous land with its people bound together by common ties of confidence and affection, and common aspirations toward duty and purpose." This was not mere political rhetoric; it was reflected, for example, in Johnson's view of the struggle for full civil rights for black Americans as an effort to incorporate the unincorporated, as "the reconciliation of different people into the national community." It was also reflected in the nomenclature of his "war" on poverty, sensitive as he was to war's ability to galvanize national cohesion.[22]

"As I conceive it," he remarked, "a President's first role and first responsibility is to help perfect the unity of the people." Unfortunately, however, Johnson had the unenviable fate of presiding over the most thorough shattering of the national unity since the Civil War, a development whose social, cultural, and political repercussions are still very much with us. They are, indeed, probably still too close, and too unresolved, to be scrutinized without parti pris. One thing seems clear, however: the controversial war in Vietnam catalyzed a profound weakening of the idea of national community and undermined the authority of what Robert Wuthnow has called the "legitimating myths" of American national purpose and destiny. Subsequent events have not entirely restored these central articles of national faith.[23] Appropriately, then, the symbolism of the Vietnam Veterans Memorial in Washington stands in striking contrast to the iconography of the Grand Review. Where the Grand Review subsumed the individual within the grandeur of a marching nation, the Vietnam memorial pointedly refused the allusion to the nation, offering instead the engraved individual names of the thousands of dead or missing. When visitors come to the Vietnam memorial, they do not come to gaze upon a grand monumental structure but to search for a familiar name on the collective tombstone—perhaps with some of the same feelings experienced by the narrator in Bret Harte's "Second Grand Review" when he scanned the passing crowd looking for the face of his kinsman.[24]

It also seems clear, in retrospect, that the opposition to the idea of national community had been gathering force on its own, from a variety of positions. The old Republican Right, epitomized by the doughty Senator Robert A. Taft of Ohio, had never accepted the understanding of the nation inherent in the New Deal; but this was not only a sentiment of the Right.[25] Beginning with the Port Huron Statement, intellectuals of the New Left evinced a strong inclination toward decentralized, small-scale participatory institutions, which would stand in stark contrast with the gigantic corporate, government, and academic bureaucracies that they saw dominating American life.[26] The Black Power movement also advocated community self-governance and empowerment, and some mainstream politicians, notably Robert Kennedy, looked upon the idea with favor, seeing it as latter-day Jeffersonianism.[27] The resurgence of ethnic sensibility in northern cities, partly stemming from a proud or fearful distaste for the nation's growing homogenization and partly stimulated by resentment of bureaucratic or judicial intrusions into settled neighborhoods, also had the effect of asserting particularism and ethnic identity against national identification.[28] On the level of domestic national politics, beginning with the administration of Johnson's successor Richard Nixon and continuing through the administrations of Ford, Carter, Reagan, and Bush, the rhetoric of streamlining, decentralization, and New Federalism has frequently taken precedence over the appeal to a consolidated national community.

A notable exception to this last generalization, Jimmy Carter's use of James's moral equivalent of war as the rhetorical frame for his comprehensive national energy policy, was not a notable success. In the era of Theodore Roosevelt, such appeals would surely have fallen upon more approving ears, for Carter's rhetoric drew upon that era's political vocabulary. In his 1979 "crisis of confidence," speech, Carter warned that the nation had embraced "a mistaken idea of freedom" and was heading down the path of "fragmentation and self-interest," of "self-indulgence and consumption"; he urged that Americans instead "rebuild the unity and confidence of America," because only by following the "path of common purpose" could we come into an experience of "true freedom." Resonating with the time-honored language and imagery of national community, solidarity, positive liberty, and self-transcendence ("There is," he said, "simply no way to avoid sacrifice"), Carter's eloquent political jeremiad turned out to be dramatically out of step with its historical moment. Surely one reason for this response was the waning appeal of the particular ideal of national community (though not necessarily of nationalism per se) to which he was appealing.[29]

To be sure, the movement toward political decentralization has so far been more rhetorical than actual; it is notorious how shallow the various "new federalisms" have been in practice and, meanwhile, how inexorably the size of the federal government has continued to grow during those same administrations. Such may well continue to be the case. Indeed, perhaps the popularity of Mario Cuomo's "Two Cities" keynote address at the Democratic National Convention in 1984 may be taken as a counterindication, for it too effectively invoked a wide array of classic Crolyan, national-community imagery—of the American nation as a "family," of the need for "surrender of . . . our individual interests," of the need to build a platform upon which all can be "proudly singing out the truth . . . in chorus," and of "laws written by . . . St. Francis of Assisi" rather than "laws written by Darwin."[30] Yet Cuomo spoke as a noncandidate, and in an unsuccessful cause—hardly a hopeful augury for the ideals to which his speech recurred.

It certainly would be reckless for a historian to do more than conjecture whether the social ideals capable of energizing Americans have begun to change. If they have, though, they may be changing in roughly the same direction that MacIntyre's words suggest: toward disaggregation, dispersal, decentralization, and at the same time toward more intense experiences of community—that is, toward identification with social forms intimate enough to bridge the gap between isolate, morally irresponsible self and ubiquitous, morally irresponsible organizations. Croly and Roosevelt had assumed that there could be such a thing as a national community, its life guided by a strong sense of the public interest and common weal, as a substitute for the small-scale community that had been rendered obsolete by the inexorable consolidating effects of the industrial age; that was precisely what Croly had meant by his juxtaposition of Hamiltonian means and Jeffersonian ends. The project failed, however, as political scientist Michael Sandel cogently explains, because the nation has "proved too vast a scale across which to cultivate the shared self-understandings necessary to community."[31] Since abandoning the Progressive notion of a common good, Sandel observes, we have merely limped along in a "procedural republic," in which individuals are endowed by a central state with "rights and entitlements" and rely upon the workings of disembodied bureaucratic procedures rather than on substantive and authoritative policies to produce wise social results. Such is the spectral vision of government, denuded of all drapery of virtue and all sense of the public interest, that Carter's 1979 speech reacted against.

Sandel's analysis casts doubt not only on the concept of national community to which Carter appealed but on the very project of national consolidation, in terms that recall MacIntyre's symbiosis of the emotivist self and the bureaucratic organization—as well as Mailer's radically free but radically situated hipster:

> In our public life, we are more entangled, but less attached, than ever before. It is as though the unencumbered self presupposed by the liberal ethic had begun to come true—less liberated than disempowered, entangled in a network of obligations and involvements unassociated with any act of will and yet unmediated by those common identifications or expansive self-definitions that would make them tolerable. As the scale of social and political organization has become more comprehensive, the terms of our collective identity have become more fragmented, and the forms of political life have outrun the common purposes needed to sustain them.[32]

Such an analysis suggests something very different from Dewey's Great Community. If this analysis is correct, then it cannot be presumed that nonmartial efforts to restore the ideal of national community, such as revivals of the Civilian Conservation Corps or the current proposals to establish a national service requirement, will be successful in the years to come.[33] Something else, something new, will instead have to evolve from the decline of the national ideal; but what might that something be?

Perhaps the most prominent recent work to grapple with this complex of issues in recent years was *Habits of the Heart: Individualism and Commitment in American Life* (1985), a collaborative exploration of contemporary American society whose chief author was the prominent sociologist Robert Bellah. Best known for his explication of the "civil religion" that binds Americans in a pluralistic social order, Bellah's work has nearly always been animated by the venerable liberal Protestant quest for community, chastened but not converted by the Niebuhrian reassertion of original sin.[34] The book also capitalized upon the same cultural predilection that *The Lonely Crowd* had tapped: the American public's appetite for anxious and highly generalized brooding upon our national sins, an appetite that seems to be especially whetted by times of prosperity. Indeed, the tinge of liberal Protestant uplift permeating *Habits* does not prevent it from being a more unsparing analysis even than Riesman's of thirty-five years before. The declension of the public realm, the disappearance of civic consciousness, the disintegration of marriage and family life, the increasingly tenuous and openly self-serving character of human relations, the near-disappearance of religious values from our shared existence (a subject Riesman barely touched): all these and more are laid out in considerable detail, using extensive interviews and case studies of "representative" Americans. Whatever else it may have betokened, the publication of *Habits* signaled a growing convergence in the critique of liberal individualism and of the moral calculus of emotivism.[35]

Needless to say, the postwar years had already seen a small but steadily growing traditionalist-conservative critique of individualism, exemplified by the works of Russell Kirk and Robert Nisbet, with lines of influence running back to the southern agrarians, to Catholic natural-law philosophy, and to the thought of Edmund Burke.[36] The import of this corpus had (and has) been obscured, however, partly because of the powerful intellectual hegemony of liberalism in the postwar years (including its "neoconservative" wing) and partly because American conservatism itself had been dominated by the classical-liberal and anti-Communist nationalist elements with which it became politically aligned.[37] In any event, Bellah did not draw upon such writers, although echoing many of their specific critical observations, since it was his intention to find a way to reconstitute the basis for community while remaining within the liberal and pluralist tradition. The result, however, was a book that repeatedly issued a resounding call for a restored "framework of values" upon which Americans can agree as a national community and upon which they can rebuild a common social life—but that was unfailingly nebulous in specifying what those values might be. A work that thus set out to address the disintegrative tendencies of contemporary American culture ended up capitulating to those tendencies at every crucial point. Given the book's enormous popularity, one can conjecture that for its readers, it may have played a cultural role similar to that of *The Lonely Crowd*, giving vent to widespread apprehensions and confusions as a form of exhortation and catharsis, not as a prescription for radical change.

At the heart of *Habits*'s argument was its call for a return to America's republican and biblical traditions to counterbalance the dangerously amoral, selfish, emotivist, radical-individualist tendencies of unrestrained liberalism. Yet the authors devoted only four pages to an explication of those traditions— surely insufficient space for the task of recovering what has been so pervasively lost. Even more problematic than the neglect of the traditions' content, however, which can presumably be derived from other sources, was the question of the authority these traditions are to possess. *Habits* preferred to frame the issue as one of enhancing public discourse by bolstering Americans' "second language" of republican and biblical forms and highlighting its embeddedness in the shared narratives of "communities of memory," as a counter to its "first language" of radical individualism. Allowing for the necessarily organic and mutable quality of all traditional knowledge and convictions, some very hard questions remain. What authority should be given to, for example, the Ten Commandments or to biblical teachings on sexuality? How much authority should the local community be permitted, for example, in establishing the boundaries of permissible expression or regulating the racial or ethnic makeup of its own public schools? Or were those republican and biblical traditions to be appropriated piecemeal, purged of any elements that ran contrary to conventional liberalism and pluralism? If so, how did such selectivity differ appreciably from the liberalism the authors were criticizing?

In a sense, *Habits* suffered from the same dilemma that afflicted Niebuhr's neoorthodoxy; perhaps we may therefore call its vision neotraditional. Niebuhr's reappropriation of the metaphor of original sin, cut loose from its theological, doctrinal, literalist moorings, was designed to appeal primarily on grounds of its usefulness, for the salutary effects in chastening the social gospel's social and political judgment that could flow from its acceptance. To put it bluntly, Niebuhr's immense appeal for non-Christians would certainly not have been so great had he really been in the business of reaffirming orthodoxy.[38] *Habits* took a similar approach to the two traditions it affirmed, hoping to gather the fruits of their cohesive effects without paying the price of accepting their authority. Surely, however, the term *biblical tradition*, for example, demands far more than that. The authors of *Habits* seem to envision strong personal morality without the taint of discipline or intolerance, strong communal and civic values without insularity or particularism, strong commitments without sanctions against those who disdain them, strong national self-esteem without national pride, patriotism without chauvinism, and so on. Anyone who takes seriously the binding power of the most fundamental sociological concepts, however, will have trouble seeing this wish list as more than insubstantial word combinations, wholly without plausible historical precedent.

Elements of such neotraditionalism, however, have found a growing place in the contemporary debate about issues of individualism and social cohesion. *Habits* was able, for example, to draw upon a growing body of scholarship critical of modern America as a "consumer culture" built upon a "therapeutic" understanding of the self.[39] It could make reference to a large literature built up over the previous two decades and dedicated to the proposition that, contrary to the assumptions of Riesman's generation, America had considerable nonliberal ideological antecedents, particularly those strains constituting the "republican" ideology of the revolutionary and early national years.[40] It could presume the distinguished efforts of writers who mourned the moral and political consequences of the modernist disenchantment of the world and sought a recovery of "the sacred" as an indispensable component of moral experience.[41] In virtually every case, however, a similar veil is drawn between the critiques of the present, which are often powerful and compelling, and the prescriptions for the future, which are often vague, pallid, even evasive. It is much easier to enumerate the faults of the liberal tradition than to suggest a plausible substitute for it.

Another important challenge has begun to emerge from the postwar feminist movement, in the form of an assertion that the problematic notion of autonomy, or "the discourse of self-reliance," arises from a characteristically male conceptual framework. The historian Linda Kerber has perhaps put the position most forcefully by asserting that "the classic statements of American individualism," as put forward in American literature and social philosophy, "are best understood as guides to masculine identity."[42] Individualism, in this view, far from being universal, is highly gender-specific, and as American intellectual and cultural history is rewritten and the constitution of present-day American society changes, that gender-specificity will be revealed, relativized, defanged, and transcended. Such a view, however, though undoubtedly not without historical support—eighteenth-century notions of individualism generally did not include women within their purview—seems hard to credit without a good deal of qualification, once modern feminism's own history and its characteristic liberatory agenda are taken into account.

For one thing, as we have seen, *The Feminine Mystique*, the critical text in the postwar intellectual and political revival of feminism, rested upon paradigmatic assumptions closely akin to those of the other postwar guardians of the self. Its argument consistently revolved around the concepts of autonomy, independence, liberation, and emancipation and stressed the demolition of barriers to women's equal economic opportunity and to full and separate human self-realization. Such a line of argument stood in a long tradition of feminist thought, stretching back to Margaret Fuller's stubborn call for self-sufficiency, to the language and style of the Seneca Falls declaration, to Elizabeth Cady Stanton's argument for the ultimate solitude and responsibility of each individual self in a Protestant culture, and to Charlotte Perkins Gilman's schemes for the liberation of women through abolition of the family as an economic unit.[43] In the nineteenth century, such had been clearly minority voices, setting themselves against the prevailing Victorian conviction that men and women were fundamentally different, a fact that in turn was thought to entail a difference in appropriate gender roles and a stark division between public and private spheres. A transitional figure like Jane Addams searched for a balance between the two worlds, seeking to reconcile the independence of a professional and public figure with the nurturant and maternal qualities that had been traditionally associated with woman and woman's work in the private sphere and to extend those benefits into public life. Friedan's work, however, and the woman's movement that arose with it in the postwar era, followed the more egalitarian line of descent and brought that line, with great success, into the political and intellectual environment of the postwar era.

A single-minded emphasis upon equality, however, has never been the whole story with modern feminism, as the complex case of Margaret Fuller, for one, readily suggests. The struggle for political rights never entirely eclipsed a struggle for distinctiveness, for a respectful recognition of women's dramatically different contributions, experiences, perspectives, and values. The concept of sisterhood, so notable in the rhetoric of postwar feminism, was meant to suggest and foster a sense of relatedness and mutuality that would be distinct from male competitiveness. In the end, sisterhood may have served chiefly as a rallying cry for middle-class feminism, a sentimental expression of solidarity that, though it employed universalistic language, in fact derived its energizing power from a common sense of very particular and class-specific grievances, directed against equally particular and class-specific enemies.[44] But such language also gained some of its force from its deep roots in women's long-standing experiences of mutual sustenance and comfort within their distinctive sphere, a potential source of strength that modern feminism has sometimes tapped and sometimes ignored or disdained.[45]

The view of individualism as a gender-specific phenomenon has perhaps gained its greatest impetus from the influential work of educational psychologist Carol Gilligan.[46] Trained in Eriksonian developmental psychology, Gilligan was struck by the degree to which studies of moral development excluded women from their samples and omitted a consideration of gender from their theoretical framework and research design. The Eriksonian bildungsroman, built around the passage from infantile dependence to adult autonomy, reflected an imbalanced, excessively male conception of adulthood, she felt, which favored the separateness of the individual self over its connection to others and sought an autonomous life of work rather than the interdependence of love and care. Gilligan proposed that women showed a strikingly different trajectory of moral evolution and a different style of moral judgment than the characteristic male pattern, and that researchers who habitually treated the male pattern as "normal" needed henceforth to take respectful account of woman's difference. The sexuality of women, she argued, was more diffuse than that of men; women's perception of self was much more consistently embedded in relationships with others than was the case for autonomy-minded men, and their moral decisions take place "in a contextual mode of judgment" rather than by reference to the abstract and depersonalized standard of justice that had always tended to be the male pattern.[47]

More impressive in its theoretical critique of Eriksonian developmental psychology than in its own rather thinly supported empirical claims, Gilligan's work nevertheless found broad and immediate public resonance (as well as controversy) when it first appeared in the late 1970s. Its underlying theme—the effort to connect the feminist movement with the more general search for meaningful ways of recovering social connectedness in an autonomy-obsessed individualistic American culture—surely had much to do with that success. Her work, however, has been widely and sharply criticized by other feminists as little more than a postfeminist social-scientific rationalization for a return to separate spheres and the cult of true Victorian womanhood, a form of inadvertent aid and comfort to the very enemies that the women's movement had initially struggled against.[48] Her case says something about the dilemmas facing a distinctively feminist approach to social thought, which strives to explicate new models of relatedness that could supplant "male" models of bourgeois individualism, even as it insists upon its own rightful participation in the same thrust toward individual empowerment. Feminism finds itself caught between the desire for unrestricted latitude of action and the desire to retain the distinctive assets of women's experience—between a Stantonesque aspiration to secure the kind of personal autonomy that had formerly been the exclusive province of men, and a Gilliganesque insistence that women are crucially different from men and that women's heightened sense of mutuality and relationship, of caring and nurturance, are the central features of that difference. Elizabeth Fox-Genovese has stated the problem with admirable concision: "Today, as in the past, feminists divide over whether women should be struggling for women's rights as individuals or women's rights as women— whether women need equality with men or protection for their differences from men."[49] Though referring directly only to feminists, her statement has the additional virtue of applying equally well to American women who do not identify themselves as feminists, such as those whose opposition to, or ambivalence about, the proposed equal rights amendment to the U.S. Constitution reflected a wariness about sacrificing all recognition of difference on the altar of equality.[50]

In any event, postwar feminism cannot be said to have spoken with a single voice on matters of individualism, being divided between paradigms of equality and difference. The proponents of the former are likely to denounce the latter as neo-Victorians who would recondemn women to the imprisonment of their traditional gender-specific roles; the latter, on the other hand, may regard the former as women who have bought wholeheartedly into the competitive atomistic individualism that represents the worst features of the masculine orientation to the world and to which women ought to be offering a more humane, sustainable, cooperative, and communitarian alternative and corrective.[51] The categories can sometimes overlap, as was evident in the rhetoric of the women's suffrage advocates who insisted both upon women's equality as citizens and upon the purifying effects their moral superiority would bring to politics; or, for that matter, as became evident in the successive stages of Betty Friedan's own intellectual development.[52] But the conflict itself shows little sign of going away, since it rests upon a clash of fundamental visions.

Such dilemmas of modern feminism are, therefore, a particular case within the larger dilemma that the present work has attempted to engage. Indeed, the postwar feminist movement has often embodied, in its own way, the same simultaneous yearning for individual autonomy (liberation) and intense social solidarity (sisterhood) that was inherent in Marcuse's work. To be sure, the strangely dissociated symbiosis of hipster and organization man has not been characteristically feminine, not yet anyway. Nevertheless, David Potter's claim in criticism of *The Lonely Crowd* that the social character of American women had always been largely other-directed, as a function of their traditional domestic obligations, suggested why the conflict between autonomy and solidarity would be a peculiarly poignant and tangled one for postwar American women to confront—and why the personal and general stakes in their dilemma might be very high indeed. There was a historical irony at work: the critical reconsideration of individualism seemed to begin at just the moment that many women felt themselves to be finally coming into fuller possession of it—and also at a moment when the stability of American marriages and family life seemed increasingly, and to some frighteningly, tenuous.[53] Small wonder that women have found the antinomies of individualism especially painful and exasperating to negotiate, both in theory and in personal experience, and that feminist thought has therefore so often found itself torn between the choice of embracing individualism or embracing its critique—between appropriating a standard of interchangeable equality or championing a protective standard of inviolable differences.[54]

The task facing writers like Gilligan, Mary Ann Glendon, Jean Bethke Elshtain, Fox-Genovese, and others who have taken, to great or lesser degree, the latter course is that of reconciling the cultural (and in some cases, biological) implications of difference, which they feel committed to uphold, with the politics of equality and individual rights. Each has mapped some element in the beginnings of a route out of individualism, but it is not clear how consequential such initial forays can be unless and until they can establish the ability of an authoritative political-moral language, other than that of individual rights, to be admitted, legitimately deployed, and respected in the American public arena. Fox-Genovese has complained that feminism itself has increasingly become one of the chief instruments of the individualistic ethos in American culture, offering an "atomized" view of society, a "celebration of egotism," and a denial of "the just claims of the community."[55] Indeed, one need only look at the characteristic public arguments offered for unrestricted abortion rights—as well, one might add, as the counterarguments of many opponents of abortion—to see how fully an absolutist language of individual rights remains the ultimate trump card in our public discourse, with the chief disagreements merely arising over the proper application of that principle, not the principle itself.[56] Little general credence is granted, as yet, to efforts to establish (or, in the case of the religious opposition to abortion, reestablish) the public authority of other moral languages. The challenge facing such maverick communitarian feminist thinkers reflects a more general challenge: that of articulating convincing grounds for social solidarity, social cohesion, and social obligation in a culture that accords ultimate respect only to the language of individual rights and individual liberty—a language that is, moreover, manifestly unable to address the disturbing experiences of political dissociation that Sandel has so compellingly described. In Fox-Genovese's gloomy but compelling view, the clarion call of masterlessness continues to set the hegemonic tone to which all fiddles are tuned.

---

Surely the popular reception of *Habits of the Heart*, however, showed that a substantial number of educated Americans found something seriously amiss in their society and connected that something with the ubiquity of individualism in American life.[57] Indeed, the most haunting feature of *Habits* was its illustration, through quotations from its extensive interviews, of the difficulty its subjects experienced in expressing their moral sentiments in a vocabulary other than that of self-interest. It is perhaps fitting, then, that so many in the recent generation of American social thinkers, especially in the 1970s and 1980s, have seemed preoccupied by concerns that stand at the opposite end of the spectrum from Riesman's characteristic themes—concern for the nurturance of community and solidarity rather than individualism and autonomy. Certainly these authors' efforts indicate that it is as difficult as ever for Americans to formulate enduring and authoritative grounds for social coherence; in that sense, they are addressing the same problems that the postbellum and Progressive thinkers (and before them, Whigs and evangelical Protestants) had tried to address and which remain unsolved, except to the extent that a pluralistic and procedural order serves, faute de mieux, in the interim.

The grail that Bellah and company sought was the recovery of a civil-religious vision of the meaning of America, a ground of national cohesion and a moral modus vivendi for the post-Protestant era. Such emphases became clearer in *Habits*'s sequel, *The Good Society* (1991), whose very chapter titles and subheadings ("We Live through Institutions," "Seeking Common Ground," "The Public Church," "The Limits of Moral Individualism," and "A Renewed Public") telegraphed its orientation.[58] But in an increasingly diverse and self-consciously pluralistic American culture, the cultivation of a binding civil religion seems increasingly quixotic, if not covertly hegemonic, to many. We seem to be living through an era characterized by disaggregation and decentering, in America and the world, in which the idea of the nation as a principle for the organization of moral community carries less weight or prestige than at any time since the Second World War.

Images of disaggregation and decentering, along with the rise of a new generation marked by its disdain for all large-scale organizations, dominated the most recent contribution to the literature on American social character: Paul Leinberger and Bruce Tucker's *The New Individualists: The Generation after the Organization Man* (1991). A work of ambitious scope and intellectual sophistication, *The New Individualists* was a self-conscious successor to both *The Organization Man* (as its subtitle indicated) and *The Lonely Crowd* (as quickly became evident in its argument). Its sense of generational timing could not have been more acute, as immediately became clear from its opening sentence. "An unprecedented transfer of power is about to take place in American life," it began, as "the organization men" gave way to "the baby boomers, male and female."[59] The authors could not have known how richly their prediction would be confirmed in the presidential election of 1992—by the new presidents's age, by his marriage, and, in some respects, even by his political vision.

There was a personal connection between *The New Individualists* and *The Organization Man* that made for a great journalistic hook: Paul Leinberger was the son of Hugo Leinberger, a Park Forest minister who was one of the subjects discussed at length in the earlier work. But the authors actually made surprisingly little use of that personal connection, preferring to reflect more generally and abstractly upon the social character and psychological profile of baby boomers who had, like themselves, grown up swaddled in the comforts and constraints of the organizational world William Whyte had described. The book's intellectual indebtedness to *The Lonely Crowd* was actually far greater, and more evident. To Riesman's typology of tradition-, inner-, and other-direction as modes of conformity it added a fourth, meant to describe its target group: subject-direction. Such characters are "emotionally controlled" by the attitude of mourning—mourning for the "death" of their "authentic self," which general affluence and the warm family life of the organizational suburb had encouraged them to cultivate, but which the decline of the American economy as well as the unpredictable demands of the postindustrial world have rendered impossible. The rise of "a genuinely global marketplace linked by instantaneous communications," they argued, "has accelerated the diffusive processes of modernity, further destabilizing the self."[60] The new character type is *subject*-directed because it is acutely aware not only of its subjectivity, but of the ways in which it is subjected to artificial forces beyond its reach. Cut off from the cherished dream of authenticity, which has been both economically and philosophically destroyed beyond recall, such a subject-directed self copes with its mourning by developing a new conception of what it means to be an individual: it fashions itself into "an artificial person." Artificial, they insisted, was not a pejorative term; it did not mean "phony or insincere," though it might well mean "ironic." It referred to a new postmodern way of understanding what it meant to be an individual, an "ensembled individualism" that emphasized the particular forms of one's unique connectedness to the world, in all their variety—one's personae, or social selves—rather than the chimera of an authentic self, a dream that had been rendered impossible of achievement.

Such a vague and abstract formulation, which the authors sometimes made even more ineffable by using the opaque jargon of academic postmodernism, was far less convincing than any of Riesman's typologies and seemed to describe precious few people. Indeed, one could have the distinct impression that the authors of *The New Individualists* were really writing about themselves and their circle of friends, working out the psychological kinks and disappointments of their corner of baby boomerdom in public, highly theoretical, anonymity. The book begins to gain credibility, however, as it moves into more empirically grounded social analysis, where one sees, in sector after sector of American life, the decentering principle vividly demonstrated, with the resulting emergence of new, vital, and unprecedented social forms. To pick two of the most compelling examples, the authors demonstrate the radical transformation of suburban life and the radical restructuring of American business corporations—both intimately related, each representing a profound shift away from the patterns of the organization man's generation. The rise of "postmetropolitan suburbs" like Irvine, California, defies the conventional industrial-city geography of a central business area surrounded by increasingly affluent residential suburban rings; it has no center and no established relational grids but is a complex and fluid network that has evolved in response to the dynamic and ever-shifting forces of the postindustrial service economy.[61] The hierarchical, vertically stepped organizational structure of the 1950s has given way to a more horizontal, networklike structure characterized by ad hoc task-oriented work teams—a structure derived not from the rigidities of a bureaucratic chain of command, but from the decentralizing imperatives of new information technologies.[62]

Unlike the more moralistic Bellah, Leinberger and Tucker attempt little or no evaluative judgment about these developments. They simply ask that they be seen as patterns, as integral parts of a large-scale systemic change rather than as random or haphazard occurrences, and that the cultivation of artificial persons be understood as a natural part of the larger patterning. Any Riesmanesque regrets about the shape of this new form of humanity the authors regard as misdirected neotraditionalism. They also suggest that anyone, such as a corporate manager, who has to deal with baby boomers in the work force would be well advised to understand their peculiar makeup. Their tenuous and provisional relationship to the organizations for which they work, for example, may seem like rank disloyalty and self-indulgent opportunism to an old-fashioned organization man, who would never have dreamed of job hopping. But to one who knows the psychology of that generation, the authors argue, and who understands the disappointments it has had to cope with, and the uncertain organizational world in which it had to make its way, such behavior is rational and realistic.

*The New Individualists* is, then, very much the book of a particular generation—even, in its own cool and diffident way, an apologia. For that reason, the subjects it does not discuss are as revealing as those it does. Some of its silences are startling, especially given the usual tendency of studies of national character to turn into sermons on the state of the national soul. It has little to say, for example, about what the brave new uncentered world it describes might mean to the children who grow up in it—an especially strange omission, since the study itself argues that "the organizational offspring" grew up in an environment very different from the one their parents thought they were creating.

Other than a disconnected assault on "radical materialist" yuppies of the 1980s, the problems of materialism are not part of the book's agenda; neither is religion, which is summarily consigned to the past, while the neotraditionalism of *Habits of the Heart* is subjected to ridicule.[63] Politics, least of all a genuinely participatory politics, is not a part of its vision either. Perhaps most notable, the book is utterly unconcerned with the problem of national cohesion—and not because it simply presumes the nation will cohere. The bitter experiences of the Vietnam War left many of the organizational offspring, the authors assert, marked for life with an ineradicable distrust of institutions—of their legitimacy, benevolence, and even rationality. All organizations great and small had become suspect in their eyes; and the most suspect of all institutions, and the least likely to command their wholehearted loyalty, was the nation-state.

*The New Individualists* also supports a more general assertion: it is unlikely, in a posttotalitarian era, that individualism will be effectively challenged by a reprise of the consolidationist vision, whether socialist or nationalist in character. If anything, the opposite seems more likely, at least in the short run, as so many nations and empires are experiencing, or facing the prospect of, disintegration and dissolution into their constituent elements. This is not only true in Eastern and Central Europe or in Canada. The term *Balkanization* applied by Kevin Phillips to the reorientation of American political life into special-interest blocs based upon race, class, ethnicity, gender, sexual orientation, religion, or ideology seems as pertinent as ever to describe the devolution of the national community into an infinitude of subcommunities.[64]

To be sure, there is much that is deplorable or ominous, even dangerous, in such developments. But if considered in light of MacIntyre's and Sandel's observations, such reorientation may also represent the beginnings of a historically inevitable, and perhaps not entirely unhealthy, reaction against the pathologies of the unencumbered self and the limitations of the centralized and nationalized social order. In his most recent book, Christopher Lasch gives voice to a venerably conservative vision of the proper conditions of human connectedness, which pays respect to the immense and enduring power of difference: "The capacity for loyalty is stretched too thin when it tries to attach itself to the hypothetical solidarity of the whole human race. It needs to attach itself to specific people and places, not to an abstract ideal of universal human rights. We love particular men and women, not humanity in general. The dream of universal brotherhood, because it rests on the sentimental fiction that men and women are all the same, cannot survive the discovery that they differ."[65] Although addressed to the problems in sustaining notions of a "family of man," his remarks also bear on the problems of nations as well.

There are, however, distinctly negative possibilities that lurk in the decomposition of nations and empires, as the murderous conflicts in the wake of the collapse of the Soviet Union make painfully clear. We can see some of these problems closer to home. The Balkanization of American politics and social life along the lines of highly specific identifications may represent nothing more than an affirmation of narrow ethnic tribalism, or even a translation of radical individualism into group terms, making possible a more effective pursuit of the group's interests within the context of a pluralistic, bureaucratic, and procedural political order but leaving the public life of the nation impoverished, and perhaps leaving us that much further from the possibility of communities capable of sustaining healthy and enlivening differences. The debate over multiculturalism that rages in contemporary academe reflects a well-grounded fear that satisfactions achieved through the embrace of ethnic tribalism or other particularisms may come at an incalculable price to the common culture, upon whose cohesion all such self-conscious and hyphenate embraces depend.[66] Do the homogeneous American "lifestyle enclaves" explored by Frances FitzGerald in her fascinating study *Cities on a Hill*, running the gamut from the retirement towns of the Sunbelt to the Castro District in San Francisco to the Rajneeshi religious commune in Oregon, represent a recovery of the vibrancy of community life through shared values and shared narratives? Or do they represent a ghastly final adaptation of expressive individualism to the Weberian logic of bureaucratic specialization—a debased form of social association that is merely the unencumbered self writ large?[67] Do they reflect the decline of the word *community* in contemporary American parlance to the point that it has become an all-purpose noun, whose sole purpose is to give the appearance of solidity to the adjective that precedes it? Has our notion of community therefore devolved into nothing more than a homogenous and politically targetable slice of the population or a demographic population with certain distinctive consumption preferences?[68]

Those questions are difficult to answer, and in any event, the attempt do so would take us well beyond the historian's proper province. But several observations may at least help focus the questions. First, as FitzGerald's title implies, lifestyle enclaves have been a persistent feature of American history, from Massachusetts Bay to Oneida to Sun City and Castro Street. They perhaps constitute a special case of Tocqueville's more general observation that Americans have a propensity and talent for forming themselves into voluntary associations, which generally combine a functional purpose with a social one, bringing men and women together for the sake of a self-identified, homogeneous community of interest. Self-interest rightly understood, in short, includes an understanding of the individual's need to associate, and a voluntary association built upon a community of interests or desires does not rely upon an authoritative person or institution to legitimate itself to its members. Thanks to its functional, purposeful, utilitarian character, it carries its raison d'être within itself. In its ideal form, then, a voluntary association offers the prospect of a frictionless association of self and society, conceiving the latter as a receptacle into which the desires of the former may flow freely and be fulfilled, without the coercive hand of human authority intervening. Herbert Marcuse's vision of a fully human society, with its combination of radical self-determination and profound social solidarity, its denial of the friction of man-in-society, offers an especially striking example of this fantasy of seamless unity.

Marcuse was remarkably cavalier, though, in addressing himself to the question of authority, breezily endorsing a "combination of centralized authority and direct democracy" without ever troubling to explain how such an arrangement might actually operate.[69] Yet no problem is more fundamental to American social character and to the complex of issues here under examination than the locus of authority; for a large, complex society cannot be governed by the premises of a voluntary association, and even voluntary associations must wrestle, in the end, with problems of authority, as the history of churches and reform movements amply indicates. A social order that is egalitarian or (more importantly) understands itself as such grants little room for what is traditionally understood as authority, unless that authority is depersonalized and embodied in the social entity—as in the adage *vox populi, vox dei*, or in the Weberian triumph of bureaucracy over patrimonialism, tradition, and charisma. "When the conditions of men are almost equal," as Tocqueville remarked, "they do not easily allow themselves to be persuaded by one another."[70] Equals, that is, do not take orders from one another. Indeed, there is no more characteristic American attitude than disdain for anyone who would arrogate the title of master.

So observed D. H. Lawrence in the epigraph with which this book began. Yet Lawrence deplored such American rebelliousness as (among other things) an obstacle to a profound experience of community, an experience made possible not by the exercise of negative liberty and self-determination but by submission and self-transcendence. For the obsessively masterless on the American strand (Calibans who were, he lamented, also prone to be slavishly bound to the collective opinion of their neighbors), he offered a simple, if not entirely transparent, answer: "Henceforth be mastered." Despite Lawrence's idiosyncratic paganism, the command is rich with more venerable Christian overtones. Seek ye first the Kingdom of God, Christ had taught in the Sermon on the Mount; Lawrence was merely ringing his own psychodynamic change upon that imperative.[71] Seek the authority not of the conscious ego-self, but of "the IT," the transpersonal "deep self." If the precise meaning of that command seemed somewhat obscure, and wide open to various forms of self-deception, its gravamen, particularly so far as an individualistic ethos was concerned, was not. "Men are not free," he asserted, "when they are doing just what they like. . . . If one wants to be free, one has to give up the illusion of doing what one likes, and seek what IT wishes done." The echoes here are perhaps more resonant of Freud, Jung, and Frazer than of the gospels and St. Paul, but the self-overcoming commission is recognizably similar if one generously assumes for the moment that the IT is as genuinely transpersonal in practice as Lawrence presents it in theory. One also need not strain one's ears much to hear a distinct echo of Edward Bellamy—of his quasi-religious longing to surrender the ego-self to the authority of a suprapersonal second self that would bring him into solidarity with the cosmos and his fellow men. Both Lawrence and Bellamy saw the restoration, or achievement, of community as inseparable from a profound personal surrender, placing oneself under a moral authority outside one's ego-self.

Whatever else may be said of that position, it suggests that there is a considerable sacrificial price to be offered for the possibility of authentic community, a price levied, so to speak, both up and down the scale of organization: both upon the would-be autonomous self and upon the consolidated social order within which it presently lives, moves, and has its being. Such demands upon the self ran directly athwart David Riesman's assertion that the other-directed man was a "lonely member of the crowd" precisely because he attended too much to the feelings of others and too little to his own; in fact, a lonely and disconnected emotivist self with ephemeral or highly attenuated loyalties may well be the logical correlative of a centralized society. Our examination of the rise and fall of consolidation suggests that a similar reconsideration may well be in order with respect to political and social organization—a scaling back of the sheer size and comprehensiveness of modern consolidated institutions and perhaps even a reconsideration of the process of political centralization so widely and greatly feared in the early republic and so powerfully signaled and symbolized by the pageant of the Grand Review.

As Lawrence observed, however, the willingness to surrender a significant portion of individual identity to a corporate whole cannot reliably flow from a vague and uplifting desire for the warmth and supportiveness of "community-building" but will be directly commensurate to the degree of authority invested in that entity. That very thought tends to strike terror in the hearts of Americans. But there will be a master, asserted Lawrence, one way or another, even if one roundly denies its existence. By positing an obscure IT as ultimate authority—in preference to, say, a Judeo-Christian God thought to have revealed himself with disconcerting and inhibiting definiteness—Lawrence himself may well have been evading authority in practice, even as he was affirming it in the abstract. As a critique of American culture, however, his remarks are harder to dismiss. We tend to forget, in liberal societies, how often we allow the marketplace mechanism to function as our model for, or substitute for, ultimate authority.[72] While such a model opens considerable possibilities, it proscribes others; it is a source of impersonal legitimizing mastery perfectly suited to a society of would-be autonomous, masterless men and women, in much the same sense that Sandel's procedural republic can continue to function even in an authoritative vacuum. We should not be deceived, therefore, into thinking that we can combine, shuffle, and incorporate the virtues of various social arrangements and traditions at will without first inevitably refashioning them in the very image of our own present condition.

Every way of life, even a seemingly neutral and eclectic pluralism that tolerantly affirms a wide-open bazaar of ideas and values, has its built-in imperatives, its virtues, its vices, its codes, its taboos, its benefits, and its costs. Whether we wish it or not, we cannot avoid paying the price for our own. Part of that price, it seems, may be some version of the tension that Whitman exemplified in extremis: a reflexive, unvanquished individualism accompanied by a perpetual yearning for unrealizable forms of community—a dream of being both autonomous and connected, which in the end often settles for being merely lonely or crowded. Whether that tension is sustainable, waiting only for its proper reconceptualization or redefinition, or will instead turn out to have been transitional, giving way in due course to other forms of social organization and correspondingly different forms of consciousness, remains to be seen.[73] History cannot predict the future, nor does it offer the present many obvious or practical lessons. But it does teach one lesson incomparably well: that things were once very different from the way they are now. Chances are, that same lesson will be equally applicable to a future social world looking backward upon our own.

# Notes

1. *New York Times*, May 23, 1865, 1. For descriptions of the Grand Review here and following, I have relied upon the accounts published on May 24 and 25 in the *Times*, the *New York Herald*, the *New York Tribune*, the *Philadelphia Inquirer*, and the *Philadelphia Bulletin*. I am also very much indebted to the opening chapter of Stuart Charles McConnell, "A Social History of the Grand Army of the Republic, 1867–1900," (Ph.D. diss., Johns Hopkins University, 1987), although our emphases in approaching the Grand Review differ somewhat, with McConnell stressing the elements of the pageant that were either disorderly or unrepresentative of the national composition. See also the lovely evocation by Thomas Fleming, "The Big Parade," *American Heritage*, March 1990, 98–104, which stresses the opposite feature of the review: the way it served to heal the intense rivalry between the eastern and western elements of the Union army. See also Philip Van Doren Stern, *An End to Valor: The Last Days of the Civil War* (Boston, 1958), 338–51.

2. *New York Herald*, May 24, 1865, 1.

3. *New York Times*, May 24, 1865, 1.

4. Stern, *An End to Valor*, 343.

5. James Reston, Jr., *Sherman's March and Vietnam* (New York, 1984), 192. This description was taken from a contemporary correspondent, but Reston does not provide a source citation.

6. Walt Whitman, *Specimen Days*, in *Complete Poetry and Collected Prose*, ed. Justin Kaplan (New York, 1982), 769–70.

7. For a probing examination of the how public memory is constituted and embodied in public spectacles and edifices, paying particular attention to the way that the choice of these embodiments of public memory is often a battleground between "official" and "vernacular" meanings, and to the way that, in the twentieth century, the results have usually served the glorification of the nation-state, see John Bodnar, *Remaking America: Public Memory, Commemoration, and Patriotism in the Twentieth Century* (Princeton, 1992), esp. 3–38, 245–53.

8. See Richard Barksdale Harwell, ed., *The Confederate Reader* (New York, 1957), 340–50, for the general order of Secretary of War Edwin Stanton and for the text of Henry Ward Beecher's Sumter oration.

9. See Thomas Bender, *Community and Social Change in America* (New Brunswick, N.J., 1978), 88, on the local nature of antebellum American patriotism/nationalism. The useful distinction between patriotism and nationalism comes from George Orwell's 1945 essay "Notes on Nationalism," in *The Collected Essays, Journalism and Letters of George Orwell*, ed. Sonia Orwell and Ian Angus, 4 vols. (London, 1968), 3:361–80, esp. 362–63. For a more general and systematic treatment of the subject as it evolved in

American thought, see Paul C. Nagel, *One Nation Indivisible: The Union in American Thought, 1776–1861* (New York, 1964).

10. McConnell, "A Social History of the Grand Army of the Republic," 3.

11. *New York Times*, May 25, 1865, 1.

12. Joseph T. Glatthaar, *The March to the Sea and Beyond: Sherman's Troops in the Savannah and Carolinas Campaigns* (New York, 1985), 180–82.

13. James I. Robertson, Jr., *Soldiers Blue and Gray* (Columbia, S.C., 1988), 16–17; James M. McPherson, *Battle Cry of Freedom: The Civil War Era* (New York, 1988), 322–23. The latter notes that the variety of uniforms in both armies eventually led to "tragic mixups in early battles when regiments mistook friends for enemies or enemies for friends."

14. It should be noted, for the record, that the variations in the steady stream of blue uniformity included a tiny number of Zouaves in the Grand Review; see the account in the *New York Herald*, May 24, 1865, 1.

15. See T. Harry Williams, *McClellan, Sherman, and Grant* (New Brunswick, N.J., 1962), 46; and Glatthaar, *The March to the Sea*, 6.

16. One of the many ironies of Sherman's career was the fact that, though hated with legendary intensity by partisan or unreconstructed southerners, he was simultaneously regarded by so many northerners as excessively lenient toward the South. There was some basis for that reputation. What Joseph Glatthaar has pointed out about the men in Sherman's army was also true of their commander: he had more in common culturally with the Confederate soldiers than with a man like his fellow Ohioan Stanton. Indeed, Sherman had southern relations and was living and working in the South as superintendent of a military college in Alexandria, Louisiana, when the Civil War broke out. The liberal terms of surrender Sherman offered Confederate general Joseph Johnston at Durham's Station, North Carolina, after defeating him in the field, particularly raised the ire of Stanton and other "bitter-enders," however, coming as it did so hard on the heels of Lincoln's assassination. One has to take into account Stanton's subsequent efforts to humiliate Sherman publicly and to cast serious doubt upon his judgment and his loyalty to fully appreciate the full measure of personal triumph the review represented for Sherman. See Benjamin P. Thomas and Harold M. Hyman, *Stanton: The Life and Times of Lincoln's Secretary of War* (New York, 1962), 405–6; and William McFeely, *Grant: A Biography* (New York, 1981), 223–31.

17. William T. Sherman, *The Memoirs of General William T. Sherman*, 2 vols. (New York, 1875), 2:377–78.

18. On Sherman's rocky relationship with the press, one of many respects in which he pioneered modern generalship, see John F. Marszalek, *Sherman's Other War: The General and the Civil War Press* (Memphis, 1981).

19. *New York Times*, May 26, 1865, 1.

20. George E. Baker, ed., *The Works of William H. Seward*, 5 vols. (Boston, 1884), 4:292.

21. McFeely, *Grant*, 230; Fleming, "The Big Parade," 104.

22. See the excellent account of Sherman in Edmund Wilson, *Patriotic Gore* (New York, 1962), 205; and also see McFeely, *Grant*, 230.

23. Wilson G. Smith, ed., *Grand Army War Songs* (Cleveland and Chicago, 1886),

2–5. Sherman's diary does, however, record the ecstatic responses of many black Georgians; see Sherman, *Memoirs*, 2:178.

24. Glatthaar, *March to the Sea*, esp. 134–55.

25. Sherman, *Memoirs*, 2:378.

26. For a brilliant explication of the phenomenology and psychology of military ritual, dress, and implements, see James Hillman, "Mars, Arms, Rams, Wars: On the Love of War," in *Facing Apocalypse*, ed. V. Andrews, R. Bosnak, and K. W. Goodwin (Dallas, 1987), 118–36.

27. Glatthaar, *March to the Sea*, 182.

28. Matt. 11:34–39.

29. Gal. 2:19–21. See also Rom. 6:1–11.

30. G. K. Chesterton, *What I Saw in America* (London, 1922), 12.

31. Sidney E. Mead, *The Lively Experiment: The Shaping of Christianity in America* (New York, 1963); Ernest Lee Tuveson, *Redeemer Nation: The Idea of America's Millennial Role* (Chicago, 1968); Ruth H. Bloch, *The Visionary Republic: Millennial Themes in American Thought, 1756–1800* (New York, 1985); Sacvan Berkovitch, *The American Jeremiad* (Madison, 1978), and *The Puritan Origins of the American Self* (New Haven, 1975); Nathan Hatch, *The Sacred Cause of Liberty: Republican Thought and the Millennium in Revolutionary New England* (New Haven, 1977). See also the useful essays in Mark Noll, ed., *Religion and American Politics: From the Colonial Period to the 1980s* (New York, 1990).

32. Sherman, *Memoirs*, 2:179.

33. See Robert Bellah's classic studies dealing with American civil religion: *Beyond Belief: Essays on Religion in a Post-Traditional World* (New York, 1970); *The Broken Covenant: American Civil Religion in a Time of Trial* (New York, 1975); and, with Phillip E. Hammond, *Varieties of Civil Religion* (New York, 1980). The "Battle Hymn" appeared in the *Atlantic Monthly*, February 1862, 10. That text, with a commentary/history by historian William G. McLoughlin, can be found in Daniel J. Boorstin, ed., *An American Primer* (New York, 1966), 399–404.

34. Wilson, *Patriotic Gore*, 97. See James M. McPherson's analysis of Lincoln's rhetoric in *Battle Cry of Freedom*, 859; see also Nagel, *One Nation Indivisible*.

35. See John Patrick Diggins, *The Lost Soul of American Politics: Virtue, Self-Interest, and the Foundations of Liberalism* (New York, 1984), 295–333; Paul Nagel, *This Sacred Trust: American Nationality, 1798–1898* (New York, 1971), esp. 129–93.

36. The second inaugural address appears in Roy Basler, ed., *The Collected Works of Abraham Lincoln*, 9 vols. (New Brunswick, N.J., 1953–55), 8:332–33. See also Diggins, *Lost Soul*, 330.

37. Diggins, *Lost Soul*, 329–33; and, before him, Reinhold Niebuhr, *The Irony of American History* (New York, 1952), esp. 171–74. The biographical literature on Lincoln is incomparably vast, but particularly worthy of note among recent works is Dwight G. Anderson, *Abraham Lincoln: The Quest for Immortality* (New York, 1982).

38. On the political uses of Lincoln's martyrdom, see David Donald's still-useful essay, "Getting Right with Lincoln," in *Lincoln Reconsidered: Essays on the Civil War Era*, by David Donald (New York, 1956), esp. 4–5. See also Wilson, *Patriotic Gore*, 97; and Diggins, *Lost Soul*, 296.

39. Don E. Fehrenbacher, ed., *Abraham Lincoln: Speeches and Writings, 1859–1865* (New York, 1989), 215–22.

40. I refer, of course, to Lincoln's assertion that "we can not dedicate—we can not consecrate—we can not hallow—this ground. The brave men, living and dead, who struggled here, have consecrated it far above our poor power to add or detract." Fehrenbacher, *Abraham Lincoln*, 536.

41. Whitman, "When Lilacs Last in the Dooryard Bloom'd," in *Complete Poetry and Collected Prose*, 460.

42. The lines immediately after those quoted testify to Whitman's increasing obsession with death: "(Nor for you, for one alone, / Blossoms and branches green to coffins all I bring, / For fresh as the morning, thus would I chant a song for you / O sane and sacred death. / . . . / With loaded arms I come, pouring for you, / For you and the coffins all of you O death.)" ibid., 461.

43. Whitman, *Specimen Days*, 763–64.

44. Whitman, "From Paumanok Starting I Fly Like a Bird," in *Complete Poetry and Collected Prose*, 420.

45. Despite their datedness, the best starting places for tracing the trajectory of this subject are still Howard K. Beale, "What Historians Have Said about the Causes of the Civil War," in *Theory and Practice in Historical Study: A Report of the Committee on Historiography* (New York, 1946), 53–102; and Thomas J. Pressly, *Americans Interpret Their Civil War* (Princeton, 1954). Other valuable studies include Arthur M. Schlesinger, Jr., "The Causes of the Civil War: A Note on Historical Sentimentalism," *Partisan Review* 16 (October 1949): 969–81; David Donald, "American Historians and the Causes of the Civil War," *South Atlantic Quarterly* 50 (Summer 1960): 351–55; John S. Rosenberg, "Toward a New Civil War Revisionism," *American Scholar* 38 (Spring 1969): 250–72; Raimondo Luraghi, "The Civil War and the Modernization of American Society: Social Structure and Industrial Revolution in the Old South before and during the War," *Civil War History* 18 (September 1972): 230–50; Phillip S. Paludan, "The American Civil War: Triumph through Tragedy," *Civil War History* 20 (September 1974): 239–50; and Eric Foner's essays "The Causes of the American Civil War: Recent Interpretations and New Directions" and "Politics, Ideology, and the Origins of the American Civil War," both reprinted in *Politics and Ideology in the Age of the Civil War* (New York, 1980), 15–53. On the ambivalence of powerful symbols, see C. G. Jung, *Two Essays in Analytical Psychology*, trans. R. F. C. Hull (Princeton, 1966), 291, and *The Symbolic Life: Miscellaneous Writings*, trans. R. F. C. Hull (Princeton, 1976), 225, 244–53, 259. For a thoughtful examination of the contest over what the public meaning of the Civil War was to be, see David W. Blight, *Frederick Douglass' Civil War: Keeping Faith in Jubilee* (Baton Rouge, 1989), 219–39.

46. Foner, *Politics and Ideology*, 53.

47. See Luraghi, "The Civil War and the Modernization of American Society."

48. For the most celebrated attempt to compare Lincoln to Bismarck (and Lenin), as well as a ferocious attack on consolidation written in the context of the Cold War, see Wilson, *Patriotic Gore*, xvi–xxxii.

49. An insightful recent comparative examination of the American Civil War, supporting this general assertion, is Carl N. Degler, "One among Many: The United States and National Unification," in *Lincoln, the War President: The Gettysburg Lectures*,

ed. Gabor S. Boritt (New York, 1992), 89–120. See also Anthony Giddens, *The Nation-State and Violence* (Berkeley, 1985).

50. Arthur A. Stein, *The Nation at War* (Baltimore, 1978), explores the links between war and national cohesion. A classic older study is Pitirim Sorokin, *Man and Society in Calamity: The Effects of War, Revolution, Famine, Pestilence upon Human Mind, Behavior, Social Organization and Cultural Life* (New York, 1942). Although not specifically addressed to the question of modern state formation, the work of Rene Girard on the "scapegoat mechanism" has fascinating implications for the relationship between externally expressed aggression and internal social solidarity; see his *Violence and the Sacred* (Baltimore, 1977) and *The Scapegoat* (Baltimore, 1986).

51. On the evolution of the Confederacy, see Emory M. Thomas, *The Confederacy as a Revolutionary Experience* (Englewood Cliffs, 1971), 58–78, and *The Confederate Nation, 1861–1865*, esp. 120–44 and 190–214; see also James Z. Rabun, "Alexander H. Stephens and Jefferson Davis," *American Historical Review* 63 (1953): 290–321.

52. It should be noted that Charles and Mary Beard were admirers of Alexander H. Stephens; see their discussion of his "great history of the conflict" in the "Second American Revolution" chapter of their *Rise of American Civilization*, 2 vols. (New York, 1930), 2:52. An excellent biographical account of Stephens, both concise and insightful, is contained in Daniel Walker Howe, *The Political Culture of the American Whigs* (Chicago, 1979), 328–62, while a more detailed biographical study is Rudolph Von Abele, *Alexander H. Stephens* (New York, 1946).

53. Alexander H. Stephens, *A Constitutional View of the Late War between the States: Its Causes, Character, Conduct and Results*, 2 vols. (Philadelphia and Chicago, 1868–70), 1:10; see also his *The Reviewers Reviewed: A Supplement to the "War between the States," etc., with an Appendix in Review of "Reconstruction," So Called* (New York, 1872).

54. From a speech delivered in Savannah in March 1861 defending the new Confederate constitution, in Henry Cleveland, *Alexander H. Stephens, in Public and Private, With Letters and Speeches, Before, During, and Since the War* (Philadelphia, 1866), 717–29. Yet in *A Constitutional View* Stephens says that "slavery, so called, [is] but *the question* on which these antagonistic principles, which had been in conflict, from the beginning, on divers *other questions*, were finally brought into actual and active collision with each other on the field of battle" (1:10).

55. Beard and Beard, *Rise of American Civilization*, 2:52–121, esp. 54–55.

56. See Ralph L. Andreano, ed., *The Economic Impact of the American Civil War* (Cambridge, Mass., 1962), for multifaceted discussion of these issues; see also McPherson, *Battle Cry of Freedom*, 817–19.

57. Beard and Beard, *Rise of American Civilization*, 2:55.

58. It is illuminating to note, for example, that in Alfred D. Chandler's magisterial study of the organizational origins of the modern large-scale business corporation, *The Visible Hand: The Managerial Revolution in Business* (Cambridge, Mass., 1977), the Civil War plays virtually no role. See also Chandler's brief remarks in "The Organization of Manufacturing and Transportation," in *Economic Change in the Civil War Era: Proceedings of a Conference on American Economic Institutional Change, 1850–1873, and the Impact of the Civil War, Held March 12–14*, ed. David L. Gilchrist and W. David Lewis (Greenville, Del., 1965), 137–65. The other essays in the Gilchrist and Lewis

volume, in general, likewise dismiss or greatly deemphasize the war's influence upon institutional economic change—a fact that may, of course, have partly to do with the presuppositions of historians who specialize in institutional, organizational hypotheses.

59. Robert H. Wiebe, *The Search for Order, 1877–1920* (New York, 1967). For an intelligent critical engagement of the Wiebe thesis, see Bender, *Community and Social Change*, esp. 47–58.

60. Again, Bender, *Community and Social Change*, esp. 45–120, provides a useful corrective.

61. Nagel, *This Sacred Trust*, xi–193.

62. Daniel J. Boorstin, *The Americans: The Democratic Experience* (New York, 1973), constantly points to this change; see esp. 359–402.

63. W. F. Allen, *A Short History of Standard Time and Its Adoption in North America in 1883* (New York, 1904), though mainly a self-promoting puff piece on the author himself, attempting to prove his claim to have been the prime mover behind this change, is nevertheless valuable. According to Charles Ferdinand Dowd, *A System of National Time for Railroads* (1870), there were at that time some eighty different time standards on U.S. railroads. For a more general consideration of the implications of the measurement of time, see Lewis Mumford, *Technics and Civilization* (New York, 1934), and his succinct "Mechanization of Modern Culture," in *Interpretations and Forecasts, 1922–1972* (New York, 1979), 270–78; Harrison J. Cowan, *Time and Its Measurements* (Cleveland, 1958); Derek Howse, *Greenwich Mean Time and the Discovery of the Longitude* (New York, 1980); David S. Landes, *Revolution in Time: Clocks and the Making of the Modern World* (Cambridge, Mass., 1983); Stephen Kern, *The Culture of Space and Time, 1880–1918* (Cambridge, Mass., 1983), esp. 11–16; Alan Trachtenberg, *The Incorporation of America: Culture and Society in the Gilded Age* (New York, 1982), 59–60; and Michael O'Malley, *Keeping Watch: A History of American Time* (New York, 1991).

64. Kern's fascinating study suggests that the process of the internationalization of standard time coincided with an acutely private and interior sense of time, exemplified in the rarefied time sense characterizing the novels of Marcel Proust. Although one could not point to an American Proust within the time frame of Kern's study, there nevertheless may well be a general relationship, not unlike the relationship argued for in chapter 8 of this book, between the phenomenon of increasing standardization and the phenomenon of increasing subjectivism.

65. As will soon be apparent, my use of this particular term derives largely from the characteristic usage I have found in antebellum political and social discourse; but I have also been influenced by John Higham's suggestive essay *From Boundlessness to Consolidation* (Ann Arbor, 1969), although I have deviated in significant ways from the periodization for which that essay argues.

66. Trachtenberg, *Incorporation of America*, esp. 3–10. One other very suggestive example of the use of *incorporation* that Trachtenberg does not note in his book is the Fourteenth Amendment's incorporation of the Federal Bill of Rights and application of those rights to the state constitutions. Yet, as he might well point out, it was not until the 1920s that this form of incorporation became a legal reality. In the 1833 *Barron* v. *Baltimore* decision, the Supreme Court had explicitly ruled that the Bill of Rights did

not apply to the states, and as late as 1923, in *Prudential Insurance Company* v. *Cheek*, it seemed to uphold that view. In a series of contemporary decisions, including *Gitlow* v. *New York* (1925), however, the Court was also beginning to depart dramatically from that opinion.

67. See Robert Bannister, *Social Darwinism: Science and Myth in Anglo-American Social Thought* (Philadelphia, 1979), which, with Donald C. Bellomy, "'Social Darwinism' Revisited," *Perspectives in American History*, n.s. 1 (1984): 1–129, leaves the conventional account of social Darwinism's ubiquity in postbellum America in ruins. See Richard Hofstadter's *Social Darwinism in American Thought* for the conventional account. On John D. Rockefeller, see his own *Random Reminiscences of Men and Events* (New York, 1909) and David Freeman Hawke, *John D.: The Founding Father of the Rockefellers* (New York, 1980).

68. Higham, *From Boundlessness to Consolidation*, 5.

69. The reader interested in exploring this issue in primary documents will find a rich source in Philip Kurland and Ralph Lerner, eds., *The Founders' Constitution*, 4 vols. (Chicago, 1987), 1:242–97, "Federal v. Consolidated Government."

70. "Speeches of Patrick Henry in the Virginia State Ratifying Convention," June 1788. For Henry and the other Antifederalists following, I refer to the editions compiled and edited by Herbert J. Storing, *The Complete Anti-Federalist*, 7 vols. (Chicago, 1981), 5:209–27 (or, in Storing's own system of numbering by volume, article, and paragraph, which is occasionally quite cumbersome to use), 5.16.1–2.

71. "The Address and Reasons of Dissent of the Minority of the Convention of Pennsylvania to Their Constituents," in Storing, *The Complete Anti-Federalist*, 3:157 (3.11.30).

72. "Address of the Albany Antifederal Committee," in ibid., 6:123 (6.10.2).

73. "Letter of Agrippa," December 3, 1787, in ibid., 4:76–77 (4.6.16–18).

74. Herbert J. Storing, *What the Anti-Federalists Were For* (Chicago, 1981), 11 (also vol. 1 of *The Complete Anti-Federalist*).

75. Clinton Rossiter, ed., *The Federalist Papers* (New York, 1961), 240–46. See also Madison's remarks on consolidation for the *National Gazette*, December 3, 1791, in *The Papers of James Madison*, ed. Robert Rutland et al. (Chicago, 1962–), 14:137–39.

76. Rossiter, *The Federalist Papers*, 294–95; this is from no. 46, by Madison.

77. Thomas Jefferson, "Draft of the Kentucky Resolutions," in *Writings*, ed. Merrill Peterson (New York, 1984), 449–56; quotation is from 455.

78. Clyde N. Wilson et al., eds, *The Papers of John C. Calhoun* (Columbia, 1976), 10:442–539. This edition provides a side-by-side comparison of Calhoun's original handwritten draft (on verso pages) with the committee document (on recto pages); the quotation cited in the text comes from the latter, p. 537. But a similar use of *consolidation* runs through Calhoun's draft, as in the following: "to divide power and to give to one of the parties the exclusive right of judging of the portion allotted to each is in reality not to divide at all; and to reserve such exclusive right to the General Government (it matters not by what department to be exercised) is to convert it in fact into a great consolidated government with unlimited powers, and to divest the states in reality of all their rights" (506). See Wilson's useful discussion, "Exposition and Protest," in the introduction to this volume, xli–xlvi.

79. *Speech of Daniel Webster on the Subject of The Public Lands, etc., Delivered in the*

*Senate of the United States, January 20, 1830* (Washington, D.C., 1830), 13–14; *Speeches of the Hon. Robert Y. Hayne and the Hon. Daniel Webster Delivered in the Seante of the United States, Jan. 21 and 26, 1830, With a Sketch of the Preceding Debate on the Resolution of Mr. Foot, Respecting the Sale, &c, of Public Lands* (Boston, 1830), 28–31; *Speech of Daniel Webster in Reply to Mr. Hayne of South Carolina: The Resolution of Mr. Foot, of Connecticut, Relative to the Public Land Being under Consideration* (Washington, D.C., 1830), 41.

80. Maurice G. Baxter, *One and Inseparable: Daniel Webster and the Union* (Cambridge, Mass., 1984), 59–62, 505. Note his remarks in his January 26, 1830, response to Hayne: "I have nothing to do, sir, with the Hartford Convention. Its Journal, which the gentleman has quoted, I never read" (16).

81. Webster's influence upon Lincoln is suggested in Waldo W. Braden, *Abraham Lincoln: Public Speaker* (Baton Rouge, 1988), 58.

82. Charles F. Adams, Jr., "The Railroad System," in *Chapters of Erie, and Other Essays*, by Charles F. Adams, Jr., and Henry Adams (Boston, 1871), 335.

83. Lewis Mumford, *The Golden Day: A Study in American Experience and Culture* (New York, 1926), 140–42.

84. Ernest Samuels, ed., *The Education of Henry Adams* ([ca. 1918]; reprint, Boston, 1973), 240.

85. William James, "The Moral Equivalent of War," in *Writings: 1902–1910*, ed. Bruce Kuklick (New York, 1987), 1281–93.

86. Ibid., 1292.

87. Samuels, *Education of Henry Adams*, 232.

88. Henry Adams to Charles Francis Adams, Jr., October 2, 1863, in *The Letters of Henry Adams*, ed. J. C. Levenson et al., 6 vols. (Cambridge, Mass., 1982), 1:395–96.

89. Samuels, *Education of Henry Adams*, 396.

90. Ibid., 397–98.

91. Ibid., 249.

92. Ibid., 344.

93. Ibid., 344–45.

94. On the Adams family character, see Peter Shaw, *The Character of John Adams* (New York, 1976); and Paul C. Nagel, *Descent from Glory: Four Generations of the John Adams Family* (New York, 1983). See Samuels, *Education of Henry Adams*, 21, for Adams's own description of that quarrel.

95. Henry Adams, *Democracy: An American Novel* (New York, 1880).

96. Henry Edwin Tremain, *Last Hours of Sheridan's Cavalry* (New York, 1940), 549.

97. A first-rate biographical and psychological study of Harte has yet to be written; the existing literature offers no clue to the origins of this poem. See Henry Childs Merwin, *The Life of Bret Harte* (Boston, 1911); George R. Stewart, Jr., *Bret Harte: Argonaut and Exile* (Boston, 1931); and Patrick Morrow, *Bret Harte* (Boise, 1977).

98. As it happens, in 1860 a great equestrian statue of George Washington by sculptor Clark Mills was placed at Washington Circle, toward the Georgetown end of Pennsylvania Avenue. Since the Washington Monument was not completed until well after the Civil War, this statue constituted the district's principal public monument to the first president at the time of the Grand Review.

99. The poem appears in *The Poetical Works of Bret Harte* (Boston, 1912), 17–19.

100. Ernest Hemingway, *A Farewell to Arms* (New York, 1929), 177–78: "I was embarrassed by the words sacred, glorious, and sacrifice and the expression in vain. We had heard them, sometimes standing in the rain almost out of earshot, so that only the shouted words came through, and had read them, on proclamations that were slapped up by billposters over other proclamations, now for a long time, and I had seen nothing sacred, and the things that were glorious had no glory and the sacrifices were like the stockyards at Chicago if nothing was done with the meat except to bury it. There were many names you could not stand to hear and finally only the names of places had dignity."

CHAPTER TWO

1. Jackson would in fact be just as plausible a choice as Washington, in light of the fact that an equestrian statue had been erected in *his* honor within a few yards of Pennsylvania Avenue in Lafayette Park, directly facing the White House and therefore close to the reviewing stands for the Grand Review. Jackson's statue, also the work of sculptor Clark Mills, was actually the older of the two, having been erected in 1853 — the first such equestrian statue made in the United States.

2. In James D. Richardson, ed., *A Compilation of the Messages and Papers of the Presidents, 1789–1897*, 10 vols. (New York, 1900), 3:292–308.

3. For a sense of those corrections, revisions, etc., see Edward Pessen, *Jacksonian America: Society, Personality, and Politics* (Homewood, Ill., 1969), 384–93; and Sean Wilentz, "On Class and Politics in Jacksonian America," *Reviews in American History* 10 (December 1982): 45–63.

4. Alexis de Tocqueville, *Democracy in America*, trans. Henry Reeve, 2 vols. (New York, 1945), 2:104–8. Also see the valuable essays in Abraham S. Eisenstadt, ed., *Reconsidering Tocqueville's "Democracy in America"* (New Brunswick, N.J., 1988), esp. Seymour Drescher, "More Than America: Comparison and Synthesis in *Democracy in America*," 77–93; Arthur M. Schlesinger, Jr., "Individualism and Apathy in Tocqueville's *Democracy*," 94–109; and Daniel T. Rodgers's rather critical "Of Prophets and Prophecy," 200.

5. See the magisterial work of André Jardin, *Tocqueville: A Biography*, trans. Lydia Davis with Robert Hemenway (New York, 1988), which traces both intellectual and personal influences going into Tocqueville's outlook; see Jardin's summation, 534–36.

6. Tocqueville, *Democracy in America*, 2:104–6.

7. Ibid., 109.

8. Ibid., 110–11. It is revealing of Tocqueville's intellectual independence that he should take this anticonsolidation position despite the extensive contact he had with Federalists (like John Quincy Adams) in his American trip.

9. Ibid., 129–31.

10. Ibid., 346–52; see also Jardin, *Tocqueville*, 278.

11. Tocqueville, *Democracy in America*, 2:131.

12. Ibid., 132.

13. Sean Wilentz, "Many Democracies: On Tocqueville and Jacksonian America," in Eisenstadt, *Reconsidering Tocqueville's "Democracy in America*," 207–28; Lynn L. Mar-

shall and Seymour Drescher, "American Historians and Tocqueville's *Democracy*," *Journal of American History* 55 (December 1968): 512–32; and Edward Pessen, *Riches, Class, and Power before the Civil War* (Lexington, Ky., 1973), and *Jacksonian America*.

14. From Theodore Sedgwick, ed., *A Collection of the Political Writings of William Leggett*, 2 vols. (New York, 1840), 1:162–66.

15. Marvin Meyers, *The Jacksonian Persuasion: Politics and Belief* (Stanford, 1957), 3–15. On the last point, see Jackson's farewell address, in Richardson, *Compilation*, 3:292–308.

16. Daniel Walker Howe, *The Political Culture of the American Whigs* (Chicago, 1979), 4.

17. See ibid. for a discussion of each of these points. The "ironist" argument relating humanitarian social reform to the specific labor demands of an industrial capitalist economy is most closely identified with David Brion Davis, *The Problem of Slavery in the Age of Revolution* (Ithaca, 1975), and *Slavery and Human Progress* (New York, 1984). That thesis has evoked a number of sharp challenges, but none more searching and sustained than Thomas L. Haskell, "Capitalism and the Origins of the Humanitarian Sensibility," pts. 1 and 2, *American Historical Review* 90 (April, June 1985): 339–61, 547–66. See also the stimulating exchange between Haskell and his critics: David Brion Davis, "Reflections on Abolitionism and Ideological Hegemony," *American Historical Review* 92 (October 1987): 797–812; John Ashworth, "The Relationship between Capitalism and Humanitarianism," *American Historical Review* 92 (October 1987): 813–28; and Thomas L. Haskell, "Convention and Hegemonic Interest in the Debate over Antislavery: A Reply to Davis and Ashworth," *American Historical Review* 92 (October 1987): 829–78.

18. Daniel Walker Howe, "The Evangelical Movement and Political Culture in the North during the Second Party System," *Journal of American History* 77 (March 1991): 1216–39, esp. 1220; see also Howe's "Religion and Politics in the Antebellum North," in *Religion and American Politics: From the Colonial Period to the 1980s*, ed. Mark Noll (New York, 1990), 121–45.

19. Howe, "The Evangelical Movement," 1216–22.

20. William Ellery Channing, *Self-Culture* (London, 1844), 8–9, 24–25.

21. See Haskell, "Capitalism and the Origins of the Humanitarian Sensibility."

22. See Isaiah Berlin, "Two Concepts of Liberty," in *Four Essays on Liberty* (New York, 1969), 118–72. Lee Benson, *The Concept of Jacksonian Democracy: New York as a Test Case* (Princeton, 1961), 103, employs a version of this terminology. For a critical view, however, see Howe, *Political Culture of the American Whigs*, 20.

23. Roy Basler, ed., *The Collected Works of Abraham Lincoln*, 9 vols. (New Brunswick, N.J., 1953–55), 4:24–25.

24. Ibid., 478–79.

25. Abraham Lincoln, "Address Delivered Before the Springfield Washington Temperance Society, on the 22nd February, 1842," in Basler, *Collected Works*, 1:271–79.

26. J. G. A. Pocock, *Politics, Language, and Time: Essays on Political Thought and History* (New York, 1973), esp. 3–41 and 233–72.

27. Karl Marx, *The Eighteenth Brumaire of Louis Napoleon*, in *The Marx-Engels Reader*, ed. Robert C. Tucker, 2d ed. (New York, 1978), 594–5.

28. For examples of this backward-looking quality of Jacksonianism, see Meyers, *The*

*Jacksonian Persuasion*, 3–15. Theodore Sedgwick's work centered around a social vision of a morally revitalized Christian community; see Joseph Dorfman, ed., *Public and Private Economy*, 2 vols. (New York, 1836–39; reprint, Clifton, N.J., 1974). See also Jackson's farewell speech, in Richardson, *Compilation*, 3:298, in which he asserts that "no free government can stand without virtue in the people and a lofty spirit of patriotism, and if the sordid feelings of mere selfishness shall usurp the place which ought to be filled by public spirit, the legislation of Congress will soon be converted into a scramble for personal and sectional advantages."

29. Robert Owen, "Address Delivered by Robert Owen, April 27, 1825," in *Antebellum American Culture: An Interpretive Anthology*, ed. David Brion Davis (Lexington, Mass., 1979), 445–46.

30. See the classic study by William A. Hinds, *American Communities and Cooperative Colonies* (Chicago, 1908); and John Humphrey Noyes, *History of American Socialisms* (Philadelphia, 1870); Ronald G. Walters, *American Reformers, 1815–1860* (New York, 1978); Thomas Bender, *Community and Social Change in America* (New Brunswick, N.J., 1978), 115–17.

31. Haskell, "Capitalism and the Origins of the Humanitarian Sensibility," esp. pt. 2.

32. Nancy Cott, *The Bonds of Womanhood: "Woman's Sphere" in New England, 1780–1835* (New Haven, 1977); Jean V. Matthews, *Toward a New Society: American Thought and Culture, 1800–1830* (Boston, 1991), 77–79; Tocqueville, *Democracy in America*, 2:222–25.

33. See, for example, the discussion of Elizabeth Cady Stanton's "natural rights" orientation at the time of Seneca Falls in Elisabeth Griffith, *In Her Own Right: The Life of Elizabeth Cady Stanton* (New York, 1984), 47–61, esp. 54.

34. Margaret Fuller [Ossoli], *Woman in the Nineteenth Century, and Kindred Papers Relating to the Sphere, Condition and Duties, of Woman* (Boston, 1855).

35. There seems little reason to revise the judgment in this matter of Carl Degler, *At Odds: Women and the Family in America from the Revolution to the Present* (New York, 1980), 190.

36. Kathryn Kish Sklar, *Catharine Beecher: A Study in American Domesticity* (New Haven, 1973), esp. 151–67.

37. Fuller [Ossoli], *Woman in the Nineteenth Century*, 115. See Susan Phinney Conrad, *Perish the Thought: Intellectual Women in Romantic America, 1830–1860* (New York, 1976), 45–92, for an account of Fuller in all her complexity. On the ambivalences of nineteenth-century feminism, see Jean Bethke Elshtain, "Feminism and Citizenship: Liberalism and Its Discontents," in *Meditations on Modern Political Thought: Masculine/Feminine Themes from Luther to Arendt* (New York, 1986), 55–70.

38. Ralph Waldo Emerson, *Nature*, in *The Portable Emerson*, ed. Carl Bode and Malcolm Cowley, new ed. (New York, 1981), 7–8.

39. Emerson, "Circles," in ibid., 232.

40. Emerson, "The Over-Soul," in ibid., 226. As Len Gougeon has pointed out, the interpretation of Emerson and his view of society has long suffered from a false dichotomy: either he must be seen as a fervent social-reform activist, as in Ralph Rusk's classic 1949 biography, or he must be regarded as a disengaged and quietistic loner, as in Stephen Whicher's 1953 biography, *Freedom and Fate*. Gougeon's study *Virtue's*

*Hero: Emerson, Antislavery, and Reform* (Athens, Ga., 1990) strongly asserts a version of the former view, which might seem to stand in opposition to the way Emerson is being characterized here. (See, in Gougeon, esp. 1–23, 337–48, 395–97.) Similarly, Mary Kupiec Cayton's *Emerson's Emergence: Self and Society in the Transformation of New England, 1800–1845* (Chapel Hill, 1989) shows how Emerson shunned the label of subjectivism (320–21). Yet Cayton's description of a larger social transition, exemplified in Emerson's person, from a "republican" to a "liberal" constellation of the self (or as she sometimes prefers to put it, to "bourgeois individualism") is very much in line with my own understanding of Emerson. Nothing in my rendering of Emerson is meant to preclude an interest in, and even a commitment to, social reform. My interest in Emerson revolves around a certain figuration of the self, and such a conception need carry no necessary disposition toward, or against, social reform.

41. Emerson, "Self-Reliance," in *Portable Emerson*, 141–42.

42. See, for example, the variant draft of "Why I Am So Clever," from Friedrich Nietzsche, *Ecce Homo*, trans. Walter Kaufmann (New York, 1967), 339: "Emerson with his essays has been a good friend and cheered me up even in black periods: he contains so much skepsis, so many 'possibilities' that even virtue achieves esprit in his writings. A unique case!"

43. Emerson, "The American Scholar," in *Portable Emerson*, 70.

44. Ibid., 52.

45. Emerson, *Society and Solitude*, in *Portable Emerson*, 393.

46. Emerson, "Self-Reliance," 142.

47. Emerson, "The American Scholar," 63.

48. Emerson, *Nature*, 19–25, esp 20.

49. Barbara Novak, *Nature and Culture: American Landscape and Painting, 1825–1875* (New York, 1980), 15.

50. Emerson, "The American Scholar," 71.

51. Emerson, "Historic Notes," in *Portable Emerson*, 594–95.

52. Whitman, "The Eighteenth Presidency," in *Complete Poetry and Collected Prose*, ed. Justin Kaplan (New York, 1982), 1324–25.

53. Whitman, "By Blue Ontario's Shores," in ibid., 475–76.

54. From preface to the 1855 edition of *Leaves of Grass*, in ibid., 14.

55. Whitman, *Leaves of Grass*, in ibid., 27–51.

56. Whitman, "Song of the Open Road," in ibid., 305.

57. M. Wyunn Thomas, "Walt Whitman and Mannahatta-New York," *American Quarterly* 34 (Fall 1982): 362–78.

58. See Paul Zweig, *Walt Whitman: The Making of the Poet* (New York, 1984), 262, where it is argued that *Leaves* is an "engine of self-making" for Whitman.

59. Whitman, *Leaves of Grass*, 214.

60. Whitman, "Crossing Brooklyn Ferry," in *Complete Poetry and Collected Prose*, 307–13.

61. Quentin Anderson, *The Imperial Self: An Essay in American Literary and Cultural History* (New York, 1971), 88–165.

62. Whitman, *Leaves of Grass*, 138.

63. Ibid., 57.

64. Ibid., 42–43.

65. Ibid., 48.

66. Ibid., 50.

67. Emerson, *Nature*, 7.

68. See James Bryce's discussion "The Fatalism of the Multitude," in *The American Commonwealth* (New York, 1888).

69. Tocqueville, *Democracy in America*, 2:92–93, argued that historians writing in democratic ages "deprive the people themselves of the power of modifying their own condition, and they subject them to an inflexible Providence or to some blind necessity."

70. Ibid., 310–11.

71. Haskell, "Capitalism and the Origins of the Humanitarian Sensibility," esp. pt. 2.

72. Thomas L. Haskell, "Persons as Uncaused Causes: John Stuart Mill, the Spirit of Capitalism, and the "Invention" of Formalism," in *The Culture of the Market: Historical Essays*, ed. Thomas L. Haskell and Richard F. Teichgraeber III (New York, in press).

73. Charles Grandison Finney, *Lectures on Revivals of Religion*, ed. William G. McLoughlin (Cambridge, Mass., 1960), 9–15; see also McLoughlin's *Modern Revivalism: Charles Grandison Finney to Billy Graham* (New York, 1959), 3–121; and Keith J. Hardman, *Charles Grandison Finney, 1792–1875: Revivalist and Reformer* (Syracuse, 1987).

74. For contemporary criticism of Finney and his New Measures, and more generally of mid-century American evangelicalism, see the works of Mercersburg theologians John Williamson Nevin, *The Anxious Bench* (1843); and Philip Schaff, *The Principle of Protestantism* (Chambersburg, Pa., 1845; reprint, New York, 1987); as well as James Hastings Nichols, *Romanticism in American Theology: Nevin and Schaff at Mercersburg* (Chicago, 1961).

75. An excellent discussion of this point is in R. Jackson Wilson, *In Quest of Community: Social Philosophy in the United States, 1860–1920* (New York, 1968), 1–31.

76. Whitman, *Leaves of Grass*, 28, 55.

77. Edward Shils, *The Intellectuals and the Powers, and Other Essays* (Chicago, 1972), 3–22, 154–95.

78. Whitman, *Leaves of Grass*, 27.

79. Emerson, "The Poet," in *Portable Emerson*, 258.

80. Whitman, *Leaves of Grass*, 44.

81. Ibid., 5–8.

82. Whitman, *Democratic Vistas*, in *Complete Poetry and Collected Prose*, 937, 988–90.

83. Zweig, *Walt Whitman*, 321.

84. Drew Gilpin Faust, *A Sacred Circle: The Dilemma of the Intellectual in the Old South, 1840–1860* (Baltimore, 1977).

85. Whitman, *Democratic Vistas*, 991.

86. Whitman, *Leaves of Grass*, 89.

87. Ibid., 611.

88. Yet it is also true that Whitman was very concerned with, and felt responsible for, his own family. See Zweig, *Walt Whitman*, 38–39.

89. Whitman, *Leaves of Grass*, 281.

90. Ibid., 248.

91. Ibid., 265.

92. Ibid., 280.

93. Emory Holloway, ed., *The Uncollected Prose and Poetry of Walt Whitman*, 2 vols. (Garden City, N.J., 1921), 2:95–96. "164" almost certainly stands for the sixteenth and the fourth letters of the alphabet: P and D, for Peter Doyle.

94. Whitman, "I Saw in Louisiana a Live-Oak Growing," in *Complete Poetry and Collected Prose*, 279.

95. Whitman, "A Noiseless Patient Spider," in ibid., 564.

96. Whitman, *Leaves of Grass*, 30. See also Holloway, *Uncollected Prose and Poetry*, 2:66: "I cannot understand the mystery: but I am always conscious of myself as two (as my soul and I)." See C. G. Jung, *Two Essays in Analytical Psychology*, trans. R. F. C. Hull (Princeton, 1966), 188–211; and the treatment of this issue in Martin Bickman, *American Romantic Psychology: Emerson, Poe, Whitman, Dickinson, Melville* (Dallas, 1988).

97. Fredson Bowers, ed., *Whitman's Manuscripts: "Leaves of Grass" (1860)* (Chicago, 1955), 68.

98. Whitman, "As I Ebb'd with the Ocean of Life," in *Complete Poetry and Collected Prose*, 395.

99. Zweig, *Walt Whitman*, 301, offers this speculation.

100. Whitman, "As I Ebb'd with the Ocean of Life," 394–95.

101. Whitman, "Out of the Cradle Endlessly Rocking," in *Complete Poetry and Collected Prose*, 388–94. The version of the poem that appeared in the 1860 edition of the *Leaves* differs from the *Saturday Press* version, and these differ in turn from the 1881 edition, which is used in the Library of America volume, which I employ here. See R. W. B. Lewis, ed. *The Presence of Walt Whitman* (New York, 1965), 1–109, 190–205, for examination of these variant texts. The differences are significant, for our purposes, in that the boy's cry is even more tortured in the 1860 edition, as in the following words, deleted from the later versions:

O if I am to have so much, let me have more!
O a word! O what is my destination!
O I fear it is henceforth chaos!
O how joys, dreads, convolutions, human shapes, and all shapes, spring as from graves around me!
O phantoms! you cover all the land, and all the sea!
O I cannot see in the dimness whether you smile or frown upon me!
O vapor, a look, a word! O well-beloved!
O you dear women's and men's phantoms!

102. Whitman, *Specimen Days*, 706.

103. Charles B. Strozier, *Lincoln's Quest for Union: Public and Private Meanings* (New York, 1982), makes a similar argument for the conflation of the public and the private, the political and the psychological, in Lincoln's political career.

104. *The Collected Writings of Walt Whitman: The Correspondence*, ed. Edwin H. Miller, 6 vols. (New York, 1961–77), 1:77.

105. Ibid., 122.

106. Whitman, *Leaves of Grass*, 610.

107. Ibid., 165.

108. Ibid., 350.

109. Whitman, "By Blue Ontario's Shore," 480.

110. Whitman, "Origins of Attempted Secession," in *Complete Poetry and Collected Prose*, 994. Again see Strozier, *Lincoln's Quest*, for a parallel aspect of the life of Lincoln.

111. Tocqueville, *Democracy in America*, 2:116.

112. Whitman, *Complete Poetry and Collected Prose*, 661.


CHAPTER THREE

1. Mary Dearing, *Veterans in Politics* (Baton Rouge, 1952); and Stuart Charles McConnell, "A Social History of the Grand Army of the Republic, 1867–1900" (Ph.D. diss., Johns Hopkins University, 1987).

2. Elizabeth Sadler, "One Book's Influence: Edward Bellamy's *Looking Backward*," *New England Quarterly* 17 (December 1944): 530–55. Also see John Hope Franklin, "Edward Bellamy and the Nationalist Movement," *New England Quarterly* 11 (December 1938): 739–72; and Kenneth M. Roemer, "Contexts and Texts: The Influence of *Looking Backward*," *Centennial Review* 27 (Summer 1983): 204–23. The quotation comes from R. Jackson Wilson's extremely insightful, and characteristically irreverent, introduction to the Modern Library edition of *Looking Backward* (New York, 1982), vii–xxxiv. See also Sylvia Bowman et al., *Edward Bellamy Abroad: An American Prophet's Influence* (New York, 1962), which catalogues the international influence of Bellamy and particularly of *Looking Backward*.

3. W. Arthur Boggs, "*Looking Backward* at the Utopian Novel, 1888–1900," *Bulletin of the New York Public Library* 64 (June 1960): 329–36.

4. Everett W. MacNair, *Edward Bellamy and the Nationalist Movement, 1889–1894: A Research Study of Edward Bellamy's Work as a Social Reformer* (Milwaukee, 1957); Arthur Lipow, *Authoritarian Socialism in America: Edward Bellamy and the Nationalist Movement* (Berkeley, 1982); and Franklin, "Bellamy and the Nationalist Movement."

5. Edward Bellamy, "Why I Wrote 'Looking Backward,'" in *Edward Bellamy Speaks Again! Articles, Public Addresses, Letters*, 2d ed. (Chicago, 1938), 199.

6. Ibid., 200–201.

7. Ibid., 202–3. Bellamy excepted, however, such "laggard" countries as Turkey, whose backwardness would probably retard the development of Bellamy's original "homogeneous world-wide social system" until 3000.

8. Autobiographical fragment, Edward Bellamy MSS, Houghton Library, Harvard University, Cambridge, Mass., cited in John L. Thomas, *Alternative America: Henry George, Edward Bellamy, Henry Demarest Lloyd and the Adversary Tradition* (Cambridge, Mass., 1983), 29.

9. Edward Bellamy, "The Religion of Solidarity," in *Edward Bellamy: Selected Writings on Religion and Society*, ed. Joseph Schiffman (New York, 1955), 26.

10. Ibid., 3–11.

11. Ibid., 14–23.

12. Sylvia E. Bowman, *The Year 2000: A Critical Biography of Edward Bellamy* (New York, 1958), 16–18.

13. Ibid., 4; George Fredrickson, *The Inner Civil War: Northern Intellectuals and the Crisis of the Union* (New York, 1965), 225.

14. Bellamy, "The Religion of Solidarity," 21.

15. Arthur Morgan, *Edward Bellamy* (New York, 1944), 145; and Bowman, *The Year 2000*, 4.

16. Edward Bellamy, "An Echo at Antietam," in *The Blindman's World and Other Stories* (Boston, 1898; reprint, New York, 1968), 42.

17. Ibid., 46.

18. Ibid., 54–58.

19. See discussion of this in Wilson's introduction to Bellamy, *Looking Backward*, xx–xxi.

20. Bowman, *The Year 2000*, 21.

21. Edward Bellamy, "How I Wrote 'Looking Backward,'" in *Edward Bellamy Speaks Again!*, 217.

22. It is a mystery why Bellamy did this. There is no clear consensus among Bellamy's biographers as to the precise motives behind his sudden abandonment of a legal career. The reason frequently given is that Bellamy's first case required him to press for the eviction of a widow, and in a fit of disgust and self-loathing he decided to close his practice immediately. See, e.g., Bowman, *The Year 2000*, 37. Apparently this story originated with Bellamy himself, who related it to his *New Nation* editorial colleague Mason Green, whose unpublished biographical account of Bellamy on deposit at the Houghton Library was in turn the sole source for Bowman's statement. But see Wilson, in Bellamy, *Looking Backward*, xviii, who is extremely skeptical about the veracity of this story—although it must be pointed out that Wilson cites no specific reason for disbelieving it. Surely he is right, however, to point out that the sudden abandonment of this career before it had even properly begun probably had more to do with the promptings of Bellamy's own psyche than with any external conditions that might be cited as pretexts for his actions.

23. Bowman, *The Year 2000*, 127–31.

24. The eighty-seven pages of Bellamy's handwritten and unpublished "Story of Eliot Carson" are in a notebook on deposit in the Bellamy Collection, MS45M–552(11), Houghton Library. See Wilson, in Bellamy, *Looking Backward*, xxvii, for a brilliant critical analysis of it; also see the excerpts in Morgan, *Edward Bellamy*, 87–89; and Bowman, *The Year 2000*, 33–36.

25. [Edward Bellamy], *Six to One: A Nantucket Idyl* (New York, 1878).

26. Bellamy, *Blindman's World*, 129–56.

27. Ibid., 104–28.

28. Edward Bellamy, *Dr. Heidenhoff's Process* (New York, 1880).

29. Bellamy, *Blindman's World*, 1–29, esp. 16–18.

30. On the concept of *puer aeternus*, see Marie-Louise von Frantz, *Puer Aeternus*, 2d ed. (Santa Monica, 1981); and James Hillman, *Puer Papers* (Dallas, 1979).

31. Edward Bellamy, *The Duke of Stockbridge: A Romance of Shays's Rebellion*, ed. Joseph Schiffman (Cambridge, Mass., 1962). For a sense of the interpretations Bellamy was overturning, see two classic historical works by his contemporaries: John Bach

McMaster, *A History of the People of the United States* (New York, 1885), 1:280–81; and John Fiske, *The Critical Period of American History* (Boston, 1888), 179–86. For the more modern reinterpretation, see David P. Szatmay, *Shays' Rebellion: The Making of an Agrarian Insurrection* (Amherst, Mass., 1980); and of less recent vintage, Robert J. Taylor, *Western Massachusetts in the Revolution* (Providence, R.I., 1954); and Marion L. Starkey, *A Little Rebellion* (New York, 1955). For a novelistic imitation of *The Duke of Stockbridge*, see George Robert Russell Rivers, *Captain Shays, a Populist of 1786* (Boston, 1897).

32. Bowman, *The Year 2000*, 68–70. It is revealing to note that one of Bellamy's most passionate infatuations was with Julia Putnam Cross, a first cousin, whom he could not have married due to family objections.

33. Bellamy, "How I Wrote 'Looking Backward,'" 222–23.

34. Bowman, *The Year 2000*, 73.

35. Paul Avrich, *The Haymarket Tragedy* (Princeton, 1984).

36. See, for example, chapter 1 of *Looking Backward* (New York, 1960), 29–32. Pagination used hereinafter refers to the New American Library Signet edition.

37. James Hillman, *Re-Visioning Psychology* (New York, 1975), esp. 115–23; and Robert Romanyshyn, *Psychological Life: From Science to Metaphor* (Austin, 1982). The latter's phenomenological and historical approach to psychological life, indebted to the little-known work of the Dutch psychologist J. H. van den Berg, deserves to be more widely recognized among intellectual and cultural historians.

38. Bellamy, "Why I Wrote 'Looking Backward,'" 202.

39. Bellamy, *Looking Backward*, 36.

40. Ibid., 45.

41. Ibid., 53.

42. Ibid., 132.

43. Ibid., 165.

44. Ibid., 77.

45. See Sylvester Baxter's essay, "Why the Name Nationalism?," from *The Nationalist*, July 1890, reprinted in *Edward Bellamy Speaks Again!*, 29–32.

46. For discussion of these and their possible influence on Bellamy, see Bowman, *The Year 2000*, 94–118.

47. Bellamy, *Looking Backward*, 171.

48. Ibid., 65–66.

49. Ibid., 200–201.

50. Ibid., 203–14.

51. Ibid., 215.

52. Ibid., 218–19.

53. Ibid., 215.

54. Cf. Matt. 5:10.

55. See, for example, 1 Cor. 15:22, Rom. 14:08, and Gal. 2:20.

56. Matt. 7:13–14.

57. Walter Rauschenbusch, *Christianity and the Social Crisis* (New York, 1907), is the representative text in this respect; see esp. 422.

58. Louis Filler, "Edward Bellamy and the Spiritual Unrest," *American Journal of Economics and Sociology* 8 (April 1949): 239–49.

59. See Bellamy, *Edward Bellamy Speaks Again!*, 132–33, where he talks about Brook Farm. "In a broad sense of the word the Nationalist movement did arise fifty years ago, for in spirit if not in form it may be said to date back to the forties. Those who are not familiar with the history of the extraordinary wave of socialistic enthusiasm which swept over the United States at that period and led to the Brook Farm Colony and a score of phalansteries for communistic experiments, have missed one of the most picturesque chapters of American history." That these movements did not enjoy more success is attributed by Bellamy—and here, too, he anticipates the opinions of more recent scholars—to the preeminence of the struggle to abolish slavery, which came to monopolize the attention of leading reformers.

60. See the discussion of Bellamy in Paul F. Boller, Jr., *Freedom and Fate in American Thought: From Edwards to Dewey* (Dallas, 1978), 133–58; and Michael Fellman, *The Unbounded Frame: Freedom and Community in Nineteenth-Century Utopianism* (Westport, Conn., 1973).

61. Bellamy, *Looking Backward*, 189.

62. Ibid., 194.

63. Ibid., 191.

64. Ibid., 184.

65. Ibid., 183.

66. Ibid., 192–93.

67. J. Hector St. John de Crèvecoeur, *Letters from an American Farmer* (New York, 1981), 71.

68. Thomas L. Haskell, *The Emergence of Professional Social Science: The American Social Science Association and the Nineteenth-Century Crisis of Authority* (Urbana, 1977), 24–47, 58 (including n. 28). In *Looking Backward*, Dr. Leete heaps contempt upon the notion of the independent individual: "Who is capable of self-support?" he asked sardonically. "There is no such thing in a civilized society as self-support. . . . As men grow more civilized, and the subdividion of occupations and services is carried out, a complex mutual dependence becomes the universal rule. Every man . . . is a member of a vast industrial partnership, as large as the nation, as large as humanity" (98).

69. Haskell, *The Emergence of Professional Social Science*, 176.

70. Kenneth Lockridge, *A New England Town: The First Hundred Years* (New York, 1970); George L. Haskins, *Law and Authority in Early Massachusetts* (Chapel Hill, 1960), 84.

CHAPTER FOUR

1. Kenneth S. Lynn, *Mark Twain and Southwestern Humor* (Boston, 1959), esp. 230–31, 246.

2. Mark Twain, *The Mysterious Stranger and Other Stories* (New York, 1922), 137–40. The unsuspecting reader should be aware of the controversy surrounding this story, which was posthumously constructed by Albert Bigelow Paine from three unfinished manuscripts. In William M. Gibson, ed., *Mark Twain's Mysterious Stranger Manuscripts* (Berkeley, 1969), the charge is made that Paine's text was nothing more than an "editorial fraud," and the three manuscripts are presented in original form.

Whatever may be the case, virtually the same words here cited appear in the Gibson book as well (cf. 405).

3. See John F. Kasson, *Civilizing the Machine: Technology and Republican Values, 1776–1900* (New York, 1976), 183–234, for a study of a related conflict, the tension between republicanism and industrial society, in both Bellamy and Twain.

4. Ray Allen Billington, *Frederick Jackson Turner: Historian, Scholar, Teacher* (New York, 1973), 124–31.

5. Ibid.

6. George Rogers Taylor, ed., *The Turner Thesis: Concerning the Role of the Frontier in American History*, 3d ed. (Boston, 1972), is a good introduction to the debates, with a helpful bibliography. Also see Ray Allen Billington, *The Genesis of the Frontier Thesis: A Study in Historical Creativity* (San Marino, 1971); Per Sveaas Andersen, *Westward Is the Course of Empire: A Study in the Shaping of an American Idea* (Oslo, 1956); Lee Benson, *Turner and Beard: American Historical Writing Reconsidered* (Glencoe, Ill., 1968); David W. Noble, *Historians against History: The Frontier Thesis and the National Covenant in American Historical Writing since 1830* (Minneapolis, 1965); and Richard Hofstadter, *The Progressive Historians: Turner, Beard, Parrington* (New York, 1968). Perhaps the best succinct recent reconsideration of Turner within the larger context of a reinterpretation of the meaning of the American West is an elegant and stimulating work of historical synthesis, Patricia Nelson Limerick, *The Legacy of Conquest: The Unbroken Past of the American West* (New York, 1986), esp. 20–32; see also its useful selective bibliography for additional relevant literature.

7. Frederick Jackson Turner, "The Problem of the West," *Atlantic Monthly*, September 1896, 297.

8. Turner's essay "The Significance of the Frontier" appears in the *Annual Report for 1893* of the American Historical Association, 199–227. I have used the more readily available text in Ray Allen Billington, ed., *Frontier and Section: Selected Essays of Frederick Jackson Turner* (Englewood Cliffs, 1961), 62.

9. Limerick, *Legacy of Conquest*, 20.

10. Turner, "The Significance of the Frontier," 56: "It was this nationalizing tendency of the West that transformed the democracy of Jefferson into the national republicanism of Monroe and the democracy of Andrew Jackson. The West . . . had a solidarity of its own with national tendencies. On the tide of the Father of Waters, North and South met and mingled into a nation. . . . Slavery was a sectional trait that would not down, but in the West it could not remain sectional. It was the greatest of frontiersmen who declared: 'I believe this Government can not endure permanently half slave and half free. It will become all of one thing or all of the other.'"

11. Ibid., 38.

12. Ibid., 61.

13. Ibid.

14. Ibid., 39.

15. Billington, *Frederick Jackson Turner*, 454–56.

16. Turner, "The Significance of the Frontier," 39.

17. Ibid., 38–39, 56–62.

18. Ibid., 43.

19. Ibid., 61–62.

20. See Walter Prescott Webb, *The Great Frontier* (Boston, 1952). For a suggestive historical treatment of the Turner thesis since World War II, as mediated by Walter Prescott Webb, adapted by NASA chief (and "Big Operator") James Webb (no relation), and applied to the rationale for space exploration, see Walter A. McDougall, *The Heavens and the Earth: A Political History of the Space Age* (New York, 1985), esp. 387–88.

21. Turner, "The Significance of the Frontier," 58.

22. The relentless attacks of Republican stalwarts against the University of Wisconsin during Van Hise's presidency played an important role in dislodging Turner from his position in the beloved institution. See Billington, *Frederick Jackson Turner*, 281–307.

23. Herbert Hoover, *American Individualism* ([ca.1922]; reprint, Garden City, N.J., 1934); Hoover greatly admired Turner's frontier essay. See Billington, *Frederick Jackson Turner*, 438–42.

24. On Hoover, in addition to George Nash's monumental multivolume biography and Joan Hoff-Wilson's *Herbert Hoover: Forgotten Progressive* (New York, 1975), see Ellis Hawley, *The Great War and the Search for Order: A History of the American People and Their Institutions, 1917–1933* (New York, 1979); Ellis Hawley, ed., *Herbert Hoover as Secretary of Commerce: Studies in New Era Thought and Practice* (Iowa City, 1981); and Lee Nash, ed., *Understanding Herbert Hoover: Ten Perspectives* (Stanford, 1987), esp. the contributions by George Nash and Ellis Hawley.

25. In a period of overcommitment in his own life, Max Farrand quipped to Ferris Greenslet in 1922 that "I feel as if I should have to do as Turner threatened at one time, namely, to declare intellectual bankruptcy"; cited in Michael Kammen, "Vanitas and the Historian's Vocation," *Reviews in American History* 10 (December 1982): 16.

26. Billington, *Frederick Jackson Turner*, 364–419.

27. Hofstadter, *The Progressive Historians*, 114.

28. Cited in Billington, *Frederick Jackson Turner*, 385.

29. Van Wyck Brooks, *The Ordeal of Mark Twain* (New York, 1920).

30. Frederick Jackson Turner, "The West and American Ideals," *Washington Historical Quarterly* 5 (October 1914): 243–57, reprinted in Billington, *Frontier and Section*, 98–114. The essay was originally a commencement address delivered at the University of Washington on June 17, 1914.

31. W. J. Rolfe, ed., *Complete Poetical Words of Tennyson*, Cambridge ed. (Boston, 1898), 221–23.

32. Frederick Jackson Turner, "The Significance of the Section in American History," in Billington, *Frontier and Section*, 124.

33. Frederick Jackson Turner, "Sections and Nation," in ibid., 136–37.

34. Turner, "The Significance of the Section," 126.

35. One could hardly point to a better example of the continuing power of regional distinctiveness than that of the South, as one finds it described, for example, in the writings of Chapel Hill sociologist John Shelton Reed; see his *The Enduring South*, among other works. Such work seems generally to have proceeded from the critique of conceptions of America as a homogeneous "mass society," however, rather than from neo-Turnerian notions of persistent sectionalism.

36. See Billington, *Frederick Jackson Turner*, 468.

37. Turner, "The Significance of the Section," 131.

38. I am indebted to David Shi for pointing out James's fondness for porch sleeping. This aspect of James's nature is well discussed in George Cotkin, *William James, Public Philosopher* (Baltimore, 1990), esp. 95–122.

39. On the problematic character of the idea of the closing of the frontier, see Limerick, *Legacy of Conquest*, 23–26.

40. David Mogen et al., *The Frontier Experience and the American Dream: Essays on American Literature* (College Station, Tex., 1990), esp. Mogen's essay "The Frontier Archetype and the Myth of America," 15–30; also see David W. Noble, *The Eternal Adam and the New World Garden* (New York, 1968); Edwin Fussell, *Frontier: American Literature and the American West* (Princeton, 1966); and, of course, Henry Nash Smith's *Virgin Land* (Cambridge, Mass., 1950). On Wister, see the splendid biographical sketch in John Lukacs, *Philadelphia: Patricians and Philistines, 1900–1950* (New York, 1981), 240–57, including the verso photograph of Wister on 240.

41. Warren Susman, "The Frontier Thesis and the American Intellectual," in *Culture as History: The Transformation of American Society in the Twentieth Century* (New York, 1984), 27–38.

42. Henry Steele Commager, ed., *Lester Frank Ward and the Welfare State* (Indianapolis, 1967), 130–31. Such language supports Dorothy Ross's contention, in her *Origins of American Social Science* (New York, 1991), that the notion of American exceptionalism was central to the early practitioners of American social science.

43. Lester Frank Ward, *The Psychic Factors of Civilization*, 2d ed. (Boston, 1906), 323–24.

44. Clifford H. Scott, *Lester Frank Ward* (Boston, 1976), 33. This is in sharp contrast to the claim of Henry Steele Commager, *The American Mind: An Interpretation of American Thought and Character since the 1880s* (New Haven, 1950), 214.

45. Commager, *The American Mind*, 199–226; see also Sidney Fine, *Laissez Faire and the General-Welfare State: A Study of Conflict in American Thought, 1865–1901* (Ann Arbor, 1956), 252–88; and a cloyingly adoring but still-indispensable study of Ward, Samuel Chugerman, *Lester F. Ward, the American Aristotle: A Summary and Interpretation of His Sociology* (Durham, N.C., 1939), esp. 302–48.

46. Burton J. Bledstein, *The Culture of Professionalism: The Middle Class and the Development of Higher Education in America* (New York, 1976), 46–128. On Ward's being a founder without heirs, see Robert Bannister's careful study of Ward in *Sociology and Scientism: The American Quest for Objectivity, 1880–1940* (Chapel Hill, 1987), 13–31.

47. Lester Frank Ward, *Dynamic Sociology*, 2 vols. (New York, 1883), 2:443.

48. Lester Frank Ward, *Glimpses of the Cosmos*, 6 vols. (New York, 1913–18), 1:lxvi.

49. Ibid.

50. Bernhard J. Stern, ed., *Young Ward's Diary: A Human and Eager Record of the Years Between 1860 and 1870 as They Were Lived in the Vicinity of the Little Town of Towanda, Pennsylvania; in the Field as a Rank and File Soldier in the Union Army; and Later in the Nation's Capital, by Lester Ward Who became the First Great Sociologist This Country Produced* (New York, 1935). On Byrd, see Lynn, *Mark Twain and Southwestern Humor*, 3–22; and Kenneth A. Lockridge, *The Diary, and Life, of William Byrd II of Virginia, 1674–1744* (Chapel Hill, 1987).

51. Stern, *Young Ward's Diary*, 166.

52. Ibid., 127 (January 2, 1864).

53. Ibid., 166. See also his comments on 104.

54. Ibid., 167.

55. On Ward's relationship with Powell, see Ross, *Origins of American Social Science*, 90. On Powell, see Wallace Stegner, *Beyond the Hundredth Meridian: John Wesley Powell and the Second Opening of the West* (Boston, 1954); Paul Meadow, *John Wesley Powell: Frontiersman of Science* (Lincoln, Neb., 1952); and William Culp Darrah, *Powell of the Colorado* (Princeton, 1951).

56. Ward, *Dynamic Sociology*, 1:142. See the rather condescending letter from Spencer in Ward, *Glimpses*, 3:214.

57. Lester Frank Ward, *Pure Sociology: A Treatise on the Origin and Spontaneous Development of Society* (Boston, 1906), 20.

58. Ward, *Psychic Factors*, 16; Ross, *Origins of American Social Science*, 90–93.

59. Ibid., 286.

60. Ward, *Dynamic Sociology*, 1:57–58.

61. Ibid., 1:60–61. See also Bannister, *Sociology and Scientism*, 13.

62. Ward, *Psychic Factors*, 325–31.

63. Ward, *Dynamic Sociology*, 2:108.

64. Ibid., 2:147; Ward, *Psychic Factors*, 74.

65. Lester Frank Ward, *Applied Sociology: A Treatise on the Conscious Improvement of Society by Society* (Boston, 1906), 72–73.

66. Ward, *Psychic Factors*, 75–80.

67. Ward, *Dynamic Sociology*, 1:468–69.

68. Matthew Arnold, *Poems* (New York, 1886), 211–12.

69. Lester Frank Ward, *Outlines of Sociology* (New York, 1898), 258.

70. Ward, *Psychic Factors*, 75–80.

71. Ross, *Origins of American Social Science*, 90–91.

72. Ward, *Psychic Factors*, 99–101.

73. Ward, *Glimpses*, 6:62–63. On Ward's view of man's not being social by nature, see Ward, *Outlines*, 90–91.

74. Ward, *Psychic Factors*, 299.

75. Ibid., 316.

76. Ibid., 315.

77. See Chugerman, *American Aristotle*, 473–74.

78. Ward, *Dynamic Sociology*, 2:575.

79. See Ward's use of Helvetius in *Psychic Factors*, 447.

80. Ward, *Outlines*, 292–93.

81. Ward, *Applied Sociology*, 14–17.

82. Scott, *Lester Frank Ward*, 23–24.

83. Even he acknowledged that the new order would be "dynamic"; see Ward, *Psychic Factors*, 99–101.

84. From ibid.: "Psychology is the physics of the mind, and its phenomena are as uniform and its laws as exact as are those of the physics of the inorganic world. If this were not so it would not be a science, and there would be no use in attempting to treat it at all" (94).

"The central and all-important truth toward which all that has been said thus far in this work has tended, is that *desire is a true natural force*. There is not the least figurativeness, metaphor, or analogy in this formula. It is the expression of a literal truth. The psychic force conforms to all the established criteria of the nature of a force and is capable of an unlimited number and variety of concrete illustrations. It obeys the Newtonian laws of motion. An animal body like a physical body, acted upon by a single force will move in a straight line in the direction in which that force acts" (34).

85. Ibid., 310.

86. Ibid., 311.

87. Ward, *Applied Sociology*, 275–76; and Ward, *Dynamic Sociology*, 2:583–84.

88. Ward, *Glimpses*, 5:270–81.

89. I am very much indebted to Bannister, *Sociology and Scientism*, esp. 26, for my understanding of these features of Ward's thought. See also, in this context, Ward, *Applied Sociology*, 339: "The goal . . . would be a state of society in which no one should be obliged to do anything that is in any way distasteful to him, and in which every act should be so agreeable that he will do it from personal preference."

90. See the excellent discussion of Hegel's place in distinctively German social thought in Leonard Krieger, *The German Idea of Freedom: The History of a Political Tradition* (Boston, 1957). Krieger underlines the corporate nature of German conceptions of freedom; individual rights were "absorbed into corporations and the national framework which were also expressions of the moral power of the state." Hegel's system was, he concluded, a "system for the binding of individualism."

91. See Walt Whitman, "Carlyle from American Points of View," in *Complete Poetry and Collected Prose*, ed. Justin Kaplan (New York, 1982), 890–99.

92. Whitman, "Origins of Attempted Secession," in ibid., 994–1000.

93. Denton J. Snider, *The St. Louis Movement in Philosophy, Literature, Education, Psychology, with Chapters of Autobiography* (St. Louis, 1920), 9–10.

94. Harvey Gates Townsend, "The Political Philosophy of Hegel in a Frontier Society," in *William Torrey Harris, 1835–1935*, ed. Edward L. Schaub (Chicago, 1936), 76; Neil Gerard McCluskey, *Public Schools and Moral Education: The Influence of Horace Mann, William Torrey Harris, and John Dewey* (New York, 1958), 109.

95. Denton J. Snider, *Abraham Lincoln* (St. Louis, 1908), and *The American Ten Years' War* (St. Louis, 1906), 50–53.

96. Snider, *The St. Louis Movement*, 27–29; Henry A. Pochmann, *New England Transcendentalism and St. Louis Hegelianism: Phases in the History of American Idealism* (Philadelphia, 1948), 11–14.

97. Michael Fellman, *Inside War: The Guerrilla Conflict in Missouri during the American Civil War* (New York, 1989).

98. Kurt F. Leidecker, *Yankee Teacher: The Life of William Torrey Harris* (New York, 1946), 197–211.

99. McCluskey, *Public Schools and Moral Education*, 111.

100. Denton J. Snider, *The State* (St. Louis, n.d.); and Robert Clifton Whittemore, "Hegel in St. Louis," in *Makers of the American Mind* (New York, 1964), 281.

101. Snider, *The State*, 405.

102. Daniel T. Rodgers, *Contested Truths: Keywords in American Politics since Independence* (New York, 1987), 166.

103. John W. Burgess, *Reminiscences of an American Scholar: The Beginnings of Columbia University* (New York, 1934), 3–4.

104. Ibid., 10–11.

105. Ibid., 21–22.

106. Ibid., 28–29.

107. Ibid., 32.

108. Ibid., 96–97.

109. Bernard Edward Brown, *American Conservatives: The Political Thought of Francis Lieber and John W. Burgess* (New York, 1951), 107; Ross, *Origins of American Social Science*, 71–77.

110. Besides the books cited above, notable works by John W. Burgess include *Political Science and Comparative Constitutional Law*, 2 vols. (Boston, 1893); *The Civil War and the Constitution, 1859–1865*, 2 vols. (New York, 1901); *The Reconciliation of Government with Liberty* (New York, 1915); *Recent Changes in American Constitutional Theory* (New York, 1923); *The Sanctity of Law: Wherein Does It Consist?* (Boston, 1927); and *The Foundations of Political Science* (New York, 1933).

111. Burgess, *Political Science and Comparative Constitutional Law*, 1:50–56, and *Reminiscences*, 250–51.

112. Burgess, *Political Science and Comparative Constitutional Law*, 1:67.

113. Ibid., 1:52–54.

114. Ibid., 1:56.

115. See Burgess, *Reminiscences*, 51–56, on the Amherst background of his idealism, and see 86–137 for the German years.

116. The terms *formalist* and *antiformalist* derive from Morton White, *Social Thought in America: The Revolt against Formalism* (Boston, 1949), esp. 11–31.

117. Burgess, *Political Science and Comparative Constitutional Law*, 1:98–108.

118. Brown, *American Conservatives*, 115; Burgess, *Political Science and Comparative Constitutional Law*, 1:98–101, 105, 107–8, 230.

119. Burgess, *The Civil War and the Constitution*, 1:134–35.

120. See Burgess, *Political Science and Comparative Constitutional Law*, 1:100: "From the first moment of its existence there was something more upon this side of the Atlantic than thirteen local governments. There was a sovereignty, a state; not in idea simply or upon paper, but in fact and in organization. The revolution was an accomplished fact before the declaration of 1776, and so was independence. The act of the 4th of July was a notification to the world of *faits accomplis*. A nation and a state did not spring into existence through that declaration, as dramatic publicists are wont to express it. Nations and states do not spring into existence."

121. Ibid., 59–62.

122. Ibid., 88, 175–76.

123. Ibid., 89.

124. Bernard Crick, *The American Science of Politics: Its Origins and Conditions* (Berkeley, 1964), 97–99; Rodgers, *Contested Truths*, 164–65. Small wonder Burgess opposed the annexation of the Philippines; see Robert Beisner, *Twelve against Empire: The Anti-Imperialists, 1898–1900* (Chicago, 1968), for discussion of that brand of racially based opposition.

125. Burgess, *Political Science and Comparative Constitutional Law*, 1:56.

126. For Burgess's distinction between the concept of the state and the idea of the state, see *Political Science and Comparative Constitutional Law*, 1:49–58.

127. Burgess, *Reconciliation of Government with Liberty*, 376.

128. Burgess, *Political Science and Comparative Constitutional Law*, 2:365.

129. Burgess, *Reminiscences*, 254.

130. Ibid., 321.

131. Burgess, *Recent Changes in American Constitutional Theory*, 1–2.

132. See Burgess, *Reminiscences*, 254–55, for Burgess's paraphrase of his own argument in *Political Science and Comparative Constitutional Law*; see p. 47: "Finally, we must conclude, from the manifest mission of the Teutonic nations, that interference in the affairs of populations not wholly barbaric, which have made some progress in state organization, but which manifest incapacity to solve the problem of political civilization with any degree of completeness, is a justifiable policy. No one can question that it is in the interest of the world's civilization that law and order and the true liberty consistent therewith shall reign everywhere upon the globe. A permanent inability on the part of any state or semi-state to secure this status is a threat to civilization everywhere. Both for the sake of the half-barbarous state and in the interest of the rest of the world, a state or states, endowed with capacity for political organization, may righteously assume sovereignty over, and undertake to create state order for, such a politically incompetent population. . . . They are under no obligation to await invitation from those claiming power and government in the inefficient organization, nor from those subject to the same. The civilized states themselves are the best organs which have yet appeared in the history of the world for determining the proper time and occasion for intervening in the affairs of unorganized or insufficiently organized populations, for the execution of their great world-duty."

133. Burgess, *Foundations of Political Science*, 45–49.

134. Burgess, *Reminiscences*, 29, 255–57.

135. Ibid., 29.

136. Ibid., 245–57.

137. See Woodrow Wilson, "A System of Political Science and Constitutional Law," in *The Public Papers of Woodrow Wilson*, ed. Ray Stannard Baker and William E. Dodd, 6 vols. (New York, 1925), 1:96.

138. Crick, *The American Science of Politics*, 97.

139. Burgess, *Political Science and Comparative Constitutional Law*, 1:66–67; Brown, *American Conservatives*, 136.

140. Rodgers, *Contested Truths*, 165.


CHAPTER FIVE

1. Morton White, *Social Thought in America: The Revolt against Formalism* (Boston, 1949); for a critical reassessment, see James T. Kloppenberg, "Morton White's *Social Thought in America*," *Reviews in American History* 15 (September 1987): 507–19.

2. Hilary Putnam, *The Many Faces of Realism* (La Salle, Ill., 1987), 70.

3. James Kloppenberg, *Uncertain Victory: Social Democracy and Progressivism in European and American Thought, 1870–1920* (New York, 1986), 3–195; for a lucid

treatment of pragmatist epistemology, see "William James and the Culture of Inquiry" and "The Problem of Pragmatism in American History," in David Hollinger, *In the American Province: Studies in the History and Historiography of Ideas* (Bloomington, Ind., 1985), 3–43.

4. Daniel J. Wilson, *Science, Community, and the Transformation of American Philosophy, 1860–1930* (Chicago, 1990); Thomas L. Haskell, *The Emergence of Professional Social Science: The American Social Science Association and the Nineteenth-Century Crisis of Authority* (Urbana, 1977); Thomas L. Haskell, ed., *The Authority of Experts: Studies in History and Theory* (Bloomington, Ind., 1984); Alexandra Oleson and John Voss, eds., *The Organization of Knowledge in Modern America, 1860–1920* (Baltimore, 1979).

5. From Henry James, ed., *The Letters of William James*, 2 vols. (Boston, 1920), 2:164. See also Bruce Kuklick, *The Rise of American Philosophy: Cambridge, Massachusetts, 1860–1930* (New Haven, 1977).

6. Wilson, *Science, Community, and the Transformation of American Philosophy*, 1–11.

7. See the chapter entitled "Interests" in Daniel T. Rodgers, *Contested Truths: Keywords in American Politics since Independence* (New York, 1987), 176–211.

8. An excellent brief overview of the tangled interpretive problems in defining Progressivism is Daniel Rodgers, "In Search of Progressivism," *Reviews in American History* 10 (December 1982): 113–32.

9. See the account of Ely offered in Dorothy Ross, *The Origins of American Social Science* (New York, 1991), esp. 110–13.

10. Richard T. Ely, *The Social Aspect of Christianity and Other Essays* (New York, 1889), 122. See Benjamin G. Rader, *The Academic Mind and Reform: The Influence of Richard T. Ely* (Lexington, Ky., 1966); and Richard T. Ely, *Ground under Our Feet: An Autobiography* (New York, 1938), 136.

11. Robert Crunden, *Ministers of Reform: The Progressives' Achievement in American Civilization, 1889–1920* (New York, 1984), 81; see also Lewis Coser, "American Trends," in *A History of Sociological Analysis*, ed. Tom Bottomore and Robert Nisbet (New York, 1978), 287–320; and Dorothy Ross, *Origins of American Social Science*, esp. 139, which persuasively links this development with the persistence of "American exceptionalism" and other similar assertions of America's millennial mission.

12. Albion Small, *The Meaning of Social Science* (Chicago, 1910), 11–11; Crunden, *Ministers of Reform*, 82–83; and Vernon K. Dibble, *The Legacy of Albion Small* (Chicago, 1975), 54.

13. The classic study is Henry May, *Protestant Churches and Industrial America* (New York, 1949).

14. Bruce Kuklick, *Churchmen and Philosophers: From Jonathan Edwards to John Dewey* (New Haven, 1985), 228–29.

15. Walter Rauschenbusch, *Christianity and the Social Crisis* (New York, 1907), 209.

16. Thomas L. Haskell, "Professionalism *versus* Capitalism: R. H. Tawney, Emile Durkheim, and C. S. Peirce on the Disinterestedness of Professional Communities," in Haskell, *The Authority of Experts*, 180–225, esp. 202–14.

17. Charles S. Peirce, "Some Consequences of Four Incapacities," *Journal of Speculative Philosophy* 2 (1868): 140–57, esp. 156–57.

18. Philip P. Wiener, ed., *Charles S. Peirce: Selected Writings (Values in a Universe of Chance)* (New York, 1958), xx (emphasis added).

19. Ibid., xix.

20. Charles S. Peirce, "What is Christian Faith?," in Wiener, *Selected Writings*, 357.

21. R. Jackson Wilson, *In Quest of Community: Social Philosophy in the United States, 1860–1920* (New York, 1968), 32–59.

22. Wiener, *Selected Writings*, xix.

23. Jane Addams, *Twenty Years at Hull-House, with Autobiographical Notes* (New York, 1910), 115–27.

24. Carl Degler, *At Odds: Women and the Family in America from the Revolution to the Present* (New York, 1980), 298.

25. Jane Addams, "Why Women Should Vote," in *The Social Thought of Jane Addams*, ed. Christopher Lasch (Indianapolis, 1965), 144.

26. See Marjorie Housepian Dobkin, ed., *The Making of a Feminist: Early Journals and Letters of M. Carey Thomas* (Kent, Ohio, 1979); and M. Carey Thomas, "The Passionate Desire of Women . . . for Higher Education," in *Women's America: Refocusing the Past*, ed. Linda K. Kerber and Jane DeHart-Mathews (New York, 1987), 263–73. The latter is excerpted from Thomas, "Present Tendencies in Women's College and University Education," *Educational Review* 30 (1908), 64–85. Thomas is a fascinating figure who is only just beginning to receive the attention she deserves. A forthcoming biography of her by Helen L. Horowitz may stimulate such attention; see also the valuable study by Barbara Landis Chase, "M. Carey Thomas and the 'Friday Night': A Case Study in Female Social Networks and Personal Growth," (master's thesis, Johns Hopkins University, 1990).

27. See the insightful discussion of Addams in Jean Bethke Elshtain, *Meditations on Modern Political Thought: Masculine/Feminine Themes from Luther to Arendt* (New York, 1986), 71–84, esp. 79. On the conception of Republican motherhood, see Linda K. Kerber, *Women of the Republic: Intellect and Ideology in Revolutionary America* (Chapel Hill, 1980), esp. chaps. 7 and 9. See also Kathryn Kish Sklar, "Hull House in the 1890s: A Community of Women Reformers," *Signs* 10 (Summer 1985): 658–77. As a corrective to an excessive reliance on the concept of separate spheres here and elsewhere, one should also consult Linda Kerber, "Separate Spheres, Female Worlds, Woman's Place: The Rhetoric of Women's History," *Journal of American History* 75, no. 1 (June 1988): 9–39, which is not only a valuable survey of the historiographical twists and turns of the concept but contains an interesting discussion of Hull-House on 33–36. Kerber suggests how permeable and shifting the concept of separate spheres can be and, correspondingly, how frequent have been the intersection and interpenetration of spheres in the actual lives of American women.

28. Allen F. Davis, *Spearheads for Reform: The Social Settlements and the Progressive Movement, 1890–1914* (New York, 1967), is the classic study.

29. Addams, "Why Women Should Vote," 151: "Is that dreariness in city life, that lack of domesticity which the humblest farm dwelling presents, due to a withdrawal of one of the naturally cooperating forces? If women have in any sense been responsible for the gentler side of life which softens and blurs some of its harsher conditions, may they not have a duty to perform in our American cities?" On the combination of the amateur and the professional in the Hull-House vision, see Crunden, *Ministers of Reform*, 68.

30. On the social-control-versus-democracy tension in the movement, see Judith

Ann Trolander, *Professionalism and Social Change: From the Settlement House Movement to the Neighborhood Centers, 1886 to the Present* (New York, 1987), 7–21; and Thomas Lee Philpott, *The Slum and the Ghetto: Neighborhood Deterioration and Middle Class Reform, Chicago, 1880–1930* (New York, 1978). For a thoughtful and balanced assessment of the Hull-House experiment's approach to the phenomenon of urban cultural pluralism, and its role in the gradual redefinition of liberal attitudes toward assimilationism, see Rivka Shpak Lissak, *Pluralism and Progressives: Hull House and the New Immigrants, 1890–1919* (Chicago, 1989).

31. Allen F. Davis, *American Heroine: The Life and Legend of Jane Addams* (New York, 1973), 47–50.

32. Ibid., 143.

33. Jean Bethke Elshtain, *Women and War* (New York, 1987), 234–36. Lillian Faderman connects these views not only with Addams's "cultural feminism," but with her lesbianism, though this characterization of her has been disavowed by Allen Davis. See Faderman's *Odd Girls and Twilight Lovers: A History of Lesbian Life in Twentieth-Century America* (New York, 1991), 24–28, 269.

34. Jane Addams, "Women, War and Babies," in *Jane Addams on Peace, War, and International Understanding*, ed. Allen F. Davis (New York, 1976).

35. Elshtain, *Meditations*, 82.

36. On Croly's life and the importance of the Comtean influence, see David W. Levy, *Herbert Croly of "The New Republic": The Life and Thought of an American Progressive* (Princeton, 1985); for the "christening," see 3–4.

37. Herbert Croly, *The Promise of American Life* (New York, 1909), 409.

38. Ibid., 411–12.

39. Ibid., 409.

40. Ibid., 211.

41. Ibid., 139.

42. Ibid.

43. Ibid., 414.

44. Ibid., 29.

45. Ibid., 43.

46. Ibid., 65.

47. Ibid., 86.

48. Ibid., 156–58.

49. Ibid., 91.

50. Ibid., 97.

51. See *The Little Flowers of St. Francis*, ed. and trans. Raphael Brown (Garden City, N.J., 1958), esp. 207–16. Croly surely also knew the famous prayer attributed to St. Francis, which concludes, "O divine Master, grant that we may not so much seek to be consoled as to console; to be understood, as to understand; to be loved as to love; for it is in giving that we receive; it is in pardoning that we are pardoned; and it is in dying that we are born to eternal life."

52. Croly, *The Promise of American Life*, 94–98.

53. Ibid., 99.

54. Ibid., 167–75.

55. See John Milton Cooper, Jr., *The Warrior and the Priest: Woodrow Wilson and Theodore Roosevelt* (Cambridge, Mass., 1983), 144–49.

56. Hermann Hagedorn, ed. *The Works of Theodore Roosevelt*, 20 vols. (New York, 1926) 17:5–22.

57. See J. G. A. Pocock, *The Machiavellian Moment: Florentine Political Thought and the Atlantic Republican Tradition* (Princeton, 1975), for a discussion of *virtù*, especially in contrast to *fortuna*. Pocock's account of Andrew Jackson's presidency in these terms (535–38) suggests that Americans might be especially drawn to find these qualities in, or project them onto, their presidents. Also see Machiavelli's own account of how "fortune is a woman" who must be conquered by the ruler's audacity and force, in *The Prince*, chap. 25.

58. Edmund Morris, *The Rise of Theodore Roosevelt* (New York, 1979), 273.

59. T. J. Jackson Lears points out Roosevelt's use of Tennyson, and the popularity of "Ulysses" among many critics of "overcivilization," in his *No Place of Grace: Antimodernism and the Transformation of American Culture, 1880–1920* (New York, 1981), 222.

60. Herbert Croly, *Progressive Democracy* (New York, 1914), 168–69.

61. See the conclusion of Croly, *Progressive Democracy*, 427–30.

62. Such, at any rate, is the verdict of Levy, *Herbert Croly*, 171–74.

63. Croly, *Progressive Democracy*, 35.

64. Ibid., 118–19.

65. Van Wyck Brooks, "America's Coming-of-Age," in *Van Wyck Brooks, The Early Years: A Selection from His Works, 1908–1921*, ed. Claire Sprague (New York, 1968), 81–95, 148–50, 157.

66. For an excellent discussion of the concept of personality in Brooks's and Bourne's usage, as well as other usages and meanings, see Casey Nelson Blake, *Beloved Community: The Cultural Criticism of Randolph Bourne, Van Wyck Brooks, Waldo Frank, and Lewis Mumford* (Chapel Hill, 1990), 50–52, 87.

67. Randolph Bourne, "Trans-National America," reprinted in *The American Intellectual Tradition*, ed. David Hollinger and Charles Capper (New York, 1989), 2:162. Bourne's article originally appeared in *Atlantic Monthly*, July 1916, 86–97. See also Blake, *Beloved Community*, 76–121.

68. Brooks, "America's Coming-of-Age," 95.

69. Blake, *Beloved Community*, 86–93, takes explicit note of Dewey's influence upon these writers, especially Bourne.

70. John Dewey, *The School and Society* (Chicago, 1900; rev. ed., 1915), 7.

71. Robert B. Westbrook, *John Dewey and American Democracy* (Ithaca, 1991). On the last point, see, for example, his citation (42) of a passage from Dewey's "Ethics and Democracy": "In one word, democracy means that *personality* is the first and final reality. It admits that the full significance of personality can be learned by the individual only as it is already presented to him in objective form in society; but it holds, none the less, to the fact that personality cannot be procured for any one, however degraded and feeble, by any one else, however wise and strong."

72. See Westbrook's clarifying explanation (ibid., 301–6) of Dewey's understanding of a public and how it comes into being.

73. John Dewey, *The Public and Its Problems* (New York, 1927), 213–19.

74. See Westbrook, *John Dewey and American Democracy*, 170; and Kloppenberg, *Uncertain Victory*, 384.

75. John Dewey, *Individualism, Old and New* (New York, 1930), 36.

76. Ibid., 65.

77. Dewey, *The Public and Its Problems*, 191.

78. Dewey, *Individualism, Old and New*, 69.

79. Ibid., 70.

80. Ibid., 99.

81. Dewey, *The Public and Its Problems*, 185.

82. Perhaps the best-known and most striking one was his vehement endorsement and promotion of American entry into the First World War, largely on the rather breathtaking grounds that a war would help promote socialization and a "more conscious and extensive use of science for communal purposes" through the "creation of instrumentalities for enforcing the public interest in all the agencies of modern production and exchange." Dewey was roundly rebuked for such arguments by critics like Randolph Bourne, who accused him of succumbing to the cant of "war liberalism"; his doing so was further taken as evidence of the moral inadequacy of Dewey's "acquiescent" pragmatism, its incapacity to challenge real-life situations of power and conflict outside the schoolroom, and its inherent inability to distinguish the idea-as-instrument from the idea-as-rationalization. John Dewey, "The Social Possibilities of War," and "America and War," in *Characters and Events: Popular Essays in Social and Political Philosophy*, ed. Joseph Ratner (New York, 1929), 2:551–65. See the scathing analysis of Dewey's wartime commitments by Christopher Lasch in *The New Radicalism in America, 1889–1963: The Intellectual as a Social Type* (New York, 1965), 202–24. Randolph Bourne, "Twilight of Idols," in *The History of a Literary Radical and Other Papers by Randolph Bourne*, ed. Van Wyck Brooks (New York, 1956), 241–59. See also Westbrook, *John Dewey and American Democracy*, 195–227.

Despite his sympathy for Dewey's project, Robert Westbrook is equally scathing about *The Public and Its Problems* and its conspicuous avoidance of crucial practical questions. Duly noting Dewey's own dictum (in *Human Nature and Conduct: An Introduction to Social Psychology* [New York, 1922]) that one who fails to make a "realistic study of actual conditions" is merely indulging ideals that are "dreams . . . romanticism and phantasy-building," Westbrook unflinchingly points to Dewey's own disappointing omissions on just these counts: Dewey's "assertion that the local community might be reconstructed in the midst of the Great Society," Westbrook observes, "seemed wistful in the absence of specific suggestions for doing it. . . . He appeared to have given little thought to the problems and possibilities of participatory democracy. . . . For a philosopher who put democratic ideals at the center of his thinking, Dewey had surprisingly little to say about democratic citizenship."

83. Alexis de Tocqueville, *Democracy in America*, trans. Henry Reeve, 2 vols. (New York, 1945), 2:73–74. Daniel Rodgers's *Contested Truths* is a splendid example of a book built around the ambiguity of many of the central words in the lexicon of American political speech.

84. Dewey, *The Public and Its Problems*, 184.

85. See his *A Common Faith* (New York, 1934) for an example of how Dewey hung onto elements of Christian solidarity in a post-Christian context.

86. Dewey, "The American Intellectual Frontier," in Ratner, *Characters and Events*, 1:448, originally appearing in *New Republic*, May 10, 1922.

87. Charles A. Beard, *An Economic Interpretation of the Constitution of the United States* (New York, 1913), 151–79, 290–91, 324–25. For a biographical study of Beard, see Ellen Nore, *Charles A. Beard: An Intellectual Biography* (Carbondale, Ill., 1983); also helpful is Bernard C. Borning, *The Political and Social Thought of Charles A. Beard* (Seattle, 1962). An incisive short study is Forrest McDonald, "Charles A. Beard," in *Pastmasters: Some Essays on American Historians*, ed. Marcus Cunliffe and Robin W. Winks (New York, 1969), 110–41; see also McDonald's attack on Beard's *Economic Interpretation*, in *We the People: The Economic Origins of the Constitution* (Chicago, 1958), as well as that of Robert E. Brown, *Charles Beard and the Constitution: A Critical Analysis of "An Economic Interpretation of the Constitution"* (Princeton, 1956).

88. Walter Lippmann, *The Phantom Public* (New York, 1925), 198 (emphasis added).

89. Dewey, *The Public and Its Problems*, 142.

90. Walter Lippmann, *Men of Destiny* (New York, 1927), 228.

91. On Darwinism, see Walter Lippmann to Newton D. Baker, May 15, 1929, in *Public Philosopher: Selected Letters of Walter Lippmann*, ed. John Morton Blum (New York, 1985), 240–41.

92. Walter Lippmann, *A Preface to Morals* (New York, 1929), 130–31.

93. Ibid., 193–95; see also Lippmann to Baker, May 15, 1929, in Blum, *Public Philosopher*, 240–41.

94. Lippmann, *Preface to Morals*, 238–39, 311–13, 326–28.

95. Ibid., 313, 329.

96. George Santayana, *Persons and Places: Fragments of Autobiography*, ed. William G. Holzberger and Herman J. Saatkamp, Jr. (Cambridge, Mass., 1986), 421.

97. Ronald Steel, *Walter Lippmann and the American Century* (New York, 1980). See also Louis Auchincloss, *The House of the Prophet* (Boston, 1980), a fictionalized version of a clearly Lippmannesque journalist, written by Lippmann's own attorney. For an incisive look at both books, and a compelling sketch of Lippmann in its own right, see Kenneth S. Lynn, *The Air-Line to Seattle* (Chicago, 1983), 172–84. Lynn is particularly persuasive in demonstrating Lippmann's propensity for treachery and betrayal, exemplified by his initiating an affair with Helen Armstrong, wife of his very close friend Hamilton Fish Armstrong, the longtime editor of *Foreign Affairs* (178–80).

98. Harold D. Lasswell, *Politics: Who Gets What, When, How* (New York, 1936); E. E. Schattschneider, *Politics, Pressures and the Tariff: A Study of Free Private Enterprise in Pressure Politics* (New York, 1935); Thurman Arnold, *The Folklore of Capitalism* (New Haven, 1937), and *The Symbols of Government* (New Haven, 1935); Charles Merriam, *Political Power* (New York, 1934). For a discussion of this development in political science, see Edward A. Purcell, Jr., *The Crisis of Democratic Theory: Scientific Naturalism and the Problem of Value* (Lexington, Ky., 1973), esp. 95–114.

99. Ellis Hawley, *The New Deal and the Problem of Monopoly: A Study in Economic Ambivalence* (Princeton, 1966); Eric Gorham, "The Ambiguous Practices of the Civilian Conservation Corps," *Social History* 17 (May 1992): 229–49; William Leuchten-

burg, "The New Deal and the Analogue of War," in *Change and Continuity in Twentieth-Century America*, ed. John Braeman, Robert Bremner, and Everett Walters (Columbus, Ohio 1964), 81–143.

100. See Walter Lippmann, *The Good Society* (Boston, 1937), and *The Public Philosophy* (New York, 1955); see also Morton White's response to Lippmann in *Social Thought in America*, 2d ed. (Boston, 1957), 264–80; and for the more general critical reception to these books (including the favorable response of General Charles De Gaulle to *The Public Philosophy*), see Steel, *Walter Lippmann*, 323–26, 494–96.

101. Reinhold Niebuhr, *Moral Man and Immoral Society: A Study in Ethics and Politics* (New York, 1932), xiii.

102. Ibid., xiv.

103. Reinhold Niebuhr, "Intellectual Biography," in *Reinhold Niebuhr: His Religious, Social and Political Thought*, ed. Charles W. Kegley (New York, 1956), 15: "The faith of modern man contains two related articles: the idea of progress and the idea of the perfectibility of man. The latter is frequently the basis of the former article. . . . This essential religion of modernity is no less 'dogmatic' for being implicit rather than explicit, and it is no more true for being arrayed in the panoply of science."

104. Quotation from Donald Meyer, *The Protestant Search for Political Realism, 1919–1941* (Berkeley, 1960), 241. See Richard Wightman Fox, *Reinhold Niebuhr: A Biography* (New York, 1987), 143–47, for H. Richard Niebuhr's decisive role in this change of Reinhold's theological mind.

105. Dewey, *Individualism, Old and New*, 63–65. See what Dewey says about religion in this context: "There are those who realize what is portended by the loss of religion as an integrating bond. Many of them despair of its recovery through the development of social values to which the imagination and sentiments of individuals can attach themselves with intensity. They wish to reverse the operation and to form the social bond of unity and of allegiance by regeneration of the isolated individual soul. . . . This injunction puts the cart before the horse. Religion is not so much a root of unity as it is its flower or fruit. The very attempt to secure integration for the individual, and through him for society, by means of a deliberate and conscious cultivation of religion, is itself proof of how far the individual has become lost through detachment from acknowledged social values."

106. Niebuhr, *Moral Man*, xi–xxv.

107. Ibid., 9.

108. Ibid., 271–73.

109. Reinhold Niebuhr, "The Nation's Crime against the Individual," *Atlantic*, November 1916, 614. See discussion of this article, and Niebuhr's shifting views on the First World War—he would change his mind twice more—in Fox, *Reinhold Niebuhr*, 46–47.

110. Niebuhr, *Moral Man*, 91.

111. Ibid., 95.

112. Ibid., 94–95, 106–7.

113. Ibid., 96–97.

114. Ibid., 212–13.

115. Ibid., 177. See Fox, *Reinhold Niebuhr*, 41–121 (esp 41–42), as an antidote to

the widespread notion that Niebuhr's Detroit church was in a working-class neighborhood with a working-class congregation.

116. Richard's masterwork, perhaps the most enduring work of theology that either brother produced, is *The Kingdom of God in America* (New York, 1937).

117. Fox, *Reinhold Niebuhr*, 136–37, 164–66, 216–17. See also Rauschenbusch, *Christianity and the Social Crisis*, 421: "In asking for faith in the possibility of a new social order, we ask for no Utopian delusion. We know well that there is no perfection for man in this life: there is only growth toward perfection. . . . The kingdom of God is always but coming."

118. Reinhold Niebuhr, *Beyond Tragedy* (New York, 1937), 130–31.

119. Matt. 22:35–40.

120. Reinhold Niebuhr, *The Self and the Dramas of History* (New York, 1955), 242; see also Niebuhr, "Intellectual Autobiography," 17: "The eternal in the human spirit . . . reveals itself in the capacity of the self to transcend not only the processes of nature but the operations of its own reason, and to stand, as it were, above the structures and coherences of the world."

121. Niebuhr, *The Self and the Dramas of History*, 37–38.

122. Ibid., 220–21.

123. Ibid., 222.

124. Ibid., 225.

125. Reinhold Niebuhr, "Reply," in Kegley, *Reinhold Niebuhr*, 520.


CHAPTER SIX

1. On the Catholic church as a totalitarian organization, see Sidney Hook, *Reason, Social Myths, and Democracy* (New York, 1940); on Plato, see I. F. Stone, *The Trial of Socrates* (Boston, 1988); more generally, see Karl Popper, *The Open Society and its Enemies* (London, 1945).

2. Leonard Schapiro, *Totalitarianism* (New York, 1973).

3. Ibid., 13.

4. Giovanni Gentile, *Genesi e struttura della società*, and "Dottrina del fascismo," *Opera* 34:117–20, cited in *The Ideology of Fascism: The Rationale of Totalitarianism*, by A. James Gregor (New York, 1969), 220–24.

5. John Patrick Diggins, *Mussolini and Fascism: The View from America* (Princeton, 1972).

6. Edward A. Purcell, Jr., *The Crisis of Democratic Theory: Scientific Naturalism and the Problem of Value* (Lexington, Ky., 1973), 135.

7. "Manifesto," *Nation*, May 27, 1939, 626.

8. Purcell, *Crisis of Democratic Theory*, 135–38.

9. Ibid., esp. 297–317.

10. Ibid., 150–52, 212.

11. There have been many studies of the refugee intellectuals, from a variety of perspectives. The earliest studies tended to focus upon the personal vicissitudes of the refugees themselves; see, for example, such still-indispensable works as Maurice R. Davie's *Refugees in America* (New York, 1947) and Donald Peterson Kent's *The Refugee*

*Intellectual* (New York, 1953). A second wave of interest concentrated more on their intellectual achievements: Laura Fermi, *Illustrious Immigrants: The Intellectual Migration from Europe, 1930–41* (Chicago, 1968); Donald Fleming and Bernard Bailyn, eds., *The Intellectual Migration: Europe and America, 1930–1960* (Cambridge, Mass., 1969); Robert Boyers, ed., *The Legacy of the German Refugee Intellectuals* (New York, 1972); Martin Jay, *The Dialectical Imagination: A History of the Frankfurt School and the Institute of Social Research, 1923–1950* (Boston, 1973); and H. Stuart Hughes, *The Sea Change: The Migration of Social Thought, 1930–1965* (New York, 1975). More recently there have been Anthony Heilbut's *Exiled in Paradise: German Refugee Artists and Intellectuals in America from the 1930s to the Present* (New York, 1983); Martin Jay's *Adorno* (Cambridge, Mass., 1984) and his collection of essays, *Permanent Exiles: Essays on the Intellectual Migration from Germany to America* (New York, 1985); Lewis Coser's *Refugee Scholars in America: Their Impact and Their Experiences* (New Haven, 1985); and Elisabeth Young-Bruehl's biography *Hannah Arendt: For Love of the World* (New Haven, 1982). An interesting sociological analysis of one prominent refugee community (not entirely made up of intellectuals, to be sure) is Steven M. Lowenstein's *Frankfurt on the Hudson: The German-Jewish Community of Washington Heights, 1933–1983, Its Structure and Culture* (Detroit, 1989); though somewhat bloodless, it makes a good companion volume to some of the more general accounts.

12. Erwin Panofsky, "Three Decades of Art History in the United States: Impressions of a Transplanted European," in *Meaning in the Visual Arts* (New York, 1955), 332.

13. H. Stuart Hughes, "Social Theory in a New Context," in *The Muses Flee Hitler: Cultural Transfer and Adaptation*, ed. Jarrell C. Jackman and Carla M. Borden (Washington, D.C., 1983), 111–20; see also 15–26. For an interesting theoretical exploration of these issues, see Raymonde Carroll, *Cultural Misunderstandings: The French-American Experience* (Chicago, 1989); and Hanna Scolnicov and Peter Holland, *The Play out of Context: Transferring Plays from Culture to Culture* (Cambridge, Mass., 1989); in the latter, see esp. 1–24, 99–109, 214–23.

14. W. Rex Crawford, ed., *The Cultural Migration: The European Scholar in America* (Philadelphia, 1953), 19.

15. Leon Bramson, *The Political Context of Sociology* (Princeton, 1961), 89.

16. Henry Pachter, *Weimar Etudes* (New York, 1982), 315.

17. Theodor Adorno, *Minima Moralia: Reflections from Damaged Life*, trans. E. F. N. Jephcott (London, 1974), 25–26, 33.

18. Malcolm Cowley, *Exile's Return* (New York, 1934), 46–47.

19. Erich Fromm, *Escape from Freedom* (New York, 1941), 90–92, 173–80.

20. Ibid., 163.

21. Ibid., 173–80.

22. Ibid., 19.

23. Ibid., 93, 263.

24. For an excellent general study of the struggles of German liberalism, see James J. Sheehan, *German Liberalism in the Nineteenth Century* (Chicago, 1978).

25. A richly detailed biography is Alexander Altmann, *Moses Mendelssohn: A Biographical Study* (University, Ala., 1973). A less comprehensive but insightful introduction to his work is Eva Jospe, *Moses Mendelssohn: A Selection from His Writings* (New

York, 1975); see esp. 3–14. See also Gordon Craig, *The Germans* (New York, 1982), 27, 129–31.

26. George Mosse, *German Jews beyond Judaism* (Cincinnati, 1985), 4, 14, 54, 55, and "Jewish Emancipation: Between *Bildung* and Respectability," in *The Jewish Response to German Culture: From the Enlightenment to the Second World War*, ed. Jehuda Reinharz and Walter Schatzberg (Hanover, N.H., 1985), 1–16; in the same book, see also Jacob Katz, "German Culture and the Jews," 85–99, which is an elaboration upon and expansion of the argument Katz first put forward in his influential 1935 doctoral dissertation. As Marion A. Kaplan has pointed out, German-Jewish women bore most of the responsibility for *Bildung*; see her book *The Making of the Jewish Middle Class: Women, Family, and Identity in Imperial Germany* (New York, 1991), which is a subtle and useful corrective to Katz's classic scholarship.

27. Jacob Katz, *From Prejudice to Destruction: Anti-Semitism, 1700–1933* (Cambridge, Mass., 1980), 148.

28. Katz, "German Culture and the Jews."

29. This is nicely conveyed in Arthur A. Cohen, *An Admirable Woman* (Boston, 1983), 21–34; and Hannah Arendt, *Men in Dark Times* (New York, 1968), 179–80. See Egon Schwartz, "Melting Pot or Witch's Cauldron: Jews and Anti-Semitism in Vienna at the Turn of the Century," in *Germans and Jews from 1860–1933: The Problematic Symbiosis*, ed. David Bronson (Heidelberg, 1979), 262–87. Also see Robert Wistrich, "Dilemmas of Assimilation in Fin-de-siècle Vienna," *Wiener Library Bulletin*, n.s. 32 (1979): 15–28, *Revolutionary Jews from Marx to Trotsky* (London, 1976), and *Between Redemption and Perdition: Modern Anti-Semitism and Jewish Identity* (New York, 1990).

30. For biographical details of the Frankfurt school, for example, see Jay, *The Dialectical Imagination*, 6–40.

31. Erich Fromm, *Beyond the Chains of Illusion: My Encounter with Marx and Freud* (New York, 1962), 5.

32. Ibid.; see also Rainer Funk, *Erich Fromm: The Courage to Be Human* (New York, 1982), 1; and Daniel Burston, *The Legacy of Erich Fromm* (Cambridge, Mass., 1991), 8–10.

33. Fromm, *Beyond the Chains*, 5–6; Gershom Scholem, *From Berlin to Jerusalem: Memoirs of My Youth* (New York, 1980), 156.

34. Fromm, *Beyond the Chains*, 9.

35. Scholem, *From Berlin to Jerusalem*, 156; Lewis Coser, *Refugee Scholars in America*, 69–70.

36. Jay, *Adorno*, 24–25, and *The Dialectical Imagination*, 21–23.

37. Hughes, *The Sea Change*, 142–43.

38. Adorno, *Minima Moralia*, 192–93.

39. A useful discussion of the universality of such strategies for overcoming the stigma of marginality appears in Stanley Rothman and S. Robert Lichter, *Roots of Radicalism: Jews, Christians, and the New Left* (New York, 1982), 118–20.

40. Jay, *The Dialectical Imagination*, 3, 36; see also Jay, *Permanent Exiles*, 28–61.

41. Hughes, *The Sea Change*, 139–40. For a general view of this subject, see George Lichtheim, *From Marx to Hegel* (New York, 1971).

42. Hughes, *The Sea Change*, 185.

43. Burston, *The Legacy of Erich Fromm*, 16–17.

44. See Lewis Feuer, "The Frankfurt Marxists and the Columbia Liberals," *Survey* 25 (Summer 1980): 156–78, esp. 176, for a negative assessment of this aspect of the Frankfurt school; see also Karl Korsch's view in *Karl Korsch: Revolutionary Theory*, ed. Douglas Kellner (Austin, 1977), 284. Also see Coser, *Refugee Scholars in America*, 91, 94; and Jay, *The Dialectical Imagination*, 36.

45. Max Horkheimer, ed., *Studien über Autorität und Familie* (Paris, 1936). I use the translation provided in Jay, *The Dialectical Imagination*, 126–27.

46. See the useful discussion in Coser, *Refugee Scholars in America*, 72.

47. Erich Fromm, "Sozialpsychologischer Teil," in Horkheimer, *Studien*, 77–135. For Freud's own view, see "Character and Anal Eroticism," in *Collected Papers of Sigmund Freud*, 5 vols. (London, 1924–50), 2:45–50.

48. Jay, *The Dialectical Imagination*, 98–101. Daniel Burston is right in chiding those writers who (perhaps under Marcuse's influence) disdain Fromm as "some sort of Pollyanna," a view that finds little support in a careful reading of his work; see Burston, *The Legacy of Erich Fromm*, 14–15.

49. Herbert Marcuse, *Eros and Civilization: A Philosophical Inquiry into Freud* (Boston, 1955).

50. Jay, *The Dialectical Imagination*, 143.

51. Theodor W. Adorno, with Else Frenkel-Brunswik, Daniel J. Levinson, and R. Nevitt Sanford, *The Authoritarian Personality* (New York, 1950), xi.

52. Ibid., ix–x.

53. Erik Erikson, "The Legend of Hitler's Childhood," in his *Childhood and Society* (New York, 1950), 326–58.

54. Ibid., 759.

55. Max Horkheimer, "The Lessons of Fascism," in *Tensions That Cause War*, ed. Hadley Cantril (Urbana, 1950), 230.

56. Theodor W. Adorno, "Scientific Experiences of a European Scholar in America," in Fleming and Bailyn, *The Intellectual Migration*, 363. Penetrating critiques of *The Authoritarian Personality*, including an especially telling one by Edward Shils, uncovering the book's political tendentiousness, can be found in Richard Christie and Marie Jahoda, eds., *Studies in the Scope and Method of "The Authoritarian Personality"* (Glencoe, Ill., 1954).

57. See Hughes, *The Sea Change*, 152–53.

58. Jay, *Adorno*, 36–43.

59. Adorno, *Minima Moralia*, 58.

60. Leo Lowenthal, "Historical Perspectives of Popular Culture," in *Mass Culture: The Popular Arts in America*, ed. Bernard Rosenberg and David Manning White (Glencoe, Ill., 1957), 55. See also Heilbut, *Exiled in Paradise*, 120.

61. Adorno, *Minima Moralia*, 200–201.

62. Theodor W. Adorno and Max Horkheimer, *Dialectic of Enlightenment*, trans. John Cumming ([ca. 1972]; reprint, New York, 1988).

63. Theodor Adorno, *Negative Dialectics*, trans. E. B. Ashton (New York, 1973), 381; also see Adorno, *Minima Moralia*, 192–93.

64. Richard Pells, *The Liberal Mind in a Conservative Age* (New York, 1985), 85. Two recent admiring studies are Stephen Whitfield, *Into the Dark: Hannah Arendt and*

*Totalitarianism* (Philadelphia, 1980); and Dagmar Barnouw, *Visible Spaces: Hannah Arendt and the German-Jewish Experience* (Baltimore, 1990), the latter of which is especially valuable in relating Arendt's thought to the particularities of German-Jewish experience.

65. See the revised third edition of Hannah Arendt, *The Origins of Totalitarianism* (New York, 1966), 460.

66. Judith Shklar, "Hannah Arendt as Pariah," *Partisan Review* 50:1, 64–77, esp. 70. Also see Ronald H. Feldman, ed., *The Jew as Pariah: Jewish Identity and Politics in the Modern Age* (New York, 1978).

67. Shklar, "Hannah Arendt as Pariah," 71. See Emil Lederer, *The State of the Masses: The Threat of the Classless Society* (New York, 1939); and Peter M. Rutkoff and William B. Scott, *The New School: A History of the New School for Social Research* (New York, 1986), 96–101, 112–13, for a crisp summary of Lederer's work.

68. Hannah Arendt, *The Origins of Totalitarianism*, 2d ed. (New York, 1958), 475.

69. The details of Arendt's life are rendered in Young-Bruehl, *Hannah Arendt.*

70. Young-Bruehl, *Hannah Arendt*, 109.

71. See, e.g., Hannah Arendt, *On Revolution* (New York, 1963), 285.

72. Young-Bruehl, *Hannah Arendt*, 139.

73. Shklar, "Hannah Arendt as Pariah," 65, 75. This disposition may also help account for the importance to Arendt of insisting upon the separation of social and political spheres, which is so important to her later work, including *The Human Condition* (Chicago, 1958). In this view, what was wrong with the kibbutz was its deliberate merging of social and political modes of being.

74. For an examination of this influence, one must begin with Young-Bruehl, *Hannah Arendt*, with its then-startling revelation of Arendt's secret personal relationship with Heidegger during her student days. A suggestive analysis of his continuing influence, especially remarkable for having been published well before the revelations of Young-Bruehl's biography, is Martin Jay, "The Political Existentialism of Hannah Arendt," in *Permanent Exiles*, 237–56. See also Vincent Vycinas, *Earth and Gods* (The Hague, 1961); Thomas Sheehan, ed., *Heidegger: The Man and the Thinker* (Chicago, 1981); and John Loscerbo, *Being and Technology: A Study in the Philosophy of Martin Heidegger* (The Hague, 1981). See Hans Siegbert Reiss, ed., *The Political Thought of the German Romantics, 1793–1815* (New York, 1955). Also see Martin Heidegger, *Introduction to Metaphysics*, trans. Ralph Manheim (Garden City, N.Y., 1961); despite the postwar date of the book's publication, it represented an elaboration of lecture materials from the 1930s.

75. This background is summarized with clarity in Alan Beyerchen, "Anti-intellectualism and the Cultural Decapitation of Germany under the Nazis," in Jackman and Borden, *The Muses Flee Hitler*, 29–41.

76. Robert Nisbet, *Sociology as an Art Form* (New York, 1976), 44–49.

77. Karl Mannheim, *Man and Society in an Age of Reconstruction: Studies in Modern Social Structure* (London, 1940), 85.

78. Edward Shils, "The Theory of Mass Society," in *America as a Mass Society: Changing Community and Identity*, ed. Philip Olsen (Glencoe, Ill., 1963), 30–31.

79. As Dagmar Barnouw points out, a point that has never (so far as I know) been systematically pursued by an intellectual historian of the United States, such concern

with the recovery of antiquity was a point of commonality linking Arendt with two other influential (and more identifiably conservative) German refugee political thinkers: Leo Strauss and Eric Voegelin.

80. Arendt, *The Origins of Totalitarianism*, 1st ed. (1951), 430–31.

81. Ibid., 2d ed. (1958), 475–78.

82. Ibid., 477.

83. Conference participants are listed in Carl J. Friedrich, ed., *Totalitarianism* (Cambridge, Mass., 1954); information on those invited obtained from Carl J. Friedrich Papers, Harvard University Archives, Cambridge, Mass. Friedrich would eventually author, with Zbigniew K. Brzezinski, one of the standard academic texts on totalitarianism: *Totalitarian Dictatorship and Autocracy* (Cambridge, Mass., 1956).

84. Friedrich, *Totalitarianism*, 29.

85. Ibid., 30.

86. George Kennan, "America and the Russian Future," in *American Diplomacy*, expanded ed. (Chicago, 1979), 153–54.

87. Kennan, "The Sources of Soviet Conflict," in ibid., 128.

88. Edward Purcell, *Crisis of Democratic Theory*, 235–72. Even with the formidable addition of émigré political philosopher Leo Strauss to the absolutist ranks, they were—at least for the time being—relegated to the wings of the debate.

89. Erikson, *Childhood and Society*, 285–325.

90. Erik Erikson, "Wholeness and Totality," in Friedrich, *Totalitarianism*, 156–71. The remarks of Leo Lowenthal in the discussion period following this paper are indicative, too, of his own perception of totalitarianism's mind-bending power: "We must accept as demonstrably feasible the restructuring of human perception. This is achieved by the totalitarian regime to such a degree that it is almost a biological change in the sensory apparatus. People are made to perceive Jews as insects, capitalists as grossly fat men, and so forth" (222).

91. Erikson, *Childhood and Society*, 247–74.

92. Peter Homans, *Jung in Context: Modernity and the Making of a Psychology* (Chicago, 1979).

CHAPTER SEVEN

1. *Life*, August 27, 1945, 21–27.

2. Ibid.; also *Newsweek*, August 20, 1945, 32–33.

3. Description of GIs taken from *Time*, August 20, 1945, 19. On the reaction of GIs to the end of the war, see the title essay in Paul Fussell, *Thank God for the Atom Bomb, and Other Essays* (New York, 1988). For much of the description here and in what follows, I am indebted to the splendid introductory pages of Jan Morris, *Manhattan '45* (New York, 1987), 3–13.

4. Morris, *Manhattan '45*, 5.

5. *Time*, August 20, 1945, 19.

6. Sloan Wilson, *The Man in the Gray Flannel Suit* (New York, 1955).

7. Ibid., 130.

8. David Wyman, *Paper Walls: America and the Refugee Crisis, 1938–1941* (Amherst,

Mass., 1968), and *Abandonment of the Jews: America and the Holocaust, 1941–1945* (New York, 1984); Henry L. Feingold, *The Politics of Rescue: The Roosevelt Administration and the Holocaust, 1938–1945* (New Brunswick, N.J., 1970).

9. Bruno Bettelheim, "Individual and Mass Behavior in Extreme Situations," *Journal of Abnormal and Social Psychology* 38 (October 1943): 417–52.

10. Ibid., 432.

11. Leo Lowenthal, "Terror's Atomization of Man," *Commentary* 1 (January 1946): 1–8. See Lowenthal's account of the lecture and article in Martin Jay, ed., *An Unmastered Past: The Autobiographical Reflections of Leo Lowenthal* (Berkeley, 1987), 134–35.

12. Bruno Bettelheim, *The Informed Heart: Autonomy in a Mass Age* (Glencoe, Ill., 1960). Such a conviction was perhaps one of the factors that led Arendt to adopt, in her intensely controversial *Eichmann in Jerusalem: A Study in the Banality of Evil* (New York, 1963), a position that seemed to implicate the European Jewish leadership in their own people's destruction—a position, moreover, that Bettelheim strenuously defended. But discriminations are in order; see the fairly evenhanded account of this still contested matter in Elisabeth Young-Bruehl, *Hannah Arendt: For Love of the World* (New Haven, 1982), 328–78.

13. Stanley Elkins, *Slavery: A Problem in American Institutional and Intellectual Life* (Chicago, 1959), 81–139.

14. Ibid., 138–39.

15. Betty Friedan, *The Feminine Mystique* (New York, 1963), 282–92.

16. Ibid., 307–9.

17. Ibid., 308.

18. Ibid., 309.

19. Alexis de Tocqueville, *Democracy in America*, trans. Henry Reeve (New York, 1945), 2:336–37.

20. Ibid., 352.

21. Robert Nisbet, "Many Tocquevilles," *American Scholar* 46 (Summer 1976): esp. 66.

22. Walt W. Rostow, *The Stages of Economic Growth: A Non-Communist Manifesto* (Cambridge, 1960); Daniel Lerner, *The Passing of Traditional Society: Modernizing the Middle East* (Glencoe, Ill., 1958). See also Alex Inkeles and David H. Smith, *Becoming Modern: Individual Change in Six Developing Countries* (Cambridge, Mass., 1974); Richard D. Brown, *Modernization: The Transformation of American Life, 1600–1865* (Prospect Heights, Ill., 1976), 3–22; and Reinhard Bendix, "Tradition and Modernity Reconsidered," *Comparative Studies in Society and History* 9 (1967), 292–346.

23. David Riesman et al., *The Lonely Crowd: A Study of the Changing American Character* (New Haven, 1969). This is the readily available Yale University Press abridged edition, which is still in print as of this writing and contains the important 1961 and 1969 prefaces; I have therefore chosen to use the pagination of this edition, except where otherwise noted. Trilling's views come from Lionel Trilling, *A Gathering of Fugitives* (Boston, 1956), 85–100.

24. James Baughman, *Henry R. Luce and the Rise of the American News Media* (Boston, 1987); Robert T. Elson, *Time, Inc.: The Intimate History of a Publishing Enterprise, 1923–1941* (New York, 1968); John Kobler, *Luce: His Time, Life, and*

*Fortune* (New York, 1968); Allan C. Carlson, "Luce, *Life*, and 'The American Way,'" *This World* 13 (Winter 1986), 56–74.

25. *Time*, September 27, 1954, cover and 22–25.

26. Steven Weiland, "Social Science Toward Social Criticism: Some Vocations of David Riesman," *Antioch Review* 44 (Fall 1986): 446–47.

27. By the time the *Time* article appeared, the amazingly productive Riesman had also published with his collaborators a sequel, *Faces in the Crowd: Individual Studies in Character and Politics* (New Haven, 1952), as well as his own *Thorstein Veblen* (New York, 1953) and a superb collection of solo essays entitled *Individualism Reconsidered, and Other Essays* (Glencoe, Ill., 1954).

28. On his upbringing, see Weiland, "Social Science Toward Social Criticism," 444–57; and several articles by Riesman: "A Personal Memoir: My Political Journey," in *Conflict and Consensus: A Festschrift in Honor of Lewis A. Coser*, ed. Walter W. Powell and Richard Robbins (New York, 1984), 327–64; "Two Generations," *Daedalus* 93 (1964): 72–97; and "Becoming an Academic Man," in *Authors of Their Own Lives: Intellectual Autobiographies by Twenty American Sociologists*, ed. Bennett M. Berger (Berkeley, 1990), 22–74. I am also indebted to a letter from Riesman to the author, April 24, 1985.

29. David Riesman, "Innocence of *The Lonely Crowd*," *Society* 27 (January–February 1990): 78.

30. Weiland points out how little is known about this phase of Riesman's life; see "Social Science Toward Social Criticism," 454. Riesman also downplays its significance, asserting that he underwent analysis "not because I thought I needed it" but "to please my mother, who wanted to be able to talk with me during the time she was an analysand of Karen Horney, who had recommended Fromm to her for me" ("Becoming an Academic Man," 45–46). Certainly, however, the protracted vocational search that Weiland argues for would also suggest that Riesman's psychoanalysis had a key, if inscrutable, position in the process of his formation.

31. Riesman, "Becoming an Academic Man," 34.

32. As a recent tribute, see the contribution by T. J. Jackson Lears to *Recasting America: Culture and Politics in the Age of the Cold War*, ed. Lary May (Chicago, 1989). See also Peter Rose, "David Riesman Reconsidered," *Society* 19 (March–April 1982): 52–61; Leon Botstein, "Children of *The Lonely Crowd*," *Change* 10 (May 1978): 16–20, 54; Anne Lowrey Bailey, "Riesman on Riesman," *Change* 17 (May–June 1985): 51–57. For comic relief, see also Michael Parenti, "How to Write a Best Seller in the Social Sciences," *Social Policy* 2 (March–April 1972): 22–24.

33. H. Stuart Hughes, *The Sea Change: The Migration of Social Thought, 1930–1965* (New York, 1975), 134.

34. See Seymour Martin Lipset and Leo Lowenthal, *Culture and Social Character: The Work of David Riesman Reviewed* (New York, 1961), 15–26; Riesman et al., *The Lonely Crowd*, 4.

35. I have left out of my account a very important part of the original argument, which any reader of the work will immediately notice, but from which Riesman quickly distanced himself when it came under attack. That was his attempt to relate his character types to population patterns, which he believed, following the biometrician Raymond Pearl and the demographer Frank W. Notestein, to have traduced an S-curve

over the long term. Tradition-direction corresponded to societies of "high growth potential" (high birth and death rates); inner-direction to "transitional growth" (declining death rate); and other-direction to "incipient population decline" (moving toward a net decrease in population) (Riesman et al., *The Lonely Crowd*, 7–31). Aside from the obvious peculiarity that Riesman put this theory forward in the midst of an American "baby boom," both the demographics and the correlations were immediately questioned, and Riesman was concerned that this might distract readers from the typologies and make his argument seem too mechanistic; so he quickly backed away from the demographic part of his argument. See Lipset and Lowenthal, *Culture and Social Character*, 156–58, 241–42.

36. Riesman et al., *The Lonely Crowd*, 25–26.

37. Ibid.

38. See ibid., 65–66, 94, for his example of Lord Chesterfield's letters to his son.

39. Sigmund Freud, *New Introductory Lectures on Psychoanalysis*, trans. James Strachey (New York, 1965), 60–62.

40. Max Weber, *The Protestant Ethic and the Spirit of Capitalism*, trans. Talcott Parsons (London, 1930).

41. See Riesman et al., *The Lonely Crowd*, 13–17, 113–29.

42. T. J. Jackson Lears, "From Salvation to Self-Realization: Advertising and the Therapeutic Roots of the Consumer Culture, 1880–1930," in *The Culture of Consumption: Critical Essays in American History, 1880–1980*, ed. Richard Wightman Fox and T. J. Jackson Lears (New York, 1983), 1–38.

43. Cf. Riesman et al., *The Lonely Crowd*, 131–32.

44. Ibid. On the matter of the new class, a useful critical examination is Daniel Bell, "The New Class: A Muddled Concept," in *The Winding Passage: Essays and Sociological Journeys, 1960–1980* (New York, 1980), 144–64.

45. Riesman et al., *The Lonely Crowd*, 130–48.

46. Ibid., 22. In the 1961 edition Riesman himself added a note mentioning the Sullivan/Freud contrast (30). See also Harry Stack Sullivan, *The Interpersonal Theory of Psychiatry*, ed. Helen Swick Perry (New York, 1953); and Perry's superb biography of Sullivan, *Psychiatrist of America: The Life of Harry Stack Sullivan* (Cambridge, Mass., 1982).

47. Riesman et al., *The Lonely Crowd*, 22.

48. Ibid., 82–83. This insight is also applicable to the professions, for what is peer review but judgment by a jury of one's peers? For an examination of the inability of professions to achieve internal disinterestedness, see Thomas L. Haskell, "Professionalism *versus* Capitalism: R. H. Tawney, Emile Durkheim, and C. S. Peirce on the Disinterestedness of Professional Communities," in *The Authority of Experts: Studies in History and Theory*, ed. Thomas L. Haskell (Bloomington, Ind., 1984), 180–225.

49. Riesman et al., *The Lonely Crowd*, 21–22.

50. Ibid., 101–2.

51. Ibid., 83.

52. John Dewey, *Individualism, Old and New* (New York, 1930), 65.

53. See Lionel Trilling, "Freud: Within and Beyond Culture," in his *Beyond Culture: Essays on Literature and Learning* (New York, 1965), 89–118. Trilling has attracted a good deal of scholarly attention in addition to the many accounts of him in memoirs and histories of the New York intellectuals. I have especially profited from William

Chace, *Lionel Trilling: Criticism and Politics* (Stanford, 1980); Stephen Tanner, *Lionel Trilling* (Boston, 1988); Mark Krupnick, *Lionel Trilling and the Fate of Cultural Criticism* (Evanston, Ill., 1986); and an account of Trilling's ideas by a sympathetic clinical psychologist, Edward Joseph Shoban, Jr., *Lionel Trilling* (New York, 1981).

54. Of course, I am speaking here strictly of its meaning in the context of moral philosophy, not in the context of political institutions or biological organisms. It is interesting that the Oxford English Dictionary gives priority to those meanings and presents the Kantian sense of autonomy as metaphorical. The liberal conception of autonomy has antecedents in Stoic writers like Epictetus and Marcus Aurelius. See John Gray, *Liberalism* (Minneapolis, 1986), 59–61.

55. Immanuel Kant, *Foundations of the Metaphysics of Morals*, trans. Lewis White Beck (Indianapolis, 1954), 54.

56. Ibid., 39.

57. Ibid., 49 (emphasis added).

58. Alasdair MacIntyre, *After Virtue: A Study in Moral Theory* (Notre Dame, 1981), 60.

59. Ibid., 65–66.

60. Ibid., 65.

61. Ibid., 107.

62. Robert Nisbet, *The Sociological Tradition* (New York, 1966), 9.

63. One should also take note of the odd combination of tribute and demystification that concepts like norms, authority, and the sacred capture. The vocabulary of social science stands in a strange, characteristically modern stance in that respect, for it renders less accessible the very things whose necessity it proclaims.

64. Robert Wiebe, *The Search for Order, 1877–1920* (New York, 1967), 144, offers a useful formulation of a similar problem.

65. *Commonweal*, October 5, 1951, 621.

66. *New Yorker*, November 4, 1950, 166.

67. Riesman et al., *The Lonely Crowd*, lvi.

68. Riesman, "Innocence of *The Lonely Crowd*," 77.

69. Carl Degler, for example, argued that Americans had always been other-directed and that, therefore, in this respect there was essential continuity between the nineteenth and twentieth centuries. See his "The Sociologist as Historian: Riesman's *The Lonely Crowd*," *American Quarterly* 15 (1963): 483–97. See also the spirited response to Degler by Cushing Strout, "A Note on Degler, Riesman, and Tocqueville," *American Quarterly* 16 (1964): 100–102.

70. David Potter's essay "American Women and the American Character" originally appeared in the *Stetson University Bulletin*; it is more readily available in John A. Hague, ed., *American Character and Culture in a Changing World: Some Twentieth-Century Perspectives* (Westport, Conn., 1979), 209–25. Linda Kerber repeats this criticism of Riesman in "Can a Woman Be an Individual?: The Discourse of Self-Reliance," in *American Chameleon: Individualism in Trans-National Context*, ed. Richard O. Curry and Lawrence B. Goodheart (Kent, Ohio, 1991), 165. The criticism is ironic (though not unjustified) in light of Riesman's long-standing, passionate, and well-known interest in promoting women's education and particularly in supporting the mission of such single-sex women's colleges as Bryn Mawr and Bennington.

71. Riesman et al., *The Lonely Crowd*, 260. In the original 1950 edition, this passage is far more rambling and obscure: "His very other-direction gives [the adjusted other-directed man] a sensitivity and rapidity of movement that may be historically new. That part of his social character which fits him for his roles at work is a smaller part of his total character than among most tradition-directed and inner-directed types. To be sure, he has been strenuously socialized and has lost much of himself in the process" (306). Surely the revision represented a clarificiation.

72. Ibid., 326.

73. Ibid., 339–40.

74. Ibid., 341.

75. A similar presumption lies at the base of another influential contemporary study of the American character, David Potter's *People of Plenty: Economic Abundance and the American Character* (Chicago, 1954).

76. Riesman et al., *The Lonely Crowd*, 210–17.

77. It is important to acknowledge, though, that Riesman was not a Veblenian, as Colin Campbell seems to assert in his *The Romantic Ethic and the Spirit of Modern Consumerism* (New York, 1987), 8. See, for example, Riesman's critical 1953 study *Thorstein Veblen*.

78. Riesman et al., *The Lonely Crowd*, 142.

79. Kenneth S. Lynn, *Mark Twain and Southwestern Humor* (Boston, 1959), 3–22.

80. See Riesman, *Thorstein Veblen*; and J. L. Simich and Rick Tilman, "On the Use and Abuse of Thorstein Veblen in Modern American Sociology, I: David Riesman's Reductionist Interpretation and Talcott Parsons' Pluralist Critique," *American Journal of Economics and Sociology* 42 (October 1983): 417–29, esp. 419–22. The latter is a somewhat unfair attack on Riesman, which nevertheless illuminates his differences with Veblen and the extent of his Freudianism and tendency to psychologize Veblen's work as an "internalized colloquy between his parents."

81. Riesman et al., *The Lonely Crowd*, 160.

82. Lionel Trilling, "A Change of Direction," *The Griffin* 1, no. 3 (1952): 5. This essay, combined with a later, even more admiring essay on *Individualism Reconsidered*, is reprinted in Trilling's "Two Notes on David Riesman," in *A Gathering of Fugitives*, 85–100.

83. See the shrewd account in James Gilbert, *Another Chance: Postwar America, 1945–85* (Chicago, 1986), 117, although it is worth noting that Gilbert makes no mention of the difference between inner-direction and autonomy.

84. Rupert Wilkinson, *The Pursuit of American Character* (New York, 1988), 71–117.

85. Riesman, "A Personal Memoir," 335.

86. Ibid., 336. See also Herbert Gans, ed., *On the Making of Americans: Essays in Honor of David Riesman* (Philadelphia, 1979), x.

87. Riesman, "A Personal Memoir," 328–29.

88. Riesman et al., *The Lonely Crowd*, 5; Gans, *On the Making of Americans*, x. See also the 1960 preface to *The Lonely Crowd*, xxvii.

89. Riesman et al., *The Lonely Crowd*, v.

90. Ibid., vii, 239.

91. Lipset and Lowenthal, *Culture and Social Character*, 41.

92. David Riesman to Hannah Arendt, February 27, 1947, Hannah Arendt Papers, Box 12, Manuscript Division, Library of Congress, Washington, D.C.

93. Riesman to Arendt, June 7, 1949, Arendt Papers.

94. Arendt to Riesman, June 13, 1949, Arendt Papers.

95. Riesman to Arendt, June 7, 13, August 26, September 10, 22, 1949, Arendt Papers. Riesman's review appeared in *Commentary* (April 1951): 392–98.

96. Lipset and Lowenthal, *Culture and Social Character*, 207, 419–58.

97. Riesman et al., *The Lonely Crowd*, lvi (1961 preface). The use of "Autonomy and Utopia" as the title for chapter 18 of *The Lonely Crowd* clearly alludes to Mannheim's *Ideology and Utopia*.

98. See Howard Brick, *Daniel Bell and the Decline of Intellectual Radicalism: Social Theory and Political Reconciliation in the 1940s* (Madison, 1986), 116–17; and Martin Jay, *The Dialectical Imagination: A History of the Frankfurt School and the Institute of Social Research, 1923–1950* (Boston, 1973), 224–25.

99. See also Erich Fromm, *The Working Class of Weimar Germany: A Psychological and Sociological Study* (Cambridge, Mass., 1984), written in the mid-1930s but unpublished until recently. A pathbreaking study that demonstrates the influence of Frankfurt school thinkers in the formulation of a "working-class authoritarianism" interpretation of the origins of Nazism is Richard F. Hamilton, *Who Voted for Hitler?* (Princeton, 1982).

100. Brick, *Daniel Bell*, 116–18.

101. Ibid.

102. Daniel Bell, ed., *The New American Right* (New York, 1955), 192–97.

103. On Hofstadter's early commitments, see Susan Stout Baker, *Radical Beginnings: Richard Hofstadter and the 1930s* (Westport, Conn., 1985); also Arthur M. Schlesinger, Jr., "Richard Hofstadter," in *Pastmasters: Some Essays on American Historians*, ed. Marcus Cunliffe and Robin W. Winks (New York, 1969), 278–315; and Daniel Joseph Singal, "Beyond Consensus: Richard Hofstadter and American Historiography," *American Historical Review* 89 (October 1984): 976–1004.

104. Bell, *The New American Right*, 35, 47.

105. Ibid., 42.

106. Ibid., 52.

107. Theodor W. Adorno, with Else Frenkel-Brunswik, Daniel J. Levinson, and R. Nevitt Sanford, *The Authoritarian Personality* (New York, 1950), 765.

108. Richard Hofstadter, *The Paranoid Style in American Politics and Other Essays* (Chicago, 1965), 29.

109. Ibid., 5.

110. Alfred Kazin, *New York Jew* (New York, 1978), 21.

111. Richard Hofstadter, *Anti-Intellectualism in American Life* (New York, 1963).

112. Hofstadter, *The Paranoid Style*, 7.

113. Ibid., 65.

114. See also Daniel Bell, *The End of Ideology: On the Exhaustion of Political Ideas in the Fifties* (New York, 1960), 369–75.

115. Dwight Macdonald, "A Theory of Mass Culture," in *Mass Culture: The Popular Arts in America*, ed. Bernard Rosenberg and David Manning White (Glencoe, Ill., 1957), 59–73.

116. Daniel Bell, "A Parable of Alienation," in *Mid-Century: An Anthology of Jewish Life and Culture in Our Time*, ed. Harold N. Ribalow (New York, 1955), 133–51, originally appearing in *Jewish Frontier*, November 1946.

117. Nathan Glazer, "The 'Alienation' of Modern Man," *Commentary* 3 (April 1947): 378–85.

118. Oscar Handlin, *The Uprooted: The Epic Story of the Great Migrations that Made the American People* (Boston, 1952), 4–6, 304–5.

119. John Lukacs, *Confessions of an Original Sinner* (New York, 1990), 216. The story appears in Shirley Jackson, *The Lottery, and Other Stories* (New York, 1982).

120. Riesman, *Individualism Reconsidered*, 38.

121. Judy Oppenheimer, *Private Demons: The Life of Shirley Jackson* (New York, 1988), 280.

122. Riesman et al., *The Lonely Crowd*, xxxii. See also Riesman's essay "Some Observations on the Limits of Totalitarian Power," which was originally read at a meeting of the American Committee for Cultural Freedom, in *Individualism Reconsidered*, 414–25.

123. Riesman et al., *The Lonely Crowd*, xii.

124. Riesman, "Innocence of *The Lonely Crowd*," 77. See also the remarks on *The Lonely Crowd* in Robert Bellah et al., *Habits of the Heart: Individualism and Commitment in American Life* (Berkeley, 1985), 49.

125. Riesman to Arendt, June 14, 1949, Arendt Papers.

126. Cited in William E. Leuchtenberg, *A Troubled Feast: American Society since 1945* (Boston, 1979), 80.

127. Lipset and Lowenthal, *Culture and Social Character*, 205.

128. Perry Miller, *The New England Mind: From Colony to Province* (Cambridge, Mass., 1953), 47.

129. Wilkinson, *The Pursuit of American Character*, 87–112.

130. Cited in Warren Susman, *Culture as History: The Transformation of American Society in the Twentieth Century* (New York, 1984), 271.


CHAPTER EIGHT

1. John Dewey, "The Crisis in Human History," *Commentary* 1 (March 1946): 1–9, esp. 8.

2. Ibid., 8.

3. Cf. the account in Allen Matusow, *The Unraveling of America: A History of Liberalism in the 1960s* (New York, 1984), 275–307; and Morris Dickstein, *Gates of Eden: American Culture in the Sixties* (New York, 1977), 3–88.

4. Norman Mailer, "David Riesman Reconsidered," in *Advertisements for Myself* (New York, 1959), 190–204.

5. Norman Mailer, "The White Negro," in ibid., 338–58.

6. Ibid.

7. Ibid.

8. Herbert Marcuse, *Eros and Civilization: A Philosophical Inquiry into Freud* (Boston, 1955).

9. Herbert Marcuse, *One-Dimensional Man: Studies in the Ideology of Advanced Industrial Society* (Boston, 1964). See also Marcuse's preface to the Vintage Book edition of *Eros and Civilization* (New York, 1961), vii–xi.

10. Marcuse, *One-Dimensional Man*, 71–83.

11. Ibid., ix; also see Anthony Heilbut, *Exiled in Paradise: German Refugee Artists and Intellectuals in America from the 1930s to the Present* (New York, 1983), 459.

12. Martin Jay, *Permanent Exiles: Essays on the Intellectual Migration from Germany to America* (New York, 1985), 54.

13. Marcuse, *One-Dimensional Man*, 3.

14. Ibid., 80.

15. Ibid., 251–52.

16. Herbert Marcuse, "Repressive Toleration," in *A Critique of Pure Tolerance*, ed. Robert Paul Wolff (Boston, 1969), 123.

17. John Patrick Diggins, *The American Left in the Twentieth Century* (New York, 1973), 194.

18. Barry Katz, *Herbert Marcuse and the Art of Liberation: An Intellectual Biography* (London, 1982), 174.

19. Herbert Marcuse, *An Essay on Liberation* (Boston, 1969), x.

20. Alasdair MacIntyre, *After Virtue: A Study in Moral Theory* (Notre Dame, 1981), 32–33.

21. Ibid., 244–45.

22. William A. Schambra, "Progressive Liberalism and American 'Community,'" *Public Interest* 80 (Summer 1985): 32–48. One of the many reasons Johnson remains an enigmatic and intriguing figure who attracts first-rate biographers is the fact that his social philosophy is not easily pigeonholed. Doris Kearns's *Lyndon Johnson and the American Dream* (New York, 1976), though its somewhat flat-footed psychologizing traces Johnson's dualities back to his parents and forces the reader to accept uncritically the author's claims of special access to her subject, is nevertheless extremely valuable; see 210–50, esp. 214–16. Since Kearns's husband Richard Goodwin drafted Johnson's Great Society speech, Kearns's observations are inevitably useful—though one remains curious about the extent to which Johnson's own social philosophy was consonant with that expressed in Goodwin's speech. Multivolume biographies of Johnson by Robert Caro and Robert Dallek are still in progress; a good brief account of the Johnson administration and the Great Society appears in Alonzo Hamby, *Liberalism and Its Challengers: F. D. R. to Reagan* (New York, 1985), 231–281, esp. 256–65.

23. Robert Wuthnow, *The Restructuring of American Religion: Society and Faith since World War II* (Princeton, 1988), esp. 241–67.

24. See the discussion of the Vietnam Veterans Memorial in John Bodnar, *Remaking America: Public Memory, Commemoration, and Patriotism in the Twentieth Century* (Princeton, 1992), 3–9, 255–56; and Jan Scruggs and Joel Swerdlow, *To Heal a Nation: The Vietnam Veterans Memorial* (New York, 1985).

25. Taft himself could be remarkably flexible on certain issues, such as federal aid to education and public housing, as James T. Patterson points out in *Mr. Republican: A Biography of Robert A. Taft* (Boston, 1972), 315–34, esp. 329–32.

26. On the Port Huron Statement and its effects, see Todd Gitlin, *The Sixties: Years of*

*Hope, Days of Rage* (New York, 1987), 101–30; also see Kirkpatrick Sale, *SDS* (New York, 1973), 53; Wini Breines, *Community and Organization in the New Left*; and Matusow, *The Unraveling of America*, 312–16. The statement itself, written by Tom Hayden, repays careful reading; it is reprinted in William H. Chafe and Harvard Sitkoff, eds., *A History of Our Time: Readings on Postwar America*, 2d ed. (New York, 1987), 289–94.

27. Stokely Carmichael and Charles V. Hamilton, *Black Power: The Politics of Liberation in America* (New York, 1967), esp. 164–85; Alan A. Altshuler, *Community Control: The Black Demand for Participation in Large American Cities* (New York, 1970); and Robert F. Kennedy, *To Seek a Newer World* (Garden City, N.Y., 1967).

28. Nathan Glazer and Daniel Patrick Moynihan, *Beyond the Melting Pot: The Negroes, Puerto Ricans, Jews, Italians, and Irish of New York City* (Cambridge, Mass., 1963); and Michael Novak, *The Rise of the Unmeltable Ethnics: Politics and Culture in the Seventies* (New York, 1972), were both symptoms of, and stimulus to, this development. See also Jonathan Rieder, *Canarsie: The Jews and Italians of Brooklyn against Liberalism* (Cambridge, Mass., 1985); and J. Anthony Lukas, *Common Ground: A Turbulent Decade in the Lives of Three American Families* (New York, 1985).

29. *New York Times*, July 16, 1979, A10.

30. Mario Cuomo, "Two Cities," keynote address to the Democratic National Convention, San Francisco, Calif., July 17, 1984, published in *Vital Speeches of the Day*, August 15, 1984, 646–49.

31. Michael Sandel, "The Political Theory of the Procedural Republic," in *Reinhold Niebuhr Today*, ed. Richard John Neuhaus (Grand Rapids, 1989), 19–32, and "The Procedural Republic and the Unencumbered Self," *Political Theory* 12 (1984): 81–96.

32. Sandel, "The Political Theory of the Procedural Republic," 32.

33. Charles Moskos, *A Call to Civic Service: National Service for Country and Community* (New York, 1988), is the most recent such effort.

34. Richard Wightman Fox, "Niebuhr's World and Ours," in Neuhaus, *Reinhold Niebuhr Today*, 15–18.

35. It is worth noting that MacIntyre and Riesman both served in an advisory capacity to the authors of *Habits*; see xii–xiii.

36. Russell Kirk, *The Conservative Mind: From Burke to Santayana* (Chicago, 1953); Robert Nisbet, *The Quest for Community: A Study in the Ethics of Order and Freedom* (New York, 1953).

37. The indispensable analysis of the full range of postwar intellectual conservatism is George Nash, *The Conservative Intellectual Movement in America since 1945* (New York, 1976); though Paul Edward Gottfried, *The Search for Historical Meaning: Hegel and the Postwar American Right* (DeKalb, Ill., 1986); and Paul Edward Gottfried and Thomas Fleming, *The Conservative Movement* (Boston, 1988), are also provocative and valuable. On the origins of neoconservatism, see Irving Kristol, *Reflections of a Neoconservative: Looking Back, Looking Forward* (New York, 1983); and Norman Podhoretz, *Breaking Ranks: A Political Memoir* (New York, 1979), as well as Peter Steinfels's *The Neoconservatives: The Men Who Are Changing America's Politics* (New York, 1979). John Judis's *William F. Buckley, Jr.: Patron Saint of the Conservatives* (New York, 1988), is insightful on the intellectual currents within which its subject swam (and swims). I have also profited greatly from a reading of Patrick Allitt's fine study of postwar Roman

Catholic conservatives, forthcoming from Cornell University Press, which will fill a conspicuous gap in the historiography of this movement.

38. For a provocative and far stronger expression of this criticism of Niebuhr, see John Murray Cuddihy, *No Offense: Civil Religion and Protestant Taste* (New York, 1978).

39. Philip Rieff, *The Triumph of the Therapeutic: Uses of Faith after Freud* (New York, 1966); Christopher Lasch, *The Culture of Narcissism: American Life in an Era of Diminishing Expectations* (New York, 1979); T. J. Jackson Lears, *No Place of Grace: Antimodernism and the Transformation of American Culture, 1880–1920* (New York, 1981); Richard Wightman Fox and T. J. Jackson Lears, eds., *The Culture of Consumption: Critical Essays in American History, 1880–1980* (New York, 1983); Donald Meyer, *The Positive Thinkers*, 2d ed. (New York, 1980).

40. Bernard Bailyn, *The Ideological Origins of the American Revolution* (Cambridge, Mass., 1967); Gordon S. Wood, *The Creation of the American Republic* (New York, 1969); and J. G. A. Pocock, *The Machiavellian Moment: Florentine Political Thought and the Atlantic Republican Tradition* (Princeton, 1975). See also the special issue of *American Quarterly* 37 (Fall 1985), entitled "Republicanism in the History and Historiography of the United States"; and Lance Banning, "Jeffersonian Ideology Revisited: Liberal and Classical Ideas in the New American Republic," *William and Mary Quarterly* 43 (January 1986): 3–19. Also see a careful skeptical assessment in Daniel T. Rodgers, "Republicanism: The Career of a Concept," *Journal of American History* 79 (June 1992): 11–39.

41. See Rieff, *The Triumph of the Therapeutic*; also Daniel Bell, "The Return of the Sacred?: The Argument on the Future of Religion," in *The Winding Passage: Essays and Sociological Journeys, 1960–80* (New York, 1980), 324–54; and Glenn Tinder, *The Political Meaning of Christianity: An Interpretation* (Baton Rouge, 1989).

42. Linda K. Kerber, "Can a Woman Be an Individual?: The Discourse of Self-Reliance," in *American Chameleon: Individualism in Trans-National Context*, ed. Richard O. Curry and Lawrence B. Goodheart (Kent, Ohio, 1991), 151–66.

43. It should be pointed out, as Jean Bethke Elshtain repeatedly does in her *Meditations on Modern Political Thought: Masculine/Feminine Themes from Luther to Arendt* (New York, 1986), that each of these thinkers has additional complexities and dimensions to her body of writings that are not covered by these characterizations. Stanton, for example, was not consistent in her gender egalitarianism, as one can readily see from her words in 1868: "The male element is a destructive force, stern, selfish, aggrandizing, loving war, violence, conquest, acquisition, breeding in the material and moral world alike discord, disorder, disease, and death. . . . The need of this hour is . . . a new evangel of womanhood, to exalt purity, virtue, morality, true religion, to lift man up into higher realms of thought and action." Citation from Elshtain, *Women and War* (New York, 1987), 6.

44. Elizabeth Fox-Genovese, *Feminism without Illusions: A Critique of Individualism* (Chapel Hill, 1991), 28–32.

45. Ibid., 11–17.

46. Carol Gilligan, "In a Different Voice: Women's Conceptions of Self and Morality," *Harvard Educational Review* 47, no. 4 (November 1977): 481–517, and *In a Different Voice: Psychological Theory and Women's Development* (Cambridge, Mass., 1982).

47. Ibid., esp. 5–23.

48. For example, see Susan Faludi, *Backlash: The Undeclared War against American Women* (New York, 1992), 329.

49. Fox-Genovese, *Feminism without Illusions*, 55.

50. See Kristin Luker, *Abortion and the Politics of Motherhood* (Berkeley, 1984); Jane Mansbridge, *Why We Lost the ERA* (Chicago, 1986).

51. Jean Bethke Elshtain, *Women and War*; and Sara Ruddick, *Maternal Thinking: Towards a Politics of Peace* (Boston, 1989).

52. Cf. the controversy over Friedan's *The Second Stage* (New York, 1981); see the attack on Friedan in Faludi, *Backlash*.

53. Fox-Genovese, *Feminism without Illusions*, 1–6.

54. Contrast, for example, Cynthia Fuchs Epstein, *Deceptive Distinctions: Sex, Gender, and the Social Order* (New Haven, 1988), with Catherine A. MacKinnon, *Towards a Feminist Theory of the State* (Cambridge, Mass., 1989).

55. Fox-Genovese, *Feminism without Illusions*, 7.

56. Mary Ann Glendon, *Abortion and Divorce in Western Law* (Cambridge, Mass., 1987), is a trenchant comparative analysis bearing on this point.

57. There is surely some significance, too, in the fact that the sequel to *Habits*, entitled *The Good Society* (New York, 1991), put together by the same group under Bellah's direction, has proved far less successful in attracting public attention, even though (or perhaps because) it suggests somewhat more specific ways the malaise in American society can be addressed. It is significant, too, that the book self-consciously appropriates its title from Walter Lippmann's 1937 book by the same name, which represented his own foray into neotraditionalism, an attempt to recover the uses of "higher law" for modern life.

58. Robert N. Bellah et al., *The Good Society* (New York, 1991).

59. Paul Leinberger and Bruce Tucker, *The New Individualists: The Generation after the Organization Man* (New York, 1991), 1.

60. Ibid., 16.

61. Ibid., 300–331.

62. Ibid., 332–51.

63. Ibid., 387.

64. Kevin Phillips, *Post-Conservative America: People, Politics, and Ideology in a Time of Crisis* (New York, 1982), 73–87.

65. Christopher Lasch, *The True and Only Heaven: Progress and Its Critics* (New York, 1991), 36.

66. Arthur M. Schlesinger, Jr., *The Disuniting of America: Reflections on a Multicultural Society* (New York, 1992).

67. Frances FitzGerald, *Cities on a Hill: A Journey through Contemporary American Culture* (New York, 1986); also see Robert Wiebe, *The Segmented Society: An Introduction to the Meaning of America* (New York, 1975), which argues that America's "remarkably tough" society has "depended upon segmentation," for "what held Americans together was their ability to live apart" (46).

68. This is well described by historian Daniel Boorstin's notion of communities of consumption.

69. Marcuse, *One-Dimensional Man*, 252.

70. Alexis de Tocqueville, *Democracy in America*, trans. Henry Reeve (New York, 1945), 2:273.

71. Matt. 6:33.

72. See the essays in Thomas L. Haskell and Richard F. Teichgraeber III, eds., *The Culture of the Market: Historical Essays* (New York, in press).

73. Marshall Berman, *All That Is Solid Melts into Air: The Experience of Modernity* (New York, 1982), is a full-throated hymn to the tensions inherent in the modernist condition. Similarly, if more subtly, Richard Sennett, *The Fall of Public Man* (New York, 1977); and Thomas Bender, *Community and Social Change in America* (New Brunswick, N.J., 1978), argue for the indispensability of an impersonal public culture and for a rethinking and redefining of sentimental *Gemeinschaftlich* notions of community. Christopher Lasch, himself coming out of a New Left intellectual tradition with an argument at once radical and conservative and exemplifying in many respects the growing interest on the Left in communitarian social thought, looks instead to a revived neopopulism in *The Culture of Narcissism* and *The True and Only Heaven*. An intriguing argument for decentralization, inspired by Lawrence Goodwyn's work on Populism, is Sara M. Evans and Harry C. Boyte, *Free Spaces: The Sources of Democratic Change in America* (New York, 1986). For a fascinating, if completely inconclusive, exploration of the sacrifices entailed in community building, see the colloquium "Who Owes What to Whom," *Harper's*, February 1991, 43–54.

# Index

McKinley, William, 113
Madison, James, 30, 31, 173, 259; on
   consolidation (*Federalist* 39), 30
Magnetism, 34
Mailer, Norman, 270–72, 274, 275,
   280
Mail-order catalogs, 26
*Main Street* (Lewis), 222
Maistre, Joseph de, 219
Malvern Hill, battle of, 38
Manhood, 164, 248, 283–86, 325
   (n. 57), 344 (n. 43)
Manifest Destiny, 42
*Man in the Gray Flannel Suit, The*
   (Wilson), 228
Mann, Thomas, 195, 253
Mannheim, Karl, 197, 219, 220
Marching, 17–22, 32, 33, 37, 73, 278;
   imagery and meaning of, 16
"Marching through Georgia," 16
Marcuse, Herbert, 194, 206, 208, 213,
   272–75, 286, 293, 332 (n. 48)
Marines, U.S., 227
Market research, 249, 250
Martial law, 23
Martial virtues, 33, 34, 39
Martians, 86
Marx, Karl, 50, 75, 147, 181, 186, 198,
   203, 205, 208, 218, 220, 236, 241,
   246
Marxism, 201, 204–6, 211–13, 216,
   219, 259, 272, 273
*Marxism and Philosophy* (Korsch), 205
Massachusetts, 12, 30, 76, 84, 88
Massachusetts Bay Colony, 292
Mass communications, 218, 243, 254,
   259, 261
Mass culture, 211, 212, 261, 263
Mass distribution, 25
Mass man, 216, 234, 255, 256, 259,
   261, 263
Mass production, 25
Mass society, 103, 208, 215, 217–20,
   224, 225, 231, 235, 256–66 passim,
   272, 316 (n. 35)
Masterlessness, 4, 287, 293, 295

Mead, George Herbert, 150
Mead, Margaret, 240
Meade, George G., 9, 14
Memory, 78, 85–87, 163, 297 (n. 7)
Mencken, H. L., 171, 177, 260, 261
Mendelssohn, Moses, 199
Mexican War, 12
Mies van der Rohe, Ludwig, 195
Military vocation, 18, 33, 80, 152
Mill, John Stuart, 59, 102, 187, 256,
   265
Millennialism, 19
Miller, Arthur, 265
Miller, Perry, 267
Mills, C. Wright, 234
Mills, Clark, 304 (n. 98), 305 (n. 1)
*Minima Moralia* (Adorno), 26, 196,
   203
Missouri, 135, 138
Modernism, 283
Modernity, 212, 213, 216, 236, 264,
   289, 328 (n. 103), 338 (n. 63)
Modernization, 22, 105, 174, 236
*Mont St. Michel and Chartres* (Adams),
   34
Moore, Barrington, 239
Moral community, 6, 184, 194, 247,
   288
Moral equivalent of war, 39, 152, 158,
   278
*Moral Man and Immoral Society*
   (Niebuhr), 177, 180, 181, 183
Moral obligation, 6, 45, 107, 223,
   287
Morgan, Hank, 105, 106
Morgan, J. P., 28, 106
Morgenthau, Hans, 194
Morris, Edmund, 164
Mount Auburn Cemetery, 92
Mount Vernon, 36
Mount Suribachi, 227
Mueller, Wilhelm, 218
Multiculturalism, 292
Mumford, Lewis, 33
Murfreesboro, Tenn., 137
Mussolini, Benito, 190, 191

Political cohesion, 138
Political economy, 153
Political religion, 19
Political science, 136, 138, 139, 143, 146
*Political Science and Comparative Constitutional Law* (Burgess), 139, 146
*Political Science Quarterly*, 139
*Politics* (magazine), 230
*Politics: Who Gets What, When, and How* (Lasswell), 176
Popular Front, 192
Popular sovereignty, 136, 137, 142, 162, 247
Populism, 162, 171, 258, 346 (n. 73)
Populists, 113, 259–60
Port Huron Statement, 278
Positive liberty, 193
Positive state, 126
Postindustrialism, 272, 289, 290
Postmillennialism, 100
Postmodernism, 289
Potter, David, 248, 286
Powell, John Wesley, 125
Pragmatism, 146, 151, 165–67, 169, 170, 190–92, 196
Praxis, 204–6, 263, 270, 275
Prayer, 34, 78
*Preface to Morals* (Lippmann), 174, 175
Preminger, Otto, 195
*Private Demons* (Oppenheimer), 265
Privatism, 43
"Problem of the West, The" (Turner), 108, 109
Professionalization, 8, 122, 151–53, 242, 284, 337 (n. 48)
*Progressive Democracy* (Croly), 165
Progressive party, 165
Progressivism, 121, 148–52, 159, 164, 165, 170–87 passim, 191, 194, 223, 257, 274, 277, 280, 288
*Promise of American Life, The* (Croly), 159, 160, 163, 165
Protestantism, 19, 59, 61, 104, 123, 153, 154, 158, 159, 177, 179, 187, 196, 241, 245, 267, 268, 273, 280, 281, 284, 288
Protocols of the Elders of Zion, 260
Prussia, 23
Pseudoconservatives, 259
"Pseudo-individuality," 212
*Psychic Factors of Civilization, The* (Ward), 120, 121, 132
Psychoanalysis, 205
Psychological understanding of ideas, 91
Public, the, 8, 43, 51, 93, 144, 148, 153, 157, 161–79 passim, 183, 237, 240, 257, 280, 281, 282, 284, 285, 287, 292, 346 (n. 73); Dewey's efforts to define, 167, 168
*Public and Its Problems, The* (Dewey), 167, 170, 172, 173, 326 (n. 82)
Public intellectuals, 7, 8, 183
Public interest, 153, 171, 172, 176, 181, 279, 280
Public opinion, 173, 175, 198
*Public Opinion* (Lippmann), 173
Purcell, Edward, 192
Pure sociology, 127, 133
Putnam, Hilary, 151

*Queen Mary*, 227

Race, 6, 277, 291
Radicalism, 270–75
Radio, 243
Railroads, 25, 26, 32, 33, 35
Rajneeshis, 292
Rath, Tom (*The Man in the Gray Flannel Suit*), 229
Rauschenbusch, Walter, 100, 150, 154, 175, 183, 187, 329 (n. 117)
Reagan, Ronald, 278
Realism, 172, 176, 183, 184
*Rebel without a Cause*, 270
"Recipe knowledge," 59, 271
Redemption, 19, 21, 39, 100
Redfield, Robert, 239
*Reflections on the End of an Era* (Niebuhr), 184

Reformation, 187, 245, 254

Refugee intellectuals, 6, 194–98, 208, 209, 213, 220, 222, 223, 230, 235, 253, 257, 259, 261, 329–30 (n. 11)

Regeneration, 19

Regionalism, 177, 316 (n. 35)

Reich, Wilhelm, 195

Reichmann, Freida, 202–3

Relativism, 142, 149, 174, 192–93, 271

Religion, 291, 328 (n. 105); of humanity (Comte), 159; of solidarity (Bellamy), 78, 81, 87, 96, 97

Religious vocation, 152

Renaissance, 4

Repression, 272

Repressive desublimation, 273

"Repressive Tolerance" (Marcuse), 274

Republic, 189; procedural, 6, 190, 280, 288, 295

*Republic* (Plato), 3, 161

Republicanism, 29, 30, 32, 36, 42–44, 51, 88, 123, 141, 164, 217, 222, 268, 275, 281–83, 294

Republican motherhood, 157

Republican party, 15, 84, 113, 124, 222, 260, 278

Revivalism, 60

Revolutionary war, 12

Rieff, Philip, 239

Riesman, David, 6, 223, 233–61 passim, 265–67, 270, 281, 283, 288–90, 294, 336 (nn. 30, 35), 338 (n. 70), 339 (nn. 71, 77)

Riesman, Eleanor, 253

Rights, 41, 47, 140, 142, 144, 199, 280, 287, 291; natural, 46, 48, 49, 136, 142, 143, 147, 149, 150, 169; women's, 285

Robinson, James Harvey, 150

Rockefeller, John D., 28

Rodgers, Daniel, 148

Roman Catholic Church, 47, 187, 189, 192, 232, 281

Roman Empire, 276

Romanticism, 217, 218

Romanyshyn, Robert, 313 (n. 37)

Roosevelt, Franklin D., 176, 230

Roosevelt, Theodore, 112, 113, 119, 120, 162–65, 180, 277–79; as embodiment of virtue, 164, 325 (n. 57); "New Nationalism" address (1910), 163–64

Ross, Edward Alsworth, 133, 150

Rostow, Walt W., 236

Rothschild family, 200

Rousseau, Jean-Jacques, 246, 275

Rousset, David, 231

Royce, Josiah, 150

Russell, Bertrand, 174

Sacrifice, 18–20, 33, 36, 39, 55, 74, 81, 89, 166, 180, 183, 184, 279, 294, 347 (n. 73)

Sadomasochism, 198, 207, 258

St. Louis Hegelians, 134–36, 142–44, 147

St. Louis Philosophical Society, 134

St. Paul, Minn., 18, 99, 100, 165, 176, 184, 294

Salt Lake City, Utah, 226

"Salut au Monde!" (Whitman), 56

Salvation, 59

Sambo personality, 231

Sandel, Michael, 6, 280, 287, 291, 295

San Francisco, Calif., 226, 227, 292

Santayana, George, 7, 151, 175, 176

Satan, 106, 124

Schattschneider, E. E., 176

Schenectady, N.Y., 83

Schleiermacher, Friedrich, 218

Schlesinger, Arthur M., Jr., 270

Schoenberg, Arnold, 195

Scholem, Gershom, 202–3

*School and Society, The* (Dewey), 167

Science, 125, 126, 128, 132, 133, 170–75, 179, 183, 188, 192, 193, 212, 251

Scopes trial, 171

Scott, Sir Walter, 106

"Second Review of the Grand Army, A" (Harte), 37–40, 278

Second soul, 78, 83, 85, 97, 99, 162

Wister, Owen, 119
Wittfogel, Karl, 194
Women: belief in moral superiority of, 286, 344 (n. 43); concept of republican motherhood, 157, 323 (n. 27); confinement to private sphere, 284; as custodians of moral virtue, 51, 344 (n. 43); as domesticating force, 159, 323 (n. 29); domestic authority of, 51; as figures of "second soul," 85; and other-direction, 248, 338 (n. 70); and the public-private distinction, 157; as source of reintegration, 51, 69, 97, 104

Work, Henry C., 16
World's Congress of Historians and Historical Students (1893), 107
Wouk, Herman, 234
Wright, Carroll D., 125
Wuthnow, Robert, 278

Yale University Press, 267
Yeats, William Butler, 64
Youth Aliyah, 217

Zarathustra, 175
Zouaves, 13